The Yishuv in the
Shadow of the Holocaust

The Yishuv in the Shadow of the Holocaust

Zionist Politics and Rescue Aliya, 1933–1939

Abraham J. Edelheit

WestviewPress

A Division of HarperCollins*Publishers*

Copyright © 1996 by Westview Press, A Division of HarperCollins Publishers, Inc.

Published in 1996 in the United States of America by Westview Press, 5500 Central Avenue, Boulder,
Colorado 80301-2877, and in the United Kingdom by Westview Press, 12 Hid's Copse Road,
Cumnor Hill, Oxford OX2 9JJ

Library of Congress Cataloging-in-Publication Data
Edelheit, Abraham J.
  The Yishuv in the shadow of the Holocaust : Zionist politics and
rescue aliya, 1933–1939 / by Abraham J. Edelheit.
    p.   cm.
  Includes bibliographical references and index.
  ISBN 0-8133-3039-4 (hc)
  1. Zionism—Palestine—History. 2. Jews—Germany—
History—1933–1945. 3. Refugees, Jewish—Palestine. 4. Jews,
German—Palestine. 5. Palestine—Emigration and immigration.
I. Title.
DS149.5.P35E34   1996
909'.049240823—dc20   96-20916
                                                                                   CIP

The paper used in this publication meets the requirements of the American National Standard for
Permanence of Paper for Printed Library Materials Z39.48-1984.

10   9   8   7   6   5   4   3   2   1

למען ציון לא אחשא

This book is humbly dedicated to
the memory of my father, teacher, co-author,
and best friend
Hershel Edelheit (1926-1995)
who taught me the Love of Zion
and the importance of Jewish History
תנצב"ה.

Contents

Illustrations

Tables

Maps

Illustrations

Preface

For nearly fifty years the history of the Holocaust and the history of the Yishuv have been written as two separate chapters in the contemporary Jewish experience: The one event viewed as the depths of tragedy reflecting the powerlessness of the Jewish community and the other reflecting its polar opposite, Jewry's emergence from powerlessness in the guise of the reborn State of Israel. Although recent historical studies have attempted to integrate these two historical trends, much more work has yet to be done in order to clearly elucidate the relationship between the two benchmark events of recent Jewish history. This book, whose origins was in my doctoral dissertation, seeks to broaden the context into which the history of rescue aliya is placed, by examining the constructive aid program in both its ideological and political contexts. The nature of the different responses to the fate of diaspora Jewry is charted and the Yishuv leadership's appraisals of the Nazi threat to European Jewry are correlated. The question of how best to aid European Jewry — a source of searing controversy among all Jews — was of daily concern to the entire Yishuv. Alternative strategies advocated by the Yishuv's leaders as they faced the painful dilemma of rescuing the Jews of Europe are therefore investigated in detail.

Finally, this book answers four critical questions: (1) Did differing party ideologies reflect clear divergences in rescue-related questions? (2) Were the policies advocated by the Yishuv's leadership (and by their opponents) reasonable responses to the actual and perceived threat? (3) Were these policies pursued creatively and energetically? and (4) To what extent did the Yishuv's disunity impact on the success or failure of the rescue program?

Numerous individuals and organizations have helped me in the completion of the manuscript. First and foremost among them are the faculty members of CUNY's graduate school who helped frame the questions and answers contained herein: Professors Howard L. Adelson, Robert M. Seltzer, Abraham Ascher, and Thomas Kessner. I would also like to thank Professor Randolph L. Braham and the CUNY Institute for Holocaust Studies for research grants in 1988/1989 and 1989/1990.

I owe a special debt of gratitude to the archivists and librarians of the following institutions: The Ben-Gurion Research Center, Kiryat Sde Boker; The Ben-Zvi Archive and Library, Jerusalem; The Central Archive for the History of the Jewish People, Jerusalem; The Central Zionist Archive, Jerusalem; The Hagana History Archive, Tel Aviv; The Histadrut Archive, Tel Aviv; The Israel Labor Party Archive, Bet Berl; The Israel State Archive, Jerusalem; The Jabotinsky Institute Archive, Tel Aviv; The Leo Baeck Institute, Jerusalem; The Leo Baeck Institute, New York; The New York Public Library Jewish Division; The Public Records Office, London; and the Yad Vashem Archives, Jerusalem. All materials from these archives are cited with permission and all copyrights are hereby acknowledged.

I would like to further take this opportunity to thank the following individuals who have had a positive input into this monograph: Professor Monty N. Penkower of Touro College, Professor Francis R. Nicosia of St. Michael's College, Professor Yoav Gelber of Haifa University, Mrs. Batya Leshem of the Central Zionist Archive, and Dr. Tuvia Friling and Howard Rosenblum of the Ben-Gurion Research Center. Hearing different parts of this work at different stages of its completion, each has contributed to fleshing out my ideas and has suggested further avenues for research. The same holds true for Rabbi Zorach Warhaftig, former Minister of Religious Affairs, who granted me an interview in July of 1990.

Thanks as well to Karin Vanderveer-Porinchak for her copyediting, to Cindy Adelstein for typing the notes, and to my friends at Westview Press — Susan McEachern, Carol Jones, Jane Raese, Alice Levine, and Lynn Arts — for helping to turn this project into a reality.

Finally, I would like to extend thanks to my family: to my cousins Rabbi and Mrs. Amos Edelheit and David and Phyllis Edelheit for their constant encouragement in facilitating all my scholarly pursuits; to my beloved Carol Ann Stein who has been a source of inspiration in my scholarly pursuits; and last, but certainly not least, to my mother, Ann D. Edelheit, for her patience and love. Completion of this work is a bittersweet moment for me as it also represents the first book I have undertaken since the passing of my father, colleague, and best friend, Hershel Edelheit. I hope this work becomes a fitting memorial to you my dear father, but in your credo I take consolation: "The teaching of the wise is a fountain of life."

Abraham J. Edelheit

Abbreviations

AJYB	=	*American Jewish Yearbook*
ATH	=	Hagana Historical Archive
BGA	=	Ben-Gurion Archive
CAHJP	=	Central Archive for the History of the Jewish People
CZA	=	Central Zionist Archive
HIS	=	Histadrut Archive
ILPA	=	Israel Labor Party Archives
ISA	=	Israel State Archives
JIA	=	Jabotinsky Institute Archive
YVA	=	Yad Vashem Archive
YVS	=	*Yad Vashem Studies*

Introduction

For the Jewish world as a whole, and the Yishuv in particular, the 1930s represented a series of increasingly severe crises. The rise of the Nazis and their antisemitic policy, the declining fortunes of Eastern European Jewry, the increasing enmity of the Arabs, and the hardening of British Mandatory policies in Palestine presented grave challenges for the Yishuv. Beginning in mid-1932, the Yishuv began to monitor events in Germany with increasing concern. The collapse of the world's economy in October 1929 and onset of the Great Depression along with the growing influence of hyper-nationalist voices in Germany, had all been seen as reasons for increased attention and concern, if not outright alarm. The Weimar Republic's steady disintegration, beginning with the inconclusive election results of June 1932 and followed by the rise and fall of the governments of Franz von Papen and General Kurt von Schleicher, culminated in the collapse of democracy in Germany.

In the Yishuv, events in Germany were seen as critically important and therefore worthy of extensive reporting. Virtually all the Jewish newspapers devoted increasingly large amounts of space to describing the events in Germany and explaining their implications. Thus, for example, *ha-Aretz* began a column titled "From the Confusion in Germany." Printed on page 1 or 2, the column usually comprised a compilation of short, unrelated items originating with one of the telegraphic agencies or with the daily's German correspondents. Simultaneously, Yeshayahu Klinov, one of the paper's German correspondents, wrote a series of articles on Hitler and Nazism that were serialized in *ha-Aretz* as well as in London's *Jewish Chronicle* and New York's *Morgen Journal*.[1]

Despite more limited financial resources, Palestine's other Jewish newspapers increasingly devoted space to describing and analyzing conditions in Germany. One particularly perceptive article was published in *Davar* by

1

Moshe Brachman, a leader of Hitachdut Olei Germania (HOG). Suggesting that German Jews should vote with their feet, Brachman analyzed the possibility of increased aliya from Germany in the near future and discussed the practical and ideological implications of such an undertaking.[2]

German Jewry's status worsened when Adolf Hitler assumed power in Germany on January 30, 1933. From that moment onward, a government-sponsored anti-Jewish campaign officially began on all levels, and the Yishuv's concern for German Jewry accelerated. Increasingly ominous reports were received and were published in the Yishuv's press. On January 30, *ha-Aretz*, *Davar*, and the *Palestine Post* all published similarly-worded articles detailing German Jewish contingencies in the event of a Nazi takeover.[3] Shortly thereafter, articles on the Nazi mistreatment of German Jewry began to appear, although some were exaggerated.[4] As an example, the first violent attack on Jews reported by the Yishuv's three major dailies concerned the murder of a Jewish student at Breslau University on February 7, 1933. Initial reports proved inaccurate, since only one student was murdered not the three that *ha-Aretz* reported.[5]

Concurrent with the Nazi assault on German Jewry was the emerging crisis for the more than five million Jews who lived in Eastern Europe. The depression, lack of traditional democratic tolerance, and outright antisemitism all contributed to a growing need for a vast Jewish emigration policy. Moreover, antisemitic agitation had increased in Poland, Romania, Hungary, and the Baltic republics well before the outbreak of World War II.[6]

Remarking on the situation in Poland in 1933, David Ben-Gurion told the British High Commissioner for Palestine, General Sir Arthur Wauchope, that "but for [Marhsal Jozef] Pilsudski's influence," the Polish Jewish situation would be even worse.[7] Similarly, in a study commissioned by the American Jewish Congress in 1935, Abraham Duker concluded that nearly one-third of Polish Jews were pauperized, and another 25 percent could maintain themselves at an acceptable standard of living only through foreign aid.[8]

After Pilsudski's death on May 12, 1935, antisemitism became Polish government policy for dealing with ever-increasing social and economic crises. In 1937 the ruling party, the Sanacja, adopted an overtly authoritarian philosophy and incorporated the antisemitic policies espoused by the Endecja. The new government, the Oboz Zjednoczena Narodowego (Camp for National Unity or OZN), sought every means to encourage Jewish emigration, including the possibility of settling Polish Jews in the French colony of Madagascar.[9]

The Jewish position in both Romania and Hungary was similar to that in Poland. Romanian Jews, numbering about 900,000 in 1939, had never gained the equality in civil status they had been guaranteed by the Congress of Berlin in 1878. Fueled by the Nazi example, Romanian antisemitic parties now demanded revocation of Jewish citizenship, the removal of Jewish influence from the Romanian economy, and limitations on Jewish participation in

Romanian culture. Direct harassment of Jews began only with the rise of the National Christian Party government of Octavian Goga and Alexandru Cuza in 1937, but for Jews conditions continued to deteriorate even after the Goga-Cuza government fell and worsened in 1938.[10] Over the course of 1937 and 1938, Hungary enacted the First and Second Anti-Jewish Laws. Patterned on the Nuremberg Laws, the Hungarian legislation was designed to limit the role played by Jews in Hungarian economic life. In 1939, a racial element was added to the Hungarian anti-Jewish legislation, paradoxically, under the impact of the anti-German antisemitism of Prime Minister Pal Teleki.[11]

In 1933 the gruesome denouement of Nazi antisemitism was not yet anticipated, even by the most pessimistic of Zionists. Albeit, much suffering was expected in the short-term. Chaim Weizmann noted in a letter to Ramsay MacDonald on June 11, 1933 that "the present German government is destroying, in a most deliberate and systematic manner, the economic life and structure of German Jewry."[12] Two points were immediately clear: that German Jewry needed a haven and that the Yishuv would play a crucial role in any solution to European Jewry's distress.[13]

In advance of the growing threat in Europe, the Yishuv and its autonomous institutions had become a tightly knit polity, considered to be the avant-garde for a movement of Jewish national rebirth. Numerically, however, the Jewish population was small and relatively weak. The 174,610 Jews living in Palestine in 1931 accounted for only 17 percent of the total population.[14] Moreover, Britain held dominion over Palestine — the result of a League of Nations Mandate issued on July 24, 1922.

Under the terms of the Mandate, the British were to help stimulate the growth of a Jewish national home. The years between 1933 and 1939 were thus crucial in the Yishuv's evolution from a small entity to "a state in the making." However, the Jewish quasi-state was riven by a number of political, ideological, economic, and social concerns. Of these, the most important was the conflict between the Mapai-led coalition that controlled the Jewish Agency (JA) and the World Zionist Organization (WZO) and the Revisionist Zionist movement.

Each of these movements had a different vision of the Jewish society it wished to build. The Revisionists adhered to a form of political Zionism that emphasized the need to create a Jewish majority in Palestine as quickly as possible. This, in turn, would establish the conditions for Jewish sovereignty and would be the first step in resettling a majority of the Jewish people in their ancestral homeland. Whereas Mapai did not necessarily disagree with this long-term goal, the party saw no need to act quickly and had no specific vision for the future beyond the desire to create a socialist (though not necessarily a Marxist) society.

In light of later events in Europe, four questions arise: (1) Did differing party ideologies reflect clear divergences in rescue-related questions? (2) Were the policies advocated by the Yishuv's leadership (and by their opponents) reasonable responses to the actual and perceived threat? (3) Were these policies pursued creatively and energetically? (4) To what extent did the Yishuv's disunity impact on the success or failure of the rescue program? These four questions, in turn, suggest a broader issue regarding intra-party rivalries within the Zionist camp: were the positions advocated by the various sides in the dispute fixed and monolithic, or porous and nuanced?

This book aims to show both the differences and the similarities in the respective approaches of the Yishuv's two main political blocs as they grappled with a variety of issues related to saving German and European Jewry. Although both the Jewish Agency Executive (JAE) and the Ha-Zohar began from the same conceptual framework — which may be termed rescue aliya — they related differently to this guiding concept. Over the course of seven years, both initial approaches were modified considerably, in light of the ever-increasing distress in Europe and the overwhelming difficulty in finding a piece of solid soil for their harassed brethren caught in a rapidly spreading quicksand.

1
Zionism Confronts the Nazi Threat

THE PERSECUTION OF GERMAN JEWRY: AN OVERVIEW

In order to understand the Yishuv's response to the Nazi threat, it is necessary to understand the context into which Zionist policy must be set. In particular, an understanding of three components is needed to place the Yishuv's response to the Holocaust in context: the slow evolution of Nazi policy during the 1930s, the response of German Jewry to their own predicament, and the options available to Jewish leaders.

The Nazi persecution of German Jewry began with the Machtergreifung on January 30, 1933. From 1933 to mid-September 1935, German Jewry was isolated by effective Nazi antisemitic propaganda and turned into a "leprous community" with which Aryans had little contact. Anti-Jewish violence was limited to sporadic and random assaults, with the precise level of violence varying according to place and time. Legislation designed to severely circumscribe the areas of economic activity and social contact permitted to Jews was emphasized in order to encourage emigration.[1]

Some Nazis gave vent to antisemitic passions through a series of sporadic attacks on Jews. The earliest attacks started in Thuringia in February 1933 and spread throughout Germany intermittently through March.[2] Press reports concerning these attacks on Jews, Communists, and Social Democrats brought about an immediate response from Jewish communities throughout the world, including a massive protest rally called by the American Jewish Congress in New York on March 27.[3] In retaliation, the Nazis declared a one-day anti-Jewish boycott for April 1. Under the auspices of Julius Streicher, armed guards of the SA and SS were posted at Jewish shops with orders to keep out all Aryan customers, by whatever means necessary.[4] The boycott did not

5

have an immediate impact on German Jewry, but did play an important role in internal Nazi politics. It allowed the SA to release tension without seriously disrupting the economy and also placed German Jewry's would-be protectors on the defensive, out of fear of provoking an even worse Nazi response.[5]

In mid-September 1935, Nazi policy reached another important turning point for German Jewry. During the Nazi Party rallies in Nuremberg in September, two new laws were promulgated. Better known as the Nuremberg Laws, these rulings served the dual purposes of defining who was considered a Jew and revoking Jews' few remaining rights. This "Reich Law on Citizenship" defined the Reichsbürger as a pure-blooded Aryan German citizen with full political rights; and the Staatsangehöriger, as a subject of the Reich, to which status German Jewry was now reduced.[6] Twenty-one other decrees were passed between the rallies of September 1935 and the outbreak of war on September 1, 1939; these finalized the Jews' fallen status and utterly destroyed whatever foundations remained to continue Jewish life in Germany.

Operating alongside the Nazi legislative program was a policy of Arisierung, that is, the Aryanization of Jewish property. Beginning in 1933, the process of Aryanization became systematic only with the rearmament campaign of 1935 and 1936. Until that time the Nazis adopted a policy of economic self-restraint regarding German Jewish businessmen (as opposed to laborers or professionals), primarily for fear of a revival of unemployment among the German masses. After 1937, however, the campaign to create a Judenrein economy began to speed up. Nevertheless, this antisemitic campaign was not fully completed until the months just before the outbreak of World War II.[7]

The expansion of Germany's territory through bloodless conquests heightened Nazi hopes for a full solution to the Jewish question. In late 1938, therefore, the Nazis accelerated emigration. In the interim the Nazis had found a simple method of reducing Germany's unwanted Jewish population: dumping thousands of East European Jews at border points between Germany and Poland. One well-known case included some 17,000 former Polish Jews who were stripped of German citizenship and dumped on the Polish border near Zbąszyn on October 28, 1938. Not permitted to enter Polish territory, they endured harsh conditions, barely existing in the no-man's-land between the two states. Herschel Grynszpan, the son of one of the unfortunates, reacted by assassinating the third secretary of the German embassy in Paris, Ernst vom Rath.[8]

Twenty-four hours later came the Nazi revenge — pogroms throughout Germany, Austria, and Bohemia-Moravia. That night, November 9–10, 1938, has become known as Kristallnacht, the Night of Broken Glass. Over the course of the evening's orgy of destruction, Jewish homes and shops were looted, scores of synagogues and Jewish communal centers — some hundreds of years old and containing priceless ritual objects — were burned, and ninety-seven Jews were murdered by the mobs. Kristallnacht marked the beginning of further radicalization and violence. Following Kristallnacht, the SS rounded up 30,000 German Jews and incarcerated them in various concentration camps. These new inmates could buy their freedom only by showing proof that they would emigrate in the span of weeks. The Nazis would no longer permit a slow and orderly emigration; flight was the only escape. In addition, Hermann Göring saw fit to levy a collective fine of 1 billion Reichsmarks on German Jewry to cover insurance company expenses for the Nazi destruction of Jewish property. Kristallnacht clearly represented a further decline in the German Jewish position and also demonstrated for the first time that the Nazis sought to solve the "Jewish Question" through violence.[9]

THE GERMAN JEWISH SITUATION IN 1933

Life as an unwanted minority in a country whose official antisemitic policies increasingly placed Jews outside the bounds of state protection required a Jewish communal response. As a result, efforts to reshape German Jewry were largely based on the long-standing critique of assimilation. German Jews, some of them argued, had gone too far in attempting to be Germans and had almost completely abandoned their Jewish identity. Now that they could no longer be Germans, they ought to become Jews again.[10] Yet, the assumption that German Jewry could weather the storm was inherent in this notion. Proponents assumed that eventually Nazi antisemitism would lose its appeal. They argued that the regime could not last long and that better days were ahead.[11] The nature of the Nazi threat must be kept in mind when analyzing this line of reasoning: until 1938, most German Jews believed that such measures could be tolerated, since Jews were still permitted an amount of economic survival within what was widely perceived as a "new ghetto."[12] Indeed, even German Zionists advocated the continuation of some form of Jewish life in Germany, as long as the regime agreed to guarantee the material existence of German Jewry and their physical lives and honor.[13] The assumption that some form of Jewish life would be possible in Germany was even more prevalent among non- and anti-Zionist organizations. In 1934, for instance, the Hilfsverein der deutscher Juden issued a statement that emphasized the "inner bond" that German Jews felt for "their Fatherland."[14]

Despite efforts to protect Jewish rights in Germany, emigration became increasingly attractive to Jews, especially after 1938. However, the Reichsvertretung der deutschen Juden and other German Jewish organizations still opposed flight, condemning it as an effort to escape from communal responsibilities.[15] Although German Jewish organizations later modified their approach, they continued to oppose mass flight until 1938, when it became clear that no *modus vivendi* was possible.[16]

In the summer of 1938 the major German Jewish institutions turned from advocating limited emigration to urging evacuation, stating that the German Jews could no longer bear their suffering. Even in 1938 and 1939, German Jewish leaders opposed flight, preferring an organized exodus. Despite this policy, a total of 273,000 German and 118,000 Austrian Jews left the Grossreich before the outbreak of war.[17]

JEWISH RESPONSES TO THE NAZI THREAT

Notwithstanding all the problems facing world Jewry, its main focus, from 1933 to 1939, was geared toward the threat to German Jewry. Jewish communities outside the Nazi sphere of influence sought to continue the well established struggle to defend Jewish rights, for both practical and ideological considerations. Practically, an attack on Jews anywhere would encourage anti-semites everywhere to attack Jews, thus creating a snowball effect and broadening the amount of distress among Jews.[18] Ideologically, such concern dovetailed well with the humanitarian orientation of most diaspora agencies and offered, in essence, their raison d'etre. By and large, these organizations pursued four spheres of activity. First, was the effort to publicize Nazi misdeeds, in the hope of mobilizing public opinion against the Nazis thus forcing them to ease their stranglehold on the German Jewish community. Second, was the pursuit of legal action through the League of Nations. Third, was the attempt to use economic warfare to cause the downfall of the Nazi regime. Fourth, was the task of finding a safe haven for Jewish refugees. All of these options were responses to the specific nature of the Nazi threat as perceived by Jews during the 1930s. Not included in these options was the use of violent means against the Nazis, as exemplified by the February 4, 1936, assassination of the Nazi Landleiter (district leader) for Switzerland, Wilhelm Gustloff, by rabbinical student David Frankfurter, and Herschel Grynszpan's November 7, 1938, attack on Ernst vom Rath, the third secretary of the German embassy in Paris.[19] Although daring, these actions could not have an impact on the Nazis, since Jews lacked any military power to follow up the acts of individual assassins. If only for that reason, these were the only two violent anti-Nazi acts by Jews before the outbreak of World War II. Jewish leaders argued that anti-Nazi violence worsened the German Jews' situation: Grynszpan's act resulted in Kristallnacht and Frankfurter's attack might also have resulted in Nazi reprisals had the summer olympics not provided the Nazis with a better opportunity for propaganda. In short, to be successful, Jewish efforts needed a reasonable chance of ameliorating German Jewry's plight.

Mobilizing Public Opinion

Two questions are relevant to studying how press reports about Nazi antisemitic excesses were treated during the 1930s: To what extent was the persecution of Jews in Germany reported (and reported accurately)? What, if any, impact did such reports have on the Nazis' treatment of Jews?[20]

The first question may be answered by noting the fairly extensive reportage in the world press of the Nazi persecution of German Jewry in 1933. Most press reports were considered accurate and provided a succinct perspective on the brutish application of Nazi antisemitism. After 1933, however, the persecution of German Jews ceased to be front-page news and, with the exception of Kristallnacht, would not return to the front pages until after the war.[21]

The Jewish press, however, continued its extensive coverage throughout the 1930s, slacking off after 1939 because of diminished communications after the war broke out. In 1943 and 1944 it resumed extensive (although, again, not always accurate) coverage. But, the Jewish press lacked influence outside the Jewish community. In advocating rescue, therefore, it was limited to preaching to the converted. Influential American papers like the *New York Times, Washington Post*, and *St. Louis Post-Dispatch* largely remained aloof, and neither reported on the persecution of German Jewry extensively in the 1930s nor advocated rescue. At the same time, almost all the major American newspapers continued to support strict adherence to immigration quotas, in some cases as late as 1948.[22]

In contradistinction to the American press, the British press was slightly more forthright in publishing news about Nazi mistreatment of German (and later European) Jewry. Nevertheless, willingness to report the news and advocacy of rescue remained an unbridged chasm in Britain, as in America. Numerous studies have noted the general ambivalence expressed by British politicians toward the rescue issue, reflecting their fear that a Jewish tidal wave would inundate Britain, Palestine, or both.[23] In both America and Britain, there was little Jewish influence within the corridors of power, rather than a lack of precise information on Nazi actions. This most singularly demonstrates the weakness of Jewry at the time: the Jews could not turn their communal agenda into the agenda of any country or any discernible group throughout the diaspora.

The Bernheim Petition

Since the Jews lacked a sovereign state, the potential for independent diplomatic action to prevent or at least mitigate Nazi antisemitism was severely circumscribed. As a result, legal action through the offices of the League of Nations represented the only possible recourse Jews had to obtain redress for Nazi discrimination. Eastern European Jews were considered a "national minority," and their rights as members of such had been guaranteed by the League in a series of Minorities Treaties signed with the so-called successor states (Poland, Hungary, and the Baltic Republics) in the years after

World War I.[24] It seemed reasonable to assume that German Jews could also benefit by using the League to pressure the Nazis into canceling their anti-semitic campaign. On this basis, a number of Jewish organizations planned to petition the League. Since Germany had not signed a broad minorities treaty and was thus not bound by any legal precedent, this idea proved faulty. Moreover, German Jewry had not been considered, nor did it consider itself, a national minority since the emancipation in 1871. As a result, these initial efforts to place the Jewish issue on the League's spring agenda failed, as did efforts to persuade Britain to sponsor a pro-Jewish resolution in the League Council.[25]

A change in tactics became necessary. Although Germany was not a signatory to any of the broad Minorities Treaties, the nation was bound by a little-used provision of the 1922 Convention on Upper Silesia signed by Germany and Poland. Five articles of this convention (Articles 66, 67, 75, 80, and 83) promised full equality for all persons living in Upper Silesia, and Article 66 explicitly specified that such protection would be granted "without distinction of birth, nationality, language, race or religion."[26] Based on this convention, a Silesian Jew named Franz Bernheim approached Nathan Feinberg and Emil Margulies, lawyers for the Comité des Délégations Juives (CDJ, the umbrella organization for all Jewish agencies represented at the League of Nations). Together, they crafted a petition in Bernheim's name that was presented to the League Council on May 12, 1933.[27] Despite strong German objections, the League took up the petition and on May 31 it concluded that Bernheim's protest was valid.[28] Since it was temporarily in Germany's interest to maintain the Silesian convention, the Nazis deferred to the League of Nations on this issue and exempted Silesian Jewry from all antisemitic legislation until 1937, when the treaty was not renewed.

This was a minor victory, but it was a victory nonetheless. The CDJ planned to carry the victory further by submitting more petitions to the League Council. Feinberg, for instance, spoke of starting a "petition movement," but the campaign did not come to fruition.[29] In part, the long-term failure to bring diplomatic pressure to bear on Nazi Germany reflected the intense disunity of Jewish organizations outside Germany, since they could not agree on a joint anti-Nazi position.[30] The failure of the League of Nations petition campaign to effect a substantive change in Nazi policy also reflects the general weakness of the League. Additionally, the unwillingness of any country to sponsor the Jewish anti-Nazi campaign demonstrates just how powerless the Jews really were, and offers an early indication of the widespread disinclination to rescue threatened European Jewry.[31]

The Boycott

While some Jewish efforts were dedicated to using diplomacy for defensive purposes, others attempted to use economic warfare, with the hope of toppling the Nazi regime or at least forcing the Nazis to moderate their antisemitic campaign. Anti-Nazi boycott groups sprang up spontaneously among Polish, American, and Palestinian Jews in February and March 1933, in response to the first news of Nazi antisemitic persecution.[32]

The difficulty faced was not in declaring a boycott, but in becoming organized and building up sufficient support to make it work. The boycott needed to be united and to represent a clear majority of Jewish groups. It also required the support of consumers, Jewish and non-Jewish alike. Despite high hopes, however, the boycott had a limited impact, causing only minor ripples in the German economy. Four factors must be considered when assessing the boycott's ultimate failure: Jewish disunity; the failure to fully enlist gentile anti-Nazi organizations and businesses; governmental intervention in some countries; and the Haavara (Transfer) agreement negotiated between Zionists and the Nazi regime.

While a unified boycott effort may have affected the German economy, unity proved difficult to obtain. The various boycott groups differed among themselves, and some of the most important Jewish communal organizations around the world — including the Board of Deputies of British Jews, the Anglo-Jewish Association, the Alliance Israélite Universelle, and the American Jewish Committee — opposed the idea of boycotting Germany.

There were a variety of arguments both for and against the boycott. At the very least, supporters argued, Jewish honor demanded a boycott.[33] Given what appeared to be the weak state of the German economy, reeling from the catastrophic effects of the depression, a vigorously pursued boycott seemed to have a good chance of success.[34] Some thought that the boycott, combined with diplomatic action, could result either in the collapse of the Nazi regime or, at the minimum, in a mitigating of its antisemitic campaign.[35]

Opponents of the boycott countered that a Jewish-sponsored anti-Nazi boycott would play into antisemitic propaganda, which claimed that there was a worldwide conspiratorial Jewish shadow government. Making Nazism a Jewish issue, as opposed to a nonsectarian one, was seen as unwise, and its scope too narrow for success. Many Jewish organizations argued that boycotting Germany at a time when friendly relations prevailed would open Jews to accusations of dual loyalty or of warmongering. Opponents of the boycott also feared retaliation against German Jewry.[36] The Board of Deputies of British Jews, for instance, opposed any officially declared Jewish boycott, but quietly supported some of the spontaneous boycott groups.[37]

We may surmise, however, that the real opposition to the boycott by most Jewish organizations was their aversion toward any public Jewish actions against Nazi Germany. Those opposed to the boycott preferred that Jewish organizations work privately to help German Jewry, and pointed to precedents of quiet *shtadlanut* (intercession) for persecuted Jewish communities.[38]

Until World War II the boycott movement in the United States remained largely a sectarian issue, attracting only a small number of non-Jews sympathetic to the plight of German Jewry and failing to provide a sufficient incentive for American businesses to break their German connections.[39]   The Jewish anti-Nazi boycott also aroused considerable criticism and suspicion. For example, an editorial in the highly influential *Christian Science Monitor*, dated April 4, 1933, stated: "Hate has begot hate, bitterness has rebounded in bitterness. Jews outside Germany have brought down trouble upon their fellows within the Reich." This editorial continued by noting that Jewish atrocity stories would be "accepted only by the gullible," and scoring the Jews' "commercial clannishness which often gets them into trouble." In the end, the *Christian Science Monitor* condemned as equally unjustified both the Nazi anti-Jewish boycott and Jewish efforts at self-defense.[40]

In Poland governmental intervention played a decisive role in deterring the boycott. There, the Jewish anti-Nazi boycott enjoyed the support of almost all Jewish political parties, a degree of unity almost unprecedented in Polish Jewish history in the interwar years. In a gesture of friendship toward the Reich after the signing of the German-Polish nonaggression pact on January 26, 1934, the Polish government unilaterally suppressed the boycott organization by banning its publicity.[41]

Finally, an apparent factor in the failure of the boycott, at least in Palestine, was the Haavara (Transfer) Agreement. The subject of much heated debate at the time, Haavara is still the source of considerable recrimination. Although relevant to diaspora Jewish responses to the Nazis, the Haavara Agreement requires more detailed discussion and will be taken up below.

Yet, it cannot be said unequivocally that a more forcefully pursued boycott would have succeeded. Jews simply did not possess sufficient economic power to adversely effect German exports in any country except, perhaps, Poland. In stark contrast, Jews received almost no support for their boycott: neither from consumers nor from retailers.[42]   R.H. Macy's, for example, stated its intention to comply with the boycott in principle, but only after all orders for German goods made before March 1, 1933, were completed.[43]   It is too much to expect that a minority group composing a few percents of a population could radically effect imports to that country without keeping in mind the actual state of the German economy. During the 1930s, Germany appeared to be on the verge of economic collapse, and Nazi leaders played up this weakness. Since World War II, however, historians have concluded that the German economy, although seriously affected by the depression, was stronger than most contemporaries realized. It follows, then, that Nazi statements regarding the economy should be dismissed as propaganda designed to justify the severe economic measures that the Nazis applied. A few statistics may help to place this into context. Between 1932 and 1936, at the height of Nazi economic propaganda, Germany's Gross National Product grew by 43 percent (from RM58 Billion to RM83 Billion) while unemployment fell by 71 percent (from a height of 5,600,000 to 1,600,000).[44]

Economic growth was the order of the day in German exports as well. In 1929 Germany had a positive trade balance of only RM36,000,000. By 1932, at the height of the depression, Germany's positive trade balance *grew* to RM1,072,000,000. Wile the balance of trade fell from that height to "only" RM667,000,000 in 1933 (and then fell negative by RM284,000,000 in 1934), in 1936 Germany's balance of trade was still in the black by RM550,000,000.[45] The reason for this was that Germany's export economy was protected in the Balkans and Eastern Europe by a series of forty clearing agreements that replaced foreign currency payments (for German imports from the relevant countries) with barter (via the export of equivalent values in German goods).[46]

The Jewish anti-Nazi boycott continued, with only minimal results, until the outbreak of World War II, when the boycott became non-sectarian. Again, however, the boycott shines a spotlight on Jewish powerlessness during the Holocaust era, and portrays a picture of world Jewry vastly different from that painted by the Nazis. "International finance Jewry" could not, it turned out, wage a successful economic campaign against its premier foe.

Aid to Refugees

Less glamorous than either the petition campaign or the boycott was the day-to-day work needed to help the ever-swelling numbers of German Jews who left the country. A total of 52.7 percent of the 1933 Jewish population of what eventually became the Grossreich left Germany and Austria prior to the outbreak of World War II: 273,000 from Germany and 118,000 from Austria. These figures must be further sub-divided into two groups: those Jews leaving between 1933 and 1937 (175,000 persons in all), and those leaving in 1938 or 1939 (103,000, not counting Jews from Austria). At least 35,000 of the former group remained in continental Europe, with the other 140,000 seeking refuge elsewhere, primarily in Palestine and the United States.

The international climate these refugees encountered was anything but friendly. As a result of continued economic dislocations caused by the depression, few countries sought penniless refugees, while only a handful of countries actively sought immigrants at all.

Although it had an otherwise liberal and tolerant reputation regarding Jews, Holland attempted to keep Jewish (and, to a lesser degree, non-Jewish) refugees from remaining in the country. No impediments were initially placed on refugees who used Holland as a transit point, but after 1934 the Dutch made concerted efforts to keep Jewish refugees (except for select individuals possessing economic assets in Holland) out of the country altogether, and to make the residence of those who did enter the country as brief as possible.[47]

In 1939 the Dutch set up a central detention center for illegal Jewish immigrants in the town of Westerbork.[48]   Again, the basis of this policy was an effort to convince Jewish refugees to use Holland only as a transit point.

Canada's policy on Jewish refugees was even simpler, and was considerably less sympathetic. For the entire period from 1933 to 1939 (and well into the 1940s), Canada's doors were closed to refugees, and especially to Jewish refugees from Germany. By 1938, it was virtually impossible for European Jews to enter Canada.[49]   Norman Robertson, an assitant to Minister of External Affairs O.D. Skelton, summarized Canada's refugee policy thus: "We don't (sic) want to take too many Jews, but, in the present circumstances particularly, we don't want to say so."[50]

Even in the few areas where immigration was still possible, such as South America, only individuals (regardless of religion) with specific skills — primarily medical professionals — were actively sought.[51]   When asylum was found, the refugees invariably needed much financial aid to build their new lives. Legislation enacted by the Weimar Republic on August 8, 1931, in the aftermath of the great inflation (1923-1924), had strictly controlled the export of capital from Germany.[52]   As a result, Jews leaving Germany (except via the Haavara agreement) were virtually reduced to penury. The economic impact of this legislation seems to explain, in part, the unwillingness of many already established German Jews to emigrate.

The need to help German Jews reestablish themselves reinforced the need for philanthropic work to help Jews trying to emigrate from eastern Europe. Jewish philanthropies, especially international aid organizations such as the American Jewish Joint Distribution Committee (JDC), had been severely hurt by the depression. Finances were severely cut back between 1929 and 1932 and the was JDC unable to fully recover its financial position by 1933. Nor had other philanthropic agencies, which often relied on the JDC for their funding.[53]   The German Jewish crisis forced the various philanthropic agencies to pool resources, by joining united committees to establish rescue priorities and financial goals.[54]   Financial difficulties would continue to plague refugee aid efforts throughout the Nazi era.

European aid efforts enjoyed some success, even though they tended to concentrate on philanthropy, rather than resettlement. European campaigns were thus able to capitalize on the immediacy of the need because of the proximity of events, and raised considerable sums, especially in 1933 and 1934.[55]

It appears, paradoxically, that the most successful fund-raising drives were in precisely those countries that attempted to exclude Jewish refugees, notably Sweden and Switzerland, although funds existed in every country.[56]   Italian Jewry also collected the considerable sum of 600,000 lire ($30,000) between January and July of 1933.[57]   Other Jewish communities collected lesser amounts, but experienced difficulty in turning the monies to any practical use owing to local currency transfer restrictions. A case in point was the Jewish community of Bulgaria, whose entire collection effort was jeopardized by the government's unwillingness to allow export of capital.[58]

As may be expected, most of the money for relief work came from the United States and Great Britain. Zionist and non-Zionist fund-raisers discovered the crucial importance of American Jewry already before World War I. Even after the Great Depression, America remained the main target for fund-raisers of all political persuasions.[59] Thus, in 1930 and 1931 Keren ha-Yesod (KHY) collected a total of £P327,293 ($1,636,465), of which £P61,291 ($306,455), or 19 percent, came from the United States.[60] In 1933 a special effort was made to collect funds for refugee relief. Although this effort accomplished much, the sums collected never equaled what was needed.[61]

In Great Britain, efforts to aid refugees culminated in the creation of a united organization, the Central British Fund for German Jewish Relief (CBF), which began operation on May 18, 1933. The CBF was organized by a distinguished committee of sponsors, including Chief Rabbi Joseph Herman Hertz, Haham Moses Gaster, Lord Reading, Lionel de Rothschild, Chaim Weizmann, and Nahum Sokolow.[62] The CBF also sponsored a Conference for Relief of German Jewry, which met in London between October 29 and November 1, 1933. Represented at the conference were all the European activists working on behalf of German Jewish refugees; their discussions centered on the coordination of activities and on the high hopes assigned to the newly appointed League of Nations High Commissioner for Refugees, James G. McDonald.[63]

To one degree or another, all of these fund-raising efforts also set monies aside for work in Palestine. They provided the resources that the Yishuv utilized in carrying out its program of "constructive" aid, which emerged in the spring of 1933 as the only practical way to offer a long-term solution to Jewish distress in Germany and Eastern Europe.

THE YISHUV IN 1933

Historians have long noted that modern Zionism developed, in part, as a response to antisemitism. Where western European Jewry adopted individual salvation and assimilation into the host nation as a result of emancipation during the nineteenth century, this was not possible for the Jews of eastern Europe. Instead, eastern European Jewry turned to self-emancipation through Jewish nationalism. Theodor Herzl argued that only through creation of a Jewish state in their ancestral homeland could Jews normalize their relations with the non-Jewish world. The immediate result was the First Zionist Congress in 1897 and the birth of modern Jewish nationalism. However, political Zionism was only one aspect of the nascent Jewish nationalist movement. Because political Zionists were initially unable to secure an internationally recognized Jewish national home, practical Zionists emphasized the day-to-day process of building the Yishuv one immigrant at a time. Even though the Balfour declaration obviated the dispute, differing definitions of Zionist goals — political versus practical — remained.

Whereas all Zionists agreed on general principles, their goals were open to widely differing interpretations. Thus, although aliya was recognized as central to the goal of creating a Jewish national home, a highly politicized atmosphere was created within the World Zionist Organization (WZO), resulting in the development of a multiplicity of political parties. Disagreements arose primarily over the parties' interpretation of three basic issues: (1) the nature of the new Jewish society to be created in Palestine; (2) the means and timetable for creating that new society; and (3) the long-term impact on Jewish social, intellectual, and political life.

Disagreements on these three issues led to the creation of four blocs of parties: Labor Zionists, General Zionists, Religious Zionists, and Revisionist Zionists. Each offered a different interpretation of the meaning and specific goals of Zionism. Calling for the fusion of socialism with Zionism, Labor Zionists emphasized the need to recast Jewish society as a whole. By a policy of limiting aliya to halutzim — young, healthy pioneers — Labor Zionists aimed to create a Jewish society in Palestine that would ultimately transform Jewry.[64] In contrast, General Zionists sought a Jewish state that would follow in the traditon of nineteenth-century liberal nationalism. Accepting the need to transform Jewry, General Zionists wanted to achieve Zionist goals through a policy of private investment and individual initiative. Nonetheless, the General Zionists, deeply divided on almost all other issues, accepted the premise of halutzic aliya.[65] Religious Zionists also accepted limited aliya, since they saw the creation of a Jewish national home in traditional terms. The establishment of Jewish control over the ancestral homeland was, in the eyes of Religious Zionists, only the first step (*Athalta d'Geulta*) toward full redemption. The final step, in the form of the long-awaited Messiah, would come only after a limited Yishuv had been established.[66]

Nevertheless, it is clear that all three of these blocs accepted aliya as a goal. They also accepted the premise that eventually a Jewish majority would be established in Palestine and that some form of sovereignty would follow, although the attainment of both was postponed to an undefined future. For now, all would work toward a sufficiently large rate of aliya to place the new Yishuv on a secure basis.

In contradistinction, Revisionist Zionists emphasized the need to offer an immediate solution to Jewish distress. They urged that a Jewish majority be established as quickly as possible, and that sovereignty not be delayed for longer than absolutely necessary. The founder of Revisionist Zionism, Zeev (Vladimir) Jabotinsky, formulated this argument in the light of his perception of antisemitism. Although he distinguished between the "antisemitism of men" and the "antisemitism of things," Jabotinsky was very pessimistic about European Jewry's immediate future. As early as 1915, he had predicted a major catastrophe would strike European Jewry; this premonition persisted throughout the 1920s and 1930s and even played a prominent role in his last work, *The War and the Jews*.[67] Jabotinsky concluded that, "The war will have been fought in vain, the victory will be worse than a lie if that seed is left in the ground to poison the future."[68]

TABLE 1.1: Political Parties Active in the Yishuv, 1930-1939

Party Name	Year	Orientation	Affiliation
A. Labor Bloc			
1. Mapai	1930	Socialist, Zionist	WZO, JA, KI
2. ha-Shomer ha-Zair	1916	Marxist	WZO, KI
3. Poale Zion Smol	1920	Marxist	WZO, KI
B. Religious Bloc			
4. Mizrachi	1902	Religious Zionist	WZO, JA, KI
5. ha-Poel ha-Mizrachi	1924	Religious Zionist	WZO, JA, KI
C. General Zionists			
6. Faction "A"	1931	pro-Weizmann, Liberal	WZO, JA, KI
7. Faction "B"	1931	anti-Weizmann, Liberal	WZO, JA, KI
D. Revisionists			
8. Hitachdut ha-Zionim ha-Revisionistim	1925	Nationalist, Liberal	Ha-Zach[69]
E. Non-Zionist			
9. Communist Party	1924	Marxist	COMINTERN
10. Agudas Israel	1912	Orthodox, anti-Zionist	None
11. Poale Agudas Israel	1925	Orthodox, Socialistic	None
F. Ethnic			
12. Yemenites	1920	Ethnic	KI
13. Sephardim	1920	Ethnic	WZO, KI
14. Ahdut ha-Am	1938	Ethnic	WZO, KI

Source: Bernard D. Weinryb, "Jewish Political Parties in Palestine," *Palestine Affairs*, vol. 2 # 4 (June, 1947): 61-64.

TABLE 1.2: Election Results for the Zionist Congress, In Percentages[70]

Congress	17th	18th	19th	20th	21st
Labor	62.0	68.0	66.8	69.5	70.6
Mizrahi	9.1	8.0	13.9	15.4	10.4
Revisionists	16.8	12.2	----	----	----
General Zionists	7.8	6.6	16.0	14.9	17.6

Source: Dan Horowitz and M. Lissak, *Origins of the Israeli Polity*, Chicago: University of Chicago Press, 1978, pp. 90-91.

The four Zionist blocs constituted a total of eight parties: three Labor, two General Zionist, two Religious, and one Revisionist. Six other parties, three ethnic, two religious non-Zionist, and the Palestine Communist Party, rounded out the Yishuv's polity in the 1930s.

Despite the deep divisions that existed between Mapai and the more radical Socialist Zionist parties Labor represented the largest single bloc in the World Zionist Congress and the WZO. Its relative strength may be gauged by Table 1.2, which indicates the percentage of shekalim bought for each bloc.

Two-thirds of the votes cast for Labor were cast for Mapai, which thus became the dominant party in the Yishuv and its institutions. Even so, Mapai was never able to establish full hegemony over the national institutions. Instead, it operated in coalition with the non-Marxist, non-Revisionist parties.

Mapai, or Mifleget Po'ale Eretz Israel (The Workers' Party of the Land of Israel), was founded in 1930 with the merger of ha-Poel ha-Zair (The Young Worker) and le-Ahdut ha-Avoda (For the Unity of Labor), two diaspora-based Socialist Zionist parties. Both had roots that could be traced back to the rise of Labor Zionism in Europe and to the Second Aliya.[71] Upon merging, the new party approved a platform that pledged itself to the goal of becoming "responsible for the pioneering fulfillment of the Zionist movement and a faithful member of the International Socialist Labor Movement."[72]

Central to Mapai's ideology was the concept of "constructive socialism," by which was meant a fusion of the concepts of Jewish national rejuvenation and a broadly Socialist Weltanschauung, with the ultimate goal of creating an Am Oved, a laboring people. Mapai concentrated on each small step — one more settler, one more dunam of land under Jewish cultivation, one more settlement. As further developed in the 1930s by Mapai leaders, primarily David Ben-Gurion, Chaim Arlosoroff, and Berl Katznelson, constructive socialism would operate in two main stages. First was to create an Am Oved, which would be realized when the Jewish masses had been converted to productive labor on the soil of Eretz Israel. At that point, Jews would become Am Mamlachti, a sovereign people. As formulated by Ben-Gurion,

Mamlachtiut (statism) involved three components: (1) cooperation with non-Socialist Zionists in building Eretz Israel; (2) abandonment of class struggle as the primary defining feature of Socialist Zionism; and (3) assumption of responsibility for fulfillment of traditional Zionist goals.[73] In his major ideological work of the 1930s, *From a Class to a Nation*, Ben-Gurion wrote:

> The time has come for our movement to cease to be one
> branch of the Zionist movement and take upon itself the
> yoke of, and responsibility for, the entire Zionist organi-
> zation . . . Our movement demands . . . [that] . . . we
> identify completely with the Zionist Organization, that
> we be a majority in the Congress and the Zionist Organi-
> zation, and stand at its head. This does not mean that we
> must turn the Zionist Organization into a socialist organi-
> zation, nor does it mean that we must abandon socialism or
> become less socialist than we have been.[74]

In essence, Ben-Gurion's argument was that there were two focal points Mapai owed loyalty to. Doing so, however, required that Labor Zionists behave responsibly within both orbits. It followed that an orthodox Marxist approach, emphasizing class struggle and internecine warfare, was not necessarily the best tactic for Socialist Zionism. Instead, an evolutionary (or reformist) approach would accomplish Mapai's twin goals more efficiently.

Arlosoroff, too, expressed significant doubts about orthodox Marxist theories. In *Der Jüdische Volkssozialismus*, he contended that European Socialists refused to permit Jews the same national consciousness that was taken for granted by all other nations. Therefore, Jews were not compelled to adopt orthodox Marxism. "For us," he stated, "Socialist struggle does not mean the struggle of one class with another. Our goal is the positive construction of a society."[75] Arlosoroff further refined his position in the early 1930s. For instance, in an article in *Davar*, he argued that the Zionists had developed Palestine too slowly: at contemporary rates of aliya, Jews would need 163 years to constitute a majority. Given the Arab population growth, the Jews would need even more time than that to develop as a majority in their national home.[76]

The implication of Mamlachtiut was that at different times, and under different specific circumstances, either the nationalist or the Socialist elements of Mapai's ideology were given greater emphasis. Between 1930 and 1933, for example, Mapai had chosen to emphasize Socialist goals and the primacy of the Histadrut labor exchanges, to the extent of generating a violent conflict with the Revisionists. At the time, conflict appeared to be the only way to fulfill party goals. Similarly, the persecution of German Jewry would be a major test to determine which element would gain priority: Would Mapai emphasize broad national goals, even if that meant the surrender of Socialist goals, or would it continue to adhere to a policy of "business as usual"?

Mapai's position was open to considerable criticism by parties on both the left and right. Those of the far left viewed Mapai's reformist tendency as nothing more than a rehashing of "Bernsteinism," or the surrender of true (from the Marxist perspective) goals for illusory ones.[77] An influential minority within Mapai also rejected reformism. This internal opposition crystallized into Siya-Bet (Faction-B) in 1937.[78] Itself a coalition of an urban group from Tel Aviv and a group of ha-Kibbutz ha-Meuhad members, Siya-Bet initially operated as an internal influence group, hoping to persuade Mapai's majority to return to the correct path of Socialist Zionism. Unlike its parent body, Siya-Bet articulated a clearly Socialist platform, which was given equal emphasis to national goals. Siya-Bet's leaders would thus strongly oppose the abortive Ben-Gurion-Jabotinsky agreements and would support an aliya policy limited to halutzim.[79]

Three other parties also articulated a Marxist ideological attack on Mapai's orientation: Ha-Shomer ha-Zair (the Young Watchman), Po'ale Zion Smol (Leftist Zionist Workers), and the Palestine Communist Party (PCP). The former two parties officially adhered to a Zionist orientation, but stood well to Mapai's left on social issues and on most, but not all, political issues as well.[80] Simply put, both ha-Shomer and Poale Zion saw Zionism as the device to create a socialist state, in contrast to Mapai which saw socialism as the means to achieve the goals of Zionism.

Rounding out Palestine's Jewish socialist parties was the small PCP. The PCP played only a minor role in the Yishuv during the 1930s and can only marginally be considered Jewish. Its unquestioningly anti-Zionist position relegated the party to the outermost fringes of Jewish society and the its unequivocally pro-Arab position also did not find many sympathetic ears in a Yishuv built on the Zionist ideal.[81]

In point of fact, all three parties remained relatively small in comparison to Mapai. Their influence, when felt at all, was felt only in limited circles and then only intermittently. They thus became oppositional movements hoping to attract a portion of the population on single issues. Rarely called on to establish policy, they were relegated to arguments about ideological purity and constant schisms and recombinations which reflected the shifting self-definitions of party members.

A substantially different form of opposition to Mapai's leadership in the WZO was encountered from the right. Founded in 1925 by Jabotinsky, Hitachdut ha-Zionim ha-Revisionistim (Ha-Zohar, the Union of Zionist Revisionists) was the only party in Palestine capable of fighting against Labor's hegemony over the Yishuv.[82] Unlike Mapai, which sought to fuse Jewish nationalism with socialism, Ha-Zohar had one goal: the attainment of a Jewish majority in Palestine, followed as quickly as possible by the creation of a sovereign Jewish state.

Jabotinsky's Zionism was founded on a number of guiding principles, of which two stand out. The first was the principle of monism, or, as Jabotinsky termed it, hadness (unity). He argued that all forms of "hyphenated" Zionism should place their individual agendas on hold. No substantive decisions needed to be made regarding the policies of the Jewish state before its creation. Rather, the Jewish need of the hour was the creation of a disciplined, though not autarkic, Zionist movement.[83] The second guiding principle was his emphasis on hadar (self-respect), an idealized code of aesthetics and behavior whose purpose was to create a "new Jew." According to Jabotinsky, hadar "combines various conceptions such as outward beauty, respect, self-esteem, politeness, [and] faithfulness."[84]

In practice, Jabotinsky emphasized three concrete aspects of his ideology: (1) the immediate need for Zionists to announce their ultimate goal, which he defined as the establishment of a Jewish state; (2) immigration "for all who want it" with the creation of an immigration policy devoid of any limitations, including supposedly objective ones such as economic absorptive capacity; and (3) the conversion of Palestine into the political, social, and intellectual center of the Jewish world.[85] It is fair to say that Jabotinsky defined Zionism exclusively in terms of sovereignty and the goal of a Jewish state.

Jabotinsky's brand of Zionism has been viewed in a number of different ways. Historians have noted similarities between Revisionist Zionism and the liberal nationalism of Giuseppe Mazzini.[86] Jabotinsky repeatedly referred to the role that the Italian *Risorgimento* played in his ideological development. "All my views," he wrote, "on problems of nationalism, the state and society were developed during those years under Italian influence."[87] Socialist (and some non-Socialist) Zionist opponents, however, condemned Revisionism as a form of "integralist" nationalism or fascism.[88] This identification was widely used by opponents to attack Ha-Zohar and deny its legitimacy. Thus, for example, Chaim Weizmann vituperatively attacked Jabotinsky, comparing him — on the basis of an incorrectly reported speech about Jewish relations with the British Empire — to Germany's National Socialists.[89]

For his part, Jabotinsky strongly condemned this anti-Revisionist libel. In a letter to Shlomo Y. Jacobi, he identified only one similarity between Revisionism and Italian fascism — the rejection of Marxist concepts of class struggle — while also noting Ha-Zohar's complete rejection of all the anti-democratic elements of Fascism. Similarly, Jabotinsky strove to explain the supposedly militaristic elements of Revisionist ideology, with its emphasis on uniform and paramilitary drill (most notable in Betar, the Ha-Zohar youth movement). Far from instilling a militaristic spirit, Jabotinsky believed, the uniform and drill served to instill a dignified bearing.[90] He was careful to add, however, that although militarism had intensely negative connotations — especially for Jews — there might be a positive element in the militaristic bearing: specifically, the discipline instilled in Betar members. In Jabotinsky's view, this form of discipline symbolized the fundamental difference "between a multitude, a mob, and a nation."[91] In view of Jabotinsky's concentration on the specific goal of statehood, his focus on discipline is understandable; however, it would, in part, also contribute to the crux of an increasingly violent conflict between Ha-Zohar and Mapai.

Despite his impassioned defense, the identification of Revisionism with fascism remained a sore point in intra-Zionist relations throughout the 1930s and well into the 1940s.[92] Moreover, while the Fascist label did not fit Jabotinsky very well — especially in light of his essentially pro-British and liberal attitudes — the same cannot be said to hold true for all his followers. When combined with syndicalist economic theories, romantic notions about organic nationalism, and hero worship, Revisionism could indeed develop into a quasi-fascism. This fact held especially true among some of Jabotinsky's younger followers — notably Abraham Stern and Abba Ahimeir — and was prominent among the members of a shadowy organization which called itself Brit ha-Biryonim (the Covenant of Terrorists).[93] Zvi Kolitz, a Revisionist leader from Tel Aviv wrote a biography of Benito Mussolini in 1936 that may be seen as typical; the publisher appended a small preface to the book that read in part: "Italy can teach us something. In particular, we Jews . . . should study the miracles which the fascist movement has brought about, especially in the area of nationalism." Jabotinsky was sufficiently concerned about this trend that he condemned it strongly in an article entitled "Basta!"[94] In a letter Jabotinsky wrote to the editors of *Hazit ha-Am* (Ha-Zohar's daily organ) he condemned even grudging admiration for Mussolini and Hitler in no uncertain terms: "The articles and notices on Hitler . . . are to me, and to all of us, like a knife thrust in our backs. I demand an un-conditional stop to this outrage."[95]

Yet, the supposed relationship between Revisionism and Fascism became the center of a manifold divergence between the two major Zionist blocs.

INTRA-ZIONIST CONFLICT: THE OPENING CHAPTER

When Jabotinsky established Ha-Zohar, his purpose was to influence the WZO and bring Zionism back to its stated goals. As early as 1925, he emphasized the need to create an "immigration regime" that would foster the mass transfer of Jews to Palestine. His proposal was for an organized aliya of 40,000 Jews per year for twenty-five years. Jabotinsky correctly reasoned that adoption of this plan would translate into a Jewish majority in Palestine, and with it, the creation of an independent Jewish state as defined by the League of Nations Mandate.[96]

However, in 1925 Jabotinsky's Revisionist movement was not part of the

WZO majority. Instead, the WZO majority followed the more moderate position articulated by Weizmann and the General Zionists. Although they agreed with Jabotinsky's rejection of Socialist Zionism, this did not lead to the creation of a liberal-capitalist coalition between the General Zionists and Ha-Zohar. Instead, disagreement over Weizmann's role and his minimalist position in the failure to achieve Zionist goals, led to a fallout between the two blocs.

Once the dominant party in the WZO, the General Zionists had been displaced by the Labor Zionists beginning in the mid-1920s. At the Seventeenth World Zionist Congress in 1931, they lost the final traces of their former influence to Mapai. Three reasons account for the party's collapse. Mapai's ascent coincided with the rise of the Yishuv as a political factor in the Zionist movement. The center of General Zionist power lay in the diaspora, and as the Yishuv grew in importance, the party's influence and power were reduced. Second, the Great Depression and subsequent economic dislocations hurt the General Zionists more than other Zionist parties precisely because the bulk of their support lay in the diaspora's Jewish middle class; as a group the Depression effected them the most. Finally, ideological factors caused by an identity crisis also played a role, since many General Zionists could not point to anything they stood for, only what they stood against. Examples of infighting include the Brandeis-Weizmann dispute of the early 1920s and the debate among Polish General Zionists over attitutdes toward the government. Both eneded in divisive schisms that weakened the party.[97]

The General Zionist collapse and the rise of Mapai also must be viewed in political context. Beacause of Arab riots in Palestine in August 1929 the British government sent the Shaw Commission to investigate conditions in the country. The commission's report advocated a complete halt to aliya. Sidney J. Webb (Lord Passfield), the Colonial Minister, issued a White Paper that incorporated the commission's proposals and signaled virtual repudiation of the Mandate. To avert the obvious disaster that such a policy represented, all Zionists united briefly in a pressure campaign that succeeded in having the provisions of the Passfield White Paper overturned in 1931.

As part of the protest strategy, Weizmann wrote a searing public letter of resignation from the presidency of the WZO. Delegates at the Seventeenth World Zionist Congress reasoned that Weizmann's minimalist policy had failed and were ready for a change. For the first time, Mapai, with the largest single bloc of delegates at the Congress, was in a position to attain control of the WZO, although it still required a coalition to secure its leadership.[98]

The second largest bloc of delegates at the Congress was from Ha-Zohar. Its role of opposition to Mapai had come to the fore, and many Revisionists hoped to achieve more than mere influence within the Congress. With Weizmann out of the picture even capturing the presidency seemed possible to Jabotinsky. Weizmann evidently thought this was the logical next step for the Congress, and he even seems to have anticipated a coalition between Mapai and Ha-Zohar.[99] Exactly the opposite took place. A coalition of Mapai, Mizrachi, and General Zionists elected Nahum Sokolow president of the WZO, and Emanuel Neumann (an American General Zionist) chairman of the Jewish Agency Executive (JAE). Any hope of influencing the WZO was destroyed when the majority of the delegates refused to even consider Jabotinsky's resolution on the so-called Endziel issue.[100]

Thus, by the time the Congress convened in 1931, conflict had replaced cooperation as the defining feature of interparty relations. That spring, a Betar work company accepted agricultural work in Kfar Saba without Histadrut consent. An attempt to prevail on the Betar members to join the Histadrut failed, prompting their forcible removal from the workplace. This incident caused a violent three-way confrontation between the Histadrut, Betar, and the growers, resulting in a stalemate at the end of the harvest season. In the interim, other farmers began hiring non-Histadrut labor, and a lockout ensued.[101] The struggle was exacerbated in the autumn of 1932, when violent clashes erupted between Betar and Histadrut members during a strike against the Froumine Biscuit Company.[102] Yet another outbreak of violence took place on the last day of Passover, April 17, 1933, when a peaceful march in Tel Aviv by uniformed members of Betar was interrupted and attacked by workers, a majority of whom were Histadrut members.[103]

More fuel was added to the fire by a series of ideological clashes. In 1932, Joshua H. Yeivin, editor in chief of Ha-Zohar's newspaper, *Hazit ha-Am*, published a novel containing a thinly veiled attack on both the Histadrut and Mapai, accusing Socialist Zionist leaders of venality and a lust for power.[104] Jabotinsky also contributed to this atmosphere, with his stand on Mapai's *"sha'atnez."* In response to the publication of Ben-Gurion's *Me-Ma'amad la-Am*, Jabotinsky challenged Mapai to truly place national goals ahead of class interests by surrendering the right to strike. In exchange, Jabotinsky proposed a national arbitration board to adjudicate labor disputes.[105] Mapai leaders this proposal as nothing more than an attempt to defend middle-class interests, a class struggle in reverse, and an effort to deny workers the chance to better themselves. In view of the voluntary nature of the Yishuv's institutions, Jabotinsky's proposal could not be taken seriously, since even a *"mandatory"* arbitration board would have no means to enforce its decisions. Moreover, the entire proposal smacked of the integralist, *"corporate"* economics prevalent in contemporary fascist Italy. Convinced that Jabotinsky was an implacable enemy, the Histadrut rejected his proposals out of hand.[106]

Such perceptions of Jabotinsky's enmity were not incorrect, although, in view of the disparate sizes of the two movements (42,000 members for Mapai, compared to 2,000 members for Betar), most Mapai members exaggerated the actual threat. In an essay entitled *"Yes, Break It,"* Jabotinsky had placed himself squarely in the ranks of opponents of the Histadrut as an institution:

> No-one seeks the destruction of the Hebrew workers'organi-
> zation — heaven forbid. There is, however, the will to
> break *one* of the workers' organizations. More precisely —
> the will to break . . . the [Histadrut's] claim to a mono-
> poly and for dominion. This is justified. Yes, break it.[107]

Jabotinsky's view was seen by the labor leaders as a declaration of war.
Violent clashes became one element in the ideological conflict. Whether
violent or not, however, this conflict between Mapai and Ha-Zohar would
impact on the Yishuv's response to the Nazi threat.

2
First Steps

RESCUE ALIYA: A CONCEPTUAL ANALYSIS

Before we can analyze the Yishuv's policy rescue policy, it is necessary to understand the Zionist decision making process. The Jews' limited options in response to the Nazis also bear remembering, since, in many ways, the Yishuv's options were even more limited than the rest of world Jewry's. The Zionist press, for example, could (and did) devote considerable space to reports on the German Jewish situation, although the Yishuv's press was limited in its influence. With the exception of the *Palestine Post*, the only English-language daily published in Palestine, none of the papers were regularly read by members of the government. Since most newspapers were party-sponsored and were read by party members, they were writing for a majority who already accepted certain Zionist premises regarding the proper response to an antisemitic attack. This prejudice did not ipso facto mean the rejection of other policies, but it did establish a clear preference regarding the kind of policy a majority of the Yishuv, and virtually all its leaders, would support.

The same may be said to hold true for the Bernheim petition, and the entire petition campaign. Although considered important by diaspora Jewish organizations, the petition did not get much support from the Yishuv. This was true for two reasons. First, the Yishuv lacked a clearly defined diplomatic status, and second, the British government refused to lend its support to these Jewish efforts. Therefore, although the WZO supported the petition campaign, it could not act as a sponsor.[1] Moreover, as the primary purpose of the petition was to regulate Jewish life in Germany, it could not act as an anchor for the Yishuv's policy of aid to German Jewry.[2] Sponsoring an anti-

Nazi boycott was also rejected by the majority of Zionists as "inexpedient and dangerous."[3] To be sure, not all Zionists accepted that idea. Zeev Jabotinsky saw the boycott as an effective defensive weapon. So did Berl Locker, Mapai's representative at the London JA Executive. Nevertheless, the JAE decided to hold off on an official boycott policy.[4]

Furthermore, the majority of Zionist institutions uncategorically rejected empty, symbolic acts that drew adverse attention to Jews and Zionists but did not offer any real benefits to the Yishuv or to German Jews. For example, on May 19, 1933, members of Betar tore the Nazi banner down from a flag-pole on the property of the German consulate in Jerusalem. Ironically, one of those involved in this act, which was condemned as vandalism by many Zionists, was Abraham Stavsky, whose name is more often associated with the death of Chaim Arlosoroff.[5] The majority rejected such acts, and the boycott as well, primarily for fear of retribution, since numerous Nazis made thinly veiled threats during speeches and meetings with German Jewish leaders.[6]

Economic, political, and social realities in the Yishuv in addition to the small influence of the WZO therefore oriented most Zionists toward what they called constructive aid. By this they meant the maximization of Jewish immigration to form a policy of rescue by means of aliya. The justifications for this policy were both ideological and pragmatic. Ideological, insofar as all Zionist ideologies were based on the premise of aliya, and practical because the Yishuv stood to gain considerably by the influx of German Jews who possessed wealth and technical know-how. In turn, rescue aliya also provided the benefit of a permanent safe haven for German Jews who, other-wise, would have to remain in Germany or chance finding temporary shelter elsewhere.

Regrettably, rescue aliya has been much misunderstood in recent years. In particular, historians have come to emphasize the problems that the rescue aliya program experienced. With perfect hindsight these historians note how completely unprepared to meet the crisis Jews, the Yishuv, and the Zionist movement were. Moreover, they also note a paradox: grandiose rhetoric about rescue in the abstract, coupled with an attitude of "business as usual" when concrete steps were to be taken. As a result of these considerations, and many others, some historians have distinguished between "rescue" and "salvation." They claim that the former was conceptually incompatible with the latter. Rescue, of necessity, always meant the immediate evacuation of German and European Jewry while salvation meant the rescue of only a "saving remnant." This line of analysis hinges on the assumption that German goals were always clear and that all Nazi actions led inexorably to the extermination of European Jewry. As the debate between the so-called intentionalist and functionalist historians shows, such a conclusion cannot presently be upheld, especially not before the mass outburst of anti-Jewish violence that culminated on Kristallnacht.[7] Thus, when author Anita Shapira concluded that even by 1939 Zionists "had not read the handwriting on the wall," she was telescoping events and assuming that in 1939 — or earlier — the Final Solution was obvious to all who viewed the events properly.[8] At the time, however, Nazi plans still concentrated on emigration. Indeed, during the summer of 1940 they had laid extensive plans to deport European Jewry to the island of Madagascar.[9] Jewish emigration from the Reich itself was not banned until October 19, 1941, fully four months after the Einsatzgruppen began mobile killing operations in the occupied Soviet territories.[10]

Yet, although this position cannot be fully upheld, it also cannot be unequivocally rejected. Moreover, the painful paradox facing the Yishuv cannot be denied. While some Zionists were unable to rise above their petty concerns, the same was true for virtually every other Jewish party and group at the time. Not even the most pessimistic of them could foresee the direction that Nazi antisemitism was taking until it was too late to save more than a remnant of European Jewry. That Zionists often used grandiose rhetoric regarding the extraordinary means needed to undertake the program of rescue aliya, and that an attitude of "business as usual" pervaded the program once it actually began cannot be denied. Blaming Zionists — accusing them of "egotism" for example — misses the point.[11] Had a sovereign Jewish State existed during the 1930s then such accusations would be valid. In reality, Britain and not the Jewish Agency, ruled Palestine. Given the Yishuv's limited resources, Dina Porat's conclusion regarding Zionist responses to the extermination of European Jewry must be kept in mind when seeking to assess guilt:

> Israelis of today have long since forgotten or are unaware
> of the difficulties facing the Yishuv at the time. It was
> a minority in a country ruled by foreigners. It was a
> social-national experiment in its early stages. Its
> resources — in manpower, money, and arms — were small.
> Nor do they realize that, for all its limitations — and in
> the face of the efficiency of the   German death machine and
> the interference of the Allies — the Yishuv in fact did
> more than it was ever given credit for — either then or now.[12]

THE YISHUV'S INSTITUTIONS REACT

The first Zionist institution to respond to the German Jewish crisis was the Va'ad Leumi. Founded in 1920, it was the executive branch of the autonomous Jewish institution, the Knesset Israel. In theory, the Va'ad Leumi acted in tandem with Asefat ha-Nivharim, the seventy-one-member elected assembly of Jewish Palestine. The Va'ad Leumi articulated the broad parameters of the Zionist policy regarding the mistreatment of German Jewry during an emergency meeting that took place on March 30, 1933. Eschewing an official anti-Nazi boycott, the Va'ad Leumi approved a resolution that was published the next day.[13]

Although the manifesto was approved unanimously, members of the Va'ad Leumi debated the practical implications of fighting for German Jewry. The debate centered on the possibility of an anti-Nazi boycott. Rabbi Moshe Ostrovsky (Mizrachi) and Aharon Zisling (Mapai) strongly opposed the boycott, which was likely to do more harm than good.[14] Jacob Weinshall (Ha-Zohar) was also opposed; instead he advocated action to rescue an initial 25,000 German Jews.[15]

The Va'ad Leumi met again on April 27 to deal with the German crisis. The Executive took upon itself full authority to coordinate appropriate rescue activities, in conjunction with other Jewish organizations throughout the world. Pleading for interorganizational unity in the vital undertaking, the Va'ad Leumi called upon the JAE to draw up a plan to deal with the expected influx of German refugees.[16] The Va'ad Leumi Executive then urged WZO President Nahum Sokolow to participate in the growing movement to help German Jewry, noting that "full cooperation [of the Jewish] Agency, Yishuv, imperative for their success."[17] Four days prior, the Va'ad Leumi Executive had joined the chorus of Zionist voices calling upon Chaim Weizmann to head the relief efforts, both in Palestine and abroad.[18]

The Nazi purge of "Jewish" books, which culminated in the mass bonfires of May 10, 1933, reinforced the Va'ad Leumi's decisions to give rescue priority over anti-Nazi pronouncements. The latter, it was argued, would be high-sounding but would bring no long-term practical results.[19] On May 11, the Va'ad Leumi issued another manifesto, calling on the entire freedom-loving world to aid German Jewry in its war for survival, and demanding that Jewish organizations mobilize to defend German Jewry. The manifesto also specified the Yishuv's role in rescuing thousands of German Jews by encouraging aliya.[20]

Other institutions also sought a response to the growing crisis. At a meeting on April 13, 1933, the Histadrut Executive approved a resolution calling for action to increase the number of immigration certificates available. It also created a committee to deal with German Jewish aliya.[21] But these decisions had no immediate impact, since they merely restated the Va'ad Leumi's previous decisions.

However, political considerations within the Yishuv complicated rescue. Under Article 4 of the Mandate, the Va'ad Leumi was not Palestinian Jewry's sole governing agency. The Jewish Agency (JA) also existed to represent the Yishuv's interests. The JA was like a shadow government; its departments were equivalent to ministries, and its Executive was arranged like a cabinet. By design, the president of the WZO sat ex officio as head of the JA, and also headed the WZO's Va'ad ha-Poel ha-Metzumtzam (Inner Actions Committee, or Executive).

TABLE 2.1: Composition of the Jerusalem Executive, 1933

Name	Party Affiliation	Department
Chaim Arlosoroff	Mapai	Political
I. B. Berkson	non-Zionist	Education
Joshua H. Farbstein	Mizrachi	Industry
Maurice B. Hexter	non-Zionist	Settlement
Eliezer Kaplan	Mapai	Finance
Emanuel Neumann	General Zionist	Chairman
Arthur Ruppin	General Zionist	Agriculture
Werner D. Senator	non-Zionist	Immigration

Source: *Jewish Agency Report*, 1933.

Within the JA, the Jerusalem Executive predominated, although it operated in coordination with a parallel Executive Committee in London and a political advisory committee in New York. The JA was not an exclusively Zionist organization. In 1929, an agreement had been reached with American non-Zionists, granting them representation on the Jewish Agency Executive (JAE). The non-Zionists, however, never dominated the JAE. The most sensitive departments and the chairmanship of the Jerusalem Executive always remained in the hands of the Zionist coalition, dominated by Mapai.

The Va'ad Leumi's decisions in March and April of 1933 might have created tension with the JAE, had Mapai not controlled both organizations. The fact that the JAE had not formulated a policy of its own to aid German Jewry helped defuse potential difficulties with overlapping authorities. To be sure, the broad parameters of a policy had already been considered by JA members. Thus, Georg Landauer, one of the leaders of the Zionistische Vereinigung für Deutschland, wrote to Dr. Werner D. Senator that a maximum number of available certificates should be granted to Germany, including as many as possible for men between the ages of 35 and 45. Landauer noted that German Jewry had not yet panicked, but he cautioned that "the need [for certificates] is great and immediate."[22]

The delay in formulating JAE policy was due in part to a lack of accurate information, as well as being caught "unprepared and defenseless."[23] Acess to precise information was especially problematic, and by mid-March the JA contemplated the establishment of "listening posts" in Czechoslovakia (at Mährisch-Ostrau) and in Holland.[24] The London Executive could not assist in this regard, and admited that all it knew was that the "German situation [is] bad. No other details beyond information [from the] press."[25] Although the Yishuv's leadership had a variety of press sources available to them, in addition to reports by Zionist shelichim in Germany (and other European countries), these sources provided only partial information and thus offered only a partial glimpse of the Nazi threat. From such incomplete sources the exact nature of the emergency could not be gauged.

Unfortunately, no written record exists of when and by whom the decision to emphasize aliya was made. At the JAE's first session on German Jewry, held on April 9, 1933 the discussion centered on how to carry out the policy, not on what policy to adopt. The decision, whoever made it, provided the foundation for virtually all Zionist work over the next decade. Moreover, rescue aliya was consistent with Mapai's pragmatic approach and with the general operations adopted by the JA. The JA, however, moved cautiously to avoid any excuse for German "retaliatory" measures against German Jews. This appears to be the cause of Senator's otherwise inexplicable memo to the JA staff dated March 17, 1933: "In light of the specific situation in Germany I request that you refrain from writing personal letters to Germany on Jewish Agency stationary."[26] Senator stated his fear that a staff member might write something which would be attributed to the JA and harm all involved.

By March 24, the specific needs of German Jewish émigrés were becoming clear. From Berlin, Landauer wrote of the urgent need for at least 700 certificates. Landauer also noted that with visitors to the Palestine Office in Berlin reaching as many as 100 a day, further grants of emergency certificates would be needed.[27] This request was strongly supported by the London Executive in a telegram to Arlosoroff. The London JAE proposed a direct apeal to the High Commissioner, General Sir Arthur Wauchope, requesting that he take the initiative to ease the procedures for "independent means immigrants" — that is, the various categories of Capitalists (A-class certificates).[28]

The call to grant as many certificates as possible to German Jews was further reinforced by the HICEM, a refugee aid organization founded in Paris in 1924 by representatives of the Hebrew Sheltering and Immigrant aid Society (HIAS), Jewish Colonization Association (ICA), and Emigdirect (United Committee for Jewish Emigration).[29] Now HICEM cabled:

> Anticipation Jewish emigration Germany beg you for
> support. Please assign important number certificates
> behalf German Jews and obtain special admission
> Category unable avail certificates [it] being under-
> stood we guarantee immigrants not public charge.
> Trusting your solidarity expect favorable reply.[30]

From the organizational perspective, this was an important cable. Previously, HICEM had shied away from direct support for Zionist activities in Palestine. Under the emergency situation, however, HICEM's policy was modified to include at least some financial support for Zionist activities, primarily for persons who could not otherwise get certificates (the special-admission category referred to as "unable avail certificates"). To this, the agency replied: "endeavoring [to] obtain advance [on] next schedule of which [a] large number will be allocated [to] German Jews. Glad [for] your cooperation, shall keep you informed."[31]   Finally, on March 31, the Hitachdut Olei Germania (HOG) Executive wrote to the JAE, requesting that the maximum number of immigrant certificates be made available for Jews from Germany.[32]

By April 1933, the Yishuv had made its decision. In a letter to the leaders of HOG, Senator summarized the program of aid. It emphasized constructive work to bring German Jews to Palestine and to keep them there, since bringing olim only to have them emigrate elsewhere — or even return to Germany (which was possible in 1933 and 1934) — would not be conducive to a long-term solution.[33] Such a bold program required both systematic planning and financial support; while the JAE could see to the former, financing would be a problem.

In order to obtain the needed financing, the JAE had to elaborate its specific plans for German aliya. Indeed, the last business that Chaim Arlosoroff completed on the day he was murdered (June 16, 1933), was the sending of a terse three-word telegram to Landauer in Berlin: "cable final plans."[34] Interestingly, the last communication that Arlosoroff received also dealt with German Jewry: a letter from the Histadrut Labor Committee containing a broad proposal for aliya-related work.[35]

In essence, the Histadrut proposed the following: (1) a request from the British for a 1,500 additional emergency certificates; (2) agreement with the council of Moshavot for a public works program, and agreement with farmers to absorb as many employees as were available; (3) increased absorption in the construction industry; (4) JAE demands for increasing the number of Jews in the civil service; (5) simplification of the process of obtaining D-class certificates (family members); and (6) predesignation of an appropriate number of certificates for artisans and skilled workers.[36]

From his vantage point as head of the JA Immigration Department, Senator was also in a position to propose policy. In April 1933 he formulated a detailed proposal for the rescue aliya program.[37]   Recognizing that non-Zionist philanthropic agencies such as the American Jewish Joint Distribution Committee (JDC), whose European branch Senator had headed from 1925 to 1930, would not support any statement of Zionist goals that included statehood, he still emphasized the crucial role that the Yishuv could play in rescuing German Jewry. Of critical importance, according to Senator, was the need for an orderly exodus: he cautioned that "spontaneous, uncontrolled and uncoordinated activities of the various sections of world Jewry will do more harm than good."[38]

Senator proposed a coordinated policy, based on three elements. The first was to create "a reliable information service," important because of repeated complaints regarding news coverage from Germany.   Expanding on the idea of two "listening posts" that he had earlier proposed to Berl Locker, Senator now said that they should be created "at three or four points" near the German border: in Czechoslovakia (Mährisch-Ostrau), in Switzerland (Basel), in the Netherlands (Amsterdam), and, if needed, in either Denmark (Copenhagen) or Poland (Posen).[39] The second element was creating a committee to "coordinate the political work of world Jewry for the behalf of their brethren in Germany."[40] "Such a political committee," Senator argued, "should be formed by representatives of the Joint Foreign Committee [of Anglo-Jewry], the Alliance Israélite Universelle, the American Jewish Committee, and by representatives of the Zionist Organization or the Jewish Agency for Palestine."[41] The committee, in coordination with ICA and the JDC, would plan and carry out an appropriate political program, including possible use of an anti-Nazi boycott, to aid German Jewry and defend Jewish rights.[42] Finally, Senator proposed the establishment of a humanitarian committee, parallel to the political committee, to look after the needs of German Jewish refugees. This committee, he assumed, "would have to look for more far-reaching and more constructive measures" to assist Jewish emigration.[43] Senator continued:

> The German Jews, with their skill, ability and capital, as
> far as they will be allowed to export at least part of it,
> may be a very valuable element in the country. Palestine
> will be not only a haven of physical refuge for them, but
> a spiritual re-creation after the disastrous disappointment
> and the tragic times through which they are now passing.[44]

Inherent in Senator's position was the assumption that German Jewry could be divided into three unequal groups. One third would seek to emigrate to Palestine. Another third would emigrate to points other than Palestine. The last third would wish to remain in Germany, regardless of the hardships of the "new ghetto."

FINANCES, RESCUE ALIYA, AND "BUSINESS AS USUAL"

One hindrance to action was the Yishuv's delicate financial situation. On April 9, 1933, Senator, following up on the contacts in March, wrote to the leaders of HICEM requesting extensive financial assistance so that constructive work, primarily housing, for the new olim could begin immediately.[45] In its April resolutions, the Va'ad Leumi spoke of the need to establish a worldwide fund-raising effort, to be headed by Weizmann.

Similarly, the London Executive called for a fund for German Jewry that would be launched by the publication of a manifesto to world Jewry written by Chaim Nachman Bialik. This fund would be designated exclusively for the settlement of "thousand(s) [of] German Jewish families [in] Palestine."[46] Of necessity, such a fund would cooperate with the various relief efforts being proposed in Great Britain and America. "In general," reported Locker, "the time is now ripe to ask Jews for financial sacrifices, although we cannot predict if the mood will last."[47]

The general consensus in London was that a figure of stature — specifically Weizmann — would be needed to give the fund credibility.[48] But in both Palestine and London, considerable personal, political, and ideological opposition existed to his involvement in such an undertaking. For example, WZO President Nahum Sokolow saw Weizmann's prominent role in the fund as a possible means for his return to the WZO presidency.[49] This opposition hindered creation of the fund, and almost aborted the Yishuv's program of constructive aid before it began. While broad positions were derived from a widely held Zionist consensus, many details still required elucidation, and the JAE still had to approve London's proposals. At the Executive's first meeting on the fund, three options were proposed: (1) not to become involved at all; (2) to use the presently existing fund-raising apparatus of Keren ha-Yesod (KHY); or (3) to create a new apparatus as part of the JAE. The first position, advocated by Mizrachi representative Joshua H. Farbstein, was rejected almost immediately. So was the use of the KHY, out of fear that its other fund-raising activities (dedicated exclusively to buying land in Palestine) would be watered down.[50] That left creation of a new committee under the auspices of the JAE.

At this meeting, Arlosoroff noted: "The German crisis is a difficult test for Zionism and its results will be of great importance for our movement." Therefore, he proposed concentration on: "1) political work, 2) preparation of concrete plans, 3) attainment of means [to carry out the plans], and 4) assistance to refugees and those [Jews] still in Germany."[51]

The Executive's agreement to Arlosoroff's proposals now raised the specter of two competing funds being called into existence, one by the JA and the other by the Va'ad Leumi. Moreover, the Va'ad Leumi had been involved in the numerous international contacts needed to create the fund although, strictly speaking, any such undertaking was the responsibility of the JAE.[52] Therefore, a series of tripartite negotiations between the Jerusalem JA, London JA, and Va'ad Leumi Executives began. Three issues needed settling during the negotiations. First, in which organization would primary responsibility for aid to German Jewry be vested? Second, what type of fund would be established, and how would that fund relate to the other Zionist national funds? Third, what would Weizmann's role in these activities be? In view of the opposition to any role for Weizmann, one can appreciate that the negotiations regarding the fund were delicate. Nor was Weizmann's attitude helpful. Refusing to consider returning to the presidency of the WZO except on his own terms, he nevertheless refused to surrender his position on the fund in deference to Sokolow. He also poured scorn and vituperation on his rivals, including Stephen Wise and Henrietta Szold, accusing them of "Fascist-Revisionist tendencies" because of their opposition to his role in the fund.[53] Clearly, these maneuvers politicized what should have been a humanitarian issue. For all these reasons, the JAE found itself deadlocked and unable to take decisive action on behalf of the German Jews.

A number of compromises were proposed to break the deadlock. London proposed the creation of two committees: one political, headed by Sokolow, and the other humanitarian, headed by Weizmann. Approached by Sokolow to lead the fund, but without any authority over political matters, Weizmann initially declined.[54] Matters were further complicated by the need for the Yishuv to create a local fund while simultaneously being involved in the global Zionist fund-raising campaign. In view of the need to begin work immediately, the Executive proposed a compromise whereby a fund would be set up under JAE control, with the participation of all relevant agencies. This fund would be run by a temporary executive that would be appointed by the JAE and would be responsible to it.[55] Turning to the larger fund-raising effort, the JAE approved a resolution suggested by Emanuel Neumann that read:

> The Executive approves of the suggestion regarding active participation of representatives of the Zionist Organization and the Jewish Agency in the project designed to create a world fund on the condition that sufficient guarantees will be made in advance for the transfer of sufficient funds for constructive work in Eretz-Israel and that such funds will be made available to the German fund set up by the Jewish Agency.[56]

The resolution is important for a number of reasons. With it, the JAE cemented its role as the premier representative of Jewish interests throughout the world. The JAE also established its veto over the use of funds collected on behalf of German Jewry. At first glance this would appear to be an example of the so-called "business as usual" that has been severely criticized by historians, but there were valid reasons for the JAE to behave in this fashion. Since Jews lacked a sovereign state, they had no government that could represent their interests. Because of its unique legal status and its nature as a coalition of Zionists and non-Zionists the JAE — unlike any other Jewish organization — could claim to represent all Jews (even those who rejected its authority). Furthermore, effective rescue work required the concentration of available money where it was needed. Without the guarantees offered by JAE dominance, it was not clear that any funds would be made available for Palestine, because many of the fund-raisers in America and Britain were non- (or even anti-) Zionists. But since Palestine was the primary destination of most émigrés (willingly or otherwise) that was where the money was needed most.

On the strength of this resolution, the JAE cabled London to proceed with the plans for a world fund that had been held in abeyance awaiting Jerusalem's decision.[57] In the meantime, the Executive of Mapai met on April 11, and called upon the Yishuv to take the lead in any program of rescue, thus also giving its approval to the actions of the JAE and WZO.[58]

Resistance to the fund's organization arose almost immediately. On April 13, JA Recording Secretary Moshe Medzini circulated a note among the members of the Executive at Senator's request. This note detailed opposition to the policy adopted by the JA from the leadership of HOG and from Tel Aviv's Mayor Meir Dizengoff. The HOG leaders were disturbed that they had not been consulted in the decision-making process. Dizengoff, on the other hand, felt strongly that the fund represented too narrow a cross section of the Yishuv's leadership.[59]

As a result, the entire issue of the fund was reopened. A meeting was arranged with the HOG leaders that was intended to clarify and alleviate their objections. At the meeting, the leaders of HOG admitted that they had inadvertently caused some of the friction over the JA's authority by also seeking to involve the Va'ad Leumi in a sphere of activity properly belonging to the JAE.[60] This admission reopened the entire question as to the role that the JAE should be playing in the fund-raising scheme, and it threatened to halt all activity. At this point, Arlosoroff argued that a "series of contradictory policies" had been proposed that would, "threaten the entire operation." He specifically referred to the two Yishuv funds (one under the JA's authority and the other under the Va'ad Leumi's), both of which would be competing with the world fund. Arlosoroff felt that nothing should delay the Yishuv from beginning work, even if details had yet to be hammered out regarding the exact relations between different agencies.[61] While it accepted Arlosoroff's position, the JAE did not take any substantive steps at the time, breaking off the discussion while it was still deadlocked over the most basic questions. Once again, all details were open to debate.

The documentation relating to much of this problem is only partial, and consequently the precise terms of the debate are not always clear. In essence, we may discern three positions regarding the fund. The first concentrated on the need to offer immediate assistance to German Jewry. The HOG leaders adopted this position, with its implication that any action for German Jewry, even if the status of the JAE was not guaranteed, was preferable to no action. At the opposite extreme, Joshua Farbstein still maintained that the JAE should not become involved in the matter at all. Between these two positions was that of the majority, which agreed that action was necessary, but felt that the position of the JAE in relation to other agencies had to be established in order to guarantee the national orientation of the undertaking. The alternative, they feared, was anarchy and failure. Aware of the historical importance of the German Jewish downfall, the members of the JAE understood that failure would be disastrous for Zionism.[62]

Part of this fear was, in fact, being realized. While the JAE deliberated, other Zionist figures were making their own independent rescue proposals. Among these, the most important proposal was that of Pinhas Rutenberg, a veteran Zionist who saw himself as above party or institutional politics. Rutenberg's scheme called for a fund for German Jewry of which as much as half of the collected monies would be used for land acquisition and settlement building.[63] Most Zionists found Rutenberg's proposals an acceptable basis for negotiations, and sought his cooperation in the common work ahead.[64] Unknown to members of the JAE, however, Weizmann had unilaterally begun his own contacts with Rutenberg.

Despite the delay in official approval, some initial organizational work was begun on the Yishuv's local fund. Organized under JAE supervision the fund was to be a collaborative effort, beginning with the publication of a manifesto. In turn, the manifesto was to be signed by delegates of the Keren Kayemet le-Israel (KKL), KHY, the Va'ad Leumi, HOG, the Tel Aviv municipality, the Chief Rabbinate, the Farmers' Association, and the Palestine Chamber of Commerce. Each would select two representatives (for a total of eighteen) who would, in turn, select eleven trustees and a presidium of three.[65]

This proposal also met with opposition. Farbstein noted that representatives of Mizrahi, the General Zionists, and the Revisionists were not asked to participate on the manifesto committee and were underrepresented on the fund since Ha-Zohar was not represented at all and Mizrahi and the General Zionists were represented only indirectly.[66] Having initially opposed JAE involvement in the worldwide fund, Farbstein appears now to have suddenly reversed himself, although that was not actually the case. Despite alignment with Mapai, Mizrahi was dedicated to the establishment of the broadest possible national coalition. Since the JAE had taken upon itself the task of trying to rescue German Jewry, Mizrachi's position was that all Zionist groups should participate equally in all related activities. Without denying the validity of Farbstein's criticism, Arlosoroff attempted to keep the matter moving, noting that no time could be wasted. However, he had reservations about the size of the board of trustees, believing that five ought to be the maximum. Arlosoroff expressed these criticisms in the name of the Va'ad Leumi, although Neumann was under the impression that the Va'ad Leumi was satisfied with the way the fund was organized.[67] With no consensus developing — the JAE was being pulled in three directions simultaneously — the meeting again ended in deadlock, although tentative work continued.

It appears that at some time between April 16 and 19, 1933, JAE Chairman

Neumann found out about Weizmann's contacts with Rutenberg and became disenchanted with the undertaking, refusing to participate any further. Neumann's resignation slowed the matter down even more, and led to a bitter dispute between him and Arlosoroff at the JAE meeting of April 19 about who was behaving responsibly and who was not. The JAE at this point not only was divided on the question of how to proceed, but was not even able to establish a consensus on how to decide what to do next.[68]

Neumann's position, as explained by Moshe Shertok at a meeting of the Mapai Executive, was that only the JA had the authority to make foreign policy decisions for the Yishuv. Any authority granted to organizations or individuals, Weizmann included, derived from the authority of the JAE and had to take account of the Executive's need to be informed of all activities undertaken in its name. By engaging in unauthorized talks with Rutenberg, Weizmann had reneged on the discipline imposed upon him by the JA, and had harmed the Agency's reputation.[69] In reply, Avraham Katznelson observed that weeks had been wasted in fruitless arguments while the need for timely aid to the Jews of Germany was becoming more urgent.[70] Speaking for Weizmann, he stated that action on behalf of German Jewry was more important than concern for organizational propriety, especially since the latter could be worked out at a later date.

On the evening of April 19, 1933, the Va'ad Leumi sent a formal letter to Weizmann requesting that he take the lead in the fund-raising efforts for German Jewry.[71] While representing a continuation of the ongoing crisis, the Va'ad Leumi's action also permitted a compromise of sorts to be worked out. The Yishuv's fund would be an independent agency under the aegis of the JA and would be responsible only to it, although representing the entire Jewish population. Weizmann would lead the worldwide fund-raising effort in London, in cooperation with other notables, both Jewish and non-Jewish. By separating the two fund-raising efforts, it was unnecessary for the JAE to decide anything about the world fund, and its work could proceed. In addition, a means was worked out permitting the continuation of Rutenberg's independent activities on behalf of German Jewry.[72]

As a result, on April 30, 1933, the Yishuv's fund emerged. The fund would have thirteen representatives, including two from the JAE (Senator and Neumann). The others would be Menahem Mendel Ussishkin, representing the KKL; Arthur Hantke of the KHY; Abraham Berlin and Yitzhak Ben-Zvi of the Va'ad Leumi; Mayor Dizengoff of Tel Aviv; Victor Cohen of PICA; Moshe Smilansky of the Farmers' Association; Berl Katznelson, representing the Histadrut; and three representatives of HOG (Hermann Struck, Ludwig Pinner, and Moshe Landsberg). Henrietta Szold of Hadassah was asked to organize a limited-duration fund in the Yishuv in the interim, so that fund-raising could commence.[73]

Another month was to pass before the Yishuv could actually get to work.

The Jewish Agengy's Manifesto of May 29, 1933
Courtesy of the Central Zionist Archives, Jerusalem

Weizmann began contacting individuals whose cooperation he felt was necessary to give the fund credibility. Among the figures he contacted were Jan Christiaan Smuts, the South African statesman who was one of the authors of the Balfour Declaration; Felix M. Warburg, a well-known American Jewish banker and philanthropist; and Viscount Herbert Samuel, the first British High Commissioner for Palestine.[74] The fund's manifesto, titled "To the Jews of All the Countries," was published in English, Hebrew, and German versions on May 29.[75] At the same time, the national funds for Palestine were guaranteed by a resolution of the trustees of the world fund, who agreed to time their activities so as not to compete with KHY and KKL fund-raising.[76] The JA would now be able to turn its full attention to creating its own fund and putting the policy of constructive aid into operation.

As against the stated need to act immediately in order to help German Jewry, the JAE showed itself to be mired in petty partisanship. The sense of impending catastrophe did not yet overpower the concept of business as usual. In turn, the behavior of the JAE raises what appear to be serious questions regarding the commitment of Zionists to rescue German Jewry. In a recent essay, Ze'ev Tzahor argues that Chaim Arlosoroff "did not regard . . . [events in Germany] as a catastrophe of unusual proportions in Jewish diaspora history."[77] There is more than a grain of truth to the criticism inherent in Tzahor's evaluation, but something else was also at work in this case.

First, the rise of the Nazis confirmed for the Zionists exactly what they had been arguing all along: that unless Jews returned to their homeland, catastrophe would devour not only German Jewry, but east European Jewry as well.[78] David Ben-Gurion, for example, warned the Histadrut Plenary Council on January 10, 1934: "Hitler's rule in Germany imperils the entire Jewish people."[79] Furthermore, Zionists feared the possibility of British noncooperation, which would result in a closing of immigration and thereby deny the Yishuv the only realistic form of aid it could offer European Jewry. In other words, a sense of powerlessness temporarily paralyzed the members of the JAE and placed them in a situation where they raised trivial issues to a level of primary importance. This was because, ultimately, they did not control even the constructive aid program they argued over: a single decree by the British Palestine administration banning new aliya — a distinct possibility given the background of the Passfield White Paper — could halt the entire program before it began.

The debate over the fund also raised the specter of Zionists acting exclusively for their own interests. What is remarkable about the Zionist response to the crisis is precisely that many of the Zionist leaders argued against a narrowly constructed policy designed to help only Zionists, thereby abandoning so-called assimilationists to their fate. To be sure, some Labor Zionists advocated such an approach; the majority, however, advocated helping any Jew who could be helped without regard to previous Zionist association.[80]

Thus, although caught unprepared, the leaders of the Yishuv recognized the need to act and to offer a meaningful response to the plight of those German Jews who took flight to seek a truly safe haven. By the end of April 1933, rescue aliya (or, as it was called at the time, "constructive aid") had begun.

TO BOYCOTT OR NOT TO BOYCOTT?

While members of the Zionist establishment were debating the most effective means of alleviating German Jewry's suffering, Zeev Jabotinsky offered an alternative policy. As early as May 1933, he urged that economic warfare be pursued against the Nazis on behalf of German Jewry.[81] That summer, at the Eighteenth World Zionist Congress, Ha-Zohar's fiery leader proposed a strongly worded resolution advocating the incipient anti-Nazi boycott. The Congress, however, rejected the resolution by a vote of 240 to forty-eight.[82] Undeterred, Jabotinsky declared the boycott to be Ha-Zohar's official policy.[83] By the end of October Ha-Zohar's boycott was organized, with the central office in Paris taking the name "Center for Economic Defense."[84]

In April the JAE had also briefly explored the possibility of joining the boycott, after receiving a telegram requesting support from Rabbi Stephen S. Wise, President of the American Jewish Congress. The American Zionist leader strongly advocated the boycott, although he was a strong opponent of Jabotinsky. Dr. Georg Halperin, a HOG leader, responded to the boycott telegram quite simply: "An unofficial boycott is a good idea; an official boycott is insanity."[85]

Halperin's belief was that an open boycott would play directly into the hands of Nazi propaganda. Even without a boycott, the Nazis were claiming the existence of a Jewish world conspiracy. The JAE concurred with Halperin; so did many other Yishuv leaders. A similar analysis was offered by Siegfried Hoofein, head of the Anglo-Palestine Bank, in a memorandum he penned in early June 1933.[86] Hoofein, particularly feared that boycotters would be unable to distinguish between items recently imported and those in Palestine for a considerable amount of time. He also observed that a boycott would render disservice to German Jews by preventing them from exporting their capital.[87] Still, Hoofein suggested that the boycott be used as a bargaining chip to elicit concessions from the Nazis regarding the treatment of German Jewry.[88]

The Zionist majority did not follow Hoofein's advice; instead a dual policy was adopted which neither openly supported nor rejected the anti-Nazi boycott. This policy was followed until the public debate over the Haavara agreement climaxed in 1935 and forced a change in the JA's alignment.

THE JOINT COMMITTEE TO SETTLE GERMAN JEWS

The direct result of the Va'ad Leumi Executive's decisions in March and April 1933, a time when the JA was still bogged down attempting to establish its course, was the creation of a fund to oversee the "massive program of absorption of German immigrants in the Yishuv."[89] In early May 1933, this fund-raising drive crystallized into the Joint Fund to Settle German Jews in Eretz Israel. Chaired by Henrietta Szold, the fund served the twin purposes of collecting and distributing monies to help newly arriving German olim. For that reason, the fund also was known as the Joint Committee to Settle German Jews in Eretz Israel or, more commonly, just the Joint Committee.

The Joint Committee began to operate in earnest in June 1933, although the earliest document relating to its work dated to early May. This was a proposal to settle 1,100 German Jews in agricultural work.[90] From inception until October 1933, the Joint Committee provided the principle source for aid to German Jews. Subsequently, it slowly wound down its operations until all its functions ceased in February 1935.

The Joint Committee spent most of May gearing up for the tasks ahead. Cooperation with the HOG and the Tel Aviv municipality was guaranteed after a meeting on May 18, when the latter also agreed to donate office space for the committee.[91] On Monday, May 29, 1933, the Joint Committee officially anounced the debut of its fund-raising activities.[92] Shortly thereafter, the Ashkenazi Chief Rabbi, Avraham Isaac ha-Cohen Kook, agreed to lend his name to the campaign's list of sponsors, provided that the committee set aside a percentage of the monies collected for aid to Russian Jews.[93] The request was accepted in principle at a meeting of the Joint Committee Executive on June 8.[94] In doing this, Rav Kook, and the Joint Committee, broadened the definition of their activities from the more limited rescue of German Jews to the rescue of all Jews who could be rescued. Also on June 8, the Executive dealt with a series of questions regarding the creation of the Joint Committee's infrastructure. Basically, four issues arose: (1) how many members the Executive should comprise; (2) where the Executive should meet; (3) how much autonomy should be granted to the various subcommittees created by the Executive; and (4) whether the fund should register with the government.

Although Szold sought a small board of three to five members, the result was an Executive of ten members, which elected a presidium of three.[95] The selected Executive consisted of Menahem M. Ussishkin, Arthur Hantke, Yitzhak Ben-Zvi, Emanuel Neumann, Leon Pinner, Meir Dizengoff, Abraham Berlin, Berl Katznelson, Mendel Sirkis, and Henrietta Szold, who was selected as chairwoman. No explicit decision was taken concerning the status of the five specialized subcommittees, that were created, each headed by a person with appropriate expertise. Given relatively wide powers to define and suggest policies, these committees still needed Executive approval to carry out their proposals. Finally, the Executive decided to register with the government as a corporation.[96]

TABLE 2.2: The Joint Committee's subcommittees

Committee	Chairperson
Aliya and Hachshara	Dr. Werner D. Senator
Social Work	Henrietta Szold
Agricultural Settlement	Dr. Arthur Ruppin
Urban Settlement	Hillel Shenkar
Education and Culture	Dr. Abraham Luria

Source: Central Zionist Archive.

Szold apparently bore the main responsibility for daily affairs, especially fund-raising. In mid-June, the Executive was reorganized into a seventeen-member board of trustees, working with a three-member presidium composed of Szold, Hantke, and Berlin.[97]

Almost immediately, the Joint Committee had to deal with fund-raising problems. One contributor, a Mr. Horowitz, complained that up until then, "the Committee has not thought fit to take the public into its confidence by formulating, in however vague and general a manner, a programme or scheme to which sums collected are to be devoted and which will be plain to the ordinary man in the street."[98] But the fund also gained some friends, especially among British non-Jews living in Palestine.[99]

Even before funds actually became available, attention was focused, primarily by the subcommittees, on the issues of how much money was needed and how best to spend the little that was available.[100] In virtually every case, the relevant subcommittee made its proposals in coordination with other bodies, primarily the Va'ad Leumi, especially in matters pertaining to education and culture.[101] Although rescue aliya did not specifically require expenditures on education and culture, such undertakings did promote the absorption of new olim.

As a means of raising funds, the Joint Committee sponsored a public appeal to the Yishuv's population.[102] Two identical proclamations were published in Jerusalem: one bore the signature of the Sephardi Chief Rabbi, Jacob Meir, and the other was signed by David Yellin, a distinguished political and social leader of the Yishuv who also served as chairman of the Joint Committee's Jerusalem branch.[103] Entitled "Resident of Jerusalem and Man of Judah" (R. Meir's proclamation was entitled "Jews, Residents of Jerusalem," but was otherwise identical) the proclamation used stirring Zionist and Jewish terms to call for raising funds. A circular letter by the Tel Aviv Mayor Dizengoff served the same purpose.[104]

In addition to the proclamations and circular letters, the Joint Committee advertised to gain contributions. The ads were brief and to the point. Among the themes were "The Exodus" and "The Need to Respond to Hitler's Challenge".[105] Although never explicitly stated, it is clear that these headings deal with the Joint Fund, as can be seen directly from the ad printed on page 3 of *ha-Aretz* for Thursday, June 6, 1933: "With a large and proud settlement program we will respond to the tragedy in Germany." These ads apparently brought some results, for on June 9, *ha-Aretz* reported that the first outlays had been made by the Joint Committee for the construction of a settlement near Rishon Le-Zion.[106] By the end of June, £P12,500 ($62,500) had been pledged to the fund, raising the question of its use.[107] At a meeting on July 9, the Joint Committee Executive solved that problem by adopting Ussishkin's proposal to divide the funds thus: 33 percent for land acquisition, 25 percent for building settlements and housing, 25 percent for educational and cultural work, and 17 percent for emergency aid.[108] The funds dedicated to education and culture served a number of purposes, primarily related to teaching Hebrew and to vocational retraining, when needed.[109]

At this time, Szold began negotiations with Agudas Israel regarding the fund, thus representing a step in Yishuv unity for German Jewish rescue.[110] The fund also established contact with the World Jewish Congress through the office of Dr. Nahum Goldmann. In a letter of July 11, Goldmann sought information on the activities of the Joint Committee for inclusion in a memo he was preparing on the course of relief efforts for German Jewry.[111] In her response, Szold stressed the need for money, a theme she would reiterate on a number of further occasions.[112] This communication resulted in further publicity for the Joint Committee, as well as for HOG, although it is not possible at present to gauge just what practical benefits the publicity had.[113]

The Joint Committee also took care to publicize its activities in Palestine, primarily through the press. Besides advertising to gain donations, communiques and progress reports were sent to *ha-Aretz* and *Davar*, in the hope that they would be used as articles, thus giving some free publicity to the cause.[114] It appears, however, that only *ha-Aretz* made use of these press releases, which formed the basis for a number of short pieces.[115]

Fund-raising and public relations were not by any means the only activities in which the Joint Committee was involved. The Joint Committee channeled much of its creative energies into social, educational, and cultural work. As early as June, an agreement had been worked out with the Va'ad Leumi Education Committee for an educational plan for German Jewish youth from kindergarten to high school.[116] Similarly, the issue of those new olim who found it difficult to obtain employment because they had to care for their young children was high on the agenda of both the social work and the aliya subcommittees.[117] In September, Szold suggested that some of these families be transferred to kibbutzim or moshavot where resident families might be willing to look after their children. Although the parents would be responsible for reimbursing the babysitters, the Joint Committee was prepared to help those unable to afford the service.[118] A press release was prepared, asking those willing to help to contact HOG. Later, it appeared in *ha-Aretz, Davar,* the *Palestine Post*, and *Doar ha-Yom*.[119]

Despite the publicity, however, the fund never quite reached its potential. Of the total amount pledged in June and July, only £P9,000 ($45,000) from individual or corporate donors was collected. One hundred donors gave (or pledged) at least £P25 ($125), although a number of corporations followed the example of *ha-Aretz*, which pledged 1 percent of its income for the months of August, September, and October.[120] In the Joint Committee's summary report (published in 1935), the actual total collected is given at £P10,488.949 ($52,444.75).[121] Sixty percent of this sum was collected in Tel Aviv.

Already in October, Abraham Rozenboim, general secretary of the Joint Committee, noted in a memo to Szold that the fund never reached its target goals, in part because donors "did not, with few exceptions, give as much as they could."[122]

As a result, a number of the more grandiose schemes had to be severely curtailed or abandoned altogether, in favor of less expensive but equally important tasks. The latter included giving short-term low-interest loans of between £P5 ($25) and £P50 ($250). Despite the relatively low prices in Palestine at the time, such loans probably offered assistance only at the outset of settlement. HOG also received a grant to maintain an employment office that helped roughly 1,000 immigrants find jobs, and made a variety of expenditures for social work.[123]

The committee's expenditures, which Szold had her assistants record carefully, totaled £P4,676.322 ($23,281.61) in Tel Aviv, £P4,168.522 ($20,842.61) in Jerusalem, and £P1,744.100 ($8,702.50) in Haifa, for a grand total of £P10,588.944.[124] The gap between the amount collected and the vast amounts needed explains why the Joint Committee was continually involved in new fund-raising efforts, with Szold seeking financial assistance wherever possible.[125] Given the huge sums required — the Urban Settlement Committee alone had potential building projects totaling £P150,000 ($750,000) — approaches to Jewish philanthropic agencies outside Palestine were also necessary.[126] These included requests for help from the Zionist Organization of America, from the JDC, and from the Geneva-based Union Internationale de Secours aux Enfants.[127] Nevertheless, the Joint Committee spent most of its efforts on raising funds in Palestine. Two form letters were mailed by the committee in August 1933, of which the earlier one contained a tear-off to be returned with the donation.[128]

The financial difficulties that the Joint Committee experienced may be explained by a number of considerations. First, the Yishuv as a whole was dependent on financial aid from abroad and, as a result, should have expected individual donations to be on the small side. Second, the fund itself experienced a number of organizational difficulties. When it began to operate, facilities were (at best) inadequate.[129] Szold had wanted to organize the fund-raising efforts on American lines, but she was not supported on this issue by either the Joint Committee Executive or the plenum.[130] Indeed, Szold had been feuding for years with a number of local Labor Zionist institutions (including Kupat Holim, the Histadrut health service) over the issue of "American" versus "Palestinian" methods.[131] As a consequence, inefficiency became a hallmark of the fund, and of virtually all the Joint Committee's activities. Complaints about this inefficiency were heard often, especially in Tel Aviv and Haifa, and they help to explain why the fund did so poorly in the Haifa area.[132] The situation in Haifa, unlike that in Tel Aviv, did not improve with time, and seems to have worsened. At least one local member complained: "It would have been possible to do great things here, if only we had the right person leading the fund. Not only does [Mr.] Wilensky not work properly, but he prevents others from accomplishing anything."[133]

A third factor that weakened the fund was the almost constant partisanship in and around the Joint Committee. Thus, almost every public body sought representation on a relevant subcommittee, if not on the Executive. Such demands were voiced, in turn, by the Federation of Teachers, which complained that one of its members was not on the Education Committee, and by the Keren Hayesod, which demanded a seat on the Executive in June.[134]

More significant were the occasionally stormy relations between the Joint Committee and HOG. On the one hand, HOG played a crucial role in many of the educational, social, and settlement projects of the Joint Committee. Many HOG leaders were also members of the Joint Committee's various specialized subcommittees, including Dr. Abraham Levi, one of the HOG co-chairmen, who became chairman of the Joint Committee Aliya Committee when Senator left.[135] HOG was also singularly involved in researching settlement projects that the Joint Committe pursued (when possible).[136] Equally important were HOG's social and employment projects, which gave moral and financial assistance to destitute German refugees. All these activities, however, required large sums of money. Budgetary problems were almost always at the root of friction between HOG and the Joint Committee. In July, HOG requested that a budget of £P3,000 ($15,000) be granted for social welfare activities in Tel Aviv, Haifa, and Jerusalem.[137] When the Joint Committee budgeted a considerably smaller sum, HOG's co-chairmen wrote an angry letter pointing out that the granted sum barely covered one activity.[138] Realizing that this attitude was not aiding their cause, the HOG leaders also praised Szold for her "singular and loyal work" on behalf of German olim — work, they noted, that was done in a trying period under difficult circumstances.[139]

Nevertheless, difficulties remained. Szold wrote an angry letter to the HOG leaders in January 1934, accusing them of purposely downplaying the fund's role in helping German olim, in an article published in *Der Mitteilungsblatt*. In response, HOG admitted an error of omission caused by the overlapping roles of many individuals in both HOG and the Joint Committee with the resulting confusion as to which organization was responsible for what. Promising to clarify the matter, *Der Mitteilungsblatt* published an article in its March 1934 issue giving full credit to Szold and the Joint Committee.[140]

Relations with the Histadrut also complicated the work of the Joint Committee. Initially, the Histadrut gave strong support to all work for German Jewry. After the murder of Chaim Arlosoroff, however, the workers' committee sought an appropriate means of commemorating its slain leader. In the last week of June the Arlosoroff Fund was established to collect money to buy land for settling German and other olim. From the perspective of the

Joint Committee this was an acceptable goal, although the Executive feared that if the Histadrut limited its aid to halutzim, every party would establish a fund for the benefit of its own constituency, thereby undermining the Joint Fund.[141] Arthur Ruppin opposed the Arlosoroff Fund because he felt that another fund-raising effort — even one limited to Histadrut members — would wreak havoc with the Joint Committee and other Zionist funds. Nevertheless, the Histadrut and Mapai decided to carry on, turning the idea of a commemoration for a fallen leader into reality.[142] As a result, the Joint Committee opened negotiations with the Arlosoroff Fund, hoping to establish clear parameters for each and thereby avoid friction and needless duplication of effort.[143]

The negotiations led to a proposed agreement, which became the basis for all relations between the two fund-raising organizations:

> (1) The Histadrut shall anounce the beginning of a land
> and settlement fund in memory of Chaim Arlosoroff.
> (2) This fund shall be limited to Histadrut members only.
> (3) The [Arlosoroff] fund will not accept donations from
> individuals who are not Histadrut members as long as they
> have not already fulfilled their obligations to the
> general fund for German Jewry.
> (4) In all proclamations and publicity materials the
> Histadrut will note the relation between its fund and the
> fund for German Jewry and will reiterate the respon-
> sibility of every Jew to contribute to the fund for German
> Jews.
> (5) The Histadrut will transfer £P1,500 from the fund it
> collects to the [Joint Committee] Executive as a contri-
> bution of Histadrut members and institutions to the
> general fund for German Jewry.[144]

Since the terms of the agreement came to be a source of argument between the Joint Committee and the Arlosoroff Fund, the agreement requires further examination. In particular, its third paragraph begged the question of which fund could raise money from which individuals. On the surface, the Histadrut appeared to concede the non-labor public to the Joint Fund. In reality, how-ever, all Paragraph 3 required was that the Arlosoroff Fund inquire whether potential donors had made a token donation to the Joint Fund. Then too, Paragraph 5 implies that the Histadrut, as the organizer of the Arlosoroff Fund, realized the negative impact that multiple fund-raising drives would have on the Joint Committee's operations. In that case, a clear argument could have been made against the Histadrut's even starting a new fund-raising drive. Though such arguments were not made at the time, the Arlosoroff

Fund was a clear example of the Histadrut's seeking to protect its institutional fiefdom. Despite such seemingly obvious potential pitfalls, the agreement was ratified by the Joint Committee on July 13 and by the Histadrut shortly afterward.[145] As a result of the agreement, Szold was asked to make an official statement on behalf of the Arlosoroff Fund, which she delivered on July 20.[146]

Almost immediately, however, relations between the two funds soured. Barely one day after Szold's statement, Rozenboim, the Joint Committee's general secretary, wrote to the leaders of the Arlosoroff Fund, airing complaints about breaking the agreement. According to Rozenboim's informants, Arlosoroff Fund collectors had requested donations from individuals who were not members of the Histadrut, and had implied that contributions to the Arlosoroff Fund fulfilled all obligations to the German fund.[147] For its part, the Arlosoroff Fund denied the accusation, and denied that it had misrepresented its purpose.[148] Joseph Baratz, director of the Arlosoroff Fund, also approached his workers, cautioning them about the terms of the agreement, but to little avail.[149] There was at least one more case, in July, of an individual inferring (or being told directly) that a contribution to the Arlosoroff Fund fulfilled all obligations.[150]

In August, the Arlosoroff Fund accused the Joint Committee of violating the agreement by approaching Histadrut members for donations. This accusation was disingenuous, since the original agreement did not explicitly enjoin the Joint Committee from doing so.[151] In response, the Joint Committee decided to approach the Histadrut Executive, hoping to resolve the simmering dispute and also seeking the £P1,500 promised at the inception of the Arlosoroff Fund.[152]

Szold and Rozenboim wrote to the Histadrut Executive, denying charges that the Joint Fund had approached Histadrut members, but their letter did not ease relations.[153] A few days later, the Joint Committee Executive unanimously approved a resolution protesting Arlosoroff Fund interference.[154] One more series of accusations was traded in September, but that did not signal an end to the difficulties.[155] By the time a truce was established, the Joint Committee was no longer in operation. Nevertheless, until the end, the Histadrut leaders seemed intent on vexing Szold by changing their commitments and not living up to their agreements.[156]

In contrast to relations with the Histadrut, which severely hampered Joint Committee operations, the JAE always maintained a cordial attitude toward Szold and the Joint Committee. This demonstrates the JAE's pragmatic approach to the vital work to be done, and anything that hindered success was discouraged. Thus, for example, when the JAE committed itself to building emergency housing for new immigrants, it had counted on an £P30,000 ($150,000) grant from London. By September, the money had still not arrived. Although itself short of necessary funds, the Joint Committee proposed a loan to the JAE, which was accepted in principle.[157]

In the interim, in late September 1933, the KKL complained that continuation of the Joint Committee (and the Arlosoroff Fund) imperiled its own annual drive.[158] Since the JAE had, by this time, created its own German Department and since the fund had failed to live up to its potential, the Joint Committee Executive decided to disband, handing refugee projects over to the authority of the JAE in the process.[159] Dismantling proved complicated, however, because the German Department would not be able to begin operations immediately. Therefore, the Joint Committee initially agreed to discontinue fund-raising while continuing all other functions.[160] This new lease on life was never meant to be more than a temporay reprieve and, over the course of 1934, Joint Committee was absorbed into the German Department and the Youth Aliya program.

Was the Joint Committee, then, a success? Clearly, the answer will depends perspective. From the broader viewpoint, the answer is no, since the committee neither collected the vast sums needed nor helped thousands of German Jews. This evaluation, however, must be tempered by the fact that a fund was created virtually from scratch. Since the Joint Fund's income ledger book was water damaged, exact income cannot be ascertained. But based on expenses, at least £P10,488.944 was collected. Except for 12.4 percent used by the Joint Committee to cover its own expenses (including salaries), the money was used for settlement and other projects.[161] The Joint Committee's Aliya Committee helped place 553 olim in kibbutzim during its first six months of operation, while HOG's labor office (funded by the Joint Committee) helped find jobs for 2,516 olim during the same period.[162] In addition, 5,569 persons received help from the Social Work Committee in 1933 and 1934.[163] Given the Yishuv's meager resources and the fact that total German aliya numbered only 7,544 for all of 1933, these were not small accomplishments, and they are indicative of both the Yishuv's strengths and weaknesses.

3
Rescue By Means of Immigration, 1933-1936

INVOLVING THE BRITISH

Since encouraging Jewish immigration was the Yishuv's primary response to National Socialism, it should not come as a surprise that thirty-eight conversations held between 1933 and 1935 by members of the JAE with the High Commissioner for Palestine General Sir Arthur Wauchope, dealt in whole or in part with aliya. The significance of this figure should not be underestimated, since it represented 60 percent of the time.[1]

By the end of 1933 a total of 60,000 Germans, of whom about one-third were Jews, became refugees. In the earliest months of the Nazi persecution, several European countries relaxed their restrictions on the entry of refugees somewhat, but almost immediately they were again put in force, and most countries sought to convince those refugees already accepted to leave for Palestine or the Americas.[2] Thus, it is no surprise that Zionists saw the potential to greatly increase the Yishuv's population and to benefit its economy by channeling as many of the German emigrants as possible to Palestine. Given the nature of immigration law under the Mandate, it should also be obvious that in such an ambitious undertaking the cooperation, or at least the acquiescence, of the British Palestine administration would be of crucial importance. For this reason, the London Executive suggested the the JAE consider sending a deputation to urge Wauchope to open Palestine's gates.[3]

Arlosoroff had already been in touch with Wauchope, when he requested the advance on the Labor schedule. In early April 1933, the JA asked for 1,000 certificates (rather than the 700 spoken of in March), and the grant was made on April 6.[4] The British also agreed to review liberally applications for certificates in other categories (primarily Capitalist ones).[5] Once these certificates actually became available, the JAE unanimously decided that they should be given to members of he-Halutz in Germany who had completed a hachshara (agricultural training) program. Such a decision was in consonance with the JAE's long-standing policy of halutzic immigration. A request for 500 more certificates was made, this time to be taken from the Palestine government's reserve. The government refused to consider any further advances, and, at least for the time being, the request was not followed up.[6]

If for now the British appeared to cooperate, it was also clear that such a positive attitude did have its limits. Wauchope, for example, adamantly refused to allow the JA to publish the facts of the extraordinary certificate grant, for fear of being seen as favoring one of the nationalities in Palestine.[7] Similarly, although he somewhat liberalized legal immigration to help German Jewry, Wauchope considerably tightened government policy regarding "illegal" immigrants, primarily those entering Palestine as tourists. At this point in time a number of anti-tourist sweeps were conducted by the Palestine police, to the great chagrin and embarrassment of all involved.[8]

Some of the British government's ambivalence could be seen as early as March 1933. On March 29, the Passport Control Officer in Berlin, Frank E. Foley, complained that he was "overwhelmed with applications from Jews."[9] The same attitude was exemplified by Britain's refusal to verify atrocity reports, when asked to do so by British Jews, and by the Foreign Office's unwillingness to sponsor the Bernheim petition at the League of Nations.[10] The British also created trouble defining who was and who was not to be considered a refugee. Thus, Otto Schiff complained to the WZO that the Palestine administration established an arbitrary date of May 26, 1933, as the cutoff after which a German Jewish emigrant could no longer be considered a refugee. He also noted that this was the opposite of British policy regarding the entry of refugees into Great Britain proper, where anyone leaving Germany after March 5, 1933, was considered a refugee.[11]

To add to the confusion the Palestine administration created legal problems for refugees attempting to come to Palestine that derived from their general lack of personal documents, except for "personalausweisen" or "fremdpassen" issued by the Germans and identifying the individual as stateless. These documents were not considered legal under the immigration statutes of the Mandate since they did not carry the guarantee implied in a passport that the bearer, as a national of the issuing country, could always return to his or her point of origin.[12] Another complication developed later. Insofar as a person was admitted to Palestine, he could be deported (for judicial or other reasons); yet, stateless persons could not be so deported since there was no guarantee that any country would accept them.[13] In both cases, British policy initially was liberal. Palestine's attorney general decided not to establish a deportation policy until such a time as one was needed, while the immigration department decided to accept all forms of personal identity papers, even the so-called Nansen Passports issued by the League of Nations.[14]

Thus, for the time being at least, the British were cooperating with the Yishuv and thus making the policy of rescue aliya possible. However, British cooperation could not be taken for granted, as may be seen by the uncategorical refusal of the immigration department to even consider granting immigration certificates for German Jews en masse. Instead, the British insisted that they would continue to issue certificates only qualified individuals.[15] Indeed, British cooperation would become more difficult to obtain as conditions in Europe worsened.

THE EIGHTEENTH ZIONIST CONGRESS

After considerable haggling between the various organizations over the Yishuv's role in global efforts to raise money for German Jewish relief, the JA was finally able to turn its full attention to the tasks at hand in May 1933. On July 3, the leaders of HOG reiterated their advocacy of rescue aliya in a letter to the Executive:

> In our opinion the report[s] we have received regarding
> the situation in Germany and the mass demand for aliya
> require urgent steps and extraordinary means to gain the
> maximum number of extra certificates for the Zionist
> Federation of Germany.[16]

Proposals concerning how best to help had been examined all spring, although no specific decisions were made.[17] Special attention was paid to the issue of how many new immigrants could be housed in various agricultural colonies, although industrial development and urban settlement schemes were considered as well.[18] The Histadrut estimated, for example, that a total of 3,830 German olim could be absorbed in kibbutzim belonging to the various kibbutz movements, including those of Mizrachi. The Histadrut economists further estimated that expenses for each new settler would be at least £P6.500 ($32.50), thus requiring the Yishuv to invest an initial sum of £P24,895 ($124,475) for the project.[19] The JA's Aliya Department also studied the issue, concluding that 1,000 settler families could be accommodated on lands belonging to the KKL.[20] At this same time, the German Zionists as well were busy laying out plans for work on behalf of the new olim. HOG prepared a memorandum for the delegates of the Eighteenth Zionist Congress calling for four substantive changes in the way that German affairs were handled. The first was to concentrate all work on behalf of German Jews in a special department of the JA. The second was to increase the aliya and labor budgets of the JA in proportion to the needs of the new olim. The third was to focus on obtaining maximum financing from abroad for the resettlement program in Palestine. The fourth demand of the German Zionists was the immediate absorption of 3,000 immigrants in training and work, the settlement of 1,500 families, new land purchases, social welfare work, and the transfer of children.[21] Once this task had been achieved, HOG assumed, even more extensive aliya-related projects could be undertaken.

The Congress, which met in Prague from August 2 to September 4, 1933, cleared up any remaining ideological and organizational issues, including that of authority. At this point, all decision-making authority regarding German Jewry was transferred from the Va'ad Leumi to the JA. As HOG had suggested, all JA work was to be concentrated in a German Department. Chaim Weizmann, working primarily in London, was made responsible for the overall relief campaign and Arthur Ruppin was to head the German Department in Jerusalem.[22] Although not the exclusive business of the Congress, the German Jewish issue was given prominent attention. The Congress's second plenary session, held in the evening of August 22, was devoted almost entirely to German Jewry. WZO President Nahum Sokolow delivered a speech which included a lengthy analysis of the situation in Germany.[23] In his conclusion, Sokolow called upon Zionists to "hurry to articulate, in an urgent way, a large-scale aid program, for there is no end to the suffering of our brethren in Germany."[24] According to Sokolow, the Zionists:

> Protect all Jewish hearts from debility and despair, remind
> them that history will note that precisely at the moment
> of darkest crisis for Jacob he will find salvation and there-
> by reach the highest step, the summit of his powers. As
> they torture us so shall we be strengthened and so shall
> we strengthen ourselves.[25]

Ruppin spoke in a similar vein, concentrating on the resettlement work that was needed to help German Jewry. Relating the tasks ahead, Ruppin refused to cite exact numbers, but mentioned the need for the emigration of between 200,000 and 250,000 German Jews. He also provided a detailed analysis of the various options for resettlement in Palestine. Ruppin anticipated that the new German immigrants would be divided in three groups: those who would settle in agricultural colonies, primarily young persons who had completed hachshara programs; those who would settle in urban centers and work in industrial plants; and those who would settle in so-called mixed-economy settlements and would engage in both agriculture and commerce.[26]

Ruppin also noted that many delegates had called on the Congress to issue a protest against the Nazi persecution of European Jewry. Included among these delegates were the Revisionists, whose proposed protest resolution, calling for an anti-Nazi boycott, was rejected by a large majority of the delegates.[27] Ruppin responded to them with the argument that: "The *best protest* against the Jewish policies of the German Government, or so it seems to me, is the *rescue effort*."[28]

During the seventh, eighth, and ninth sessions of the Congress, the floor was open to debate. Two Revisionist delegates, Meir Grossman and Joseph B. Schechtman, condemned the anti-Nazi resolutions passed by the Congress as too weak.[29] David Ben-Gurion spoke of the need to absorb "large numbers of Jews," as did Nahum Goldman and Morris Rothenberg of the Zionist Organization of America.[30] Finally, Rabbi Stephen S. Wise called on both Mapai and Ha-Zohar to cease their internecine struggle in order to con-centrate all Zionist forces on the task of rescuing German Jewry.[31]

After the debate, the Congress adopted two resolutions relating to Germany. The first protested the "theft of Jewish rights" by the Nazis and called on

> the entire civilized world, especially the League of
> Nations, to aid Jewry's war for the return of German
> Jewry's rights. The Congress requests that all countries
> and their governments take any steps necessary to ease
> the emigration of German refugees and the creation
> of possibilities for resettlement.

The resolution further called on Great Britain to open Palestine for as large an immigration as possible, and requested that friendly countries express solidarity with this goal.[32] The second resolution called for Jewish solidarity and for the financial and political support needed to make the rescue program a reality. At the Congress a new JAE was elected, as related in Table 3.1.

TABLE 3.1: Jewish Agency Executive, 1933

Department	Chairman	Affiliation
Chairman	Ruppin	General-Zionist A
Political	Shertok	Mapai
Colonization	Ruppin/Hexter	GZ/Non-Zionist
Finance	Kaplan	Mapai
Immigration	Gruenbaum	General Zionist
German	Ruppin/Senator	GZ/Non-Zionist
Education	Berkson	Non-Zionist
No Portfolio	Ben-Gurion	Mapai[33]

Source: *Jewish Agency Report*, 1935.

THE RESCUE ALIYA PROGRAM TAKES SHAPE

In the aftermath of the Congress, serious rescue work began. In October the JA German Department began to operate under Ruppin's direction. In turn, the Joint Committee was disbanded and absorbed by the JA. On September 27 the Executive decided to hasten planning work and to send all practical proposals to London for final consideration and financing.[34] The Executive remained fairly careful with finances, in part because the available resources were meager and in part to "achieve the maximum of efficiency possible."[35] Total expenses for initial settlement work were estimated at £P50,000 ($250,000).[36] Again, however, care in the use of funds was stressed, as when the JAE budgeted a total of £P300 ($1,500) for the first three months of the German Department's operation.[37]

Given the numbers of Jewish refugees leaving Germany, the JAE forwarded Weizmann's request for 700 additional emergency certificates, to be used to relieve the large number of German Jews in refugee reception centers in Belgium and France. Arguing that they could not make a further advance on the next schedule, the British rejected this request.[38]

By the end of 1933, one report listed a total of seventeen different projects that the JA was involved in, all on behalf of German Jewry.[39] The JA provided a more detailed report for the Vaad ha-Poel ha-Mezumzam, which met in Jerusalem in March 1934. According to the report, a total of £P66,318 ($331,590) was collected for Palestinian rescue work in 1933. Over the course of that year, 6,803 German olim entered Palestine, along with 4,372 tourists. Of the former, 3,055 bore Capitalist (A-I) certificates, and 3,129 received certificates from the Labor schedule.[40] Other statistics included the number of families settled in various agricultural colonies (almost 200), the amount of short-term low-interest loans given to German olim who preferred city settlement (£P2,400), and the number of families receiving social welfare assistance from the JA (595). Looking to the future, the report noted that 1,000 additional settlers could be accommodated on lands already held by the KHY for the relatively small outlay of between £P400 and 700 ($2,000 to $3,500), a sum needed mainly for the development of new sources of water.[41]

At this point, the Yishuv began its program of rescue aliya, with much fervor. For the program of rescue aliya to be considered successful, it had to provide the realistic possibility of aliya for as many German (and eastern European) Jews as possible. Aliya increased 317 percent in 1933 over 1932: total aliya in 1932 was 9,553, as against 30,327 in 1933.[42] Although scholars continue to disagree over the precise tabulation for total immigration, the aliya figures for the period may be summarized by reference to statistical material prepared by the JA in 1947. The figures for the years between 1933 and 1937 are summarized in the following table:

TABLE 3.2: Aliya Figures, 1933-1937[43]

Year	Total Aliya	German Aliya	Percent
1933	30,327	7,444	24.5
1934	42,359	9,923	23.4
1935	61,854	9,561	15.5
1936	29,727	8,792	29.6
1937	10,536	3,604	34.2
Total	174,803	39,324	22.5

Source: D. Gurevich (comp.), *Statistical Handbook of Jewish Palestine*, Jerusalem: Jewish Agency for Palestine, 1947, pp. 98-108

While these figures are tentative, it may be concluded that from 1933 to 1937, German Jews represented 22.5 percent of all olim. In the same period, olim from Poland numbered 75,622, or 43.3 percent of the total. Other aliya figures were as follows: Austria, 2,338 (1.3 percent); Czechoslovakia, 3,063 (1.7 percent); and Romania, 8,360 (4.8 percent).

Since aliya was restricted only by the number of certificates granted, these figure may seem low. Rhetoric aside, however, three considerations must be kept in mind when analyzing the numbers. First, few German Jews, and almost none of the German Jewish leaders (even those advocating emigration), spoke in terms of total evacuation. Ruppin, too, spoke of only 200,000 emigrants in his speech at the Eighteenth Zionist Congress. Such a figure represented approximately one-third of German Jewry in 1933. As late as 1937, the majority of German Jews did not see emigration as their sole recourse, even though "there was agreement on the desirability, even necessity, of facilitating the exodus of the young."[44] The total German emigration did reach 50 percent (considering Germany in her pre-Anschluss borders), but a clear majority of Jews left only after the events connected with Kristallnacht, that is, in 1938 and 1939.[45]

The second consideration was the attitude and policy of the British Palestine administration. The British position was ambivalent from the beginning, and it became increasingly hostile as time wore on. Humanitarian considerations notwithstanding, the Palestine administration existed to serve Great Britain's strategic interests. Primary among those interests was maintaining peace in Palestine and retaining the goodwill of the independent (or semi-independent) Arab states, especially Egypt and Iraq. Against such interests Jewish needs Jews were seen as secondary, at best, and declined in importance after 1936.

The third consideration, finally, was the Zionist rescue policy, which often reflected ideologically adumbrated rescue priorities. Although this factor should not be exaggerated, it also cannot be wholly ignored. Numerous disagreements arose within the Yishuv regarding the new aliya and its implications. Such disagreements were not primarily over which policy to adopt, but rather over how best to apply the policy already adopted. This was especially true as better information on the situation in Germany and in eastern Europe became available after the autumn of 1933. For two years, Mapai's shelichim in Berlin, Eliezer Liebenstein and Chaim Enzo Sereni, kept the Yishuv's decision makers well informed on the march of events in Germany and in the neighboring states that had become temporary havens for Jews.[46] Then too, when Zionist leaders spent time abroad they usually immersed themselves in local affairs. Upon their return, they invariably reported to the party or the Zionist institution on whose behalf the trip had been made. Thus, when he returned from Germany, Arlosoroff reported extensively to the Mapai Executive on June 15. This proved to be one of Arlosoroff's last official acts before his murder.[47]

Similarly, Berl Katznelson spent six weeks in Europe after the Eighteenth Zionist Congress. Observing firsthand the fate of Jews in eastern and central Europe, he concluded that the Jews of Germany, Poland, and Slovakia were in particular danger as a result of rising antisemitic agitation.[48]

These three factors — the attitudes of German Jewry, of the British government, and of the Zionist movement — were responsible for shaping the outcome of the program of rescue aliya begun in 1933. In a conversation with High Commissioner Arthur Wauchope on February 22, 1934, Moshe Shertok observed that, despite increases in aliya, Palestine still faced a labor shortage.[49] The purpose of Shertok's statement was to encourage further increases in the number of certificates granted. Weizmann, too, became an enthusiastic proponent of German aliya, introducing a report by the German Department with a cover letter in which he stated: "We know that there exist definite opportunities whereby the Jewish population of Palestine might be doubled within four or five years."[50] Such a proposition would require, at the least, British acquiescence, if not full and eager cooperation.

1934-1935

Hints that the Palestine administration was not as cooperative as it could be were already evident in 1933, and by 1934 they were becoming more and more glaring. Closer inspection of the immigration figures in Table 3.2, for example, yield most interesting results. Thus, in March 1934, negotiations began between the JAE and the British regarding the schedule for the following six months (April to October 1934). The JAE requested just over 22,000 certificates: 17,938 to be granted outright, 1,500 to be held in reserve by the High Commissioner, and a supplement of 15 percent (roughly 2,900) for family reunions. The British responded by offering 11,859 certificates — 8,859 for the JA and the rest to be used by the High Commissioner or to be kept in reserve.[51] During the debate over the schedule, Selig Brodetsky, then in Palestine as a representative of the London Executive, noted that the previous schedule (covering October 1933 to March 1934) had undergone the same process: of 24,000 certificates requested, 5,500, or fewer than one-fourth, were granted.[52]

The British also became more restrictive of olim from European countries other than Germany, especially Russia. For the Zionist activists, conditions in Russia were almost as bad as in Germany. Since the 1920s the Communist authorities used imprisonment, random searches and seizures, and other police-state tactics to decimate the Russian Zionist movement. Rescuing Russian Zionist activists was also, therefore, a priority for the Yishuv throughout although on a lower level during the 1930s. Thus, when the British proposed a bond for olim from Russia (£P10 per adult and £P6 per child), the JA viewed the proposal as an attempt to slow down or even prevent such aliya, and protested strongly.[53]

By then, Zionist leaders had become more or less accustomed to seeking any help they could get from political leaders throughout the world. For instance, much of Weizmann's conversation with Benito Mussolini on February 23, 1934, was taken up with the plight of Jewish refugees. Mussolini's profession of support for a Jewish state, that could absorb all of the Jews wishing to leave Europe, was not seen as serious, but was nonetheless appreciated.[54]

The certificate situation would worsen in October 1934, again in conjunction with negotiations for a new schedule. At this time the British requested that, as the quid pro quo for a larger schedule, the JA issue a declaration denouncing illegal immigration. This the JAE declined to do, because it saw the proposal as a trap linking future immigration to JA compliance with British demands. The JAE's refusal to publicly condemn illegal immigration should not be construed as support for aliya bet. Indeed, a majority of the members of the Executive opposed illegal immigration. Nahum Sokolow, for example, flatly stated that it brought an "unwanted element" — in other words, Revisionists — into the Yishuv.[55] Since the High Commissioner was in London when this proposal was made, it became clear to many of the Yishuv's leaders that the focal point for discussions on aliya had shifted (at least temporarily) from the High Commissioner's residence in Jerusalem to London, although the results of such a shift were not clear. At the least, the Zionist leaders thought, pressure had to be brought to bear on the British administration to prevent a catastrophe. Some consolation, however, could be gleaned from the fact that the British retained their relatively liberal attitude toward Youth Aliya.[56]

In addition to its work directly benefiting immigrants, the JA was also involved in fund-raising and related political work in the diaspora. Much of the work was undertaken in the United States, although it should be noted that extensive fund-raising was carried out in Europe as well.[57] Funds raised in the diaspora and donated for specific purposes created their own problems. First, these funds had to be overseen, creating questions of authority. In addition, care had to be taken to ensure that fund-raising for German Jewry did not interfere with KKL or KHY financial activities.[58]

Still, immigration remained the JAE's main focus with regard to German Jewry. Thus, for example, Shertok noted in his office diary the terms of a discussion with Yitzhak Gruenbaum regarding the British-proposed Legislative Council. Basically, Gruenbaum suggested that Zionists demand a quid pro quo: "Regarding mainly the size of immigration and the area of land the acquisition of which would be allowed in the next five years, as the terms,upon which we should be prepared to join the Council" even if the council was not based on the concept of parity between Jewish and Arab delegations.[59]

By the year's end, immigration reached new heights, despite British demurral. The 6,000 olim who entered Palestine in October of 1934 represented the largest one-month figure in the history of the Mandate.[60] This increased aliya reflected the success of Zionist attempts to convince Jews that the Yishuv was Jewry's only safe haven. In turn, the Zionists' newfound ability to convince European Jews on this score reflected a hardening of the refugee policies of countries that had been relatively liberal. France represented a special case in point. Whereas it had offered considerable assistance to Jewish refugees in the early months of the Nazi regime, the French later rapidly decreased all forms of aid, especially regarding refugee resettlement in administered territories such as Syria and Lebanon.[61] Moreover, Nazi antisemitism semed to be spreading, even outside of Europe. In October 1934, Bukharian Jewish leaders requested help, citing recently intensified anti-Jewish propaganda that, they argued, "might also be assigned to Nazi influence."[62]

1935-1936

By 1935 the main crisis faced by the JAE was no longer to obtain adequate funding, but to secure an adequate supply of certificates. A JAE financial report, for example, noted that the London fund-raisers had transferred £P109,478.153 ($547,290.75) in 1933 and an additional £P68,500 ($342,500) in the first six months of 1934.[63] As a result, the schedules became the object of intense negotiations and haggling.[64] A clear example is provided by the arguments over the schedule of April to October 1935, with its 7,600 certificates. The debate over who should be given how many certificates continued into May 1935, leading an exasperated Gruenbaum, who had taken over the Aliya Department, to remark at length about "the intense pressure for certificates from every side."[65] Whereas the Zionist experience of the 1920's had been the availability of an adequate, if limited, number of certificates with few takers, in the 1930's the situation was reversed, leading to many more demands for certificates that were in short supply.

Disputes within the Yishuv over rescue priorities, between the advocates of limited halutzic aliya and those of mass resettlement, became more intense.[66] So did the amount of criticism to which the JAE received. Thus, representatives of HOG accused the Executive of "not doing everything necessary" to help German olim, especially regarding diplomatic contacts to facilitate the exodus from Germany.[67]

This already difficult situation did not improve with time. In the aftermath of the Nuremberg Laws (September 15, 1935), the entry of Jewish refugees into most European countries was severely restricted, yet again increasing demands placed on the Yishuv. In September 1935, the JAE received 1,000 requests for certificates from Germany alone.[68] Government agreement in October 1935, to provide another emergency advance of 1,000 certificates — half reserved for German Jews — did not substantially lessen the shortage of certificates.[69] By that point requests for certificates exceeded 200 per day and 6,000 per month. The JA became so desperate for certificates that it requested 2,000 emergency certificates as an advance on the next schedule.[70]

The adoption of the Nuremberg Laws also heightened the crisis atmosphere for the leadership of Mapai and the JAE. At a meeting of the Mapai Political Committee on October 27, 1935, Levi Skolnik (Eshkol) noted that for the time being, the radical Nazis who advocated the confiscation of all Jewish wealth had been held in check. "Nevertheless," he said, "for all intents and purposes this is only a question of time, and if [confiscation] does not take place now, it will in a few months' time."[71] The obvious upshot of such concern was to increase rescue work. Even the Haavara agreement, which had created a swirl of controversy when first announced, was accepted by the majority of Zionists as a practical way to rescue German Jews and their property.

The appearance of unanimity among the Zionists was also reflected at the Nineteenth Zionist Congress, held in Lucerne, Switzerland, between August 20 and September 4, 1935. Sokolow again delivered the keynote address, and again he chose to concentrate on the fate of Jewry in eastern and central Europe. Of special interest in Sokolow's speech is the way the WZO president placed the Jewish condition in a global context, concentrating on the theme of Nazism as a threat to all Jews, not only to the Jews in Germany.[72] David Ben-Gurion's speech expressed grave fears about the future, but it ended with a rousing call for the "settlement of one million families, one million economic units in the homeland."[73] Finally, in an address that actually concentrated on Youth Aliya, Henrietta Szold reported on the settlement program.[74]

Basically dedicated to continuing its current course, the Congress's only substantive resolutions dealt with the JAE's assumption of responsibility for supervising the Haavara agreement.

Zionist unity was only a facade, for several reasons. As a result of the accumulated frustrations of the previous four years, and since it no longer seemed even remotely possible to influence the majority of the WZO, Jabotinsky seceded before the Congress took place. The majority of Ha-Zohar followed suit, crystallizing as the New Zionist Organization (known in Hebrew by the initials Ha-Zach) in late September. Only the Jewish State Party, led by Meir Grossman, remained in the WZO as a "loyal opposition," but with little actual influence. Similarly, while the Haavara was ultimately accepted by the Congress, approval did not come before an acrimonious debate led by advocates of the anti-Nazi boycott, which included the American rabbis Stephen S. Wise and Abba Hillel Silver. Finally, although the Congress approved a settlement project to honor Szold's seventy-fifth birthday, that did not result cooperation:[75] In particular, Histadrut participation was reluctant.[76]

In general, the Congress advocated continuating the policy already approved. Yet, there still remained two major impediments to the success of the task at hand. First, although seeking Jewish emigration from Germany, the Nazis, paradoxically, made emigration difficult for Jews. Financial restrictions were especially problematic, since Jews leaving Germany (except for the few able to participate in Haavara) were effectively reduced to penury. By 1935, only the Yishuv actively sought penniless Jewish refugees. However, German refugees competed for the precious certificates with equally poor, and almost equally desperate, Jews from Poland and other countries.[77]

Second, since the British position regarding Jewish immigration to Palestine was, at best, ambivalent, there seemed to be no end in sight to German Jewish distress. Thus, when the JAE requested a total of 38,100 certificates for the two schedules of 1935/36 (that is, April-September 1935 and October 1935-March 1936), the government granted only 21,250 (55.8 percent of the number requested). It must also be noted that the 1935/36 schedule was the largest, both in absolute numbers and in the proportion of certificates granted to those requested. As a result, increasingly desperate activists in Europe resorted to illegal immigration. The British government therefore tended to limit the size of schedules as a result, creating a vicious cycle broken only when Britain withdrew from Palestine in 1948.

In 1936, the issue of how much aid could be given and who should have priority reached a crescendo. Thus, for example, a request for 2,000 emergency certificates for Germany was made in the days after the assassination of the Swiss Nazi leader, Wilhelm Gustloff. The logic behind the request was the belief that the Nazis might use violence to avenge Gustloff's death.[78] As had happened on a number of previous occasions, the British turned down this request.

At a Mapai Political Committee meeting on March 30, 1936, Ben-Gurion evaluated the situation thus: "Yet, we face one burning question: the condition of Jews in Poland and Germany and the necessity to bring them to Eretz-Israel."[79] He repeated his evaluation on April 16:

> Eretz-Israel must provide an answer for Jewish suffering,
> if not the complete answer at least a major portion of the
> answer that must be given immediately for the Jews of
> Germany, Poland, and other countries — then it is in-
> cumbent on us to see our principle work in attaining the
> maximum [aliya rate] . . .   barring this, not only
> will there be no escape from the Jews' fate, but there
> will be no remedy for the fate of Zionism.[80]

Ben-Gurion's statements must be seen as the logical follow-up to talks he held in London during December 1934, in which he proposed that the British government guarantee an aliya rate of 50,000 Jews per year for at least ten years.

The problems were not ideological but practical. The Yishuv could dedicate itself to an idea, but increasing Arab frustration, fueled by the increase in aliya from 1933 to 1935, incited by the Grand Mufti of Jerusalem, and fanned by Italian and German radio propaganda, flamed into an all-out Arab revolt beginning in April 1936. The revolt turned the Yishuv's attention away from Europe at the worst possible time, reinforcing the second thoughts for many figures in the British government regarding the Zionist endeavor. As a direct result, the gap between certificates requested and certificates granted grew. For the two schedules of 1936, the JA requested 21,985 certificates; the British granted only 6,300, or 28.6 percent.[81] By the spring of 1936, the future of the policy of rescue aliya was in doubt, although it would continue under even more trying circumstances for nearly three more years.

4
The Politics of Aliya

ZIONIST RESCUE PRIORITIES

Beginning in 1933 the Yishuv embarked upon a program of rescue aliya as the primary Zionist response to the Nazi persecution of German Jewry. Such importance was attributed to the program that the editors of the *Jewish Agency Report* for 1933 listed the German aliya as one of four crucial events that had transpired since the previous report (published in 1931).[1] Given the recurring theme of immigration as the quintessential Zionist response to crisis, it is not surprising that the rescue aliya program retained its primacy in the Yishuv throughout the 1930's. The emphasis on aliya as a means of defense established a positive goal. This was a goal that, even if sought in only a limited fashion, could garner much success, unlike other political, economic, or diplomatic weapons available to Jews, whose success was difficult to measure at the time. The relative success or failure of rescue aliya rested on three factors: ease of emigration from Germany, cooperation of the British administration, and proper Zionist appreciation of the Nazi threat and its implications.

In 1933 the Yishuv began its campaign of rescue aliya. Despite its success at bringing in 174,803 olim between 1933 and 1937, of whom 39,324 were from Germany, disputes arose over virtually every aspect of the aliya campaign. The Joint Committee to Resettle German Jews in Eretz Israel, for example, was constantly beset by internal and external disputes over authority. One dispute, between the Aliya and Social Welfare subcommittees, was not satifactorily resolved until October 1933, by which time the Joint Committee had declared itself defunct.[2] Similarly, when the JA announced its creation of a department for German affairs, the Histadrut demanded representation.[3]

Even fund-raising provoked disputes, since much of the money collected came from the diaspora and was earmarked for specific purposes. The JAE was responsible for the money, but most often it had no say on how the sums were to be spent. One member, Joshua H. Farbstein, demanded as early as 1933 that the JAE use "all the money" that was collected in London for German Jews on behalf of Eretz Israel without specifying whether or not it was used for German olim. Farbstein was not supported by the Executive, since it feared that such a policy might lead to adverse publicity, which would impact negatively on the Zionist national funds (the KKL and KHY).[4]

These arguments represented different viewpoints on rescue aliya, but they still reflected a general consensus on the need to work for increased aliya and absorption. Not everyone was concerned that rescue aliya be unlimited. Some of the Yishuv's parties tempered their hopes for increased immigration by emphasizing the "type" of olim they sought. In particular, two different orientations existed: one emphasized mass aliya (or evacuation), and another emphasized the quality of the olim. The latter has come to be known as halutzic aliya and is primarily identified with parties of the Zionist left, although in actuality a majority of Zionists accepted the premise that only the young, skilled, and healthy should immigrate.

At the annual conference of ha-Kibbutz ha-Meuchad (the United Kibbutz, the association of kibbutzim aligned with Mapai), held at Kibbutz Yagur from April 16 to 19, 1933, all speakers called for increased aliya, but representatives of many of the kibbutzim also complained about the lack of Socialist orientation among the German olim.[5] Some kibbutzim, both those associated with ha-Kibbutz ha-Meuchad and those associated with other movements, refused to accept members with families. These kibbutz members argued that the Yishuv "should select immigrants more carefully" — that is, it should limit aliya to male bachelors between the ages of 17 and 35 who had completed a hachshara program. In opposition, the chairman of ha-Kibbutz ha-Meuchad's Executive, Yitzhak Tabenkin, argued that "whoever he-Halutz [Mapai's youth and training movement in the diaspora] sends us, we must accept without complaint."[6] Tabenkin did not mean to advocate that only he-Halutz members should be permitted to immigrate but rather that the kibbutzim should not be concerned with the qualifications of the new immigrants. At the Congress, Joseph Sprinzak boldly called for a mass aliya movement. "We cannot be satisfied with 60,000 immigrants a year," he argued, "we must bring [in] 100,000!"[7] At about the same time Moshe Beilinson, another Mapai and Histadrut leader, wrote that:

> The Jews of Germany never leave my heart, which beats —
> day and night — with only one thought: The Exodus
> from Egypt has arrived. Oh what we could accomplish if
> we were a proper movement! Not only to save [the

German Jews], but to establish our foundations on the
land in one stroke . . . I am not thinking of a year or
two, but of ten years — the Exodus took forty years or
more. I am not concerned with language and culture. I
need Jews. And as to the absorptive capacity of the land,
I firmly believe that it can absorb 2-3 million, . . . Not
only is there room for German Jewry, but for Polish and
Russian Jewry as well.[8]

In analyzing the differing positions, both similarities and differences must
be noted. Tabenkin's position, reflecting that of Mapai's majority, accepted
the premise of halutzic immigration but hoped to steer some Jews with skills
to the Yishuv other than those learned in agricultural training. Viewing the
matter from their more narrowly Socialist ideology, the kibbutz movements,
along with members of Siya-Bet, ha-Shomer ha-Zair, and Poale Zion Smol,
not only sought limited aliya, but actually sought exclusive aliya of the "right"
kind of olim. In 1933, the advocates of mass aliya represented a small
minority within Mapai. Sprinzak, Beilinson, and Berl Katznelson — comple-
mented by JAE members David Ben-Gurion and Moshe Shertok — were the
only major Mapai leaders to have advocated anything approaching "non-
selective" aliya.[9] At a meeting of the Histadrut Aliya Committee on January
10, 1934, Ben-Gurion admitted that the JAE had erred by being committed
to economic absorptive capacity as the criterion for immigration schedules.
The Zionists had thus not demanded unlimited immigration, although, now it
appeared necessary to do so.[10]

The non-Socialist members of the JA coalition, Mizrachi and the General
Zionists, agreed with the position enunciated by Tabenkin and the Mapai
majority: an appeal for an aliya program limited to those with the capital or
skills needed to help build up the Yishuv, including those young enough to
eventually acquire such needed skills. The same was true for the German
Zionists (in Palestine and in Germany). They felt that Palestine could never
offer a complete solution to the German Jewish problem, but it needed to be
available.[11] At least as far as rescue aliya was concerned, this position was
not based on the heartless acceptance of an ideological idee fixe. Rather, it
was based on the assumption that the Nazi threat was not that serious and
that Jews could find a modus vivendi in Germany.

Most indicative of Zionist policies and priorities, in this case, was the issue
of aliya for men (and women) over the age of 35. As already noted, the
kibbutz movements and many Socialist Zionist leaders had severe doubts
about the utility of such olim. The JAE, despite its Mapai majority did not
pursue such a narrow policy, however, and repeatedly (and usually fruitlessly)
sought to ease the British stranglehold on certificates for olim over 35. In
addition, the JAE sought (somewhat more successfully) to gain easier access

to certificates for women of all age groups.[12] The JAE's efforts were only partly successful. In August 1933 the JAE requested 100 certificates for men and women over 35, but received only twenty-four.[13]

A further case that exemplifies the complexities of Zionist rescue policy was the JAE discussion of the April to September 1934 schedule, which involved only 5,500 certificates. Yitzhak Gruenbaum, chief of the JA Labor Department, suggested that half the certificates be given to halutzim, on the proviso that each recipient agreed to work in an agricultural settlement for at least one year. In response, Ben-Gurion suggested that 60 percent of the certificates be dedicated to halutzim, 10 percent used to unite family members, and the remainder distributed proportionately to different regional Zionist organizations. Eventually, the division that was accepted granted 50 percent directly to he-Halutz for distribution, 10 percent to Jewish farmers not associated with he-Halutz, 10 percent to reunite families, and the remaining 30 percent to be used for skilled laborers, professionals, and others.[14]

The position adopted by the JAE toward the immigration of Jews not associated with the coalition parties can also illustrate the debates over JAE rescue priorities. Thus, the Lublin Yeshiva's December 1934 request for a grant of ten Labor certificates for students of the academy developed into a debate between Ben-Gurion, who suggested that a grant from the JA reserve be given to the yeshiva by Mizrachi, and Yitzhak Gruenbaum, who opposed the grant altogether.[15] In addition to the fact that yeshiva students were not working men and, strictly speaking, not qualified for Labor certificates, the case in question relates to the attitude toward Agudas Israel, the orthodox anti-Zionist party. Aguda routinely received certificates from the JAE; other parties opposed to the WZO posed similar problems. Thus, when Ha-Zohar withdrew from the WZO in 1935, the question of granting certificates to Betar members arose. The JAE decided, with only Gruenbaum dissenting, to continue granting certificates to Betar on an ad hoc basis — as had been decided in the unratified Ben-Gurion-Jabotinsky agreement of 1934 — so long as Betar agreed not to disrupt the activities of the national funds.[16] The JAE adopted a similar position regarding aliya by members of Poale Zion Smol: if they did not attempt to disrupt Zionist activities, the party would receive between five and ten certificates per month each schedule period.[17]

Again, however, these decisions were not achieved without opposition. In a meeting of the JAE on June 23, 1935, Eliezer Kaplan, head of the JA Financial Department and a member of the Mapai Executive, expressed his uncategorical opposition to granting certificates "to organizations that fight against the [World] Zionist Organization." The Executive, by 2 to 1 did not support Kaplan's position.[18] In all these cases certain types of immigrants were encouraged and others discouraged, by different elements of the Yishuv.

All these examples also share a common denominator that runs through the ideological history of rescue aliya. With a few noteworthy exceptions, most

TABLE 4.1: Labor (C) Schedule Requests, 1933-1937

Schedule	Requests	Granted	Percent
April-September 1933	12,750	5,500	43.0
October 1933-March 1934	24,490	5,500	22.5
April-September 1934	20,100	6,800	33.8
October 1934-March 1935	18,600	7,500	40.3
April-September 1935	19,160	18,000	94.0
October 1935-March 1936	19,000	3,250	17.0
April-September 1936	11,290	4,500	40.0
October 1936-March 1937	10,695	1,800	16.8
TOTAL	136,065	52,850	38.8

Source: *JA Report*, 1935, p. 15 and *JA Report*, 1937, pp. 26-32.

Zionist leaders distinguished between "salvation" and rescue. Given the goal of attaining national salvation, rescue appeared to take second place. They thus operated on the belief that Palestine represented only part of the solution for the immediate distress of German and eastern European Jewry.

Furthermore, most Zionists accepted — as a fait accompli — the principle of "economic absorptive capacity" as a valid criterion for establishing the size of immigration schedules. Had the British accepted 100 percent of every requested schedule that the JAE proposed, the level of Labor immigration would have reached only 136,065, as against the millions of Jews in Germany and eastern Europe awaiting rescue. To provide a better perspective on the issues, Table 4.1 lists the Zionist labor schedule requests for 1933 to 1937.

Publicly, Zionists continued to emphasize that they expected approximately one-third of German Jewry to be uprooted over the long-run.[19] By January 1934, however, almost every European country had closed their doors to refugees; coming on the heels of the failed Lausanne Conference of the Refugee Council (initiated by the League of Nations High Commissioner for Refugees) this emphasis on a small numbers of expected refugees is startling.

Finally, there was also a marked lack of a sense of urgency in planning for both emigration and immigration. In the years between 1933 and 1935 it seemed that a modus vivendi was possible for German Jewry.[20] Zionists of all stripes certainly recognized that Germany had declared war on Jews; a smaller number also realized that the Nazi war had the potential for violence. But for the time being Germany's anti-Jewish campaign was being conducted on an ideological and economic plane and was not marked by violent outbursts by and large.[21]

Almost all Zionist leaders and their organizations issued clarion calls for increased rescue work after the Nuremberg Laws. But, Zionist rhetoric was not always matched with specific action. Even German Zionists already in Palestine were troubled by the apparent lack of urgency in the Yishuv's activities: they complained bitterly that the 16 percent of certificates granted for German Jews in the Spring 1935 schedule was inadequate.[22]

A case in point is the November 1935 scheme for the organized emigration of German Jewry, which was given some consideration by the JAE. Emphasizing that there were approximately 73,000 German Jews between the ages of 17 and 35, the plan's author proposed to finance the relocation of 24,000 of these Jews in three years, at the rate of 8,000 per year. The anonymous author also anticipated an aliya of at least 6,000 German Jewish capitalists (2,000 per year). In this way, over the course of nine years a total of 90,000 immigrants (all those already between 17 and 35, plus all who would enter this age category during the period of operation) could be accommodated.[23]

THE EVACUATION PLAN

The November plan and all similar attempts to introduce order into the emigration of German Jewry kept to conventional numbers. Despite the worsening position of German Jewry, some form of continuing communal life still appeared possible. Such a view reflected widely held perceptions in the mid-1930's, and may be considered the conventional wisdom of the time. One visionary proposal that did not accept this view was Zeev Jabotinsky's evacuation plan, designed to remove a minimum of 1.5 million Jews from eastern Europe, primarily from Poland, and bring them to Eretz Israel over the course of ten years.

The archival material on Jabotinsky's evacuation scheme is irretrievably lost; all that remains are a series of pamphlets written in German, Hebrew, and English by Dr. Stefan Klinger, a member of the Ha-Zach presidium.[24] Since Jabotinsky's proposals remained relatively stable, the last pamphlet (published in 1938) will be summarized here.

The evacuation scheme was based on four premises. First, Jews needed to become a majority of the population of Palestine as quickly as possible. Second, only the creation of an "immigration regime" — a British administration willing to foster aliya — would make that goal possible. Third, reforms to the structure of the WZO and JA were necessary to further these goals. Fourth, the long-range goal of evacuation was the formation of a sovereign Jewish state.[25] Once completed, the evacuation plan woulbe only the first phase; the second phase would take place once a Jewish state existed, and would involve the repatriation of the entire diaspora. This, Jabotinsky stated (in his foreword), was "the real aim of Zionism."[26]

The proposal to settle one-third of the immigrants in Transjordan and the strident critique Jabotinsky leveled at his opponents, are significant. In a speech on the evacuation that he delivered in Warsaw in October 1936, Jabotinsky went so far as to call on his opponents to "either abandon Zionism or support my position."[27] Noting that the evacuation scheme was not an attempt to surrender Jewish rights in the diaspora, Jabotinsky emphasized that evacuation offered the only future for Jewry.[28] According to Jabotinsky, the counterpolicy espoused by the WZO sought to create "a garden for show, but not a land for all Jews to build."[29]

The evacuation scheme must be viewed within the context of Jabotinsky's overall approach to diaspora Jewry. Jabotinsky denied that evacuation implied the surrender of the Jews' right to live peacefully and with dignity in the diaspora. Rather, evacuation was meant to ensure that the diaspora did not liquidate Jewry. To prove his assertion, Jabotinsky cited a statement about "unnatural diasporas" by Ber Borochov, one of the fathers of Socialist Zionism.[30] Jabotinsky also recalled the 1906 Helsingfors program, which called on Zionists to work for the acceptance of Jewish national minority rights in the diaspora.[31] However, Jabotinsky cited the Helsingfors program to prove that his attitude toward the diaspora was positive, not to argue for a renewed effort at gaining Jewish autonomy. In other words, he argued that tactics appropriate for Zionist and Jewish needs in 1906 were no longer appropriate. Now, Jews had two choices: flee or be overwhelmed.[32]

At the Nineteenth Zionist Congress, in 1935, David Ben-Gurion spoke about mass aliya in similar terms: a million Jews to be resettled in Eretz Israel as quickly as possible. Although Ben-Gurion may have been trying to steal Jabotinsky's rhetorical thunder, in letters that he wrote to his wife and children, and in talks held with other Mapai leaders Ben-Gurion also spoke about schemes for increased immigration — not to the extent of millions, but at least in the hundreds of thousands.[33] Clearly Ben-Gurion, who had previously accepted halutzic aliya, began changing his position with the rise of the Nazis in 1933. At this stage, however, his views represented only an intermediate position, between limited and mass aliya.

Ben-Gurion's public actions reinforce this impression. During negotiations with the British government in the autumn and winter of 1934, he requested British guarantees for a minimum aliya rate of 50,000 per year.[34] Neither of his immigration proposals was immediately taken up by the JAE, which had not yet abandoned the more conventional approach to aliya, nor did the British grant any aid to the rescue aliya program. In contrast, Jabotinsky could have argued: Why request 20,000 certificates a year, or 50,000, for that matter — why not 100,000? His position was based on the need to act and to offer a solution to Jewish suffering, not on palliatives offered for a specific case. On the whole, Revisionists tended to be more sensitive to the plight of eastern European Jewry. In evaluating the differences between the two policies, it may be said that the JA tended to concentrate on the issue of German Jewry and on the slow but necessary steps required to offer aid to those in need. The Revisionists, on the other hand, concentrated on the crisis in Poland and on the broad terms of an encompassing solution.[35] Realities were, of course, far different from appearances. Neither policy was able to effect any long-term change in the suffering of the Jews in Germany or Poland since neither the JA nor the Revisionists controlled Palestine: the British did.

Most Zionists advocated a continuation of the existing rescue aliya program instead of evacuation. Among the Mapai leaders only Ben-Gurion broke the mold, proposing a massive increase in aliya. The majority of the Zionists did not even think in such terms until after Kristallnacht (November 9-10, 1938). As a result, the evacuation scheme remained outside the pale, although Jabotinsky continued to urge its adoption on friends and foes alike.

YOUTH ALIYA

Within the overall policy of rescue aliya, Youth Aliya played a special role especially since it was the only form of legal Jewish immigration into Palestine that the British permitted during World War II. Youth Aliya's importance has led to a number of historical analyses; here, only a few observations on the program's history will be provided, to place it in its ideological and political context.[36]

The first proposals regarding special arrangements for teenage youngsters entering Palestine without their parents were made by Recha Freier in 1932, as a response to the steadily worsening conditions in Germany.[37] Not until February 1933 were the Zionists convinced of the usefulness of such a scheme. Despite the initial reticence, Youth Aliya was accepted by all Zionists as a way of rescuing children whose parents could not, or would not, emigrate.[38]

Although the British had established a "student" category (Certificate B-III) in their immigration regulations, the certificate was limited to those attending school in Palestine and implied that the bearer was a transient whose maintenance was guaranteed by an accredited institution until he or she could become self-supporting. Such immigration required the posting of a considerable bond and also stipulated very strict age requirements. The regulations regarding the B-I certificate, for orphans to be housed in publicly supported institutions, were similarly specific.[39] Therefore, before any work could actually begin, explicit British approval of the plan was necessary.

When they were approached in the summer of 1933, the British proved willing to accept some of the proposals relating to Youth Aliya. They sought limitations on the number of settlements that would be allowed to participate, and they wanted a strict policy of responsibly supervising the youngsters.[40] Age limits were also set (they could not be under 14 or over 17 years old), and financial guarantees had to be posted for each youngster. A sliding bond was to be posted, with the amount dependent on the age of the child: £P48 for a 17-year-old, £P96 for a 16-year-old, and £P144 for children younger than 16. Henrietta Szold, who took responsibilty for Youth Aliya for the JA, noted that such strict requirements were difficult to comply with but she agreed to them, realizing that compliance was the only way to obtain approval of the scheme.[41] In response, Albert Hyamson, the director of the Department of Immigration, requested a further clarification regarding the number of youngsters and the finances available for their maintenance.[42]

While they awaited British approval, those responsible for arrangements in Palestine were busy working on organizational issues related to the Youth Aliya. These included finances, the question of which settlements should be approached, and the degree of outside supervision for the selected settlements.[43] As with the Yishuv's other rescue efforts, finances posed a pressing problem. So did relations between the various political factions and institutions. In early August 1933, Youth Aliya representatives accused the Histadrut of conducting independent negotiations relating to the aliya of young people, but that was strongly denied.[44] Whether or not such negotiations did take place, it must be noted that Youth Aliya appears to have experienced the least infighting of all the rescue programs the Yishuv pursued, since Youth Aliya's clear humanitarian goals left little room for political partisanship.

In time, the necessary financial guarantees were given, and on November 22, 1933, the British tentatively approved the Youth Aliya scheme.[45] In the interim, a number of other financial arrangements were made to permit work to begin.[46] The first forty-three olim arrived in February 1934, and by May the total had reached 115. Plans had already been set in motion to transfer as many as 500 more youngsters; many more, it was reported, could be accommodated if the proper funding were secured.[47]

As the youngsters arrived, they were accommodated in various moshavot, kibbutzim, and educational institutions. New locations were investigated throughout the Yishuv for the placement of successive arrivals.[48] The JA also inaugurated fund drives for Youth Aliya in a number of European countries and in the United States. In an effort to gain funds, a glowing and emotive description of the arrival of the first group was written by Chaim Weizmann and mailed to prospective donors.[49]

At this point, the project ran afoul of the British, as a result of the defined age limit for Youth Aliya. The JA accepted these limitations and was very careful to obtain precise information about each prospective oleh. Parents had to fill out a detailed questionnaire, and a medical report was required before the youngster was even considered.[50] Because the British interpreted "ages 14 to 17" as disqualifying youngsters who were even a few months past their seventeenth birthday, Passport Control Office in Berlin refused to grant certificates to a number of candidates who were nearly seventeen, since they would be over the age limit by the time they arrived in Palestine. In turn, Szold was forced to write to Georg Landauer, asking him to instruct the

Berlin representatives to double-check each candidate's age very carefully.[51] Szold wrote to Landauer again slightly more than two weeks later. Believing that an approach to the British could ease the age problem, she suggested that he look into the matter.[52] Landauer, in turn, wrote to the JA Political Department, requesting their intervention.[53]

The impasse thus reached was never fully eliminated, but a step in the right direction was taken in October 1935. Edward Mills, head of the Department of Statistics in the Palestine government, traveled to Berlin to consult with Passport Control officers there. According to Norman Bentwich, "Mills came back from Germany in righteous indignation and he is anxious that the Youth Alijah [sic] will be increased." Bentwich, himself just returned from America, noted that Youth Aliya "was my best selling point in America and I am sure people can be moved there and here [in Britain] for the children's cause."[54] Youth Aliya's appeal resulted in a loosening of the grip on certificates, so that by the end of 1935, more than 750 youngsters had been transferred. By the end of 1936 the number had reached 1,553.[55] In 1936 it became clear that Youth Aliya would continue to enjoy a relatively secure status. Plans were thus made to expand its activities to eastern European countries, particularly in Poland — partly to ease the pressure on Polish Jewry, then reeling from the shock of a series of pogroms — and partly as a test to see if the British would make any effort to choke off the expected increase in aliya before it began.[56] There were a few problems, primarily in assuring a sufficient number of certificates, but these were usually overcome. A careful reading of the documents shows that the British were having second thoughts regarding the easier access to certificates they had allowed to Youth Aliya, but also showing that there was no thought of stopping the program.[57]

Youth Aliya received additional drive from Hadassah (the Women's Zionist Organization of America) in a strongly worded resolution passed unanimously at Hadassah's Twenty-second National Convention, held from October 18 to 21, 1936, asking that the Mandatory government increase the number of Youth Aliya certificates for German and Polish youth:

> Hadassah, the Women's Zionist Organization of
> America, which through its sponsorship has won the uni-
> versal support and interest of the American public,
> respectfully petition[s] the Government of the Mandatory
> Power through the Jewish Agency not only for an in-
> crease in the number of Youth Aliyah certificates granted
> to the Youth of Germany, but for the extension of the
> benefits of the immigration and education scheme to the
> eager and waiting young people of Poland.[58]

Following up on the resolution, Hadassah began a publicity campaign almost at the same time the Peel Commission was in Palestine. Hoping to impress the British with Hadassah's unity behind the Youth Aliya, the American women proposed telegraphing the commission that it would be "unthinkable [that a] humane British government [could] fail [in] cooperation [with] this work. Adverse policy in salvation of children would create disastrous public opinion in America." On Szold's advice, however, the telegram was toned down considerably, to read: "Respectfully urge that mandatory makes possible [for] America[ns to] continue this humane work."[59] This approach appears to have won the day, and no changes were made to Youth Aliya.

Youth Aliya may thus be seen as a qualified success since the program enjoyed a special status and was able to operate even after the program of rescue aliya had collapsed. This success was qualified, however, by the British-imposed age and financial requirements, and by constant financial difficulties that inhibited further growth and considerably narrowed the number of families that could be helped.

THE HAAVARA AGREEMENT

Origins of the Agreement

Without a doubt, the Haavara agreement was the most controversial element of Zionist aliya policy during the 1930s. The subject of a number of studies in recent years, Haavara has been misunderstood and often misrepresented by authors seeking to use the agreement for polemical rather than scholarly purposes.[60] Here the Haavara agreement and the controversy surrounding it will be assessed only as they relate to the policy of rescue aliya.

It will be recalled that in the early spring of 1933 a series of anti-Nazi boycotts began spontaneously among different Jewish communities, most notably in the United States. The initial response of the Yishuv to this proposal was ambivalent. Some elements — primarily those connected to Ha-Zohar — enthusiastically supported the boycott; others — notably the German Zionists and their organization in Palestine (HOG) — forcefully opposed the idea. The JAE and the WZO adopted a policy of offering neither support nor opposition. The status quo lasted for almost a month. On May 4, 1933, Jabotinsky issued a strongly worded manifesto calling on all Jews to declare economic warfare on the Nazis.[61] That same month, Chaim Arlosoroff traveled to Germany. While in Berlin, he signed a document titled "Einige Thesen zur Frage der Liquidationsbank" (A Few Theses Regarding the Liquidation Bank Question), which represented an agreement in principle on the means of enlarging capitalist aliya.[62] In late June, Arlosoroff published an article in *ha-Olam* (the official WZO weekly) expanding on the idea of a liquidation bank. The organization thus created would act as a guarantor to insure the liquidation of German Jewish businesses and "thereby increase aliya." Arlosoroff felt that such a policy could only result from negotiations with the German government and the framing of "a solution . . . based on concessions and advatages for both sides."[63]

Arlosoroff's proposal on the creation of a liquidation bank represents the first official contacts regarding Haavara. Behind the proposal lay the desire to ease the financial distress of German Jews emigrating to Palestine, since German laws passed by the Weimar Republic placed severe restrictions on capital export by émigrés. Anyone leaving Germany could legally remove only RM50 in coins; cash could not be withdrawn at all.[64] Following up on the proposals made by Arlosoroff, Dr. Werner D. Senator held talks with Dr. Carl Melchior, a well-known German Jewish banker. Both concluded that only a liquidation bank would be able to offer practical assistance to German Jewry, and they proposed to establish one with the help of American and Anglo-Jewish bankers.[65]

The liquidation bank as such never came into existence. As the proposal was based on the sale of stocks, it is hard to see where sufficient funds would have been available to finance the project in any event. Instead, in June 1933, Sam Cohen, the chief executive officer of Hanotaiah and part owner of *Doar ha-Yom* (a daily closely associated with Moshe Smilansky and the Farmers' Association), began a series of negotiations with Heinrich Wolf, the German consul general in Jerusalem. The centerpiece of their deal, which was formalized as an agreement between the German Zionist Federation and the Nazi regime in August 1933, was the replacement of capital transfers with the transfer of equivalent values of German manufactured goods, raw materials, or services. Such a transfer agreement appeared beneficial: the emigrant recovered part of his capital; the Yishuv received new immigrants bringing much-needed capital, technical expertise, and materials vital for further expansion and growth; and Germany boosted its exports by a small degree without a drain on precious foreign currency.[66]

The main opponents of such a scheme were the supporters of the anti-Nazi boycott, since a reduction of German exports was their only realistic weapon. They argued that morality demanded that Jews do nothing that could be seen as helping the German economy.

Although almost every economy had been hurt by the depression, German exports, especially in eastern Europe, were protected by clearing agreements making the German economy less susceptible to boycott.[67] Exports to all of Palestine, however, amounted to less than half of 1 percent of Germany's total exports. As a result, a boycott seemed more likely to harm German Jewry than the Nazis.[68] According to this line of analysis, the rescue of German Jewish property, coupled with the rescue of at least some German Jews, was preferable to a boycott whose outcome was by no means certain.[69]

While differences in alignment regarding Haavara were largely based on party affiliation, clear lines of demarcation did not yet exist in the spring of 1933. Thus, Gershon Agronsky, editor of the left-leaning *Palestine Post*, supported the anti-Nazi boycott as a cost-effective weapon for the defense of German Jewish rights in an editorial titled "Hitlerist Germany and the Jews."[70] So did many American Zionists, including Rabbis Stephen S. Wise and Abba Hillel Silver, who both opposed Haavara because it hurt the anti-Nazi boycott and broke Jewry's united front.[71] The boycott advocates argued that Haavara harmed Jewry's moral position since one ought not do business with one's enemies.

Proponents and opponents of Haavara met officially for the first time at the Eighteenth World Zionist Congress. There the first announcements were made regarding the agreement, to the intense consternation of many members of the Executive, who claimed to know nothing about the negotiations. Much of the embarrassment arose from the fact that initial press reports spoke about an £P3,000,000 ($15,000,000) citrus deal that made no reference to emigration or rescue.[72] By then, Cohen and Wolf had negotiated an £P3,000,000 transfer scheme permitting 3,000 Jews to emigrate with A-I (Capitalist) certificates.[73]

Although £P1,000 ($5,000) per person represented a considerable amount of money, the sum was not beyond the reach of many middle- and upper-class German Jews, especially those who were professionals. Thus, the agreement offered a unique opportunity to save Jewish lives while conserving precious Labor certificates for those without means. And since a Capitalist certificate permitted the immigration of the bearer's family (up to a total of four persons), the reticence of many potential olim about breaking up their families was reduced.

Yet despite the agreement's positive elements, those who supported it did so only reluctantly. They were especially sensitive to accusations that a few wealthy Jews were being accommodated at the price of moral surrender and the abandonment of impoverished Jews to their fate. Weizmann, for example, saw Haavara as a Hobson's choice for the Zionist movement: either aiding Jewish capitalists in recovering some of their capital and guiding that capital into investment in Palestine, or abandoning both the wealthy and the poor Jews to the vagaries of the Labor schedule. The German Zionists, on the other hand, saw the issue in even simpler terms: without the agreement, most wealthy German Jews would simply stay put, hoping to weather the storm.[74]

Therefore, despite opposition, the agreement proceeded. The Palestine Manufacturers' Association promised full cooperation in the undertaking, agreeing to buy needed products from Germany as a means of funding the transfer.[75] On September 7, 1933, *ha-Aretz* reported that the Palaestina Treuhandstelle (PALTREU, the Palestine Trust and Transfer Company), in Berlin already had 650 subscribers.[76] In mid-September Haavara, Ltd. (the name PALTREU used in Palestine) and the Anglo-Palestine Bank published the first information booklet on the agreement, intended as a guide for prospective investors.[77]

Haavara in Operation

Like any clearing agreement, Haavara operated on a simple set of principles. The prospective emigrant placed his assets in one of two blocked accounts (Sonderkonto I or Sonderkonto II), in either the M. M. Warburg Bank in Hamburg or the A. E. Wasserman Bank in Berlin, the two designated

Sample Haavara Certificate
Courtesy of the Jabotinsky Institute Archive, Tel Aviv

PALTREU banks. In return he received a certificate of debenture from Haavara Ltd. that entitled him and his family either to be reimbursed in goods and services or to receive the monetary equivalent of his deposit after the sale of imported German products, once he arrived in Palestine. In theory, the émigré thus retained a relatively large percentage of his capital. In practice, however, only about 25 percent was actually transferred. The primary reason for this glaring discrepancy was the Nazi export policy, specifically, the German demand that transferred goods be sold at their full market value or higher, so as not to harm private German exporters in the Middle East. As a result, in order to transfer RM1,000,000 (£P80,000), approximately twice that amount (in goods) had to be sold. German restrictions rapidly resulted in a policy of dumping goods, i.e. of importing materials that were paid for by retailers who had little (if any) hope of recouping their expenses.

The inability to absorb such a large amount of goods led to financial limitations on Haavara in Palestine: only £P1,000 (RM12,500) was guaranteed to the oleh, although more than that amount was eventually paid out. Indeed, PALTREU was still making payments to investors as late as 1951. In spite of the financial difficulties Haavara experienced, the agreement permitted the aliya of between 20,000 and 50,000 German Jews, meaning that it was one of the most successful of all rescue aliya programs.[78]

Financial arrangements in Palestine were overseen by the Anglo-Palestine Bank (APB), although it was not responsible for actual payments. The payments, based on a schedule of funds available divided by the number of transferees, were made by Haavara Ltd in Tel Aviv, organized for this purpose as a limited stock company. Jews living in Palestine could invest in Haavara Ltd, although the purpose of the company was neither to reap a profit nor to increase the stock value.

One point must be emphasized: at this stage the Haavara agreement essentially remained a private deal that was not under the supervision of any Jewish institution. Insofar as any "dumping" took place it occurred because ha-Notaiah was a private concern and did not opertae under any form of Zionist (certainly not JAE) supervision.[79] For that reason, Haavara as such was neither debated nor often mentioned by the JAE.[80] The fact that initially Haavara supervised itself sparked a debate about the agreement's propriety, beyond its negative impact on the Jewish anti-Nazi boycott. Leo Motzkin, a veteran Zionist activist, condemned Haavara for that reason in a speech in Geneva on September 10, 1933.[81] Zionists in America and South Africa were similarly critical of the agreement.[82] The fact that private corporations were involved was a special source of concern even for those who supported Haavara. As a private corporation, ha-Notaiah, or its stockholders, could be construed as reaping a profit out of the desperate condition of German Jewry and their desire to settle in Eretz-Israel.[83] Press sources, especially in the diaspora, also distorted the agreement, leading to further controversy.[84]

German Zionists, on the other hand, were Haavara's strongest supporters. Since it was possible to qualify for a Capitalist certificate only through Haavara, the agreement was seen as the best means of helping German Jews to emigrate with enough capital to begin life anew. On at least three different occasions, leaders of the German Zionists in Palestine attempted to rally support for the agreement. On the first occasion, in August, the Haavara Executive wrote to Nahum Goldmann, hoping to prevent an anti-Haavara resolution in the World Jewish Congress (WJC). Their argument that "Jews find Haavara the sole means of rescue" convinced Goldmann, who reported that he would defend Haavara to the best of his abilities.[85]   Although it passed a pro-boycott resolution, the WJC did not condemn Haavara. Instead, the WJC requested the WZO reconsider its approval of the deal.[86]

On the second occasion, in September, Landauer wrote to Yosef Sprinzak, hoping to convince the Histadrut leader that the boycott was pointless "so long as Germany maintains trade agreements with other countries that guarantee her contingencies." In Landauer's estimation Haavara represented the only way to control the natural proclivity of Jewish emigrants to convert assets that would otherwise be lost into goods and bring them into Palestine. Haavara allowed the Yishuv to control the inflow of German products, thereby benefiting local manufacturing (Tozeret ha-Aretz), since the list of Haavara-permitted products did not include any items produced in Palestine. Without supervision of Haavara, it was seen as likely that Palestinian industries would have suffered if German Jews brought in products without any form of supervision.[87]   On the third occasion, in October 1934, the co-chairman of HOG wrote to the JAE seeking help to "ease the transfer," while noting that "the issue is urgent."[88]

The sense of urgency was created by Haavara's financial difficulties, which resulted from greater capital investment in Germany and the ensuing import of more German goods than could be absorbed into the Yishuv's fragile economy. Although RM9,795,038.75 (£P783,603.100) was invested in Germany in 1934, the actual amount transferred that year was only RM400,933.63 (£P32,074.690).[89]   By November nearly RM18,000,000 (£P1,440,000) had been deposited, but only one-third of that amount had been transferred on behalf of 1,250 families, totaling 5,000 persons.[90]   On the basis of these statistics, Landauer, in a letter to Arthur Ruppin, suggested three possible options: (1) increase German imports to Palestine, in hopes of reducing prices (by dumping products on the market), thereby increasing sales and revenues; (2) declare the transfer a failure, in hopes of dissuading German Jews from investing in it; or (3) expand the sales of Haavara-imported goods to other Middle Eastern countries, notably Egypt, Iraq, and Syria.[91]

The last proposal, however, ran afoul of the British, who feared German competition in Middle Eastern trade.[92]   The economic situation engendered by Haavara increased the reticence many Zionists had concerning the agreement, and therefore increased the insistence of opponents that the deal be scrapped. Furthermore, the JA was becoming increasingly involved in the Haavara issue, largely against its will. For that reason alone, Eliezer Kaplan suggested that the matter be brought to the Executive, since "anything that involves the Jewish Agency in the issue, even unofficially, must be approved by the whole Executive Committee."[93]

The discomfiture of the Haavara organization, surprisingly, was not the only goal of those advocating a boycott. In May 1934, the Haavara Executive suggested a joint meeting with representatives of HOG and of Palestinian newspapers and institutions, including the Revisionists, to clarify what Haavara was and what it was not.[94] Although this meeting did not take place as planned, a number of meetings with individual members of the Joint Committee to Boycott German Products did. In August, a Mr. Jemani of the Boycott Committee met with Dr. Weiss (of the Haavara directorate) and concluded that Haavara should bear responsibility for all German imports to Palestine, thereby easing both the financial problem of Haavara and the job of those overseeing the boycott (since they would only have to deal with one organization).[95]

Jewish Agency Intervention

Haavara's difficulties increased in 1935, when the Nazis increased restrictions on the amonut capital permitted for export. In April the JAE was asked to help and the Executive agreed to do so, although reluctantly.[96] Efforts were also still being made to export goods to other Middle Eastern countries originally bought from Germany through Haavara.[97] In addition, a num-ber of companies that had originally been involved in Haavara, including ha-Notaiah, sought to use the agreement to boost their own exports of citrus fruit to Germany. These efforts were opposed, even by supporters of Haavara, on moral grounds. Still, the economic pressure was so great that even the Histadrut Executive considered — and initially approved — an export deal for citrus fruit exports to Germany.[98]

Opponents of the agreement, including Yitzhak Gruenbaum, railed against such export deals. Gruenbaum, in particular, felt that in continuing normal economic relations with the Third Reich the Yishuv threatened to become "Germany's global export agents."[99] Gruenbaum's logic was that Haavara ought to serve only the role that the WZO approved: rescuing German Jews with some of their capital. If Haavara no longer served that goal, it no longer deserved the WZO's support.

This was the state of affairs when the Nineteenth World Zionist Congress convened in Lucerne. While the plenum of the Congress debated the entire agreement, representatives of organizations involved with the transfer, including Haavara Ltd., the ZVfD, the APB, PALTREU, and the JA German

Department, negotiated the transfer of authority for the agreement to the JAE.[100]

Two considerations apparently weighed heavily upon the JA leaders' minds and convinced them to become involved. By 1935, the backlog in Haavara payments had reached RM24,000,000 (£P1,920,000), meaning that transfer was slowing down at a time when greater aliya efforts were vital. Moreover, at a meeting between Shertok, Ben-Gurion, and Mills, the latter reiterated British willingness to accept Haavara debentures as proof of sufficient capital to obtain an A-I certificate. He warned that in the future, if an individual coming to Palestine on an A-I certificate did not attain the actual capital to qualify (i.e. £P1,000) the JA would be punished by forfiture of a labor certificate. He also warned that the already used capitalist certificate would not be returned, meaning that the JA would lose two certificates for one oleh.[101]

Under the circumstances, the JA now had a vested interest in the success of the Haavara agreement and pressure to become involved mounted. The result of public and private negotiations relating to Haavara was the following resolution, which passed the Congress's plenum by a wide majority: "In order to encourage the continued immigration into Palestine of Jews from Germany the Executive is instructed to take under its control all work of the Haavara."[102]

A number of limitations were placed on Haavara, especially the following: (1) Haavara would be restricted to Palestine only; (2) Haavara would deal only with the capital of individuals actually making aliya or with monies raised for the Zionist national funds (KKL and KHY); and (3) Haavara Ltd would break all contacts with Palestinian companies advocating exports (primarily of citrus fruit) to Germany.[103] Haavara was thus to be limited, in the words of a JA press release on the subject, to "enabling the transfer to Palestine of the capital of German Jews." This transfer served three goals: "(a) to render possible the immigration of Jews of means from Germany; (b) to assist thereby in the settlement of German immigrants of the labouring class and (c) to promote in general the cause of Jewish reconstruction in Palestine."[104]

Decisive support for Haavara came from a surprising source: eastern European Zionists, who were seen as competing with German Jews for the ever-decreasing number of immigrant certificates that the Mandatory administration was making available.

Two of the Congress's resolutions were put into effect relatively quickly: on October 9, the JAE unanimously voted to absorb Haavara's operations and to publicly oppose any new citrus export to Germany.[105] The third resolution, relating to money transfers, was not effected immediately, since the economic picture in Palestine had not yet changed. Not everyone, however, was satisfied. Col. Frederick H. Kisch, a veteran Zionist and former head of the Zionist Executive's Political Committee (which became the JA Political Department in 1929), wrote an anti-Haavara letter to the editors of *ha-Aretz* and the *Palestine Post*.[106]   Ha-Zach activists became more vocally opposed Haavara after the change in authority, as can be seen by the examples of anti-Haavara posters reproduced below.

As these posters clearly show, the opponents of Haavara emphasized Jewish honor and self-respect. This theme had been central to Jabotinsky's critique of the WZO for the better part of a decade, and it was made explicit in aninterview he granted in Prague immediately after the Eighteenth Zionist Congress. According to Jabotinsky, the Congress "dishonored the Jewish people in the face of the arrogance of the Third Reich."[107]   He further argued that Jews should not be assisting in the economic growth of their persecutors: to do so would be a dishonorable pursuit of money. Honor was also central to the billfold-and-broadside campaign waged by Ha-Zach against the transfer and for the boycott. One billfold called upon members of the Yishuv: "Honor yourself and others! Punish the enemy and remain loyal to your friends."   Another billfold called for support for an anti-Haavara plebiscite in the Yishuv.[108]

One may question the efficacy of this campaign. At times the posters, bill-folds, and broadsides became focal points for interparty violence. Anti-Haavara handouts were duly distributed.[109]   Circular letters calling for opposition to Haavara and support for the boycott were mailed.[110]   In December 1935, the anti-Haavara plebiscite took place, with just over 20,000

"And You Still Buy German Products?"
Courtesy of the Jabotinsky Institute Archives, Tel Aviv

"Have no fear Hitler! The Jews of Eretz Israel are helping you:
Another 'Transfer'-order"
Courtesy of the Jabotinsky Institute Archives, Tel Aviv

"Another order from Eretz Israel"
Courtesy of the Jabotinsky Institute Archives, Tel Aviv

persons casting their vote in opposition to the agreement.[111] Yet that figure represented slightly less than 10 percent of the total population of the Yishuv, which was estimated at 210,000 persons. Moreover, supporters of Haavara waged a countercampaign on behalf of the agreement. At a Histadrut Executive meeting on November 4, 1935, veteran labor Zionist leader David Remez stated that, in his opinion, joining the boycott was like "jumping from the flame into the fire." He condemned the boycott propaganda as "demagoguery."[112] "Don't Touch the Transfer!" read a pro-Haavara broadside, reproduced here in full translation:

DON'T TOUCH THE TRANSFER!

The Zionist Congress at Lucerne approved the Transfer.
Irresponsible partisans are trying to make it into a
subject of political warfare. Eretz-Israel is the only hope
for the Jews of Germany and the Transfer is their sole
and final exit. Should the Transfer be a weapon in the
hands of the Revisionists, who placed themselves outside
the Zionist Congress? Jews! Do you want to help them
and sacrifice German Jewry? Do you want to help in the
destruction of German Judaism? This is the first time in
Jewish history that Eretz-Israel is in a position to
rescue an entire persecuted community. Today the Yishuv
must prove its political wisdom. Zionism faces a historic
challenge. Jews! Do you believe these betrayers, that the
Zionist Congress, the Jewish Agency, and the other
national bodies of the Zionist movement, who took responsibility for the Transfer, are traitors to the Jewish
people?
Therefore:
No responsible Zionist should participate in the
"Haavara" plebiscite.
Do not participate in damaging rallies, and prove your
political maturity and practicality.

Defenders of Haavara based their position on three interconnected arguments. First, abrogation of the transfer agreement would lead to the collapse of rescue aliya, at least for capitalists, who, would have to leave Germany penniless. Such a result would also obligate the JA to use badly needed Labor certificates for German Jewish capitalists, in essence short-changing the poor. Second, with the cancellation of Haavara, only German Jews (and indirectly the Yishuv) would be the losers, since they would have to abandon 100 percent of their property to Germany, which had few moral compunctions, especially when it came to Jews. Third, some German Jews would still attempt to save at least part of their capital by employing unilateral and uncontrolled means, whose end results could be more harmful to the anti-Nazi boycott.[113] Pro-Haavara groups thus sought to cast themselves as pro-aliya rather than anti-boycott. Indeed, they continually emphasized the fact that Haavara gained no foreign currency for the Third Reich.[114]

Opponents of Haavara, with their advocacy of the boycott, opted to defend the honor of the Jewish people. They considered the positive benefits of Haavara too small a compensation for the price that the Yishuv had to pay.[115] Similarly, opponents of Haavara examined the meager initial results: 2,700 German Jewish émigrés on Capitalist certificates entered Palestine from inception through mid-1935. Of course, in relation to the total picture — 500,000 German Jews to be saved — 2,700 is a small number. But one must take into consideration the reasoning of a large number of German Jews in mid-1933, who thought that the worst had passed. Once the Nazis felt secure enough, they would seek world respect and at the very least ease up on their anti-Jewish drive. According to these German Jews a modus vivendi was possible with the Nazis, rendering mass emigration schemes premature.[116]

Unable to convince the majority of the population, opponents of Haavara adopted a policy of limited sniping at the agreement. Despite all this, Haavara was continued. By the end of October 1935, 3,196 payments, totaling RM30,284,560.55 (£P2,422,764.800), had been made. An additional 452 payments, worth RM5,749,720.93 (£P459,977.670), awaited transfer.[117] Yet despite these seemingly impressive numbers, financial difficulties remained. Part of Haavara's difficulty derived from the unwillingness of local Jews, of all political stripes, to buy German products: the unofficial boycott that filtered down from the leaders enjoyed considerable support within the Yishuv.[118] Now, the JAE attempted to rectify the problem, once again by means that would include exports to Middle Eastern countries such as Iraq, Persia, and Egypt.[119] On November 3, 1935 the JAE reorganized the Haavara directorate, increasing it to four members: two representatives of the JA (Senator and Landauer) and one representative each from the Va'ad Leumi and the APB.[120] One week later the board was further enlarged to five members, by the addition of a representative from HOG.[121]

In the meantime, another problem arose when a number of Palestinian citrus concerns continued their trade with Nazi Germany and used Haavara as a means of drawing in their profits, despite the Congress's resolution to desist from such acts.[122] The actions of the citrus concerns must be seen as irresponsible. This was not an effort to equalize Palestine's balance of trade with Germany, which would have been bad enough; it was simply an attempt to profit from the suffering of others. The JAE met twice to deal with the matter, and at the second meeting its unanimous resolution was: "The Executive, in accordance with the resolution of the Congress, establishes that

Haavara *is not* to be used to further the export of citrus fruit to Germany and that Haavara has no right to bring German products into Palestine in exchange for the export of oranges to Germany."[123]

Such irresponsible actions added further grist to the mill of those opposed to Haavara. Attacking it with whatever means were available, opponents raised questions regarding the factual information that Haavara Ltd published in defense of the agreement.[124] In response, advocates of Haavara challenged their opponents to "show [an] alternative method [for] saving German Jews or state publicly [that they] prefer abandoning them [to] their fate."[125]

The relative silence of Haavara's opponents concerning better ways to save German Jews does not necessarily mean that they proposed abandoning them, but it does accentuate the Zionist dilemma. Haavara Ltd. therefore appealed to members of the Yishuv's intelligentsia, hoping to convince them of the agreement's propriety and in this way to generate positive public opinion. Frequent mailings of explanatory material were made to individuals who were thought to be influential or whose support for the agreement was not assured. Among those in the latter category was Dr. Judah L. Magnes, the president of Hebrew University.[126] Apparently, Magnes was persuaded; his papers contain the handwritten notes made for a speech he delivered on the subject in December 1935 or January 1936.[127] Another new supporter of Haavara was Ben-Gurion, who had not previously expressed an opinion on the agreement in public. At a meeting of the Va'ad Leumi, on December 11, 1935, Ben-Gurion spoke forcefully on behalf of the agreement:

> Only Eretz-Israel can serve as a cure for German Jewry,
> even if not for all of them; any other "cure" is a false
> hope. We cannot topple Hitler, perhaps he will be
> toppled some other way. We must be concerned with
> the fate of the children and women, who are choking in
> this destructive hell. There is one way to rescue them —
> to bring them to Eretz-Israel, with their capital. Their
> capital — that is, merchandise, and by this I do not mean
> French or English merchandise. The only question is
> whether the money will return to Germany. This is not
> German merchandise; this is Jewish capital, belonging to
> Jews who are going to their destruction . . . we have no
> other honor except by rescuing Jews and bringing them to
> Eretz-Israel.[128]

Ben-Gurion's strong words were, of course, formulated polemically, but his note that the Yishuv could not topple Hitler was well taken nonetheless. The Yishuv's limited influence may be seen tangentially in a letter by Yitzhak Ben-Zvi, chairman of the Va'ad Leumi Executive, to the Austrian consul in

Jerusalem. Ben-Zvi asssured the consul that the Yishuv would not boycott Austrian films in the same way that it boycotted German ones unless the Austrians adopted Nazi antisemitism.[129] This letter points directly to some successes of the boycott — despite Haavara. More significantly, however, the letter implies that some countries could be approached in a more forceful manner: threats against Austria might succeed, but against the Nazis such threats elicited little concern proving how weak the Yishuv really was.

Another effort to gain support for the agreement was the December 22, 1935, press conference called by the Haavara Directorate. Twelve local and three foreign newspapers were invited, along with representatives of the Va'ad Leumi, KHY, KKL, the Manufacturers' Association, the Farmers' Association, and the Joint Boycott Committee.[130] The Haavara Directorate attempted to use the gathering as a way to respond to many of the criticisms leveled at Haavara; it is clear, however, that the only participants convinced by the speakers probably already supported the agreement. The opponents of using economic interests as a means of rescue were not convinced, and changed neither their minds nor their tactics.[131]

The Yishuv's Boycott Movement

In the main, critics of the Haavara agreement concentrated on the alternative policy articulated by Jabotinsky in his May 4, 1933, speech. The documentation is rather sketchy, however, and the history of the Yishuv's boycott organization, the Joint Committee to Boycott German Goods (JCB), cannot be fully reconstructed. From extant documents, three spheres of boycott activity become evident: first, the boycotters undertook a systematic propaganda campaign, designed to convince the populace not to buy German products (examples of the posters used are reproduced above). In August 1934, Ha-Zohar undertook a monthlong campaign to oppose Haavara and strengthen the boycott.[132] Given the counterpropaganda relating to Haavara, the boycott propaganda campaign does not appear to have been a success.

Second, the JCB attempted to convince merchants not to renew stocks of products made in Germany. Of special significance for the boycotters was cutting off the sale of Haavara-imported items, since these were seen by the JCB members as the result of a deal with the devil. Third, they attempted to convince theater owners not to show movies or newsreels produced in Germany and imported into Palestine, even though these were not part of the Haavara agreement.

In 1933 and 1934, the boycott met with mixed results. Some firms and theaters did indeed break contacts with Germany; others did not. The JCB's greatest success seems to have been with theater owners, who were asked to pay a small fee for an endorsement verifying their support for the boycott.[133] Since the theaters paid for the endorsement, the JCB had a regular source of income, but this was tenuous, and did not cover expenses. For example, during the ten weeks between August 15 and November 1, 1935, the committee earned £P35, while expenses were £P49.740.[134]

Attempts to persuade merchants to support the boycott appear to have been less successful. Refusal to support the JCB, however, did not ipso facto signify willingness to sell German products (imported via Haavara or other sources), but simply reflected the merchant's unwillingness to publicly support the committee.[135] Some companies refused to even meet with the JCB's representatives.[136] By and large, such companies simply refused to cooperate with the boycott and did not express any overt ideological posture. In this case it is not possible to indict Haavara as such for the failure of the boycott to gain the support of merchants. Although some of the approached companies did participate in the transfer, the advocates of Haavara claimed that the agreement could actually be a means of strengthening the boycott, by centralizing imports from Germany, limiting private imports, and denying the Nazis much-needed foreign currency.[137] They further claimed that such a policy was logical, and hoped to obtain the boycotters' agreement. No such agreement, however, was ever pursued, since it would have meant that the boycott advocates would have had to agree to Haavara. Another factor weakening the boycott was the import of German products by Arab and non-Jewish German residents of Palestine (e.g., the Templars).[138]

From the few documents available, it is possible to partially reconstruct the JCB's relations with the Va'ad Leumi which appear to have been proper, if not cordial. On September 20, 1935, the JCB requested that the Va'ad Leumi convene a court of honor to deal with statements made by HOG members that defamed the JCB.[139] The Va'ad Leumi refused, claiming that convening a court of honor fell outside its authority. The real reason for the Va'ad Leumi's refusal appears to be that the supposed defamatory comments were all quotes from HOG depositions accusing JCB members of threatening violence against merchants who did not comply with the boycott.[140] In October, the JCB reiterated its request, and was once again rebuffed.[141] In view of these claims and counterclaims, it is safe to assume that relations with HOG were never very cordial.

Relations with the Va'ad Leumi soured in 1936 for reasons that cannot be fully explained. It appears that the JCB offered to the Va'ad Leumi representation on a national boycott committee (until then the JCB had operated via local committees), perhaps with the hope of gaining Va'ad Leumi sponsorship of the boycott.[142] Had such support been forthcoming, it almost certainly would have led to conflict between the Va'ad Leumi and the JA. This may have been the JCB's goal, since the JAE had by then assumed supervision of the Haavara.

The involvement of the Va'ad Leumi with the JCB did not end there. A representative of the Va'ad Leumi apparently continued to attend JCB meetings, and at the end of March 1936, the JCB requested Va'ad Leumi participation in a national boycott conference designed to formulate the Yishuv's boycott strategy in time for the upcoming world conference of anti-Nazi boycott groups. Again the Va'ad Leumi refused, on grounds of authority — or, rather, of lack thereof.[143]

Surviving documents relating to JCB relations with the three other Yishuv organizations are of special significance. The earliest of the documents is a note to the Mapai Executive that encloses the handwritten protocol of a meeting between Mapai representatives and Hillel Kook, the chairman of the JCB Executive. Mapai's representatives had demanded an explanation as to why their delegate had been removed from the JCB's last meeting. Explaining that the action had been a personal and not a party matter, Kook assured his interlocutors that in the future, Mapai representatives would be permitted to attend meetings; he even proposed cooperation on the national level, something that never became a reality.[144] This requires some comment since most authors have regarded the boycott as the exclusive province of Ha-Zohar. The fact that individual members of Mapai actively participated in meetings regarding the boycott, while the party itself supported the Haavara agreement, may require a revision of the strict lines of demarcation hitherto used to categorize the different responses of the Yishuv's parties to Nazi Germany.

The same potential need for a revision of previously held positions derives from the second document: a letter from Haavara Ltd to the JCB. Referring to complaints about the importing of certain items from Germany, the correspondent denied any responsibility for those imports and expressed hope that the matter would soon be clarified.[145] Again this document appears to defy the strict division between organizations and strongly implies the existence of non-Haavara imports of German goods by German Jews.

The third document is a letter from Nir, the Histadrut-owned agricultural cooperative, to Nahum Goldmann. In their letter, the Nir representatives referred to their use of Haavara to transfer money invested by German Jews for themselves and the KKL. As to complaints that Nir thus harmed the anti-Nazi boycott, the correspondents made two points. First, they declared that, after intense scrutiny of all aspects of the issue, the Histadrut Executive concluded that transferring the capital was preferable to abandoning it in Germany. On another level, however, Goldmann's correspondents claimed that the most vocal condemnations of this use of Haavara by the Histadrut derived from supporters of Ha-Zohar in ha-Notaiah, especially Sam Cohen, and other private citrus concerns. Ironically, the writers noted that these were the same people who had negotiated the original Haavara agreement.[146]

Such a revelation of Cohen's political orientation demands an explanation. It is true that Cohen was not a supporter of the Histadrut, but he was not a Revisionist. His only association with the Revisionist movement came during the early 1930s, when a series of labor disputes during the citrus harvests —

caused first and foremost by the farmers' hiring practices, which were widely perceived as an attempt at union breaking — led to partisan strife between members of the Histadrut and the Revisionist National Labor Federation. Thus, from the perspective of the Nir representatives, Cohen might as well have been a Revisionist. He and other citrus growers had been doing business with the Germans all along: it was they who had attempted to sell fruit to Germany, hoping to use Haavara as a means to collect their profits. Essentially, the author of the letter was attempting to deny any possible wrongdoing on Nir's part by claiming that its critics were doing the same thing.

This document requires further elucidation. Hitherto, authors have established a strict division between the Haavara and the boycott as weapons in the struggle on behalf of German Jewry, since the two policies appeared contradictory — different both in approach and in ultimate goal. The boycott was an attempt to use economic warfare against Jewry's greatest enemy, in the hope of at least salvaging Jewish honor, if not achieving total victory. Haavara, on the other hand, conceded that victory over the Nazis was impossible, and sought to take as many Jews as possible out of harm's way. But because the two policies differed does not mean that one was ipso facto more moral or more correct than the other.

Many authors have simply assumed that Mapai and its allies adopted and consistently pursued a Haavara policy, while Ha-Zohar consistently pursued the boycott. Future investigations may further revise this picture, but three facts are clear: first, the argument that supporters of Haavara were not concerned with Jewish honor is untenable. The majority of Zionists supported the agreement not because they thought it was good, but because they feared it was their only choice. That was the Hobson's choice to which Weizmann and others referred on numerous occasions. Second, Haavara guaranteed the transfer of a minimum of £P1,000, gaining an A-I (Capitalist) certificate for the potential oleh. Thus, Haavara significantly increased aliya without using precious certificates from the Labor schedule, while transferring entire families to Eretz-Israel. Only the A-I certificate entitled the bearer to bring three additional family members with him. Third, Haavara also brought material benefits to the Yishuv that have too often been overlooked in this debate: the injection of German Jewish capital, even in the form of German goods, permitted further economic growth in the Jewish economy.[147] This, in turn, increased Palestine's economic absorptive capacity and made requests for larger schedules appear more reasonable to the British. One fact is irrefutable: without Haavara, the Nazi murder machine, which operated with cool and calculated efficiency in the 1940's, would have had many more victims.

Expanding Haavara

The German Jewish situation worsened in the fall of 1935 with the introduction of the Nuremberg Laws; conditions for Jews in Poland, Romania, and other parts of eastern Europe were also in a state of continued turmoil. Simultaneously, a deadlock developed in Palestine as the British decreased the size of schedules granted at a time when more certificates were needed. Clearly, the British were making a conscious effort to limit the size of Jewish immigration, in the hope of staving off a revival of Arab violence.[148]

The JA sought a means of breaking the certificate deadlock by utilizing the bylaws of capitalist immigration. Grants of Capitalist certificates were virtually unlimited, and, as noted above, the A-I certificate permitted the bearer to bring up to three family members with him. But in order to obtain an A-I certificate, the potential immigrant had to prove that he had at least £P1,000 in cash or debentures. The Capitalist certificate was limited to individuals of some means, and had been primarily used for the benefit of those making aliya under the Haavara agreement. In 1935, however, the JA began a series of negotiations with eastern European governments toward concluding a series of Haavara-like clearing agreements. Ultimately, these negotiations would encompass Czechoslovakia, Poland, Rumania, Latvia, Lithuania, Austria (before the Anschluss), and the Free City of Danzig.

An explicit call for the JAE to act in response to the suffering of Jews in eastern Europe was made by Levi Skolnik (Eshkol). "What Jews were unwilling to do when they had the opportunity," he said, "we can now get them to do under [conditions of] duress."[149] In a sense, Skolnik appeared to be welcoming antisemitism, at least insofar as pressure to emigrate became an impetus for Jews to turn to Zionism. Such, however, was not his purpose. Even if the Zionists did not properly assess the Nazi threat, none of them looked forward to the prospect of Jewish suffering. Again, a Zionist leader was caught in the same rhetorical trap analyzed by the "Catastrophic Zionism" school: for forty years, Zionists had predicted an impending assault on European Jewry. When the predicted catasrophe arrived, however, they were unable to rise above the "business as usual" attitude that permeated the Yishuv's daily politics.

The earliest eastern European contacts were with the Czechs, and, not unlike those that were made prior to the German Haavara agreement, they began as a series of unofficial contacts by Czech Zionists. The terms of this initial agreement differed from those of the Haavara. Instead of a deal involving goods, the transferee's money was deposited in a Prague bank and an equal sum in Palestine pounds was then transferred to the Philip Mayer and Associates real estate firm in Haifa. Unlike the German Haavara, this agreement allowed the full sum to be exported. The transferred capital was then invested in land bought for Czech Jews. Thus, the Czech oleh met the minimum financial requirements for the A-I certificate and also had a place in which to settle upon arrival.[150] Regrettably, these talks hit a snag, although contacts continued. Only in September 1938 was a final agreement reached regarding the transfer of 2,500 Czech Jews with £P500,000 ($100,000) of their capital. The emigrants deposited their capital in a blocked account in the Narodni Banka (Czech national bank) and were reimbursed from the Bank of England as part of a £8,000,000 ($40,000,000) loan that Britain had extended to the government of Czechoslovakia.[151]

After further negotiations, agreements were reached with the governments of Latvia and Lithuania. Signed on March 23, 1936, the Latvian agreement was a straight barter arrangement. In return for a guarantee that the Yishuv would import $500,000 in Latvian products, Latvian olim would be permitted to withdraw sufficient funds to qualify for a Capitalist certificate.[152] The Lithuanian agreement was identical, and was signed on April 20, 1936.[153] It is difficult to gauge the impact of these two agreements, since aliya from either Lithuania or Latvia never amounted to a significant proportion of any schedule.

Contacts with the Poles began in May 1936.[154] Despite lengthy negotiations, which dragged on into 1938, no agreement was ever reached. Yitzhak Gruenbaum visited Poland on a number of occasions to try to get the talks moving, to no avail.[155] The Poles, according to the Zionist negotiators, refused to negotiate in good faith, and the negotiations may be deemed a failure. Judging by the quantity of documents on the talks, failure to conclude an agreement cannot be blamed on the JA or Zionist representatives.[156]

Throughout these negotiations, the transfer agreement with Nazi Germany continued. According to an undated report of either 1936 or 1937, Haavara transferred a total of RM33,800,000 (£P2,704,000) out of a total of RM48,000,000 (£P3,840,000) invested in Germany.[157] The figures should represent approximately 2,700 transferees, although the report does not specify numbers. Nevertheless, Haavara's financial picture did not improve in 1936. The payment schedule continually fell behind the number of olim, requiring renewed attempts to export goods to the Arabs.[158] Since these efforts coincided with the declaration of an Arab general strike against the Yishuv and the beginning of an all-out Arab revolt against the Mandatory government, Haavara's success was illusory. Some Arab businessmen, in fact, proposed direct trade between themselves and Nazi Germany. This meant dispensing with the monopoly granted to PALTREU as a means to gain much-needed foreign currency for Germany, something that was not to be won from Haavara.[159]

Developments in the Middle East in 1936, including the Arab proposals regarding direct trade formed the basis for a German reevaluation of Haavara, but they did not lead to its termination. Serious reservations had always been voiced among some Nazi ideologues regarding the wisdom of support for Zionism, which, they feared, could be misconstrued as a concern for Jewry's legitimate right to exist. In view of the British proposals to create a Jewish state (the Peel plan), a proposal the Nazis rejected completely, these voices were added to those of the Arabs trying to curtail aliya. But insofar as the Nazi hierarchy sought a solution to the "Jewish problem" on the basis of emigration or expulsion, anything encouraging the exodus was to be pursued; the orders regarding the continuation of Haavara reputedly came from Hitler himself.[160]

The Jewish controversy regarding Haavara also continued. Advocates of the boycott made another effort to prevail on the WJC, which convened in August 1936, to condemn the agreement, but the anti-Haavara resolution came to nought.[161] Despite the lack of firm documentation, it can be assumed, that the JCB continued its sniping at the Haavara.[162] On the other hand, support for Haavara was gained from Walter Schevenells, a well-known leader of the Franco-Jewish Labor movement, who noted that many of Haavara's most vocal critics in the diaspora were not themselves careful about the entrance of German products into their own communities.[163]

Despite its controversial nature, Haavara played an important role in rescue aliya. From 1933 to 1936 it was a major means of encouraging emigration from Germany in a way that also improved Palestine's economic condition and thereby increased the labor schedule. Indeed, as the situation in Germany worsened (in 1938 and 1939), Haavara became the only practical means for Jewish emigration on a large scale. For that reason alone, the Zionists sought to continue the agreement, and similar agreements negotiated with eastern European countries, until the outbreak of World War II in September 1939.

ALIYA BET

As with both Youth Aliya and Haavara, the history of what the British called "illegal" immigration, but which is better known in Zionist historiography as aliya bet or ha'apala, has been reviewed a number of times.[164] Again, this section will provide only a few notes on the subject in order to place the history of ha'apala into context. First, it is necessary to clarify the terminology used. For the British, "illegal immigration" meant the unlawful entry into, or residence in, Palestine of a person not born there and lacking an immigrant certificate. Zionists, on the other hand, did not see such immigration as "illegal," and used a number of different terms for such immigration, including ha'apala (literally, struggling), aliya bet (as opposed to aliya alef, or legal aliya), and independent aliya.

Second, ha'apala must be placed into a political context. With respect to the Yishuv, aliya bet contained three elements: a protest against limits on Jewish immigration, a conscious effort to escape Europe, and — especially for Betar members — a protest against the Jewish establishment in connection with legitimizing an activist struggle against the British. As such, aliya bet was the method of choice of those too poor to afford even an A-IV (person with a guaranteed salary of £P4.000 per month) certificate and lacking the skills to qualify for a C (Labor) certificate.[165] Parenthetically, the question of Jewish illegal immigration to western European countries between 1933 and 1939 must also be considered, but has not elicited much research to date.[166]

There had always been an amount of ha'apala connected with the growth of the Yishuv. Despite Ottoman attempts to obstruct Zionist infiltration into Palestine, Jews were still able to immigrate, mostly "illegally." This process continued throughout the period of the British Mandate. Dalia Ofer, in her well-crafted study on aliya bet during the war years (1939-1945), has estimated that almost one-fourth of the Yishuv's immigrants between 1914 and 1945 were "illegals."[167] However, ha'apala really became important only after 1930, when the British doubled the minimum financial requirements for Capitalist certificates (increasing the requirement for the A-I certificate from £P500 to £P1,000, and so on).[168] Coupled with the growing Jewish desperation caused by the increasing hardship in eastern Europe, aliya bet came to reflect the frustrations of Jews faced with the immigration system created by the British Immigration Ordinance of 1930.

Aliya bet was both spontaneous and organized. The former refers to tourists who remained in Palestine after the expiration of their visas and to others who undertook the trip to Palestine without first attemting to get a certificate. Between 1933 and 1937, 9,458 tourists entered Palestine, while departures numbered only 2,058. Although not all of those who remained did so illegally, a large proportion did.[169] The British were aware of this and in 1933 be-gan a series of regular anti-tourist sweeps. This, in turn, forced both the JAE and the Va'ad Leumi to try to secure permanent residence for tourists.[170] Additionally, a small number of individuals made the arduous trek to Palestine without a certificate, hoping that intervention on their behalf would eventually gain them a certificate.[171] Fictitious marriages were also used as a means of promoting "illegal" immigration, despite the warnings of numerous rabbis that so-called fictitious marriages were real marriages in Jewish law.[172]

Until 1930, legalization had been a relatively straight-forward matter, but after that year the British became increasingly reluctant to help. In 1936 the JAE argued, to no avail, that a general amnesty ought to be granted, since the deterrent effect of continuing to punish "illegals" already in Palestine would be minimal, especially since ha'apala had tapered off at the time.[173]

Organized aliya bet began in earnest after 1934, partly in response to the Nazi threat and partly in response to the frustrations of Polish halutzim, who were made to wait for years after completing a hachshara before they could obtain a certificate. The first such undertaking, under the sponsorship of the Polish he-Halutz, was the *S.S. Velos*, which sailed from Greece in July 1934 carrying 350 ma'apilim.[174]

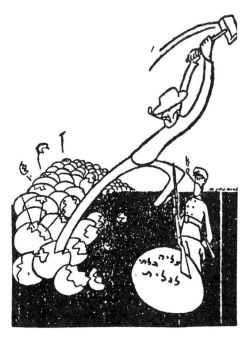

Anti-Ha'apala Cartoon from *Davar*
Courtesy of the New York Public Library

The *Velos* operation was undertaken unilaterally, and he-Halutz's decision to embark on a program of ha'apala was made without the prior consent of either the WZO or the JAE. For that reason, he-Halutz was not supported by any of the Yishuv's major organizations or parties. In the early 1930s, only Ha-Zohar and Mapai's Siya Bet unequivocally supported ha'apala.[175]   Of the Yishuv's recognized leaders, only Berl Katznelson supported aliya bet, and he was a notable exception.[176]   *Davar*, the newspaper he edited, published an editorial cartoon showing its opinion of ha'apala: "illegal" immigration destroyed the "eggs" before they even hatched.[177]

Opponents took issue with aliya bet for a number of reasons. Nahum Sokolow, for example, felt that it brought an "unwanted element" into the Yishuv. Among Mapai leaders, Sprinzak feared that it would bring economic and political disaster, while Ben-Gurion opposed aliya bet because it was not cost-effective.[178]

Ben-Gurion's position appeared to be vindicated in September 1934, when the *Velos II* was intercepted by the British and its passengers deported.[179] Further impetus for abandoning ha'apala was felt when the British enacted two new policies regarding "illegal" Jewish immigration in 1935. First, the

British began to deduct certificates from the Labor schedule equal to the estimated number of "illegals." Second, they nullified the JA's right to use certificates for persons already living in the Yishuv, a means used previously to aid individual ma'apilim to become legal.[180] Although the JA Political Department made a valiant effort to sway the High Commissioner on this matter, the effort was a failure.[181] In the aftermath of the *Velos II* incident, therefore, he-Halutz halted its ha'apala activities.

Simultaneously, but independently, Ha-Zohar began its own campaign of independent immigration, prompted by two factors. The first was the vast disparity in the proportion of certificates granted by the British, and the second was the immigration policy pursued by the JAE, which denied certificates to Betar members. As a recognized pioneering movement, Betar should have been entitled to a proportional number of certificates from the labor schedule. As punishment for breaches of WZO discipline, however, a Zionist court held during the Eighteenth Zionist Congress revoked Betar's immigration privileges. In response, Betar began its independent immigration program. Its first ship was the *S.S. Union*, which left Greece for Palestine in August 1934 with 117 ma'apilim.[182]

For the next two years, aliya bet languished. With legal immigration reaching its pinnacle in 1935 and 1936, there seemed little reason for the existence of ha'apala, although that situation would change again in 1937.

It should be clear that at this stage aliya bet played no role in the Yishuv's policy of rescue aliya. Indeed, the leaders most closely associated with the rescue aliya policy all opposed "illegal" immigration at this time. Even advocates of ha'apala, such as Berl Katznelson, were cognizant of the immense logistical and financial strain that aliya bet placed on the Yishuv for what amounted to only small gains in numbers of olim. Therefore, only the Revisionists pursued their program of independent immigration throughout the 1930s. As a consequence of the Arab revolt and subsequent changes in British attitude, however, the JAE would eventually adopt the policy of aliya bet that it had initially eschewed.

5
Aliya and Intra-Zionist Politics

IMMIGRATION AND ABSORPTION

The relative unity manifested by the Yishuv's political parties and institutions regarding rescue aliya should not be construed as indicating agreement on anything but the broadest national consensus. Such unity as existed was rather shallow, with numerous divergent opinions among and within parties. These disagreements, however, were almost all tactical — with the clear exceptions of the Haavara and boycott — and related primarily to questions regarding how best to implement agreed-upon policies. Thus, for example, the JAE adopted a resolution of protest concerning the slow and inefficient way in which the London Executive undertook its political tasks.[1]

Yet there were more serious divergences within the Yishuv, on both an ideological and an institutional level. This chapter will chart two of these major chasms that between the German olim and the rest of the Yishuv, and that between Mapai and Ha-Zohar/Ha-Zach. This examination will permit an evaluation of the impact of disunity on the program of rescue aliya, and will add meaning to both the Zionist and the human issues involved in the immigration of German Jews.

Immigration has always been seen as one of the central elements of Zionist thought. Although the Yishuv's leaders looked forward to tapping the potential of the new wave of aliya, absorption posed a problem in the economic and the socio-cultural position of the new immigrants. Although they seemed intimately related to one another, the two issues were actually independent, and despite difficulties, the economic problem was solved relatively quickly.

In essence, the economic problem posed by the German aliya was finding suitable employment for the new immigrants — the same as the problem of

TABLE 5.1: German-Jewish Occupational Distribution.

Occupational Sector	Percentage
Domestics	1
Agriculture and forestry	2
Civil service and privately employed	13[2]
Industry and artisans	23
Sales and laborers	61

Source: E. Beling, *Die gesellschafliche Eingliederung der deutschen Einwanderer in Israel*, Frankfurt A/M: P. Lang, 1967, pp. 15-16.

any mass migration. Two groups of olim found gainful employment with relative ease: halutzim, who were rapidly integrated into the structure of the kibbutz or moshav movements, and capitalists, whose income was sufficient for them to begin new undertakings.[3] As of December 1935, sixteen ha-Kibbutz ha-Meuhad kibbutzim had absorbed 1,400 halutzim of German origin, representing approximately 12 percent of the total German aliya at the time.[4]

In 1936, ha-Kibbutz ha-Meuhad placed another 1,248 halutzim in kibbutzim, representing roughly 18 percent of the olim from Germany.[5] Most of the German olim, however, were neither halutzim nor capitalists. Between 1933 and 1936, for example, 1,491 professionals — 895 doctors, dentists, and nurses; 281 lawyers; and 315 teachers and academicians — made aliya.[6] These 1,491 persons represented approximately 6.5 percent of German olim in those three years. In addition to academicians and professionals such as lawyers, many of the new olim were small businessmen. The occupational distribution of the German olim is summarized in Table 5.1. The three last categories of olim, by and large, lacked either the capital or the skills to be immediately absorbed into Palestine's largely agricultural economy. The absorption of doctors into the Yishuv, even though they had needed skills, was also difficult. Moreover, only a limited number of openings were available, since once a position was filled it was highly unlikely that it would be re-opened. For example, in 1933 the various Hadassah medical divisions in Palestine employed eleven German doctors on a full-time basis and thirty more on a part-time or voluntary basis.[7]

As a partial solution to the problem, the Histadrut proposed that four havurot (groups) be established to offer on-the-job training in agriculture or construction work to olim in need of vocational retraining. These havurot would initially operate in Petah Tikva, Nes Ziona, Rehovot, and Haifa, with an initial budget of £P5,000 each. Further expansion, if needed, was also contemplated, assuming that proper financing would be available.[8]

Vocational training programs were also established by HOG and by the JA German Department. They met with relative success in helping place olim who required help integrating into the Yishuv's economy.[9] Given the age distribution of the olim (90 percent were under 21 years old in 1933), vocational training was plausible and represented a cost-effective way of absorbing new immigrants.[10] By 1936 vocational retraining was still plausible, since the age range, although clearly changing, still reflected the fact that nearly three-quarters of all immigrants were younger than 40.[11]

Still, economic absorption was not quite so simple, and some problems did surface. In June 1934, for example, a number of German olim complained that the Histadrut labor exchange had purposely refused to assist them in finding employment in the construction industry. Their complaint of discrimination succeeded in opening the industry, but only after the intervention of HOG and of Heshel Frumkin.[12] Conversely, one month later, the Histadrut reported ten instances in which German olim had received certificates in return for promises to work in moshavot but had later reneged.[13] Records of similar problems abound; in time all (or almost all) were resolved.

In the case of the Yishuv, there appeared to be two primary causes for such differences. The Yishuv was not fully prepared for the influx of German Jews. Proper organization took time, and the stopgap measures introduced in the interim were not always effective. Second, the German olim themselves differed as compared to previous olim. Many German Jews emigrated only reluctantly, and for them Palestine was usually not a destination of first choice. A proportion of these olim had not previously been associated with the Zionist movement, and almost all had been accustomed to a higher standard of living than was possible in Palestine during the 1930s. A majority of the German olim came from urban areas and sought to remain in cities, despite the fact that, with its agricultural economy, Palestine was not heavily urbanized. Yet German olim settled in urban centers whenever possible, with the three cities of Tel Aviv, Haifa, and Jerusalem counting for more than half of all German olim.[14] The differences between the German olim and the environment that they entered should have resulted in a more careful approach to absorption. This was not always possible, however, since there was a dearth of individuals qualified for such work.[15] Thus, for example, in an effort to employ the most qualified medical personnel, the Histadrut hired a large number of German doctors who were well-known anti-Zionists before their own aliya. The German Zionists felt that protesting this policy was necessary, and suggested that henceforth national institutions should enquire from HOG about the ideological background of German immigrants.[16]

Thereafter, complaints about the officials overseeing absorption of German olim continued, with HOG and the Histadrut seeking to find a mutually acceptable solution.[17] So, too, did complaints about the German olim, although the most glaring problems were experienced in the cultural and ideological spheres. The majority of the Yishuv's population was religiously inobservant but had developed a Zionist Jewish culture that emphasized the Hebrew language and used elements of the Jewish past to form what may be termed a civil religion. The Jewish holidays were observed not primarily for their religious content, but for their historical value. This secularized Jewish culture was familiar to East European Jews but was foreign to most German Jewish adults, who had grown up in a milieu that emphasized assimilation.[18] Even the German Zionist leaders in Palestine noted crucial cultural differences, and continually referred to the need to "Zionize" the new olim.[19] For immigrants from Germany, cultural absorption in the Yishuv proved to be problematic. The question of the Hebrew language provides a good example of the cultural problems relating to absorption. As early as October 1933, members of the Yishuv united to fight the perceived intrusion of German culture into the Jewish national home.[20] Since this linguistic struggle had roots going back to the Second Aliya, it had become deeply entrenched and was not easily resolved. At a May 1935 meeting of Histadrut employees who worked with German olim, much emphasis was placed on the need to expand Hebrew education among German immigrants, despite considerable strides made in this sphere during the two previous years.[21] Further progress in language education took place over the next four years, but the problem did not entirely disappear.

As an example, we may cite the case of the *Jüdische Welt-Rundschau* (JWR). In March 1939 a number of German Zionists in Palestine, including Robert Weltsch, the former president of the Zionistische Vereinigung für Deutschland, proposed the publication of a Palestinian version of the ZVfD's newspaper, *Jüdische Rundschau* (which had been shut down by the Gestapo). The resulting outcry has come to be known as the "newspaper war": Palestine's other Jewish newspapers, including *ha-Aretz*, *Davar*, the *Palestine Post*, and the *Palestine Ilustrated News*, attempted to forestall the publication of JWR.[22] On March 24, 1939, these newspapers released an appeal for an advertising boycott against JWR, which in the meantime began to publish despite the protests. The protesters used the "lingual segregation of the Yishuv" as their justification for the boycott, drawing a number of intellectuals, including the poet Shaul Tchernikovsky, within their lines.[23] Opponents claimed that there was no need for a German-language newspaper in the Yishuv, since it would reinforce the tendency among German olim to stand aloof from the rest of the Yishuv. The first issue of JWR, published on March 10, included an editorial explaining the need for a window on the German Jewish world. News reports and notices reviewed the state of German Jewry and of German Jewish refugees throughout the world.[24]

Continued opposition by the Yishuv's Hebrew and (ironically) English press to the intrusion of a foreign-language newspaper forced the JWR's editors to modify their public approach. They claimed that JWR was edited in Tel Aviv but printed in Paris, on behalf of German Jewish refugees in the diaspora. Between March 1939 and May 1940, JWR appeared weekly, but continued pressure applied by its opponents on advertisers forced it to cease publication thereafter. In 1978, summarizing the "newspaper war," Weltsch claimed that the incident "sheds a light on the schizophrenic attitude of the Yishuv towards the new immigrants."[25]

Other complaints about the apathy of German Jews with regard to the goals of the Yishuv in general, and of the Histadrut and Mapai in particular, continued throughout the 1930s. In a diary entry for May 3, 1935, for example, David Ben-Gurion noted that from the JAE's perspective all German olim ought to land in Haifa. His reasoning was that the absorption offices in Haifa seemed better equipped to work with the Germans, as compared to offices in Tel Aviv and Jerusalem.[26]

Hans Rubin, a senior Histadrut official in Tel Aviv, complained: "Whoever looks at the life of German olim in Tel Aviv with open eyes will see — *a German ghetto . . . non-participation in organizational life; a non-Zionist orientation among a large proportion of the olim*; apathy." According to Rubin, the failure to involve the German Jews in the Yishuv's affairs derived from two causes. First, Mo'ezet Poale Tel Aviv (the local workers' council) had not taken the matter seriously and thus did not act effectively. Second, "the German oleh does not have a good attitude with the workers' council in Tel Aviv. He regards it, for different reasons, either with apathy or with bitter criticism."[27] Rubin had previously reported similar, attitudes in other cities and settlements.[28] Extensive Histadrut activities in this sphere, including night classes and seminars, improved matters to some extent, although complaints about German olim continued.[29]

From this perspective, absorption of German Jews appears to have been a major problem. The issue of how successful absorption really was, however, must be looked at from a broader perspective. The only cases documented seem to be the unusual or the controversial. When matters proceeded without problems, few records were left, since there was no need for meetings or negotiations. As a result, analysis of the documents must proceed in two directions: examination of what the documents say, as well as what they do not say. For example, the above-mentioned case of August 1934, when ten olim agreed to settle in moshavot and then reneged on their promise, may correctly be seen as a crisis of absorption. It may, and perhaps must, also be seen as a case of ten exceptions out of the thousands of immigrants who entered Palestine that year. Likewise, in a conversation with the High Commissioner, Moshe Shertok extolled the absorption of German Jews, reporting on the different industries into which they were being absorbed and concluding that it was an unequivocal success.[30] While it is unlikely that he would have concentrated on failures of absorption, since they would very likely have led to reductions in the Labor schedule, it is also clear that failure could not have been hidden from the High Commissioner for long. Shertok used a similar line of analysis in February 1934, when he requested an advance on the schedule, justified by the successful absorption of immigrants from the last schedule and by the need to ease a shortfall of workers in the Yishuv.[31]

It therefore seems likely that, despite numerous problems regarding absorption in the short term, the process was successful in the long term. Indirect support for this supposition may be gained from two other sources. First, in August 1934 a group of Polish olim announced the creation of Irgun Olei Polonia, an organization intended to parallel HOG. As part of their justification, the organizers pointed to HOG's successes in the sphere of aliya and absorption.[32] Second, we can use yerida figures to gauge the success of the absorption process: if absorption was successful, historians would anticipate lower figures for yerida, while the reverse would also hold true. The documents on yerida are very clear, even if they are not complete. There was a small percentage of yerida throughout the 1930s, including slightly fewer than 300 German Jews who sought to return to Germany.[33] In 1933 and 1934 some were actually permitted to return, although this came to a halt in 1935. At no time did yerida become sufficient to impact on the Yishuv's rate of growth. Again, we may conclude that, short-term problems notwithstanding, in the long term absorption was, in fact, successful.[34]

FROM HITACHDUT OLEI GERMANIA TO AHDUT HA-AM

Under these circumstances, we can understand why the German aliya became politicized so rapidly. It is important to note that many German olim chose not to identify with any of the established Zionist parties. Instead, they transformed the already existing Hitachdut Olei Germania (or, rather, parts of it) into a new ethnic party, initially called Ahdut ha-Am (Unity of the Nation). Ahdut ha-Am was the culmination of a process that began in 1935. HOG itself was founded in 1932, by veteran olim from Germany who saw a need for self-help work among an element within the Yishuv that was largely overlooked by other organizations. Between 1933 and 1935, HOG developed into a fully ramified social welfare agency, operating as the major contact point for the new mass aliya through a central office in Tel Aviv and through various subcommittees.[35] By 1936, it was organized into four main offices and thirty-four local committees. It kept in touch with its far-flung membership through a bulletin, *Die Mitteilungsblatt*. It has been estimated that by 1936, one-third of all German olim (including "tourists" and "illegal" immigrants) belonged to HOG.[36] Two of HOG's activities stood out: the work of the aliya Committee in promoting German immigration and lobbying for certificates, and the work of the Social Welfare Committee, whose close cooperation with the Joint Committee and the JAE has been discussed above.

A new phase in the history of HOG began in the summer of 1935. HOG presented a memorandum to the Nineteenth Zionist Congress whose main points dealt with organizational issues relating to work for increased aliya. While the Congress accepted almost all of HOG's substantive proposals, some delegates felt that the memorandum's tone was too partisan and reflected a growing politicization within HOG. This perception was reinforced when HOG decided to run its own candidate in the Tel Aviv municipal elections, justifying this political act by explaining that the only way for German Jews to be heard was to have a German Zionist in an influential public position.[37]

These trends came together at the HOG annual convention, held in Tel Aviv on March 3, 1936. Chaim Weizmann delivered the opening address, concentrating on the importance of the program of aid for German Jewry.[38] He was followed by a veritable galaxy of German Zionist leaders, who offered their opinion on the main question before the plenum: approval of a new constitution that would have turned HOG into a political body. A clear majority of the speakers enthusiastically supported the new constitution, without detailing its implications, however. One exception was Richard Lichtheim, who expressed doubts about the wisdom of politicizing the organization. From inception, Lichtheim argued, HOG had been a *Landsmannschaft*, able to bring together all German Jews living in Palestine — Zionist and non-Zionist. Converting HOG into a political body, given the way the Yishuv's organization, guaranteed a split between the Zionist and non-Zionist German Jews that would, paradoxically, weaken the very organization that was designed to increase their influence.[39]

Despite Lichtheim's opposition, the new constitution was passed by a large majority. Two years later, the German Zionist party Ahdut ha-Am appeared, eventually submitting a list of delegates for the Twenty-first World Zionist Congress, held in Geneva from August 16 to 26, 1939. The party thus established was primarily middle-class in membership, but liberal in outlook. It sought cooperation with centrist elements in the Histadrut and with the General Zionist Alliance.[40]

Ahdut ha-Am adopted a clear position on internal issues, but the party's attitudes toward aliya, relations with the British, and relations with the Arabs are of interest. While it might have been expected that a party whose constituency was based almost exclusively on immigrants from Germany would have concentrated on aliya as its main issue, in fact it did not. Ahdut ha-Am rarely criticized the JAE or the WZO for their aliya policy, and implicitly accepted the concept of halutzic aliya. It militated for the continuation of the Mandate even in 1936 and 1937, when the British had proposed partition.[41] During the debate over the Peel plan, Ahdut ha-Am expressed strong opposition to partition and to Jewish sovereignty. Its most strident criticisms of JAE policy all related to the Arabs, with the German Zionists calling for parity and for Jewish-Arab cooperation.[42] On Jewish-Arab issues, Ahdut ha-Am stood considerably to the left of the JAE and of the majority of Mapai, and it may be seen as continuing the orientation espoused by Brit Shalom and other advocates of a binational Palestine.[43]

Early in its existence, Ahdut ha-Am sought to reach an agreement with Judah L. Magnes, the president of Hebrew University and one of the most prominent members of Brit Shalom, regarding a concerted effort to reach a rapprochement with the Arabs.[44] Curiously, this attitude was exactly contrary to developments in the Yishuv as a whole. According to Susan Hatis's study on Brit Shalom, the rise of the Nazis infused the Yishuv with "a sense of urgency" regarding immigration. This made rapprochement between Jews and Arabs on the basis of limited aliya, as Brit Shalom advocated, unacceptable to the majority of the Yishuv.[45] The German Zionists retained their advocacy of binationalism throughout the 1930's, with some of the most vociferous exponents lamenting the failure of this solution as late as thirty years after the establishment of the State of Israel.[46]

Only in 1939 did Ahdut ha-Am substantially modify its position. As a result of the White Paper, it entered into a coalition with General Zionist supporters of Chaim Weizmann and strongly criticized British policy. Thereafter, the party advocated an open-door policy for aliya, but still did not support Jewish sovereignty and sought a rapprochement with the Arabs.[47]

HITACHDUT OLEI GERMANIA EXPANDS

Simultaneous with its first, tentative (and ultimately, unsuccessful) steps toward becomng a political party, HOG continued and expanded its social welfare and immigrant aid activities. As conditions in Europe worsened in 1938 and 1939 these activities became even more important. In the meantime, HOG grew to twenty branches with 5,000 members in 1938 and to 6,000 members in twenty-six branches on the eve of World War II.[48]

In March 1938 Austrian immigrants organized their own *landsmannschaft*, called Hitachdut Olei Austria (HOA); their principle activity being an ultimately fruitless effort to obtain both money and certificates for a mass rescue scheme in post-Anschluss Austria.[49] In June HOA, which claimed to have 1,215 members, requested funding from the JAE in order to open a social welfare office in Tel Aviv.[50] The JA, however, rejected this request since it needlessly duplicated the German Department's work.[51] The JA's rejection, however, seems not to have detered the Austrian Jewish activists, for they opened an office in Tel Aviv anyway.[52]

Quite rapidly, the HOA office faced financial difficulty; after careful consideration of all its options HOA began negotiations for a merger with HOG. A tentative agreement was worked out rapidly since both groups found common ground on most substantive issues.[53] However, this agreement broke down almost immediately since, despite a common interest in aliya, HOG and HOA were far apart in their institutional and political attitudes.[54] Both parties ultimately complained to the JAE, each claiming that the other was using defamatory tactics and, more importantly, was preventing action on behalf of aliya.[55]

While the argument between HOG and HOA may appear mundane at first glance the disagreement was animated by two serious (although hardly crucial) considerations. First, some of the Germans appeared to look upon their Austrian counterparts as "newcomers" and "upstarts" a level of disdain that was equalled by the Austrians in their attitude toward "Yekkes." Thus, to an extent, the dispute may be seen as another manifestation of already existing intra-communal strife that derived, in no small measure from German Jewish attitudes of moral, social, and cultural superiority over "Ostjuden."[56] Important differences in organizational orientation exacerbated this tension and briefly threatened the agreement.

HOG's leaders derived their status from the reality of a special relationship between the organization and the JA German Department. In effect, HOG acted as a conduit between the JA and the German olim. HOG thus enjoyed a status unique among ethnic parties and as a result, HOG leaders tended to construe the agency's purpose very narrowly. However, HOG's leaders feared losing this special status if their organization was "watered down" and became "merely" another *landsmannschaft*. For their part, the Austrian olim had no status to lose and sought to widen HOG into a immigrant aid agency for all European olim. These differing institutional attitudes were never fully bridged some of the Austrian activists (notably David Zvi Pinkus, one of the early founders of HOA) continued independent activity. Albeit, financial realities forced the unification process to continue and led to the final merger in mid-August 1938.[57] Hitachdut Olei Germania now became Hitachdut Olei Germania ve-Olei Austria (HOGOA). Indeed, despite centrifugal forces, the impulse toward unity was so strong HOGOA soon expanded to include Jews from Czechoslovakia and Danzig. In turn, these additions were reflected in a new name, Irgun Olei Mercaz Europa (IOME).[58]

INTRA-ZIONIST RIVALRIES, 1933-1934

In the early 1930's, relations between the Zionist groups turned violent. Part of this struggle, between Betar and the Histadrut, has already been reviewed. In the summer of 1933, however, interparty strife increased markedly. On June 16, Chaim Arlosoroff was murdered while walking with his wife on Tel Aviv's beach. Perhaps the most controversial crime in Israel's history, the Arlosoroff affair has been investigated repeatedly, but without clear results. Indeed, in 1985 an Israeli Government Commission of Inquiry concluded that although the suspects arrested in 1933 were innocent, Mapai's suspicions regarding possible Revisionist involvement were not unfounded. Despite an intensive investigation into the confessions of two Arabs, Abdul Majid and Issa el Abrass, the committee concluded that it could not determine the identity of the murderers.[59]

At the time of Arlosorpff's murder, the Yishuv was divided into two camps. After a brief inquest, the British Palestine Police, aided by members of the Hagana, arrested three Betar leaders — Abba Ahimeir, Zvi Rosenblatt, and Abraham Stavsky. All were soon tried for the crime. The prosecution claimed that their motives were political and that they were members of a shadowy terrorist group called Brit ha-Biryonim. As evidence, the prosecution pointed to a number of Ahimeir's articles in *Doar ha-Yom*, which Mapai had interpreted as death threats against Arlosoroff.[60] The defense, on the other hand, claimed that the motive for the murder was robbery, and that the accusations against the three were politically motivated and false.

Mapai's leaders were unalterably convinced that the three were guilty, though David Ben-Gurion initially suspected that Communists were responsible.[61] Zeev Jabotinsky and some influential non-Revisionists, including Chief Rabbi Abraham Isaac Kook, were equally adamant in believing in their innocence. Kook went so far as to sponsor a fund for Stavsky's defense. In this he was supported by the editors of *ha-Aretz*, who believed Stavsky to be guilty but felt that justice would best be served if he had the best defense.[62]

In the immediate aftermath of the arrests, numerous voices in the Yishuv, including members of the conservative General Zionist Alliance (the B faction), called for the outlaw of all Revisionist organizations, and especially Betar. Mapai's leaders launched a campaign in support of such an action, drowning out almost all calls for moderation. In October 1933, the Tel Aviv Kupat Holim (the Sick Fund; Histadrut-operated health clinics) dismissed a Revisionist named Pa'amoni. The fact that he was not involved with the murder, or with other anti-Mapai activities, mattered little: he was seen as guilty by association.[63] Mapai's wildly exaggerated fears about a Revisionist putsch — which they compared to the tactics used by Hitler and Mussolini — fueled a Ha-Zohar counterattack. Besides accusing the labor leaders of a "blood libel," Jabotinsky accused one of the few Mapai voices counseling moderation, Berl Katznelson, of being an informer.[64] This in turn touched off another war of words followed by violence.

At the Eighteenth World Zionist Congress, just three months after the murder, Jabotinsky and his wife were accosted by a group of young Labor Zionists. Although threatened, Jabotinsky was able to enter the Congress hall peacefully.[65] After such an inauspicious beginning, Ha-Zohar fared badly in the Congress. All of Jabotinsky's resolutions were rejected, while a Mapai resolution not to allow members of Ha-Zohar onto the WZO Presidium passed the plenum by a vote of 151 to 149.[66]

In the Yishuv, an almost daily cycle of low-intensity violence continued, with casualties on both sides.[67] Public argument continued well after the trial ended, especially after a court of appeals overturned Stavsky's conviction on a technicality.[68] The vindication of the young Ha-Zohar leaders in 1934, however, was a Pyrrhic victory. Despite Jabotinsky's protestations to the contrary (expressed, for example, in a letter to Elias Ginsburg of Brooklyn), Ha-Zohar was effectively isolated within the WZO. Jabotinsky could promise to unleash "the long pent-up energy of our Revisionist masses in Eastern Europe and Palestine," but in reality he could not even guarantee immigrant certificates for qualified Betar members.[69]

A WZO court, held during the Eighteenth World Zionist Congress, found Betar (and Ha-Zohar) guilty of what the Executive declared to be repeated breaches of Zionist discipline, primarily in relation to the national funds (KKL and KHY), and punished the party by withdrawing its right to certificates. In response, Betar Circular #60 announced a new party policy: henceforth efforts would be made to obtain certificates directly from the High Commissioner's reserve, instead of from the JAE.[70]

When the JAE received a purloined copy of Circular #60, the majority of its members viewed the newly enunciated policy as a direct threat to their authority, and demanded its immediate repudiation. The JAE noted that the new Betar policy played right into the hands of the British, who at that very moment sought to justify changing the immigration statutes.[71] Betar refused, defending the circular by noting that the JAE's monopoly over certificates was unfair: it was being used to weaken non-Socialist Zionist parties by granting certificates only to those who had graduated from a hachshara. Betar also stated that the makeup of the JAE — primarily the membership of non-Zionists — was unacceptable and that it freed Betar from the responsibility of submitting to JA authority. Moreover, the Betar leadership argued, the Immigration Ordinance of 1931 guaranteed the right to request certificates from the High Commissioner.[72]

The JAE rejected Betar's defense of Circular #60 as either irrelevant or unacceptable, and maintained that the premises on which the Betar circular based itself constituted a breach of Zionist discipline.[73] Since Betar was a duly recognized member of the WZO — a fact that granted certain rights but also brought with it specific responsibilities — Betar could not claim these rights while refusing to accept its responsibilities. Moreover, the makeup of the JAE had been accepted by a majority of the delegates at the World Zionist Congresses in 1929, 1931, and 1933. Therefore, Betar's unwillingness to accept JAE authority undermined the position of the JA and harmed the Zionist cause.

Before any further action could be taken, Ha-Zohar began a campaign to petition the League of Nations for reforms to the British Mandatory administration. The petition argued for the creation of a "colonization regime," that is, for the reorganization of the British Palestine administration into one that encouraged, rather than discouraged, Jewish immigration.[74]

Two points raised by the petition are of interest. First, this petition is one of only a few Ha-Zohar documents to deal explicitly with the plight of German Jewry, placing the Nazi persecution in the context of European Jewry's overall insecurity. Although similar to the evaluation made by the JA and WZO, the Ha-Zohar petition viewed conditions in Germany with a greater sense of urgency than did other contemporary proposals. Despite the fact that the German Jewish condition appeared less fraught with danger in 1934, Ha-Zohar's petition correctly anticipated developments that took place in 1935, and foretold a deterioration of German Jewry's plight.[75]

The second point is the petition's analysis of Palestine's economic absorptive capacity. For tactical reasons, the petition's authors did not deny the validity of economic absorptive capacity as a criterion for immigration. Realizing that any proposal for a completely open-door policy would be rejected out of hand, the petition instead claimed that the administration was improperly and unfairly assessing Palestine's capacity to absorb new olim.[76]

Although moderate in tone, the petition was condemned by the JAE as yet another breach in Zionist discipline and as a counter-productive undertaking that would undermine British support for Zionist aspirations in Palestine.[77] New reports that Betar members in Poland and Rumania had disrupted KKL and KHY fund-raising meetings brought further criticism, including a proposal by Ben-Gurion to convoke another WZO court. Only the fact that Jabotinsky had condemned such attacks in writing convinced the Executive to hold off on any action.[78] Nevertheless, the JAE did support a wide-ranging anti-Revisionist propaganda campaign to be undertaken in Germany and eastern Europe, in effect becoming a mouthpiece for Mapai.[79]

Although some Betar members were guilty of instigating violent clashes, neither Betar nor Ha-Zohar was the only guilty party in this case. Each side justified physical attacks as part of a legitimate war against the alleged enemies of Zionism. During a stormy meeting with South African Zionists Ben-Gurion, Eliezer Kaplan, and Yitzhak Gruenbaum analyzed two major issues separating Mapai and Ha-Zohar: labor relations and Zionist discipline. Ben-Gurion and Kaplan saw Betar's efforts in the sphere of labor as an attempt to destroy the Histadrut and thereby crush the movement for Avoda Ivrit (Hebrew Labor), which was one of the basic premises of Socialist Zionism. According to this line of analysis, Betar, and by extension Ha-Zohar, reflected the position of certain Jewish bourgeois circles in Palestine who, although Zionist in orientation, placed their own economic interests ahead of national interests.[80] To be sure, Jabotinsky and Ha-Zohar saw matters in a different light. In their view, they were attempting to break up a mono-polistic organization that encompassed both a labor union and an industrial employer. Jabotinsky vociferously denied that he opposed either Avoda Ivrit or the right of workers to unionize. He did, however, oppose what he saw as Histadrut's efforts to establish its hegemony over the Yishuv.[81]

The South African Zionists attempted to persuade Ben-Gurion and Kaplan to issue a public manifesto calling for an end to internecine strife, but they failed to offer convincing evidence that a manifesto would improve the situation in any way. Thus, although Ben-Gurion stated his agreement with the principle of intra-Zionist peace, he adopted a position of uncompromising enmity toward Jabotinsky and Ha-Zohar. "I tell you," Ben-Gurion stated bluntly, "that Jabotinsky will not accept any agreement except one — *the state of Hitler in Germany for Zionism.*"[82] He added: "There are some people who are bitterly complaining why cannot labour leaders be hanged in Palestine as they are doing in Vienna."[83] With these words, Ben-Gurion fell into the common trap of identifying Jabotinsky with Nazism. Nothing could have been further from the truth: despite his emphasis on the trappings of military-style discipline and uniforms for Betar members, Jabotinsky was committed to a liberal and democratic vision that represented the antithesis of Fascism. Ben-Gurion's words also reflect the depth of hatred between the two competing blocs, and the willingness of Mapai's leaders to use terminology repudiating the legitimacy of their opponents.

THE BEN-GURION-JABOTINSKY AGREEMENTS

The issue of Zionist discipline was taken up again at length during a meeting held by Ben-Gurion and Kaplan for the JAE and a number of Va'ad ha-Poel representatives in Jerusalem on August 6, 1934. A cease-fire between the Histadrut and Betar and negotiations for ending the internecine strife were proposed. Although not optimistic about the outcome of such talks, Ben-Gurion accepted their necessity on the condition that any action taken must have the authority of the JAE.[84] Pinhas Rutenberg made the initial contacts.[85] Along with David Remez, a senior Histadrut leader, Rutenberg enterred negotiations with Dr. Abraham Weinshal, a representative of Betar. Although cordial, the talks led nowhere, since neither Remez nor Weinshal held sufficient seniority to make any agreement last.[86] As a direct result of this failure, the JAE gave Ben-Gurion the authority to continue contacts.

Again initial contacts were made by Rutenberg, after which the negotiations between Ben-Gurion and Jabotinsky began. Initially kept a secret, the talks took place in London in October and November of 1934.[87] Ben-Gurion kept the JAE well informed of his progress, with reports covering every phase of the talks.[88] All outstanding issues were aired, although Ben-Gurion made it clear that the issue of WZO discipline was not negotiable.[89] Such a posture might have scuttled the talks, but both leaders sought to emphasize the areas they could agree on, rather than bog down in needless haggling.

On November 11, 1934, three agreements were concluded. The first governed Ha-Zohar's relations with the WZO and JAE. The agreement also stipulated that when Betar's Circular #60 and its boycott of the KHY and KKL were rescinded, the status quo ante regarding Betar's right to receive immigrant certificates would be restored. The agreement did not declare either party guilty of any misdeeds, but established the grounds for peaceful coexistence. The second agreement related to internecine violence, calling on both sides to work together for the goals of Zionism. Importantly, this agreement was worded in such a way that neither Mapai nor Ha-Zohar was blamed for the clashes. The third agreement dealt with relations between the Histadrut and the Revisionists: Ben-Gurion made important concessions with regard to Jabotinsky's proposal seeking arbitration, in return for concessions on strikebreaking and a hoped-for lessening of internecine violence.[90]

The JAE narrowly approved the agreements: Ben-Gurion, Sokolow, and Shertok voted in favor of them, while Gruenbaum and Arthur Ruppin voted against. Because he represented non-Zionists, Dr. Werner D. Senator abstained, since the agreements dealt exclusively with Zionist matters.[91] Gruenbaum's opposition to the proposed agreements rested on two factors. He felt that the effort to reach a compromise with Jabotinsky was misplaced, since the Revisionists either accepted WZO discipline or they did not. In the first case a compromise was unnecessary; in the second it was untenable. Regarding the labor issue, Gruenbaum argued that the JAE should not decide anything until the Histadrut had voted on the agreement. Logic was on Gruenbaum's side in this case, but the majority of the JAE felt that an agreement to end the violent clashes between the two Zionist blocs was of vital importance to the future of the Yishuv. Ruppin, who also voted against the agreements, did so for pragmatic reasons. Ha-Zohar, he felt, should implement its side of the agreement regarding Circular #60 and the Zionist funds before the JAE ratified them. In defending the agreements, Sokolow noted that although they were not perfect, approval was necessary to prevent a further rupture in the Zionist movement.[92] At a meeting held on December 16, 1934, the JAE tentatively decided to follow up and permit certificate grants to Betar members.[93] As matters turned out, the agreement was not ratified, and the issue of certificates became moot.

Primarily because of Jabotinsky's impassioned call for Zionist unity, the Eighth World Conference of Ha-Zohar, meeting in Krakow, Poland, on January 13, 1935, approved the agreements, despite the strong opposition by a majority of the Palestinian Ha-Zohar and other delegations.[94]

Matters regarding cooperation were more complex on the Laborite side. Grave doubts about Jabotinsky's goodwill were expressed in Mapai circles.[95] In an article in *ha-Olam* (the WZO's official newspaper) that was reprinted in *Davar*, Jabotinsky was accused of having delivered an ultimatum on the agreements to the WZO in one of his articles in the Polish-Jewish daily

Der Moment. In his original article, Jabotinsky had announced that Ha-Zohar could not accept the binding nature of Zionist discipline in cases where a simple majority had passed a resolution. Jabotinsky was seen as placing pre-conditions on the agreements and rendering them almost meaningless even before they were ratified, since large majorities were difficult to attain in the World Zionist Congress.[96] Jabotinsky's position was based on his belief that WZO discipline was merely a cover for silencing his independent efforts to advance the diplomatic goals of Zionism. Discipline, in this case, was a cover for doing nothing to upset the British or the Arabs.

Davar's editors argued that members of an organization, who enjoyed the benefits of WZO membership, could legitimately be compelled to desist from undercutting the position of the majority. The minority had no right to impose its will on the majority: questioning the authority of a small majority was no more democratic than questioning a large majority.[97]

Even supporters of the agreements noted their weaknesses. For example, Zalman Rubashov (Shazar) noted, in an interview he granted in New York, that the agreements banned only inter-party violence, not ideological strife or propaganda.[98]

Ben-Gurion's return to Palestine after the agreements were signed, was greeted with an emotional poster campaign opposing the agreements. One Poale Zion Smol poster "welcomed" Ben-Gurion by denouncing his agreements "with the Duce of Biryonism." Once again, Jabotinsky was associated with fascism. In this case, however, opponents of the agreements went one step further: in common with Communists in Europe, they argued that the Social Democrats (in this case Mapai) were really Fascists in disguise. The poster therefore continued to hammer away at *"Ben-Gurion's method of rescue: Cooperation with fascism, [a] coalition with Revisionism the path of destruction for the workers' movement."* Poale Zion Smol had a solution: Palestine's Jewish workers should repudiate Ben-Gurion, the agreements, and Mapai's reformism in order to ensure that "Ben-Gurion's fate does not become the fate of the working class." In the broadest sense the poster, argued that the problem was not agreement with Ha-Zohar, but reformism, which was seen as a form of proto-fascism. "Against the anti-Marxist coalition of Ben-Gurion-Jabotinsky, forge the proletarian Marxist Zionist party!"[99] In view of Poale Zion Smol's ideology, it is not surprising that the party advocated attainment of Socialism ahead of national revival.

The agreements had even more influential opponents, including many in the Mapai Executive. Although the party had given its full-fledged support to Ben-Gurion's trip and supported the negotiations, many members appear to have been unclear as to the negotiation's goals. Some of Mapai's leaders seem to have sincerely thought that an agreement was impossible, but supported the negotiations as a face-saving gesture. To their surprise, an agreement was worked out. The Mapai Executive was thus faced with the choice of approving, and possibly compromising Mapai's ideals by surrendering control over the Histadrut, or disapproving and possibly rending asunder the Zionist movement.[100]

Even before Ben-Gurion returned and briefed the Mapai Executive, the party leadership had split into three camps: agreement supporters, such as Shertok and Remez, who called for ratification of all three agreements; outright opponents, including Yitzhak Tabenkin and Eliahu Golomb; and those, including Berl Katzenelson, who opposed some parts of the agreements but not their entirety.[101] Hoping to lobby for Mapai approval, Ben-Gurion had cabled from London that the agreements were "too good to be true" — even before the final agreement was signed.[102]

On October 31 three possibilities were put to a vote, with a narrow majority supporting a compromise to call a party conference to ratify or veto the agreements. Ironically, as each individual agreement was put to a vote, the agreements on violence and labor relations (seen as an adequate basis for further negotiations) were approved by a wide majority, but the agreement on Zionist discipline was rejected by a vote of 13 to 1.[103] Since that agreement was the crucial one, at least insofar as Zionist unity was concerned, its rejection may be seen as a rejection of the entire concept behind the negotiations.

When Ben-Gurion returned from London, he reported on the agreements to a full session of the Mapai Executive. Given the opposition expressed at the previous meeting, Ben-Gurion approached the issue gravely. "We stand before a question," he said, "that will decide the future of our movement. It cannot be delayed."[104] In the interim, Ben-Gurion gained the support of Katznelson, but he continued to face opposition from the leadership of ha-Kibbutz ha-Meuhad, and especially from Tabenkin.[105] Once again, the totality of the agreements was not accepted, even though majorities supporting each discrete agreement could be found. As a result, no other means to achieve a decision seemed available, short of the Mapai conference approved on October 31.

Meetings on November 24 and December 20, 1934, removed the issue from the party altogether because it was deadlocked, and transferred it to the Histadrut. In effect, this posturing allowed a minority to impose its will on the majority. In turn, the Histadrut Executive elected to place the agreements before a party referendum.[106] On January 31, 1935, the Histadrut Executive established the procedure for the referendum: all voting would be by secret ballot, although only those whose membership in the Histadrut dated before November 1934 would be permitted to vote; even then the format would be all or nothing.[107] When Ben-Gurion proposed that the Executive publish a letter supporting passage, he was defeated by a vote of thirteen to one. Thereafter he ceased all activity in the Histadrut Executive pending the outcome of the referendum.[108]

Both supporters and opponents sought to influence public opinion on the matter. The General Zionists, who had largely remained silent during the negotiations, approved a resolution at their annual convention on November 27-28, 1934, which called for "the creation of a coalition in the Zionist Executive [i.e., JAE] composed of all Zionist factions and parties."[109] Sir Alfred Mond (Lord Melchett), the well-known British newspaper magnate and staunch Zionist, also entered into the fray, providing strong support for the agreement. Mond specifically saw the agreements as an important sign of Zionist and Jewish unity at a crucial juncture.[110]

Ben-Gurion and Katznelson worked tirelessly to convince members of the importance of consensus. The proponents argued that without the agreements, Zionism would be harmed. They feared that the Revisionists would bolt from the WZO and create a competing organization. This would weaken the Yishuv and slow down the pace of growth at a most inopportune time. In the proponents' view, even if the specific details of the agreements left something to be desired, approval was still necessary; details could be worked out later. This approach must be viewed as essentially pragmatic, placing the interests of the Yishuv as a whole before those of any one party or class.[111]

Opponents of the agreements, however, were also active in condemning the peace agreement with what they termed "Revisionist Fascism."[112] Claiming that the agreements did not coincide with working-class interests, these opponents refused any compromise with Ha-Zohar and sought complete victory over Revisionism. According to the most radical opponents of the agreements, even a coalition with the General Zionists was an unacceptable compromise of working-class interests.[113] Destroying Zionist unity — such as it was — did not appear to concern opponents of the agreements; their position was ideological and was very narrowly constructed.

Notwithstanding the stature of the proponents of the agreements, the agreement's opponents appear to have better appreciated the temper of Mapai's membership. When the referendum was held and the votes counted, the nays outnumbered the ayes by a ratio of better than 3 to 2: approximately 15,000 to 10,000 votes. The defeat was a crushing one for Ben-Gurion, who had gone from success to success during the 1920s and 1930s and was here handed his first substantial defeat.

THE REVISIONIST SCHISM

With the failure of the Ben-Gurion-Jabotinsky agreements, relations between Mapai and Ha-Zohar reached a new low. In March 1935, Ha-Zohar's petition was rejected by the League of Nations, to the great relief of many members of the JAE.[114] At this point, however, the WZO reached an important turning point. After a decade of efforts to influence the WZO, the Revisionists had accomplished little. More significantly, Ha-Zohar was almost completely isolated within the WZO by 1935. At the Seventeenth World Zionist Congress (1931), Jabotinsky had torn up his delegate card in disgust after his resolution on the Endziel was shouted down.[115] Now Labor Zionists had vetoed an agreement negotiated in good faith. Rescuing the Zionist dream required decisive action: specifically, the forming of an organization dedicated to political activism and to advancing the true goal of Zionism — the creation of a Jewish state. Previously Jabotinsky's closest followers had strongly urged that he withdraw from the WZO and establish his own organization but he had been unwilling to condone such an attack on Zionist unity. Now, convinced that continuing the fight would not yield any positive results, he decided to withdraw in May 1935.[116]

Jabotinsky's decision initiated the greatest schism in Zionism since the Uganda controversy. Following his lead, Ha-Zohar and its subsidiary agencies (notably Betar) completely withdrew from the WZO and the Va'ad Leumi. Only a small portion of the Revisionist movement, associated with Meir Grossman and organized as the Jewish State Party, remained within the WZO. The remainder of Ha-Zohar joined Jabotinsky in the formation of Histadrut ha-Zionit ha-Hadasha (Ha-Zach; The New Zionist Organization), which held its first congress in Vienna in September 1935, one month after the Nineteenth World Zionist Congress, which was held in Lucerne. In his key-note address, Jabotinsky denied creating a separatist organization and claimed to have created "the seedling for the legal development of the entire Jewish people."[117] He believed that he was rescuing the ideals of Theodor Herzl and Max Nordau, which had been destroyed by the socialists of Mapai.

Jabotinsky also briefly referred to conditions in Germany, noting the need to solve the totality of the Jewish problem, rather than concentrating on one specific aspect of it. He again offered his explanation of the crisis in Europe, saying that antisemitism was endemic and calling for evacuation as the only means of rescuing European Jewry. In essence, Jabotinsky accused the WZO leadership of missing the forest for the trees: as he observed, eastern European antisemitism was of one cloth. Today's antisemitic outbreaks in Poland would be followed by tomorrow's in Hungary or Romania. Sooner or later, European Jewry, and the Yishuv, would be faced with the bitter necessity of rescuing as many Jews as possible. Therefore, Jabotinsky said, it was better to act now, while mass rescue was still feasible.[118]

Far from ending the controversy with Mapai, the creation of Ha-Zach intensified the climate of ideological disunity. Mapai election posters prepared for the Nineteenth World Zionist Congress emphasized Mapai's role in rescue aliya, which was a function of its control of the JAE and thus of immigration certificates.[119] At the Congress, the Revisionists were never mentioned directly, although Sokolow and Ben-Gurion referred to them in passing in their respective addresses.[120]

Just before the schism, the Revisionists began a poster campaign in the diaspora to convince Zionists not to buy the shekel, thus creating quite a bit of consternation among the Zionist establishment.[121]   Relations were further aggravated when Ha-Zach began a campaign, primarily in Poland, to request immigrant certificates directly from the British. Citing the unfairness of the JA monopoly on Labor certificates, Ha-Zach representatives prepared a circular in Polish and Hebrew which included the initial documents that had to be completed.[122]

Although the incidents of interparty violence declined, there was no abatement in the propaganda war. In April 1936, Fischel Rotenstreich, chief of the Palestine Office in Warsaw, wrote Ben-Gurion that the editors of *Der Moment* were thinking of terminating their contract with Jabotinsky. Rotenstreich suggested a sustained effort to reinforce that trend, with the hope of denying Jabotinsky an outlet for his propaganda.[123]   Moreover, in May 1936, the policy whereby Betar members were systematically denied immigrant certificates was renewed.[124]

At the same time the Ha-Zach Executive organized its offices, which were located in London, Geneva, and Warsaw and were patterned after those of the JAE. Ten departments were established, as follows: 1. Presidium and Political Department (London), headed by Jabotinsky; 2. Finance (London), headed by Zinovy Tiomkin; 3. Organization and Pasports (London), headed by Dr. Jacob Damm; 4. Press and Propaganda and National Assembly (London), headed by Dr. Joseph B. Schechtman; 5. The Ten-Year Plan (London), headed by Dr. Stefan Klinger; 6. Representative at the League of Nations (Geneva), Dr. Harry Levy; 7. Legal Adviser (London) Samuel Landman; 8. Immigration, Training, and Economic Department (London), headed by Aron Kopelowicz; 9. Department for Organizing Orthodox Jews (Warsaw), headed by L. Ingster; 10. Passport Department for Poland (Warsaw), headed by Ingster.[125]   The Political Department also included an advisory committee, consisting of Landman, Klinger, Shlomo Y. Jacobi, and M. S. Schwartzman.

The next step in Ha-Zach's plan to again become a factor in Zionist affairs was to conduct a series of negotiations with the British and Poles regarding the Evacuation Plan, now renamed the Ten-Year Plan, as well as other Zionist issues.[126]

In September, Jabotinsky began negotiations with the Poles regarding the evacuation scheme. These negotiations created something of a stir among Polish Jews: in some circles Jabotinsky was accused of trying to sow discord within the Jewish community.[127]   From parallel Polish documentation recently published by Jerzy Tomaszewski, it is clear that sowing dissension and disunity within the Jewish community was indeed the Poles' purpose in these negotiations. Jabotinsky was not aware of this Polish trickery, and undertook the negotiations in good faith.[128]

In addition to Ha-Zach's negotiations with foreign sources, at least two abortive peace feelers were put out to the WZO, implying that the rift within

Zionism was reversible. In the earlier case, Josiah Wedgwood, a well-known supporter of Jabotinsky, approached Colonial Secretary John Thomas requesting that the Palestine administration act as an intermediary in negotiations between the two parties. Wedgwood was especially unsettled by the discordant fact that Betar members, accepted by all as good Zionists, were denied certificates, whereas Agudas Israel, which opposed everything that Zionism stood for, was granted them.[129] Thomas passed Wedgwood's proposals on to Weizmann, but refused to take any other action.

In May, Weizmann and Jabotinsky met in London, and the latter expressed his willingness to tone down some of the NZO's demands regarding reorganization of the WZO. The two veteran Zionists agreed that for the immediate future Zionism's goal ought to be increased immigration — although neither had ever disagreed with that premise in the past. On the whole, no substantive accord resulted from these talks.[130]

A subsequent proposal for inter-Zionist peace originated in the late summer of 1936 among Polish non-Zionists, who proposed to mediate the dispute. In this case the JA rejected the effort, more out of an unwillingness to allow non-Zionists to interfere in Zionist affairs than out of a refusal to negotiate with Revisionists.[131]

In his conversation with Weizmann, Jabotinsky expressed a willingness to consider moderating his position on intra-Zionist issues. He elucidated his positions on these issues in a speech in Vienna on November 20, 1936, and they may be summarized thus: (1) adoption of a maximalist policy regarding political demands, culminating in statehood; (2) adoption of the Ten-Year Plan as the basis for Zionist aliya policy; (3) expansion of Zionist alliances with Italy, Poland, and perhaps other states; and (4) convocation of a Jewish National Assembly that would be elected on the basis of universal male suffrage and would supersede both the WZO and the NZO.[132]

Jabotinsky's proposals did not become the basis for a united Zionist front. The JAE chose not to respond to his overture. The Arab revolt and the disagreement over havlaga between the Hagana and IZL reinforced the already existing centrifugal tendencies, meaning that substantive chances for compromise were very slim. In addition, the WZO preferred that the Revisionists return to a reunited movement rather than create a new organization. Indeed, although further efforts at attaining unity were to be made in 1937, 1938, and 1939, only the events of 1939, culminating in the outbreak of World War II, would force a semblance of unity on the Zionist movement.

EVALUATION

Zionist disunity must be kept in context: the entire Jewish world was deeply divided during the 1930s. Questions of nationalism versus internationalism, religious orthodoxy versus heterodoxy or secularism, and activism versus passivity in the face of external pressure were among the issues that divided all Jewish communities. The Yishuv, as has been seen, was also deeply split between competing ideological blocs. Despite the divisiveness of party politics in the Yishuv during the 1930s, there was an underlying unity of purpose in the positions adopted by the two main Zionist blocs. Thus, Jabotinsky's political program did not contradict the program of rescue aliya, and Mapai's pursuit of rescue aliya did not necessarily contradict Jabotinsky's belief that statehood must be the ultimate goal of the Zionist movement.

An interesting perspective is provided on this issue by Howard Rosenblum's recent doctoral dissertation. Studying a broad spectrum of Zionist issues, Rosenblum has concluded that both ideologically and practically, there were fewer distinctions between Mapai and the Revisionists than would appear at first glance.[133]   Concentrating only on two issues relevant here — immigration and statehood — Rosenblum has actually found a greater area of agreement between the two blocs. Both Mapai and Ha-Zach, according to Rosenblum, accepted the need for a Jewish majority in Palestine, and both agreed that the implication of a Jewish majority was statehood. The major area of disagreement was the timetable for the attainment of these goals. Mapai, oriented toward a policy of slow but steady development, operated on the assumption of accomplishing these Zionist goals in the long term. In contrast, Jabotinsky felt that Zionist goals must be accomplished immediately; only in this way could a catastrophe of epic proportions be averted.[134]

From the perspective of half a century, it is abundantly clear that Jabotinsky's position was justified. Any position regarding the Jewish question that did not account for the massive Jewish requirements for aid — in other words, a policy that continued business as usual — would seem inadequate when compared to the Nazi extermination program carried out from 1941 to 1945. Such an evaluation, however, is not wholly satisfactory, since it does not take chronology into account. In the 1930's the means being used by the Nazis against German Jewry appeared conventional. Conventional responses, "business as usual," seemed adequate to most analysts and gained wide support among Jewish leaders and the Jewish masses. A visionary with considerable experience regarding the European psyche, Jabotinsky was able to rise above the conventional and to perceive broader implications of the events to which he was responding.

Of his ideological opponents, only Ben-Gurion approached the breadth of Jabotinsky's analysis. As early as 1934, and perhaps already in 1933, realizing that the Nazi threat augured ill for all of European Jewry, Ben-Gurion began to considerably modify the conventional approach that his colleagues had adopted. Specifically, he began to advocate massive increases in aliya. This, in turn, would inevitably speed up the process of creating a Jewish majority and of attaining sovereignty, although at the time Ben-Gurion did not emphasize either goal. It should not come as a surprise, therefore, that only Ben-Gurion echoed ideas regarding Zionist goals that were similar to Jabotinsky's, although the process of change from the conventional Zionist approach to the radical mamlachtiut that became Ben-Gurion's major ideological fixation took until the later 1930s to develop fully.[135]   In comparison, Weizmann did not begin to advocate the aliya of hundreds of thousands until after the White Paper of 1939.

One question must still be asked: did intra-Zionist rivalries ultimately weaken the rescue aliya program? It is difficult to provide a definitive answer without using hypothetical points that cannot be proved or disproved, but the broad parameters of an answer are clear. Although it must be admitted that the reality of rescue aliya never matched the rhetoric behind it, we must also seek the cause for failure. When we do, it becomes abundantly clear that the onus of failure must be placed primarily on the British Palestine administration, and only secondarily — if at all — on the supposed timidity of the Zionist response to the Nazi threat.

6
Rescue Aliya and Zionist Foreign Relations

YISHUV DEVELOPMENTS, 1933-1936

In an office diary entry for November 27, 1933, Moshe Shertok noted the arrival of the *SS Martha Washington* in Palestine. Aboard were more than 500 olim from eastern Europe, along with many tourists. This large number of immigrants created a tumult. The authorities in Jaffa permitted only 200 of the olim to disembark, forcing the rest to remain on board until the ship reached Haifa.[1] Although the authorities were following standard procedure, the incident indicates the problematic relation of the British administration to the rescue aliya program. Ambivalent almost from the beginning, the British Palestine administration that set and implemented immigration policy for Palestine translated directly into the reduction of rescue aliya's potential for success, and ultimately caused the program's failure.

As Shertok's diary entry proves, however, the Zionists were not wholly unaware of the problem. To comprehend this situation, we must review Zionist-British relations with specific focus on the struggle to secure rescue aliya in 1936 and 1937, and we must place those relations into context. It is necessary to recall some of the Mandate's background. The League of Nations Mandate's stated purpose was the creation of a Jewish national home. The Mandate specifically recognized that Jews immigrating to Palestine did so by right, not by sufferance, and this principle was accepted unanimously when the Mandate was approved at the San Remo Conference in 1922. Despite this clear principle, aliya became a sore spot in British-Zionist relations from the beginning of the Mandate. Before 1933, aliya was halted twice: by High Commissioner Herbert Samuel in 1921, and by the Passfield White Paper in 1930. Both bans resulted from a British effort to appease the Arabs after riots.

TABLE 6.1: Palestine Immigration Certificates, 1933-1939

A	**Capitalists**
A-I	Persons with at least £P1,000 in capital
A-II	Persons with at least £P500 in capital
A-III	Persons with at least £P250 in capital
A-IV	Persons with an income of £P4 or more per month
A-V	Persons with £P500 and demonstrated ability to support self
B	**Immigrants whose self-sufficiency is secured**
B-I	Orphans in publicly supported institutions
B-II	Religious functionaries
B-III	Students
C	**Workers**
D	**Persons whose immigration is requested by resident(s)**
D-I	Relatives of immigrant/resident
D-II	Workers with special skills

Source: *Government of Palestine, Ordinances, 1933*, London: HMSO, 1934.

The concept of "economic absorptive capacity" was first used in 1922 in the Churchill White Paper, in order to establish the parameters of Jewish immigration at any given time.[2] This premise was legislated into the Immigration Ordinance of 1925, which set down the different categories of immigrants and left the establishment of each specific quota in the hands of the High Commissioner.[3] While the majority of the Zionists would have preferred a less rigid system, they accepted the principle of economic absorptive capacity as a criterion for immigration quotas.

The system thus established remained the basis for all legislation on immigration during the period of the Mandate. Legislation modifying the Immigration Ordinance was passed during the late 1920s and early 1930s as a means to refine the system but did not reflect any fundamental changes. The categories of immigration visas, as revised in 1930 and then codified in the Immigration Ordinance of 1933, are summarized by Table 6.1.

Of these categories, only C, the Labor schedule, was open to input by the JA, which made nonbinding requests for certificates based on its estimate of the number of workers needed for the Yishuv's economy. Two Labor schedules were granted per year, one covering April to September, and the other October to March. If needed, supplemental schedules could be granted, although this rarely happened, since the office of the High Commissioner usually held a number of certificates in reserve. This system left virtually the entire decision-making process regarding economic absorptive capacity in the hands of the Palestine administration, leaving the Yishuv without a form of appeal against arbitrary decisions by the administration.

Despite the pitfalls, the Yishuv continued its steady growth during the 1920s. Palestine's Jewish population, as cited in the 1931 census, was 174,610. This figure represented nearly 17 percent of a total population of 1,035,821. Immigration languished in 1931 and 1932, as a result both of an economic slowdown and of the continuing effect of the Passfield White Paper of 1930. It resumed its steady growth in 1933. The official government estimate of Palestine's population published on June 30, 1934, listed the total population as 1,171,158, of whom 253,700 were Jews. The Yishuv's growth — by some 79,000 in three years — also reflected the percentage growth of the Jewish population, from just 17 percent to 21.7 percent.[4] Similarly, the population estimate published by the government on December 31, 1938, listed the Jewish population at 411,222, or 30 percent of the total population of 1,368,732.[5]

Arab opposition to Jewish immigration — expressed by violent means virtually from the inception of the Mandate — continued unabated. Arab riots of August 1929, which led to the Shaw Commission investigations and to the Passfield White Paper, also led to a temporary disruption of aliya and an abortive effort by the British government to repudiate its commitments to Zionism. Violence was renewed sporadically in 1933 and 1934. On October 13, 1933, a rally protesting Jewish immigration turned violent, and as a result the Arab Executive called for a general strike.[6]

Arab dockworkers in both Jaffa and Haifa refused to unload ships bringing Jewish immigrants. At the same time, the Arab Executive declared a boycott of Jewish products and services that continued (with little impact) throughout the remaining years of the Mandate. Jews undertook a counter-boycott, particularly of Arab labor, that was very beneficial for the Yishuv and quite harmful for the Arabs. These incidents were not themselves significant, but they boded ill for the future of Jewish-Arab relations in Palestine, and increased the stress between the Yishuv and the Mandatory administration.

While Zionist efforts to involve the British government in the rescue of European Jewry met with an ambivalent response, the JAE's request in April 1933 for 1,000 emergency certificates from the High Commissioner's reserve was accepted. Significantly, the general trend was to drastically reduce the number of certificates granted. Moreover, a JAE request for 3,500 additional emergency certificates was flatly rejected in July 1933.[7] In September of that year, negotiations began regarding the schedule that was to last from October 1933 to March 1934. The JAE requested 24,000 certificates, but the British government granted only 5,500. Furthermore, when the schedule was officially published, 1,000 certificates (18 percent of the total grant) were automatically deducted as punishment for illegal Jewish immigration. Naturally, the JAE protested both the reduction of the schedule by 77 percent and, on top of that, the cancellation of the 1,000 certificates. JAE representatives used two principal lines of protest during a stormy meeting with High Commissioner General Sir Arthur Wauchope. They first insisted that Palestine's absorptive capacity was much larger than the schedule implied. Indeed, they noted, there appeared to be no correlation between Palestine's absorptive capacity, which was an objective criterion, and the subjective schedule grants. The JAE members' second argument was that Jewry's dire plight necessitated emergency measures. The future of Jewry depended on free immigration to Palestine. David Ben-Gurion emphasized these points in an impassioned statement:

> We are now living through a terrible tragedy, one of the
> hardest in our history . . . No Jew in the world would
> understand why at this hour, at the time of the German
> tragedy, when there was such distress in other countries
> and when such considerable development was taking place
> in Palestine owing to our efforts, the government was not
> admitting Jewish immigration up to the limit of the
> country's capacity. Jews were bound to ask themselves
> whether this was the way of fulfilling the obligations
> resting upon the Mandatory government to facilitate
> Jewish immigration.[8]

This protest fell on deaf ears, and further restrictions were not long in coming. The government sought a means of dissuading Jews from entering Palestine with tourist visas, since many such tourists remained as illegal immigrants.

In November 1933, the administration enacted a decree requiring that each prospective tourist post an £P60 bond at the Passport Control Office issuing the visa. Only tourists traveling first class — presumably capitalists — did not have to post any bond. Again, the JA saw the decree as an attempt to undercut aliya and, as before, a delegation of JAE leaders was sent to persuade Wauchope to change the policy. Ben-Gurion, Shertok, and Dr. Werner D. Senator argued to no avail, but they did convince him that written guarantees from local Palestine Offices should be considered sufficient to waive the bond. In consultation with the director of immigration and the Colonial Office, the High Commissioner also agreed to consider creating a new category, that of "permanent resident." This was defined as a person who, even if he or she had entered Palestine without an immigrant certificate, could remain there as long as he or she was employed.[9] Despite Wauchope's interest in such a category, however, the relevant legislation was never enacted. The JA delegates also countered British accusations regarding illegal immigration by noting that faster action by the Passport Control officials to grant certificates, a procedure that took a year or more, would prevent a most illegal aliya.[10]

In addition, the JA representatives sought to convince Wauchope that provision ought to be made to ease aliya for persons over 35, since the virtual ban on immigration by these individuals had no legal standing.[11] No conclusive steps were taken during this meeting. The JAE representatives simply requested that "a fair proportion" of future schedules be dedicated to olim over 35 years of age. Although an adequate policy was never established during the entire Mandatory era, the importance of the conversation transcends the JA's failure to achieve a more open immigration policy, and explains much about the ultimate failure of rescue aliya. On a number of occasions, the JAE and the WZO have been accused of emphasizing halutzic aliya. The accusers claim that the Yishuv in its entirety sought only olim between the ages of 17 and 35, thus abandoning older, and presumably less "qualified," Jews to their fate. To be sure, there were those, especially within the kibbutz movement, who used such an argument. Ben-Gurion and Shertok, two leaders of Mapai, did not follow a narrowly construed policy of halutzic aliya but sought a more open immigration policy. They were not yet close to Jabotinsky's ideas on the creation of an immigration regime in Palestine that would lead to the evacuation of all threatened European Jews, regardless of age, financial status, or employability. But, at least with respect to the issue of olim over the age of 35, they were heading in a convergent direction. Moreover, the demographic reality guaranteed an increase in aliya for persons over 35 despite British demurral: aliya by this age group rose from 19 percent of all German olim in 1933 to 27 percent in 1936 and 39 percent in 1939. The cause for this increase was demographic: German Jewry was an older community even before the Machtergreifung. The graying of German Jewry continued after 1933 as more and more young people emigrated, leaving an older community. In time, many of the more established members of the community (those over 35) also sought to emigrate, with a relatively large proportion heading for Palestine.[12]

Ben-Gurion and Shertok repeated their protests to Wauchope in a meeting on November 10, 1933. Again, the JAE leaders complained about the manner in which the administration was neutering the use of economic absorptive capacity as a criterion for aliya. Accusing Wauchope of creating a labor shortage in Palestine, both Ben-Gurion and Shertok requested an increase in the schedule grant. In response, the High Commissioner urged the Zionist leaders to consider using Arab labor, since it was both plentiful and inexpensive. This the Zionist leaders rejected. Observing that Zionism, especially Labor Zionism, was based on the premise of Avoda Ivrit (Hebrew labor), both Ben-Gurion and Shertok refused to consider replaceming labor aliya with Arab workers. Stating that most unemployed Arabs had infiltrated Palestine illegally without any British efforts to halt the flow, the JA leaders refused to accept the premise that the Yishuv's future should be contingent upon Arab employment. Following such a policy would, they said, result in the liquidation of the very idea of a Jewish national home.[13]

With the British unwilling to budge even one inch on their antitourist policy, the Va'ad Leumi and the JA met in a joint session on Sunday, November 26, 1933, to formulate a counter-policy. The Va'ad Leumi Legal Department was authorized to assist ma'apilim in becoming legal, and the JA Political Department agreed to approach the government with suggestions on how to streamline the conversion of immigrants from temporary to permanent residency status.[14] Again, nothing was gained by the effort.

The immigration schedule was the crux of the growing conflict of interest between the Zionists and the British, and would remain so beyond the rest of the decade. As a result, immigration became the main focus of Ben-Gurion's discussions with Colonial Minister Philip Cunliffe-Lister and Wauchope in London in December 1933 and January 1934. During the talks, Ben-Gurion proposed a new immigration policy guaranteeing an aliya rate of between 40,000 and 50,000 Jews per year. Although this plan covered all categories of olim, including those in the D category, according to his estimate the plan's implementation would have required the Labor schedule to double.

In concept, Ben-Gurion's plan was similar to Jabotinsky's evacuation plan, insofar as both required a major change in the British attitude toward rescue aliya. But there were also two diferences between the plans. On the simplest level, Jabotinsky's evacuation scheme dealt with a larger scale — three times that of Ben-Gurion's plan. Of greater significance, Jabotinsky's plan had as its ultimate goals a Jewish majority and a sovereign Jewish state, aims that did not explicitly animate Ben-Gurion's plan at this time.

Ben-Gurion based his plan on three principles, which he sought to impress upon the British at every available opportunity: (1) the immense needs of tempest-tossed European Jewry; (2) the need to secure the Yishuv's brittle economy by bringing in both capital and labor; and (3) the need to convert Palestine into world Jewry's center of political gravity.[15]

Although the JAE approved Ben-Gurion's, the Executive was far from unanimously committed to it. Arthur Ruppin, for example, felt that an immigration level of 50,000 per year ought to be a long-range goal. In the interim, the Zionists should concentrate on smaller increases in the Labor schedule and on shortening the delay in getting certificates to those who needed them. According to Ruppin, the problem was that the grant of an A-I certificate took between six and seven months, a D certificate usually took thirteen to fourteen months, and labor certificates often took even longer.[16]

Ruppin's minimalist position was not more acceptable to the British. Ben-Gurion reported to the JAE that his plan was received coolly by Cunliffe-Lister and Wauchope. The latter went so far as to ask Ben-Gurion, "If I grant a schedule of 20,000 certificates now, will you return in six months and request another 20,000?"[17] Nor would there be any relief in the backlog of certificate grants for either the short- or the long-term.

There were to be further confrontations over the schedule between 1934 and 1937. As noted in Table 4.1, the JAE requested a total of 136,065 certificates for the eight schedules between April 1933 and March 1937. Only 52,850 certificates, or roughly 39 percent, were granted, and only one schedule, that of April to September 1935, witnessed a grant of more than half of what the JA requested: 18,000 certificates granted, against a total of 19,150 requested (94 percent). The next schedule, covering October 1935 to March 1936, saw a return to the restrictive policy, with a grant of 3,250 certificates against a JAE request for 19,000. The diminution would become even greater in the schedule covering October 1936 to March 1937: the request for 10,695 certificates was met with a grant of 1,800, or only 16 percent.

Examined in greater detail, the problem facing the JAE becomes even more glaring. In February 1934, negotiations began for a new schedule, but again the JAE was disappointed: 20,100 certificates were requested but only 6,800 (34 percent) were granted.[18] The High Commissioner held back 800 certificates as punishment for illegal immigration. Similarly, only 540 certificates were to be made available for those over 35. None were to be granted to potential olim over 45, and only 485 certificates were held over for women of any age. Finally, the government decided to divide the certificates into three installments, rather than granting the entire schedule at one time.[19]

Perhaps to lessen the impact of the diminished schedule, Wauchope made a personal donation of £P500 to the JAE refugee relief fund. His gesture, however, made no impression, in view of the more pressing needs at hand. In fact, Ben-Gurion characterized this schedule as "cruel," asking only if the cruelty was deliberate or not.[20]

On February 22, 1934, Shertok again met with Wauchope to protest the arbitrary schedule, and requested a supplementary grant of certificates.[21] Wauchope received Shertok politely, but all members of the Executive realized that his response represented a rebuff. In April 1934 Shertok made one more effort to secure a supplemental schedule. In his conversations with Wauchope, he advanced two arguments: first, that the British were setting an arbitrary schedule based on political expediency rather than on Palestine's economic absorptive capacity, and second, that the British were turning a blind eye to illegal Arab immigration from Syria and Transjordan.[22]

The April to September 1934 schedule would witness further controversy. In May the British announced that 800 certificates would be withdrawn, again as punishment for illegal immigration. Furthermore, one-third of the certificates granted were to be dedicated exclusively for use by German olim, even if there were not 2,000 certificate requests from Germany at that particular time. This ruling essentially robbed the JA of any vestige of authority, and the diminished numbers of certificates granted threatened to choke off aliya.

Shertok warned the Executive that the developing trend seemed to presage a concerted British effort to manipulate the schedule in order to slow the growth of the Yishuv.[23] Ben-Gurion proposed that the Yishuv and its allies in London launch a public protest campaign culminating with the publication of a "Blue-White Paper" setting out concrete Zionist immigration proposals. Ben-Gurion's baseline for immigration assumed acceptance of the 50,000-olim-per-year rate that he had proposed during his stay in London.[24]

In preparation for the JAE's public campaign, Ben-Gurion and Shertok met with Wauchope once again, with dubious results. The JAE therefore resolved unanimously to advise all regional Zionist federations to publicly protest British immigration policy, in ways deemed locally appropriate.[25]

What, if anything, these protests accomplished is unclear. Whether or not a more forceful approach would have accomplished anything further is purely conjectural. To understand why this was the case, we must recall the British perspective on rescue. Wauchope, for example, presented himself as sympathetic toward the plight of the German Jewish refugees, at least in his conversations with Shertok.[26] Yet, his protestations of sympathy never translated into a more liberal immigration policy, nor any action to streamline the lengthy wait for certificates. Wauchope was not completely at fault for the lengthy backlog in certificate grants; at least part of the blame was shared by the Colonial Office in London and by other members of the Palestine administration. Two examples will suffice to explain the problem. An especially glaring example of the attitude of the administration both in Palestine and in London was the curious definition of "refugee" whereby the Colonial Office and the Palestine administration's Department of Migration and Statistics refused to consider as a refugee any Jew who left Germany after May 1933 if he or she came to Palestine. In effect, they would not consider any German Jew a refugee, and thus they could avoid doing anything that might be construed as assisting Jewish emigration. Clearly political in nature, this decision contradicted the policy of other offices in the British government. Although the JAE sought to change this definition, none was granted.[27] Similarly, in a conversation with Ruppin, John H. Hall, the Palestine government's secretary for immigration, inquired about what he saw as the similarities between Jewish insistence on Avoda Ivrit and Nazi antisemitic legislation. In essence, Hall saw no moral difference between victim and persecutor, and therefore no grounds to assist the rescue aliya program.[28]

On June 19, 1934, the JAE request for a supplemental Labor schedule was turned down.[29] Despite the limited schedule, the total aliya for 1934 reached 45,000, with much of the difference between the low Labor schedule (only 20 to 30 percent of the JA request) and the total aliya rate consisting of capitalists in the different categories.[30]

While the conflict over immigration grew worse, another element entered into the Zionist-British equation. In the fall of 1934, the High Commissioner revived a 1922 British proposal to create a Legislative Council for Palestine. To be based on a one man one vote electoral system, the Legislative Council was seen by all Zionists as a dire threat: the proposed council guaranteed an

Arab majority, which could then act to cut off aliya. Only Brit Shalom, which advocated a binational Palestine, accepted the Legislative Council as presented by the government.[31]

In 1934, the Zionist leadership remained adamantly opposed to any form of Legislative Council, except under conditions of parity (equal representation of Jews and Arabs). The only notable exception was Yitzhak Gruenbaum, the Polish Zionist leader who joined the JAE in December 1933. Hoping to manipulate negotiations over the proposed council, Gruenbaum was willing to accept the principle of one man one vote in return for British concessions regarding aliya and land acquisition.[32] The JAE majority, with the unanimous backing of the Va'ad ha-Poel ha-Zioni, declared a less equivocal policy: "We shall do everything in our power to suspend the Legislative Council."[33] The JAE also received support for its opposition from Agudas Israel, an organization that otherwise refused to cooperate with the Zionists.[34]

Recognizing the council's broader threat to the terms and spirit of the Mandate, Jabotinsky began a whirlwind lobbying campaign in Parliament and the British press.[35] Surprisingly, perhaps, the Zionists managed to stay united and also remained focused on their unalterable opposition to the plan as published by the High Commissioner.[36] Simultaneously, the JAE sought to reopen the long-standing issue of land settlement with the British. During the 1930's, two outstanding issues involving land animated Zionists, Arabs, and the British administrators: first, making land acquisition easier for Jews, and second, opening new areas for Jewish settlement. Regarding the latter, both Transjordan and the Negev weighed heavily.[37] Transjordan, as already noted, was crucial to Jabotinsky's evacuation plan. The JAE as well sought to open Transjordan, at least as a tool for further negotiaitions on western Palestine's economic absorptive capacity. In 1933 and 1934 the JAE discussed Transjordan at fourteen of its meetings, indicating the importance attached to the possibility of opening settlement opportunities there.[38]

The expansion of settlement areas in Palestine and opening Transjordan increased in importance after the French reneged on their 1933 promise to open Lebanon to Jewish refugee settlement.[39] Continuing infiltration by Arabs seeking work, coupled with the High Commissioner's demand that Arab labor be used in the Yishuv, also fed the Zionists' fears and encouraged attempts to increase the area open to Jewish settlement. These fears became so significant a feature in British-Zionist relations that in mid-October of 1933, Shertok ordered the JA Political Department to begin systematic research into the issue of Arab infiltration.[40]

There was no relief to the certificate problem in 1935. The JAE requested just over 38,000 certificates, but received about 21,000, or 55 percent. Although this represented an improvement over the figures for 1934, it was still not an adequate response to Zionist needs and the backlog of requests grew. On May 23, 1935, Felix Rosenblueth cabled from London: "Postponement despatching certificates creates [a] terrible situation, especially [in] Paris for refugees already confirmed by Berlin."[41] At that rate, not only was Jabotinsky's evacuation scheme unattainable, but even Ben-Gurion's clarion call at the Nineteenth Zionist Congress, for the relocation of 1 million Jews in twenty years, appeared unrealistically optimistic.

Nor would the British budge on granting permanent resident status to tourists who remained after their visas expired, and thus became illegal in the eyes of the administration. In one instance, the government refused to grant certificates to fifty German Jewish tourists whose visas had not yet expired and who hoped to avoid becoming illegals.[42] The government also refused to legalize Jews who requested relief directly (that is, without the help of the JA), although in the case of German Jewish refugees, many were permitted to remain in the country unregistered. Such a status, it must be noted, virtually guaranteed that family members of the ma'apil, including spouses and children, were left stranded in Europe.[43]

After numerous travails, the JA received one relatively minor concession from the British relating to Haavara: possession of a Paltreu promissory note would constitute valid proof of the £P1,000 in personal reserves needed to qualify for an A-I certificate.[44] This concession streamlined the process of gaining certificates for some groups of German Jewish Capitalists, while also making Haavara more accessible to those who could not both invest in Paltreu and retain the £P1,000 in cash needed for an A-I certificate. Late in June 1935, another concession was announced: an indefinite delay in the implementation of the Legislative Council, in view of Zionist opposition to the proposals regarding the electoral system to be used.[45]

What one hand granted, however, the other hand took away. In February 1935, the Passport Control Office — responsible for actual transmission of immigrant certificates — announced a new policy regarding Capitalist certificates of the A-II and A-III categories in all of eastern Europe: no such certificates were to be granted except by explicit orders from London.[46]

In October 1935, reacting to the heightened crisis in Germany after ratification of the Nuremberg Laws, the British agreed to grant 2,000 emergency certificates. However, these certificates were viewed as an advance on the next schedule.[47] Two caveats must be noted in this connection, and they indicate much about the British role in neutralizing rescue aliya. First, having granted the advance of 2,000 certificates, the British then reversed their seemingly liberal trend by granting a total schedule of only 3,250 certificates, as compared to the 19,000 requested by the JAE. Representing only 17 percent of the request, this was the second smallest schedule granted between April 1933 and March 1937. Second, in December, the British undermined the schedule entirely when they withdrew 1,200 certificates as punishment for illegal immigration.[48]

IMPERIAL POLICY AND THE JEWS' FATE

Based on a conversation with administration officials Shertok noted in an entry in his office diary for December 10, 1933, that the British seemed to believe that once a Jewish majority was established in Palestine, the Zionists would not be as loyal to Great Britain's strategic interests as Jewish leaders claimed.[49]   Although he vociferously denied this anti-Zionist analysis, Shertok, like all the Zionist leaders, could not help but observe that the gulf between the Yishuv and the British appeared to widen with each passing day.

It is clear that the British had originally come to Palestine primarily for strategic, not idealistic, reasons. Far from constituting an altruistic policy, the Balfour Declaration and Britain's acceptance of the Mandate reflected Great Britain's ambition to anchor its strategic interests in the Middle East by holding Palestine.   Only insofar as the Jewish goals of immigration, land acquisition, and settlement coincided with Britain's own geo-strategic interests would Britain continue to fullfil its commitments to the Jewish national home. When Jewish needs no longer coincided with Britain's imperial desires, the British would not feel compelled to keep promises made to the Zionists.[50]

This fact raises two interrelated questions. To what extent did the Zionist leaders accept the fact that Britain's true intentions were strategic and not moral, and how did they view long-term relations with the British government in view of the strategic reality? As with other issues, the traditional approach identifies two positions: that of the Zionist majority, who sought to align themselves exclusively with Great Britain, and that of a minority, primarily Jabotinsky and the Revisionist movement, who distrusted the British from the beginning and therefore focused on attaining Jewish sovereignty as quickly as possible. Viewed from the JAE perspective, this position would emphasize that the "responsible" Zionist leaders hoped to keep the conflict of interest to a minimum, in order to attain Zionist goals quietly, slowly, and without much fanfare while "irresponsible" leaders such as Jabotinsky spoke and acted in a way guaranteed to sow conflict and enmity. Viewed from Ha-Zohar's perspective, JA and WZO leadership behaved timidly and did not address Jewish needs properly; only Jabotinsky and his followers recognized the true Jewish needs of the hour and behaved accordingly.

Again, this traditional analysis fails to consider the nuances of Zionist ideology and the realities of Jewish powerlessness. Actually, both Zionist camps were pro-British in strategic orientation. Their ideas differed on the best tactics to reach Zionist golas within the pro-British orientation.

Although Jabotinsky emphasized the relatively immediate need to fulfill Zionist goals, his position was not specifically based on a conflict with the British. To the contrary, he continually noted that achieving these goals would strengthen, not weaken, Great Britain's position in the Middle East.[51] Of Jabotinsky's main opponents, only Chaim Weizmann couched his orientation in more pro-British rhetoric, although Weizmann's minimalist stance regarding aliya made him more Anglophilic in practice.[52] For their part, the British never considered Jabotinsky a long-term ally, preferring to work with the more moderate Weizmann.

The Mapai leadership adopted a succession of positions that spanned the spectrum of attitudes toward the British, with Berl Katznelson the most Anglophobic (as evidenced by his early support for aliya bet) and Shertok the most Anglophilic.[53] Ben-Gurion's position initially emphasized the concurrence of British and Zionist interests and, especially, the critical dependence of the Yishuv on British military might to maintain security. Thus, on April 16, 1936, Ben-Gurion noted to the Mapai Central Committee that dependence on the British "places us in a morally difficult position, but that is the situation." In his estimate, as long as that meant continued aliya, the Zionists had to accept reality.[54]

Ben-Gurion was thus pro-British in practice, but his position was based on the need to strengthen the Yishuv by the aliya of 1 million Jews from Germany and Poland over the course of twenty years. His statements in 1936 represented the evolution of his position from the amorphous emphasis on mamlachtiut (statism) that he had expressed in 1931. Ben-Gurion appears to have realized sooner than Weizmann that true cooperation could develop only if the Yishuv were strong enough to stand on its own if need be.

Jabotinsky had arrived at a similar conclusion, but considerably earlier than either Weizmann or Ben-Gurion. Having worked to help create the Jewish Legion in World War I, Jabotinsky hoped that the Legion would become the basis for a strong Yishuv able to defend itself.[55] The British disbanded the Legion, thus threatening the security of the entire Yishuv in Jabotinsky's view. Jabotinsky therefore began what may be termed a love-hate relationship with Great Britain. Love, because he greatly admired many elements of British culture and British politics. This element of his relationship with Britain was also tinged with gratitude for the Balfour Declaration and with the hope that the mighty British Empire would assist in fulfilling Zionist goals. Jabotinsky noted that unless Zionist-British relations were based on mutual respect and a clear statement of Zionist goals, pro-Zionist British politicians could not take the lead in carrying them out. He also believed that political work had to continue, to offset the power wielded by Zionism's many opponents in both Britain and Palestine and to project a positive image of Jews and Zionism.[56] An example of Jabotinsky's position is demonstrated by his strong advocacy of the "Seventh Dominion Scheme" proposed by Josiah Wedgwood in 1926.[57]

Labor Zionists did not necessarily disagree with the broad parameters of Jabotinsky's analysis — especially insofar as the need for continued political work was accepted by every Zionist leader — but they did not immediately follow his lead regarding the need for statehood. Until 1937, none of Mapai's leaders spoke explicitly in terms of sovereignty, at least not as an objective to be attained over the short-term. Those Laborites who did speak of statehood invariably deferred actual attainment of sovereignty to a far-off, almost messianic, future.[58] It should also be recalled that Mapai's leaders had prevented Jabotinsky from offering his resolution on the Endziel issue at the Seventeenth and Eighteenth Zionist Congresses. Only the Arab revolt would cause a change in Mapai's position, and even then, not all Labor Zionist leaders were convinced that sovereignty was the true goal.

For Ben-Gurion a new road had been opened; one which reflected a deep-seated fear about the Jewish situation in both Europe and Palestine. In a discussion with Weizmann in January 1936, for example, Ben-Gurion admitted his growing fear of an imminent and complete British betrayal of the Yishuv. The Italian invasion of Ethiopia had unleashed a new factor in Middle Eastern politics, forcing the British to consider appeasement for the Arabs (much as they were attempting to appease Hitler).[59] As a result of these fears, Ben-Gurion approached the High Commissioner with a proposal to speed up his previous aliya plan. Now, he declared, the Yishuv must attain a majority in five years or less. As with Jabotinsky's Evacuation Plan, Ben-Gurion's plan required British acquiesence, if not direct cooperation. Both plans remained on the Zionist agenda, but neither proved acceptable as a basis for negotiations with the government.[60] At the height of the Arab revolt, Ben-Gurion's fear of British betrayal actually led him to suggest that the Yishuv should attempt to sidestep the British altogether by cutting a deal with the Arabs. Although he did not elaborate what the Arabs would gain from this "peace" agreement, Ben-Gurion insisted on Arab acceptance of an aliya rate of 80,000 per year for five years.[61] This would have doubled the Yishuv's population and probably would have created a small Jewish majority in Palestine.

In January 1936 the British virtually eliminated tourism to Palestine, in an effort to halt illegal Jewish immigration. The Palestine administration also attempted to choke off capitalist immigration, by proposing that the cash holdings necessary to qualify for an A-I certificate be doubled.[62] In a meeting of the Mapai Central Committee, Shertok stated that public opinion represented the Yishuv's sole weapon in defense of aliya, especially after the Nuremberg Laws and the highly publicized resignation of League of Nations High Commissioner for Refugees James G. McDonald.[63]

THE ARAB REVOLT

Tension again mounted in Palestine. As in 1921 and 1929, when Arab violence had led to temporary stoppages of aliya, there was a short-lived series of riots in 1933. Fortunately, the High Commissioner reacted swiftly and no major damage was done. The riots soon petered out, and quiet returned. But the Arabs did not come to terms with the Yishuv; rather, they were waiting for a new opportunity to strike. On April 25, 1936, the newly created Arab Higher Committee declared a general strike against aliya, against Jewish land acquisition, and for a "responsible" Legislative Council. The strike declaration was preceded by violent assaults on Jews traveling through Tulkarm on April 15, 1936 and an anti-Jewish riot in Jaffa on April 19.[64]

The upshot of Arab agitation was the outbreak of a full-scale revolt, not only against the Yishuv but also against the Mandatory government. As security plummeted, the Yishuv's attention turned away from Europe at a time when the threat to German and eastern European Jews markedly increased. Simultaneously, the British reassessment of Imperial interests diverged even farther away from Zionist needs. While the history of the revolt and its impact on the policies pursued by Zionists of all ideological stripes has already been extensively studied, it is necessary to reconsider the impact that the revolt (and subsequent political developments) had on rescue aliya.

Already a few weeks after the revolt's outbreak, Ben-Gurion reported to the JAE that the British perceived two options for securing Palestine's future: either a round-table conference at which Jewish and Arab representatives could negotiate a peace settlement, or another royal commission.[65] Within the Yishuv and the Zionist movement as a whole, the Arab revolt renewed debate in two spheres: how best to respond to the Arab attacks, and how to adjust the rescue aliya program to the new reality. An additional issue — what response to make to the British offer of statehood in a partitioned Palestine — was added to this agenda in 1937.

For one movement, the Palestine Communist Party (PCP), the Arab revolt presented no problem. Founded in 1924, the PCP was a full-fledged member of the Communist International (Comintern), and on Comintern orders, it had supported the Arab bloodletting in August 1929. Viewing the 1929 riots as the legitimate response by downtrodden Arab masses to Zionist imperialism, the PCP split, with some members returning to the mainstream Labor Zionist parties.[66] The PCP as a whole, however, did not change its attitude toward Arab violence in 1936, and it continued to place the blame for the riots squarely on the Zionists. This line of analysis was most explicitly formulated in a poster oriented toward German olim that equated Zionists with Nazis:

Jewish worker you, who have felt national suppression in your own lifetime, should not be a tool of imperialist oppression in this land. Have not you yourself felt the conquest of Hitler? The liberation of colonial peoples advances daily; the victorious Arab nation will, in time, demand an accounting from you.[67]

The PCP cannot be characterized as a Zionist party, by any definition. By 1936 it could barely qualify as a Jewish party, since almost the entire leaders and nearly half the membership were, by Comintern orders, Arabs.[68] Still, the PCP sought to influence the behavior of Jewish workers and thus entered the Yishuv's ideological debate.

Ha-Shomer ha-Zair also expressed criticism of the Yishuv's handling of the Arab revolt. During the party's annual convention in Warsaw, the delegates approved a resolution opposing military defense and advocating "[the] neutralization of Eretz-Israel, the friendship of nations, [and] a joint organization [with the Arabs]."[69]

All the other Jewish parties in Eretz Israel were forced to grapple with the Arab revolt in one way or another. For the Zionists, the revolt raised three fundamental policy questions: how best to defend Jewish lives and property; how to respond to the political aspects of the revolt; and whether or not to continue settlement building during the crisis. More often than not, the answers offered to these questions broke down along ideological lines, although six factors influenced the answers that each party gave: (1) Zionist perceptions of the revolt; (2) perceptions of the means available to undertake effective defense measures; (3) perceptions of the impact of the revolt on the British; (4) relations between the different Zionist parties; (5) perceptions regarding the legitimacy of the use of violence; and (6) perceptions of the possibility of using the new situation for Zionist purposes, especially the legalization of Jewish self-defense forces.[70]

Since all Zionists considered defense a legitimate policy, it was the first to be pursued. Ha-Zach reprinted an updated memorandum on defense (originally published in 1929) that called upon the British to arm Jewish settlers, to legalize the Jewish self-defense organization, and to increase the number and stature of Jewish officers in the Palestine police.[71] The Hagana, indirectly under the control of the JAE, reordered itself at the time of the uprising. Seeing itself as a militia, although an illegal one, it organized its units geographically and relied on a cadre of members who lived in or close to the settlements that they defended.

The Hagana was not the Yishuv's only underground movement. In 1931, arguments over the increasingly partisan orientation of the Hagana (which was controlled by the Histadrut as a cover for its operations) and disagreement over its policy of havlaga (self-restraint) led to a schism along with the creation of the "Hagana-B" (also called the Irgun ha-Hagana be-Eretz Israel, or Irgun-B, and later the Irgun Zvai Leumi).[72] Despite ideological differences with the Hagana, the Irgun-B initially also adopted a defensive posture in face of Arab violence.[73] The Hagana's havlaga position did not advocate complete passivity, but it did commit the Hagana to a policy of waiting for attacks before engaging in armed operations. Havlaga further meant no preemptive or punitive actions, since combat was seen as only legitimate while the Arab bands were actively attacking. Only after the revolt continued with no end in sight did Hagana policy follow a more active operational role.[74]

As understood in the late 1930s, havlaga did not necessarily mean that no reprisals would ever be carried out, although in theory, self-restraint did imply such a policy. In both the Hagana and Irgun-B, reprisals were left to the discretion of local commanders. On the night of August 17/18, 1936, for example, Hagana units in Jaffa retaliated for a grenade attack by Arabs on the Jaffa-Haifa train in which a small Jewish child was killed and two women were wounded. The Hagana units, under the direct command of Eliahu Golomb, destroyed a number of Arab houses in the area of the attack, killing and wounding a large number of Arabs.[75] This example was typical; the Hagana undertook reprisals only in response to particularly unacceptable acts of Arab terror, and then only to prove that Jewish blood was not cheap.[76]

Thus, in practice, the operational differences between the Hagana and Irgun-B were minimal. Strategically, however, there was a difference between their policies. The Hagana saw havlaga as an end to be striven for; when reprisals were undertaken, they were done so reluctantly and were kept secret, since no specific didactic purpose was attached to the operations. The Irgun saw havlaga or other defensive policies as merely a means to the attainment of broad strategic goals. If havlaga became an end in itself, according to the Irgun leaders, it was nothing more than defeatism. As a result, the Irgun publicized its retaliatory operations, although Ha-Zach officially repudiated acts of counterterror, in order to maintain its legitimacy in British eyes.[77] However, the Betar leaders in Palestine maintained that the only way to secure the Yishuv was to create "a bridge of iron, not a bridge of paper."[78]

How did the havlaga relate to rescue aliya? For most Labor Zionists, there was an intimate connection between the policy of nonretaliation and rescue aliya. Indeed, in a series of four editorials in *Davar*, Moshe Beilinson argued that the only proper Zionist response to Arab terror was increased settlement work and aliya. If any further response was necessary, that response, according to Beilinson, should be directed to the British as a demand to arm Jewish youth, either as part of an expanded Palestinian police force or as an independent but legal Jewish self-defense force.[79] Katznelson also expressed his strongly held conviction that the Yishuv had to respond creatively, but ought not turn to counterterror. Despite the emotional need to respond in kind, the Yishuv needed to pursue a restrained policy — not out of "saintliness," but rather to protect its long-term interests.[80]

Ha-Zach leaders viewed Jewish needs in a similar light, but they came to radically different conclusions. Jabotinsky likened havlaga to Russian Jewry's reaction to antisemitic violence at the time of the Kishinev pogrom (April 19-21, 1903). He agreed that havlaga was the moral response. Under the circumstances, however, behaving morally would only increase immorality, since the moral posture could not be an answer to Arab terrorism. Nevertheless, Jabotinsky agreed that havlaga could be an acceptable policy if — but only if — the British rewarded havlaga by renewing the Jewish Legion.[81]

Dr. Benjamin Lubotzky, another Ha-Zach leader, noted that havlaga was problematic because of its demoralizing effect on European Jewry: the realization that even in the Jewish national home Jewish life and property were not safe resulted in mass despair. Indeed, Lubotzky asserted, Polish Jewry, then besieged by intense pogroms, had acquitted itself honorably in self-defense, as during the Przytyk pogrom of March 9, 1936. When the Jewish defenders of Przytyk were arrested by the Polish authorities, all of Polish Jewry joined in their defense. In contrast, the Yishuv publicly berated its true defenders as terrorists.[82]

Ben-Gurion upheld unqualified support for havlaga, although at times he was uneasy about its implications. In a diary entry for July 11, 1936, he wrote:

> I have never felt hatred for Arabs, and their pranks have
> never stirred the desire for revenge in me. But I would
> welcome the destruction of Jaffa, port and city. Let it
> come, it would be for the better. This city, which grew
> fat from Jewish immigration and settlement, deserves to
> be destroyed for having waved an ax at those who built it
> and made it prosper. If Jaffa went to hell, I would not
> count myself among the mourners.[83]

Despite his private dream of revenge en masse, Ben-Gurion did not waver in his public support for havlaga. In a letter to European Labor Zionists, for example, he enumerated nine arguments for retaliation in kind, including the deleterious effect of not responding on morale within the Hagana, the Yishuv, and the Jewish world as a whole. The most serious of these nine arguments, according to Ben-Gurion, was that havlaga could be interpreted by the Arabs as cowardice. Yet he did not find these arguments decisive justification for behaving in a way that was politically problematic, especially since, in his opinion, the British would view retaliation as placing the victims on the same moral level as their attackers.[84] Implicit in Ben-Gurion's position was the criticism that opponents of havlaga were immoral, although he always attacked them on pragmatic grounds. Since Ben-Gurion felt that the Yishuv was dependent on the British, his position on havlaga was based on an acknowledgement of Zionist weakness. He did not believe that the Yishuv was strong enough to act independently.

In Ben-Gurion's analysis, the Yishuv could not present a dilemma to the British on the issue of whether they should yield to the Arabs or to the Jews. Yet that was precisely the basis of Jabotinsky's policies at the time: creating a set of alliances that would give Jews the power to force Britain to take them into account in setting Palestine policy.[85] When the opportunity arose, however, Ben-Gurion opted for a change in his Zionist policy, in this case regarding the partition of Palestine.

In the interim Ben-Gurion feared that the Irgun-B would jeopardize the Yishuv by ignoring the defensive nature of operations (and thus break the terms of British-imposed martial law). To this end, Ben-Gurion proposed re-integrating the Irgun-B into the Hagana.[86] In mid-September 1936 tentative talks were held between both senior and junior Hagana officers and their Irgun-B counterparts. The upshot of these talks was an agreement to place the Irgun-B under Hagana command (and thus under indirect JAE "discipline"). However, the Irgun command, and especially Jabotinsky disagreed with the apparent subtext of the agreement, that the Irgun-B now agreed to havlaga, and refused to accept unification of the underground movements. The talks dragged on through April 1937, when the Irgun-B split, with approximately one-third of its members simply returning to the Hagana and the remainder adopting the new name of Irgun Zvai Leumi (IZL).[87]

THE PEEL COMMISSION

Following procedures established during previous outbursts of Arab violence, the British government formed a Royal Commission to investigate the root causes of the riots and to report on possible means of bringing peace to Palestine. The announcement of this commission's (which has since come to be known as the Peel Commission) creation was greeted with considerable consternation by the JAE, and especially by Ben-Gurion. Its limited scope of investigation explored only the latest series of riots, and placed little or no emphasis on their background causes. On the other hand, the Commission had almost unlimited powers of interpretation regarding the legitimate meaning of the Mandate's terms. From Ben-Gurion's perspective, this was most disconcerting.[88]

To make matters worse, on the eve of the Peel Commission's arrival, High Commissioner Wauchope temporarily suspended immigration, creating panic among JA leaders. Ben-Gurion and Shertok met with Wauchope to explain:

> [T]hat this suspension of immigration would be a most terrible and cruel blow to the Jews. This was not a question of 2,000 immigrants more or less, although that question was also of importance. He had just paid a flying visit to Warsaw and he was depressed beyond words by what he saw . . . It was much worse than Germany. The only hope was Palestine and every thousand immigrants mattered tremendously.[89]

At the crux of the matter, according to Ben-Gurion, was the fact that by suspending immigration, the High Commissioner was rewarding the rebels while penalizing the Jews for their self-restraint.[90]   Ben-Gurion implied that havlaga — hitherto framed in exclusively moral terms — also had a political element: that the Jews hoped for a reward in the form of a larger schedule. Shertok added that such a suspension could prejudice the Jewish case even before the Royal Commission began its hearings.[91]   For once the JA leaders' protest convinced the British and the ban on aliya was lifted in early July.[92]   Success emboldened Ben-Gurion to renew his call for a massive new program that would revitalize rescue aliya: specifically he proposed that the British announce that henceforth for each Jew killed by Arab terrorists 1,000 certificates would automatically be granted to the JA.[93]   The British, however, failed to respond to this initiative, which might have resulted in thousands of new olim and could have seriously altered political conditions in both Palestine and Europe.

By August, Ben-Gurion's temporary optimism again turned to apprehension. In a letter to Moshe Shertok, Ben-Gurion voiced the opinion that the Jews had no reason to participate in the Royal Commission's hearings since they could never get a fair deal. Moreover, he felt that the British might well renege on their promise not to halt aliya; that prospect, Ben-Gurion feared, would mean the abandonment of European Jewry and the Yishuv withering on the vine.[94]

Because of these apprehensions, Ben-Gurion originally planned to boycott the Royal Commission's hearings, but he later changed his mind.[95]   The JA and WZO planned to send a large delegation to the hearings, including Ben-Gurion, Shertok, and Weizmann, who had resumed the WZO presidency after Nahum Sokolow died in 1935. In addition, the JAE planned to bring extensive documentation as evidence for the Jewish case. Despite Ha-Zach's plans for an equally strong deputation, the Peel Commission permitted only Jabotinsky and Wedgwood to testify in London. While the JAE had no hand in limiting the Revisionist testimony, it also did not protest the patent unfairness of allowing such a large deputation from one part of the Zionist movement to testify along with a large number of Arabs while virtually silencing Jabotinsky. Old enmities had not yet been healed, even though the JAE could have manipulated Revisionist testimony to offer the British the alternative of dealing with the moderates with less harm yo British interests, or dealing with the radicals with grave harm to British interests resulting.

Within the JAE, opinions differed regarding the proper approach to be taken in the testimony. Senator was especially troubled by the apparent schizophrenia of many Zionist spokesmen who informed Jews that the long-range Zionist goal was a total of 5 million olim, while at the same time advising the British that the Zionists' "real" goals were considerably less. In the end, Senator said, "neither will believe us."[96]   Insofar as Senator's critique was a commentary on Zionist public relations tactics, he was correct. Zionist leaders of all stripes, except Jabotinsky, had always expressed two sets of goals: they sought to appear moderate to the British and more demanding to Jewish audiences. At this stage, Senator's words were more valuable as a warning against repeating the practice than as an evaluation of past behavior. In any case, none of the JAE members seem to have heeded his warning, and at least for the British, Senator's prediction appeared to have come true.

Menachem Mendel Ussishkin proposed that the Zionists convene a counter-commission, consisting of representatives of those nations that had sponsored the Balfour Declaration and the Mandate, but his proposal was rejected.[97] After further discussion, three different approaches were considered by the JAE: (1) one that would exclusively defend the Yishuv against Arab charges; (2) one that would exclusively air Jewish complaints; and (3) one that would adopt some elements of both approaches and demand that the British fulfill the terms of the Mandate.[98]

In the end, the JAE adopted the third position. Ben-Gurion agreed that, despite the Zionist commitment to the Mandate, the League of Nations document should "neither be seen as the basis nor the source of Jewish rights in Eretz-Israel."[99] In his estimation, Jewish rights had three bases, and the acceptance of all of them was vital to the Jewish future: the historical connection of Jews with the land; Jewish suffering in the diaspora; and the socioeconomic realities of the dynamic Yishuv.[100]

Although the Zionist testimony at the Peel Commission hearings has already been analyzed, no effort has been made to view the Zionist arguments in the context of the program of rescue aliya. Yet the relationship is obvious in almost every statement made by the various Zionist representatives. Thus, Weizmann placed much emphasis on the refugee aspect of the Jewish problem in the memorandum he wrote on behalf of the JAE for the Commission. For Weizmann, the Jewish problem was that of homelessness. European Jews were, he wrote, "doomed to be pent up in places where they are not wanted, and for whom the world is divided into places where they cannot live in peace, and places into which they cannot enter."[101] The suffering of German Jewry was not the primary threat facing Jewry: "The German tragedy," wrote Weizmann, "is of manageable proportions, and moreover, the German Jews are stronger; they can resist the onslaught much better."[102] Of far more pressing importance was the fate of East European — especially Polish — Jewry. Though suffering both from direct and indirect antisemitism as well as from intense economic distress, the Polish Jews were virtually unable to find a safe haven. For Weizmann, the only solution was the creation of a Jewish national home — the long-term goal of Zionism and the sole purpose of both the Balfour Declaration and the Mandate.[103]

Such an entity did not have to be a sovereign state, although the fulfillment of Zionist goals required a Jewish majority in Palestine.[104] But four practical problems stood in the path of fulfillment: immigration, land, labor, and self-government. Regarding immigration, Weizmann noted that the Zionists had accepted the principle of economic absorptive capacity, even though it was disproportionate to the needs of the Jewish masses. Basically, such a concept was inconsistent with the idea of a national home, since a home "is a place to which everyone may return freely."[105]   Even though the Arab revolt had changed the atmosphere in Palestine, at least from the British perspective, Weizmann concluded his memorandum by demanding that the British fulfill all their promises and obligations.

In his direct testimony at the commission, during the eighth public session, held on November 25, 1936, Weizmann continued to testify on three inter-related themes: first, that the Jewish problem could not be solved by the Jews themselves but required the participation of the entire world. According to Weizmann, Palestine would play the decisive role in any long-term solution to Jewry's needs.[106]   Second, against claims of overpopulation in Palestine, Weizmann argued that no one really knew what population could actually be absorbed. He also stated that all the key documents relating to Britain's commitments toward the Jewish national home referred to Transjordan, which, he maintained, should be opened for Jewish colonization but which had been closed to the Jews since 1922.[107]

On the other hand, Weizmann accepted the premise of economic absorptive capacity as a determinant of yearly aliya rates, but only if it was used as an objective and fair criterion. As an argument against the proposed Legislative Council, Weizmann suggested that the Palestine administration grant both Jews and Arabs more municipal self-government and local autonomy.[108]

Although Weizmann did not explicitly mention cantonization at this hearing, his position on municipal autonomy, which he saw as a first step to cantoniza-tion, is strikingly similar to a proposal for the division of Palestine into Jewish, Arab, and British cantons that he discussed in London during June and July 1936 with British politicians and with Nuri Said, the foreign minister of Iraq. Weizmann's cantonization proposal included British guarantees for the aliya of 700,000 Jews, to be spread over twenty years. He did not delve into the implication of his proposal: the maintenance of an Arab majority in Palestine. Weizmann believed that his proposal would relieve one-third of the Jewish problem in eastern and central Europe. The remaining homeless Jews, ap-proximately 2 million in Weizmann's estimate, would need refuge elsewhere.

When first presented, Weizmann's proposal proved unacceptable to many JAE members, but few supported Ben-Gurion's call to remove him from office. For Ben-Gurion, Weizmann's immigration proposal was nothing less than scandalous, since Polish Jewry alone numbered more than 3 million souls. Although Weizmann's proposal was a bold move, it fell short of Ben-Gurion's simultaneous proposal for 1 million olim in ten years, and even shorter of Jabotinsky's appeal for 1.5 million olim during the same period of time. Ben-Gurion's and Jabotinsky's proposals would have guaranteed the creation of a Jewish majority and would have gone far to relieve the distressed

Jewish communities of eastern Europe. Weizmann's proposal even fell slightly short of a British proposal made by Colonial Minister William Ormsby-Gore to allow 50,000 olim per year for fifteen years (which still would have resulted in a Jewish minority). In 1937 the Peel Commission report mentioned — but rejected — cantonization.[109]

After Weizmann, a virtual panoply of JAE figures testified: Shertok, Senator, Ruppin, Eliyahu Epstein, and Maurice Hexter, among others. In their joint testimony on immigration, Shertok and Senator concentrated on technicalities rather than ideas. They did speak of the great distress of European Jewry, admitting that the JAE used the persecution of Jews in Poland, Rumania, and Germany to demand a fuller measure of immigration requests. However, Jewish distress did not cause the JAE to "inflate" schedule requests beyond Palestine's economic absorptive capacity.[110] According to Shertok and Senator, reduction of the Labor schedule threatened Palestine's prosperity.[111] Indeed, Shertok argued that the British had created an artificial labor shortage in Palestine that could be solved only by employing Arab labor.[112] In turn, the higher standard of living that Palestine's Arab population enjoyed attracted large numbers of illegal Arab immigrants. The Commission dealt extensively with this topic during testimony by Shertok and Epstein on December 8, 1936.[113]

Further testimony by the leaders of the Va'ad Leumi, the Histadrut, and the JA continued to hammer home the basic Zionist contention that the Mandate should be maintained and that the Yishuv should be granted the fullest possible opportunity to continue growing. Leonard Stein testified on the legal ramifications of the Balfour Declaration and the Mandate, concluding: "The administration is to do something positive. That positive thing is to facilitate Jewish immigration under suitable conditions."[114] Stein also concluded that cantonization would be inconsistent with the Mandate, at least insofar as any division of Palestine along national lines would be discriminatory, since Jews would be unable to immigrate, buy land, or settle in the Arab canton (de facto if not de jure).[115]

Ben-Gurion, who testified during the forty-ninth public session in Jerusalem on January 7, 1937, ended the JA's presentation. Declaring the Bible as Jewry's mandate, he strongly defended the Jewish people's historical right to Palestine.[116] In his public testimony, Ben-Gurion supported the Mandate's continuation and campaigned against Jewish statehood, saying that Zionists did not wish to be placed in a position where they could dominate and then persecute the Arabs.[117]

The implication of Ben-Gurion's public testimony was much the same as that of other Zionist leaders. This position was forced upon Ben-Gurion by the reality that a majority of his colleagues still supported Weizmann's position or, as in the case of Berl Katznelson, still clung to Weizmann out of respect for his ability to influence the British. From Ben-Gurion's private

testimony and other sources, however, it becomes clear that he actually supported an almost contradictory position: that the Jews would accept termi-
nation of the Mandate and the creation of a sovereign Jewish state. In his in
camera testimony, Ben-Gurion also called for schedules sufficiently large to
permit the aliya of 4 million Jews in twenty years.

Throughout his testimony, both public and private, Ben-Gurion seems to
have attempted to manipulate the Commission. He sought to maneuver it into making an offer for which he could claim responsibility if it proved popular
among Jews, or which he could repudiate if it proved unpopular. The
Commission members evidently saw through Ben-Gurion's hairsplitting, however, and negatively contrasted his testimony to Weizmann's.[118] Yet in the
end they did exactly what Ben-Gurion hoped they would, offering the Jews
sovereignty in a partitioned Palestine.

The paradox of Ben-Gurion's arguing for one set of goals publicly, while
hoping for a completely different outcome privately, arose from his fear that
the British would reject any call for sovereignty that originated with Zionist
sources, and the corollary, that the result of such rejection would inevitably be
an end to aliya. This, in turn, would result in Zionism's erosion and ultimate
evapora-tion, along with the Yishuv's withering.[119] Recognizing that after
going through the motions of hearing Jewish and Arab testimony, the British
government would act in accordance with their own strategic interests, Ben-
Gurion hoped that Arab rejection of parity with Jews and the impracticality
of cantonization would lead the British to support the Zionist position on
Palestine. He hoped that ultimately the British would offer sovereignty to the
Jews as a way to cement their strategic position in the Middle East.[120]

For the time being, only Jabotinsky publicly contemplated a sovereign
Jewish state. He adopted an approach to the issue that was different from
that of Ben-Gurion, whose privately held position did not reflect official Mapai
policy. True to his long-held position, Jabotinsky demanded creation of a
sovereign, autonomous Jewish state on both sides of the Jordan River. He
left room for negotiations with the British, however, over the exact extent of
sovereignty beyond "some indispensable amount of self-government in inner
affairs."[121] Jabotinsky also denied that Jewish sovereignty would displace
Arabs: to the contrary, he argued that there was ample room in the whole of
Palestine for as many as 2 million Arabs, in addition to millions of Jews.[122]
Unlike the JAE members, however, Jabotinsky explicitly spoke of the pressing
need for an immediate rescue of European Jewry. During his testimony, he
spoke at length about the rapidly deteriorating situation in the diaspora:

> We have got to save millions, many millions. I do not
> know whether it is a question of re-housing one-third of
> the Jewish race, half of the Jewish race, or a quarter of
> the Jewish race; I do not know, but it is a question of

> millions. Certainly the way out is to evacuate those
> portions of the Diaspora which have become no good,
> which hold no promise of any possibility of a livelihood,
> and to concentrate all those refugees in some place which
> should not be a diaspora, not a repetition of the position
> where Jews are an unabsorbed minority, within a foreign
> social, or economic, or political organism.[123]

Attaining sovereignty and a Jewish majority in Palestine would be only the beginning:

> I am going to make a 'terrible' confession. Our demand
> for a Jewish majority is not our maximum; it is our mini-
> mum; it is just an inevitable stage if only we are allowed
> to go on salvaging our people. The point when the Jews
> will reach in that country a majority will not be the point
> of saturation yet, because with 1,000,000 more Jews in
> Palestine today you could already have a Jewish majority,
> but there are certainly 3,000,000 or 4,000,000 in the East
> who are virtually knocking at the door asking for
> admission — i.e. for salvation.[124]

Although he, like the Labor Zionists, spoke in terms of "salvation," in Jabotinsky's view this "humanitarian" element distinguished him from other, "spiritual," Zionists. He defined the view of the spiritual Zionists "as the desire for self-expression, the rebuilding of a Hebrew culture, or creating some 'model community of which the Jewish people could be proud.'"[125] Al- though publicly respectful of the spiritual position, Jabotinsky utterly rejected it, seeing "spiritual Zionism" as a "luxury" under contemporary conditions.[126]

On the issue of Zionist-Arab relations, Jabotinsky remained similarly un-equivocal. He claimed, to the apparent chagrin of the Commission members, that the lack of intercommunal peace was Britain's fault. Jabotinsky explained that by prevaricating in their support for the Zionist goals that the British government had accepted as legitimate, the Palestine administration had inculcated in the minds of the Arabs a belief that British support for Zionism was shallow and that pro-Zionist declarations or actions were undertaken under duress. The Arabs' past outbursts had been rewarded, rather than punished, and had culminated in the revolt, necessitating the creation of the Peel Commission.[127] To regain peace and to guarantee a peaceful future, Jabotinsky concluded, the British had to make their support for the legitimate goals of Jewry abundantly clear via a new policy that would encourage aliya and grant sovereignty to the Jewish national home.[128]

Although Jabotinsky was propounding an unequivocally maximalist position before the committee, there is evidence that he was willing to keep open options that would fulfill the basic Zionist goals while also securing the British position in the Middle East. All he sought at this stage was a Jewish majority in Palestine and the possibility of rescuing tempest-tossed Jewry. For that reason Jabotinsky did not explicitly state the extent of sovereignty beyond "the essential minimum of statehood."[129] In a letter that he wrote to Benjamin Akzin, director of the NZO Political Department, Jabotinsky expressed a willingness to accept the further partition of Palestine under certain circumstances. Specifically, he stated that he would accede to partition if sufficient territory were granted to the Jews on both sides of the Jordan River permiting a massive settlement campaign.[130] This territory could then become the Zionist "Piedmont" that would lead to an ultimate reunification of all of Eretz-Israel under Jewish control. Although Jabotinsky founded this position on the assumption that the British would actually carry through the partition scheme, he predicted that the Mandatory administration lacked the will to carry it out.

Jabotinsky's flexibility must be viewed in context. His willingness to accept another partition (after Transjordan had been removed from the Mandate by the Churchill White Paper of 1922) was based solely on the need to offer immediate assistance to European Jewry. If rescue could be accomplished only by sacrificing territory, then, in his view, rescue took precedence. Yet this flexible attitude was only fleeting, since Jabotinsky did not see any evidence of such British intent. On the other hand, Jabotinsky was uncompromising in his attitude toward the JAE and the leadership of the WZO. Asked to respond to the position espoused by the JAE, he replied with a twofold criticism. First, he said, the JAE and WZO were based on a paid franchise (the shekel), rather than on the universal suffrage of all Zionists. The implication of Jabotinsky's position was that the JA and WZO leadership could not claim to be the legitimate representatives of world Jewry, since they were self-appointed.[131] This criticism was true, insofar as the shekel was a paid franchise, although it is not clear that universal suffrage would have translated into greater support for Zionism among communities where the WZO was relatively weak. Jabotinsky's second point of contention was that the JAE lacked a blueprint regarding Palestine's future.[132] He aired only one specific grievance: that the JAE was, once again, refusing to distribute immigration certificates for members of Betar.[133] Jabotinsky concluded his testimony with an impassioned plea that the British fulfill the terms of the Mandate. A Jewish national home, he asserted, would be complete when 51 percent of the population was Jewish. Such a goal was not only plausible and fairly simple to attain, but it was the demand of the hour for both the Jews and the British Empire.[134]

Following Jabotinsky was Josiah Wedgwood, a prominent British supporter of Ha-Zach, member of Parliament, and the Privy Councillor. Wedgwood's testimony was largely technical and concentrated on the discrimination against Jews in the Mandatory government.[135] With his testimony, the commission adjourned and began to prepare its report.

The wait until publication of the Peel Commission report was a tense one for the Zionists. Shertok expressed fear that the High Commissioner would see a need to defend his own prestige and prove his policies justified by halting all Jewish immigration.[136] These fears appeared well founded when Wauchope announced a Labor schedule of only 220 certificates for the period between June and September 1937. This schedule represented only 3.1 percent of the JAE request for 7,034 certificates. Dismayed by the diminished schedule, Ben-Gurion and Shertok protested, only to discover that Wauchope considered this a reasonable compromise, since his advisers had suggested granting no schedule at all.[137] The JAE members also failed to obtain a refund of 1,350 certificates previously withheld by the High Commissioner as punishment for illegal immigration, even though the British administration had agreed that the punishment was excessive.[138] As aliya was steadily strangled, the concept of rescue aliya was rapidly reduced to a meaningless shell, with a resulting negative impact on the Yishuv's fragile economy.[139]

THE PARTITION PLAN

In addition to the severe curtailment of aliya, the ongoing Arab revolt did not afford the Zionists much optimism. Despite the institution of martial law on June 13, 1936, Arab assaults continued and mushroomed into major attacks on Jewish settlements. In February 1937, the Jewish quarter of Tiberias was attacked, and in May, men of Fauzi Al-Kaukji's Arab Liberation Army, who had infiltrated Palestine from Syria, launched all-out assaults on kibbutzim Tel-Yosef and Tirat Zvi. In both instances the attacks were deflected only with great difficulty by Hagana forces that were stretched to their limit.[140]

A training exercise by British and Jewish police that Shertok viewed seemed promising, but his optimism rapidly dissipated when Arab attacks on Jewish settlements continued with increasing intensity.[141] Zionist fears grew when ominous reports were received of the Mufti of Jerusalem's plans to organize a pan-Arab army in Syria and Iraq.[142] In the interim, a sense of mistrust arose between the authorities and the Jews. On May 31, 1937, nervous British police officials blamed Jews for an attempt on the Mufti's life. As it turned out, the Mufti's bodyguards misreported the event, which the British blew out of proportion. This pure fabrication sheds light on the ambivalence of the British authorities toward the Hagana, despite havlaga.[143] In response to the Hagana's apparent lack of commitment and the failure of restraint, Jabotinsky renewed his call to end to havlaga, ob-serving that the policy was counterproductive. His opponents, however, held firm.[144]

When the Peel Commission finally issued its report on June 22, 1937, the state of the Yishuv could be summarized as beleaguered, demoralized, and pessimistic. The publication of the report changed the equation and touched off a new debate among Zionists. Just before the actual announcement of the Peel Plan, the JAE became aware of its contents through both official and unofficial sources. The proposed borders were reported in advance; Shertok's sources, however, underestimated the size of the proposed Jewish state.[145] On the other hand, the JAE did not underestimate Arab opposition to partition, although most of its members considered such opposition only marginally important.[146] On the eve of publication, June 21, 1937, the Va'ad ha-Poel ha-Zioni met and rejected both partition and cantonization, since these would restrict the legitimate growth of the Jewish national home. Having thus undermined the JAE's position, the Va'ad ha-Poel then undermined its own position, instructing the JAE to "do everything in its power to ensure that any solution put forward by the Commission and accepted by [the] government should be the least harmful and, in the circumstances, the most advantageous to Jewish interests."[147]

The following day, the Commission issued its report, calling for partition of Palestine into three zones. The Jewish state would include Palestine's coastal plain from a point some twenty-five kilometers south of Rehovot northward to the border of French-controlled Syria-Lebanon. This zone, however, would include neither Jaffa nor a ten-kilometer passage representing the British zone to Jerusalem. In the north, the Jewish state would include the entire Emek region except for Beisan. The fate of territory on the eastern bank of the Jordan River north of the Sea of Galilee was not clearly established. In all, the Jews received less than one-third of the territory west of the Jordan, with the Arabs and British receiving more than two-thirds. All territories not included in the Jewish state and not retained by the British were planned as part of the Arab state.[148]

Two Zionist parties immediately declared themselves unalterably opposed to the partition: Mizrachi and Ha-Zach. Mizrachi's objections were based on religious considerations: the land of the divine covenant with the Jewish people could not be divided.[149] Ha-Zach's opposition was based on considerations that directly impacted on Jabotinsky's position regarding rescue. Jabotinsky had argued that the territory promised to the Jews would be insufficient to absorb the millions of Jews in need of rescue. Although he briefly toyed with the idea of partition, at least in private, he publicly rejected the notion out of hand, for two reasons: utility and honor. In a statement issued by the NZO presidency shortly after the announcement of the Peel Plan, Jabotinsky rejected partition since it would "fail to solve the Jewish problem," while constituting "a serious breach of international obligations." Partition, he said, would fail to bring peace to Palestine, and thus would fail to fulfill any utilitarian function, even from the British perspective.[150]

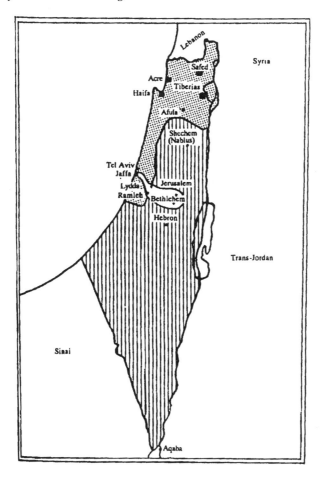

Map 6.1: The Peel Partition Plan
Source: *Palestine Royal Commission: Report, 1937*, London: HMSO, 1937

Ha-Zach took up the legality of partition in a memorandum to the League of Nations Permanent Mandates Commission in Geneva. Maintaining that partition was "unacceptable from the point of view of the principles for which the League of Nations stands," the NZO memorandum called for an objective agency — presumably the Permanent Mandates Commission — to investigate both the legality and the utility of the Peel Plan.[151] Repeating the gist of Jabotinsky's testimony at the Royal Commission hearings, the memorandum added another dimension: the creation of the proposed Jewish state would increase antisemitic agitation throughout eastern Europe, since antisemites would expect Jews to evacuate immediately to the new Jewish state despite insufficient space there for the millions of Jews rendered homeless. Having created a new "Pale of Settlement," albeit with the veneer of Jewish sovereignty, partition could make the Jewish world as a whole less, rather than more, secure.[152]

As an alternative, Jabotinsky proposed the evacuation scheme he had first put forth in 1935, now named the "Ten-Year Plan." This variant plan contained five substantive components: (1) maintainance of the Mandate, with only minor adjustments; (2) the opening of Transjordan for Jewish settlement; (3) a "Jewish National Loan" campaign to reclaim cultivatable but unused lands on both banks of the Jordan River; (4) creation of an immigration regime to absorb 150,000 Jews per year; and (5) sovereignty after ten years, when a Jewish majority existed.[153]

Jabotinsky continued to hammer away at the inter-related themes of evacuation, security, and honor for more than a year. An increasing tone of desperation can be sensed in some of his words at the time. Partition and the subsequent end of Mandatory law in the Arab state would in effect mean that Jews could live in those territories only by sufferance, not by right. Zionism would experience not a new beginning, but an end. The hope of expanding the area of the Jewish state, whether by occupying the Negev (whose status was not explicitly laid out in the original Peel report, although implicitly the area would fall into the Arab state) or through dreams of military conquest, was a false one. In one of his essays, Jabotinsky argued that partition would be a "death-blow" to aliya, and that, therefore, "no Jew can sign any agreement relating to partition."[154] In a speech, he called for renewed Zionist activity based on mass aliya to a united Palestine.[155] Accordingly, the only logical Zionist policy would call for evacuation, not partition.[156]

Realizing that the British might demand something in return from the Zionists in order to guarantee Imperial interests, Jabotinsky, who as late as the eve of the sellout of Czechoslovakia (September 1938) could not conceive of Britain totally reneging on a solemn promise, again raised the suggestion that Palestine become Britain's seventh dominion.[157] Recognizing the danger inherent in the Peel partition plan more clearly than others, Jabotinsky therefore sought to defeat this new threat to Zionism. He worked tirelessly with the Ha-Zach Political Committee in London and with the party's representatives in Geneva to have the partition scheme overturned. But his actions met with only limited success, and, in 1938, when the British government also dropped the partition plan, the replacement policy did not, in fact, prove to be any more pro-Zionist.[158]

Tnuat Bnei Chorin, a short-lived Revisionist group, espoused a position similar to Jabotinsky's. According to one of the group's pamphlets on the partition plan, the international ramifications of Nazi and Nazi-sponsored persecution of Jewry left only one option: a Jewish state in an unpartitioned Palestine. The author of the pamphlet rejected the possibility of finding temporary havens: none existed, and even if they did, a temporary haven, by definition, could not offer a permanent solution.[159] Only a Jewish state in Palestine could ensure that today's haven would not become tomorrow's new refugee problem. The pamphlet contained a fearful prophecy:

> Thus the problem simmers down to this: the eventual
> annihilation of about six million Jews of Central and
> Eastern Europe or — after a radical change of the
> British policy with regard to Palestine in favour of the
> Jews — their transfer to Palestine, their repatriation to
> the land of Israel so that they might reclaim and re-
> construct the land on both sides of the Jordan as a
> solution for themselves and with goodwill towards all.[160]

Another Tnuat Bnei Chorin booklet, entitled *A New Deal for Palestine*, also suggested that Palestine become a self-governing dominion and a member of the British Commonwealth.[161] Here too, the primary justification for Jewish sovereignty was Jewish need: a temporary refuge could not provide long-term security for German and eastern European Jewry.[162]

Yet for precisely the same reason, Ben-Gurion came to support partition, although he was not an unequivocal supporter of the Peel Plan. Ben-Gurion, like Jabotinsky, sought free Jewish settlement in all parts of Eretz Israel, including Transjordan. His disagreement with Jabotinsky — according to his own analysis — was over realism versus idealism: should the Jews accept what could be gained now by negotiation or refuse a deal in the hope that they might gain more from the British (or Arabs) in the future?[163] In light of the Nazi threat to Jewry, Ben-Gurion was convinced that a "wait and see" policy could only lead to disaster. At one point in the partition debate Ben-Gurion had stated that "in a world without evil" Jews would have to reject partition. Under the circumstances, however, Jewry had no choice but to accept whatever could be attained in the short-term in order to guarantee continued aliya.[164]

Although almost all of Ben-Gurion's references are oblique, it is clear that Nazism weighed heavily upon his thoughts. In a conversation with Pinhas Rutenberg before the Peel Plan was made public, but after the JA had already become aware of its contents, Ben-Gurion stated that Zionists must ensure that the area of the Jewish state included "a large enough territory to absorb a major immigration wave, of which a substantial part will settle on the land."[165] One week before the Peel Plan was published Ben-Gurion met with JA and WZO leaders in London. Whereas Berl Katznelson argued that Jewish activists should concentrate their efforts in the United States in the hope of cancelling the partition plan altogether, Ben-Gurion argued that the main public relations effort ought to be in London and ought to be predicated on the need to enlarge the Jewish state's borders.[166]

After analyzing all the factors involved in partition, Ben-Gurion admitted that the disadvantages of the Peel Plan far outweighed its advantages.[167] The inadequate borders granted to the Jewish state were especially problematic, and they represented a likely cause for a future war between the Arab and Jewish states.[168] Thus, although Ben-Gurion supported partition and Jewish sovereignty, he did so reluctantly.[169] Despite his misgivings, he heavily weighed the eastern European Zionists' enthusiastic support for a sovereign state, irrespective of its actual borders. For these proponents of partition, Jewish sovereignty meant the end to all restrictions on aliya. They made partition the centerpiece of any future plans related to rescue aliya.[170]

Further encouragement for Jewish statehood came from an oblique source: the High Commissioner. The virtual strangulation of aliya, especially after the May 1937 mini-schedule, raised fears among some JA leaders that very little time remained to accomplish Zionist goals, and convinced them that they must act quickly and decisively. The revelation that the Peel Commission had seriously considered only two options — partition or the imposition of a "political maximum" for aliya — did nothing to reassure proponents of the scheme.[171] Further impetus to act quickly, while the offer of a Jewish state still had validity, came from the north. On June 22, 1937, the same day that the Peel report was published, the Syrian nationalists' provisional government, then engaged in a rebellion against the French colonial regime, announced its intention to annex Palestine.[172]

THE TWENTIETH ZIONIST CONGRESS

The Zionists' accumulated fears and hopes, as well as their need to discuss the few remaining alternatives, came to the fore at the Twentieth Zionist Congress, held in Zurich between August 3 and 16, 1937. Weizmann opened the session with a keynote address that summarized recent events in Palestine and in central and eastern Europe. "Living conditions for tens of thousands of Jews in Central and Eastern Europe," Weizmann stated, "are beyond description."[173] Weizmann also touched on the partition scheme, promising a more detailed analysis later. He finished by saying that only a limited time remained to act, because the Palestine administration had already announced the establishment of a "political maximum" capping Jewish immigration at 8,000 per year (one-third less than proposed by the Peel Commission) for the duration of the Mandate.[174]

Weizmann strongly supported partition in his second address to the Congress, on the evening of August 4, 1937. In it, he requested a resolution empowering the WZO Executive to conduct further negotiations on the Peel Plan that would ultimately result in a Jewish state.[175] In view of his juxtaposition of the three themes of rescue, aliya, and partition, it is clear that

Weizmann linked them together. So did Ben-Gurion and Shertok, who also supported partition. Ben-Gurion emphasized the rescue angle, stating:

> Jewish need is very great. The pressure of masses of Jews
> as well as the pressure of countries that want to get rid
> of them is constantly growing stronger. The Jewish
> problem was never as acute as in these days, and outside
> of Palestine, there is no hope to look forward to. The
> world is barred against us.[176]

Quite perceptively, considering that his words were spoken a year before the Munich sellout of Czechoslovakia, Ben-Gurion predicted a new world war and warned of dire consequences for Zionism if the WZO were to "overlook the serious dangers which are bound up with the growing acuteness of international complications." This also led him to fear for the diaspora, and he predicted the possible cutoff of contact with other Jewish communities, paralleling the breakdown of communications with the Jews in Soviet Russia.[177] In view of the increasing Arab strength, Ben-Gurion said, Jews had to act immediately and forcefully. Thus, the transformation of Ben-Gurion's position was almost complete: in so many words he was now arguing for the evacuation scheme.

Ben-Gurion did not state that partition was good, but that it was necessary. Even he realized that the borders of the new state would not be adequate for the numbers of Jews seeking immigration. He explicitly rejected the rump state that the British were offering, but he hoped to negotiate for larger borders after the principles of partition and Jewish sovereignty were accepted. Moreover, Ben-Gurion was attracted to the idea of transferring the Arab population living in the area of the Jewish state to the Arab state. In the coastal plain alone, he estimated, such a transfer would free space for another 340,000 Jews. If all Arabs were removed from the Jewish state's territory, Ben-Gurion expected to be able to settle another 1 million Jews.[178] Only a sovereign Jewish state, in his view, could fulfill the need for mass aliya. Here Ben-Gurion appears to have borrowed (without attribution) some of Jabotinsky's rhetoric regarding mass immigration, even while publicly railing at Ha-Zach's leader's "demogoguery."

Ben-Gurion ended his address by calling for the addition of 1.5 million olim to the proposed Jewish state. The parallel to Jabotinsky's evacuation scheme, officially repudiated by the JAE, but increasingly a part of Ben-Gurion's Zionist platform since 1935, is clear. Indeed, Ben-Gurion reversed one of Jabotinsky's speeches on Arab-Jewish relations, saying that creation of a Jewish majority in even part of Palestine would break down the "stone wall" that faced the Yishuv.[179]

In opposition to the "yea-sayers," two Zionists stood out at the Congress as "nay-sayers": Ussishkin and Katznelson. Their significance increases upon recollection that the Revisionists did not attend the Congress at all. Contrasting Weizmann's apparent eagerness to accept the partition plan with the Executive's unwillingness to even consider the Endziel resolution at the Eighteenth Zionist Congress in 1933 (again Jabotinsky's idea, here used as a rhetorical tool), Ussishkin flatly rejected partition. "I must admit," he stated, "that I would be glad to support what [Weizmann] said. . . But my duty to my people, to my movement's ideals, and to my past, force me to say what I must."[180] Ussishkin then laid out his reasons for rejecting the Peel Plan: first, because he did not trust the British, and second, because partition would destroy the Zionist movement. "They [the British] have placed two choices before us: either to strangle our movement or to tear our homeland to shreds. And [we have] the task of advising them as to which we prefer: strangulation or dismemberment."[181]

Katznelson spoke in a similar vein, emphasizing the negative impact that Zionist acceptance of partition would have on the moral and ideological foundations of Zionism. Partition meant the surrender of Zionist values and, more significantly, the mortgaging of Jewry's future for a mirage.[182] He saw partition as denying the essence of Jewish rights in Palestine — contradicting both the Mandate and Ben-Gurion's assertion that the Bible, and not the Mandate or the Balfour Declaration, was the basis for Jewish rights.[183]

TIME AS AN ENEMY OF RESCUE ALIYA

Other opponents of partition included Selig Brodetsky, the political secretary of the JA London Executive, and almost all the members of Mapai's Siya Bet. Brodetsky felt strongly that Zionists should not mortgage the future because of current needs. Ideally, the JA should first increase the Yishuv's Jewish population by 1 million over ten to fifteen years, and then consider sovereignty. He concluded: "it is forbidden for us to accept a plan which is likely to build an iron wall around us in the next ten to fifteen years."[184]

The crux of the argument was not specifically the propriety of terminating the Mandate, nor was Jewish sovereignty the main issue, since it had always been an element in almost all of the Zionist ideologies. Both sides of the partition debate also used conditions in Europe in an almost identical fashion: those who supported partition did so because they saw a Jewish state as the sole means of reviving rescue aliya, while those opposing partition saw the borders of the proposed Jewish state as precluding any further large-scale aliya. It is clear ex post facto that the debate was academic: since the British did not carry out partition, it is impossible to know who was right in 1937.

What, then, were the supporters and opponents arguing over? At first glance, the main argument seems to be the question of maximalism versus minimalism that had plagued the Zionists throughout the Weizmann era. For advocates of halutzic aliya, the territory proposed for the Jewish state appeared sufficient to continue the slow but steady work of creating a Jewish majority in at least part of Palestine, one immigrant at a time.[185]

In contrast, the supporters of mass aliya, or even of evacuation, rejected the territory to be granted as woefully inadequate for the purpose of rescuing European Jewry.

While this explanation accounts for the positions adopted by most Zionist leaders, especially those who rejected partition, it does not account for all of them. While from mid-1934 onward, Ben-Gurion ceased to advocate halutzic aliya and began to advocate mass aliya, by 1937, he had come to advocate the virtual evacuation of European Jewry. Yet he strongly supported partition, thus manifesting a paradoxical combination of minimalism in relation to the British, and maximalism with regard to aliya. There is only one explanation for the paradox of Ben-Gurion's position: fear that time was running out for the Zionist endeavor. On at least two occasions prior to 1937, Ben-Gurion had publicly vented his fear: (1) during a secret meeting with representatives of the Yishuv's political parties after the British announced the severe reduction of the schedule for the period from October 1933 to March 1934, and (2) during a press conference on December 5, 1933. In both instances, the need to massively increase aliya led Ben-Gurion to the conclusion that the WZO must accomplish the maximum in as short a time as possible.[186] The partition debate merely lent new urgency to his fears, especially in view of the worsening situation in central and eastern Europe, a situation he (and others) described in almost apocalyptic terms.[187]

The skeptics, from Jabotinsky on the right to Katznelson on the left, believed that time was not an enemy. In their estimation, time was actually on Jewry's side, since eventually, the British would return to an appreciation of the moral and strategic advantages to be derived from a strong Yishuv. The skeptics too believed that only decisive action could save European Jewry, but they did not think that a partitioned Jewish state would offer anything more than token assistance.

The antipartition forces failed to convince the majority of the delegates at the Twentieth Congress. By a vote of 300 to 158, the Congress approved Weizmann's resolution. It gave the WZO Executive the authority to negotiate the partition of Palestine, while officially rejecting the borders for the Jewish state proposed under the Peel Plan. As matters turned out, however, time was not the Zionists' only enemy.

7

1937: Rescue Aliya in Crisis

DECLINING CONDITIONS IN EUROPE

The debate over the Peel partition plan represented a watershed in the history of rescue aliya. Zionists in eastern Europe saw the assumption of sovereignty by Jews, even in a rump state that represented only 10 percent of western Palestine, as the only way to continue rescue aliya in any systematic way, and lent considerable support for partition. Partition appeared preferable to those Zionists, since it offered a hope of peace and security, albeit a slim one.[1] Otherwise, the security situation in Palestine did not offer much chance for further Jewish settlement. Indeed, such concerns were expressed by many prospective olim (especially, though not exclusively, from Germany), partially explaining the dip in the rate of aliya in 1937.[2] Despite such concerns, Palestine remained central to the solution of the Jewish refugee problem, and as conditions worsened, it became even more central to the security of European Jewry.

That the condition of European Jewry fell in the years 1936 and 1937 may be seen by a few examples. On February 7, 1936, Polish Sejm deputy Janina Prystor introduced a "Humane Slaughter Bill" whose primary purpose was to ban shechita (Jewish ritual slaughter). Despite Jewish protests, the bill passed the Sejm by a clear majority on April 17 of that year. The law took effect on January 1, 1937, and virtually banned kosher slaughtering (except for chicken and other fowl) in the Polish republic. The Sejm's "Bakeries' Mechanization Bill" took effect the same day, and for all intents and purposes legislated Jewish bakeries out of existence.[3]

January 1, 1937, was an especially bad day for European Jewry. On the same day that the two pieces of antisemitic legislation came into force in

Poland, the Gestapo closed all Jewish-operated employment agencies in Germany, and the Romanian police raided the Bucharest offices of the Romanian Zionist Federation, the KKL, the KHY, and the Palestine Office, seizing numerous documents in addition to some money and temporarily paralyzing Zionist activities throughout Romania.[4] Almost a year to the day previously, a Romanian student member of the Garda de Fier (Iron Guard), Romania's premier fascist party, had attempted to assassinate Chief Rabbi Jacob I. Niemirower in Bucharest as he walked home from Sabbath services.[5] Finally, on January 4, 1937, Poland's universities reopened with a new round of antisemitic attacks by Endek youth and a renewed effort to institute "ghetto benches."[6] Antisemitism seemed to predominate throughout eastern Europe, threatening even greater distress for Jewry. This fact may easily be gleaned from the almost continuous stream of increasingly ominous reports from Europe published in the Yishuv's press.[7]

Steadily worsening conditions, combined with new currency export laws adopted by the Polish Sejm, gave further impetus to the Zionists advocating a clearing agreement with the Poles.[8] Although negotiations with the Poles had been carried out beginning in the spring of 1936, by 1937 agreement had not been reached, even on fundamentals. The Polish government viewed a clearing arrangement as an advantageous means of exporting a large number of unwanted persons (Jews) while also increasing product exports, yet it created numerous difficulties for negotiators. The Zionists, particularly JAE member Yitzhak Gruenbaum, saw the Poles' motivations as political; he believed that the Poles sought an agreement as a means to muzzle the Zionist opposition while permitting the virtual seizure of Jewish institutions in order to "oversee" the orderly transfer of Polish Jewry.[9] The Poles also sought to clarify the ways in which the JAE intended to increase aliya. The JAE responded by expressing a willingness to entertain proposals from the Polish government, but they did not offer guarantees that such proposals would be adopted.[10] These negotiations continued, with the Poles adding demands at virtually each session; in the end, no agreement was reached.[11]

Violent antisemitism made a dramatic return to Poland's public life in 1936 and 1937. A new party, the Oboz Narodowy Radykalny (National Radical Camp; ONR), played an especially important role in radicalizing Polish antisemitism. It aped Nazi-style actions and sought a comprehensive solution to the Polish Jewish "problem." To a degree, the government of the Colonels' regime took its cue from these antisemites, and the ONR members could claim, with some justification, that they directly influenced national policy even though they were not officially part of the government.

Antisemitic agitation, in turn, became Poland's systematic policy in an effort to reduce all social and economic tensions to a single issue. Thus, Polish antisemitism paralleled the policies pursued by both Tsarist Russia and the Third Reich. It may be subdivided into five broad categories of activity: (1) isolation of the Jewish minority; (2) cultural exclusion; (3) destruction of the Jewish economic position; (4) toleration of anti-Jewish terrorism; and (5) a process of breaking Jewish morale in order to drive Jews to emigrate.[12]

The march of events in Hungary and Romania was similar. In both, fascist parties — the Nyilaskeresztes Part (Arrow Cross) in Hungary and the Garda de Fier (Iron Guard) in Romania — rose to prominence after 1935 and closely modeled their Jewish policies on that of the Third Reich. The rise of the Octavian Goga-Alexander Cuza government in Romania in 1937 badly affected the Jewish population there. Toward the end of January 1937, the Goga government passed a series of antisemitic laws, that made the political climate "similar to the situation in Germany five years ago."[13] The Garda's agitation occasionally turned violent, although most Romanian politicians sought Jewish emigration rather than extermination. In 1938 the government dissolved all Jewish organizations except for the Zionist youth movements; the latter were not molested because they encouraged emigration.

Hungarian Jewry experienced much the same: Zionists were permitted to go about their business unmolested insofar as they worked for emigration. Socialist Zionists who worked for other goals in addition to emigration did so only at great risk.[14] In 1938, Hungary enacted a series of "Magyarized" Nuremberg Laws under direct pressure from Berlin, though more loopholes existed in the Hungarian legislation than in contemporary Germany.[15]

As in Germany during the earlier part of the decade, the new antisemitic assault in eastern Europe became the catalyst for a Jewish response. Once again emigration to Palestine became one of the major Jewish defense mechanisms. However, as in Germany, emigration from eastern Europe did not approach mass proportions, as may be seen in Table 7.1.

TABLE 7.1: Eastern European aliya Figures, 1933-1939

Country	Number of Olim	Percentage of Total Aliya
Austria	5,623	3.0
Bulgaria	948	0.5
Czechoslovakia	4,779	2.6
Hungary	1,107	0.6
Latvia/Lithuania	8,420	4.5
Poland	83,847	45.0
Romania	9,458	5.1
Soviet Union	2,473	1.3
Stateless/Unspecified	6,219	3.3

Source: David Gurevich (comp.), *Statistical Handbook of Jewish Palestine*, Jerusalem: Jewish Agency ofr Palestine, 1947, p. 100.

Total aliya from Poland amounted to slightly less than 3 percent of the Jewish population in the country. Even considering the limitations the British placed on aliya, and factoring in the possibility that establishment Zionists requested too few certificates for Polish Jewry, it is clear that a majority of Polish Jews were unwilling or unable to emigrate. This conclusion accords with the ideological picture of Polish Jewry, and, to a lesser degree, of Romanian and Hungarian Jewry as well. While Zionism played a major role in all of these communities, the Zionists did not dominate any one of them. Assimilationist Jewish gentry dominated the Jewish communities in both Hungary and Romania; in Poland the Bund, the Folkists, and Hasidic and ultra-orthodox groups still represented major sections of the Jewish population. The Zionist parties (taken together) were the largest Jewish parties in the diaspora, but this plurality was tenuous.[16] Indeed, a recent study has noted traces of what may be termed a defection from the Zionists toward the Bund in the last years of the Polish republic.[17]

All Polish non-Zionists rejected emigration to one degree or another. In direct opposition to the policies espoused by the Zionists, they emphasized remaining in Poland. The Bundists called this policy Daism ("hereism"). Emigration, in their analysis, was a sign of cowardice. To abandon the sites of nearly a millennium of Jewish history for what appeared to be a mirage in Palestine seemed inadvisable, at best.[18] What was true of the Bund also held true for the Folkists, whose primary ideologue, Simon Dubnow, consistently rejected Zionism as a solution to the Jewish problem.[19] In the second half of the 1930's, Dubnow modified his approach, although he continued to reject the Zionist goal of sovereignty. In "What Should One Do in Haman's Times," an essay published in 1939, Dubnow advocated emigration as a partial solution to the Jewish problem, specifically mentioning the need to find havens for Jewish refugees. He did not, however, give prominence to emigration: pride of place went to defending Jewish rights in the diaspora.[20] The same held true for the orthodox anti-Zionist party Agudas Israel. In 1942, while incarcerated in the Warsaw ghetto, Rabbi Simon Huberband, a leader of Zeirei Agudas Israel (the party's youth movement), wrote:

> The Gerer Rebbe (R. Avraham M. Alter) had a negative
> attitude toward the building of Eretz Israel, as did the
> majority of Hassidic rabbis in Poland. If the Gerer
> Rebbe would have decreed to his Hasidim — among
> whom there are thousands of rich industrialists and
> property owners — to settle in the land of Israel . . .
> then the Jewish settlement in the Holy Land and the
> Jewish community in Poland would have both been very
> different today. But the Gerer Rebbe did not issue such
> a decree.[21]

Thus, although steadily deteriorating, the Jewish situation in eastern Europe did not result in immediate pressure for evacuation until it was too late to actually effect it because of the severe limits the British placed on aliya.

GERMAN JEWRY IN THE ERA OF BLOODLESS CONQUESTS

At the same time as conditions in eastern Europe became increasingly unbearable, conditions in Germany appeared to have stabilized, if they did not improve. During 1936 and 1937 many observers, both inside and outside the Reich, assumed that the worst had passed, that the Nazi "hot-heads" had been silenced, and that a modus vivendi could be established permitting Jewish life to continue in Germany's new ghetto. For example, many of the public manifestations of antisemitism (such as the strict separation of Jews from Aryans in public places) were toned down in 1936 as a propaganda ploy during the Berlin Olympics.[22] This apparent reversal of Nazi policy proved transitory. All the old limitations on Jews, and many new ones, became operative soon after the athletes departed.[23]

Still, throughout 1936 and 1937, Nazi policy continued to emphasize emigration and the Aryanization of Jewish capital. As a result, most Jews — both in and outside Germany — remained fixed to a policy of refugee relief; here too, proposals for mass emigration did not seem necessary. While it is possible to criticize the short-sightedness of the German Jews, ex post facto, it is more important to understand the context in which the decision was made to concentrate on orderly emigration (as opposed to evacuation).

Germany, it will be recalled, still suffered from the effects of the economic depression when Hitler came to power in 1933. Nazi policies toward Jews in the first four years of the Reich were framed around the premise of removing the Jews from positions in German civil, political, and ecomonic life without creating too many obstacles for economic revival.[24] In fact, the Nazi regime had succeeded in reducing unemployment from a high of 6,013,612 in January 1933 to only 994,590 in December 1937. Military production accounted for most of the new jobs thus created, while the reintroduction of conscription in 1935 further reduced the number of workers still unemployed.[25]

During the same time period, Nazi foreign policy was capped with a series of spectacular, but bloodless, victories. On January 13, 1935, a plebiscite was held in the Saar — German territory placed under League of Nations control by the Treaty of Versailles — and the region returned to Germany. That same month, Hitler publicly announced the reintroduction of conscription and he renounced the limitations imposed on Germany by the Treaty of Versailles. In both cases actions that had been considered potential causi belli by the British and French went unanswered. In attempting to appease Hitler, the democracies hoped to avoid war but merely played into Hitler's hands.

Germany hosted both the Winter and Summer Olympics in 1936, the winter games held in Garmisch-Paternkirchen (Februry 6 to 16) and the summer games in Berlin (August 1 to September 9). The refusal of international sporting organizations to relocate the games, or to boycott them, implied either an unwillingness to punish the Reich for its antisemitic policies or even broad acceptance of Hitler's "New Order" in many circles.[26] The remilitarization of the Rhineland on March 7, 1936, in contravention of the Treaty of Versailles and the Locarno Pact, brought Germany another bloodless victory. Thus, by the end of 1936 Germany's diplomatic successes had created a new political reality in central Europe.

Why then were Jewish affairs relatively quiet in 1936 and 1937? On the simplest level it appears obvious that the Nazis were spending more effort on foreign policy in those two years and thus let the Jewish question remain fallow. Moreover, from the German government's perspective, the relative quiet did not translate into a complete halt in anti-Jewish policies. The most important policies regarding Jews — Aryanization of businesses and emigration — continued unabated.

The German Jews, of course, could not see that little had changed. 1933 had seen a flurry of antisemitic harassment and was followed by relative quiet in 1934. The introduction of the Nuremberg Laws in 1935 ushered in a new era of persecution, but from the victims' perspective the next two years were relatively quiet and thus there seemed no need for evacuation. In reality, 1937 represented a turning point in Nazi policies toward German Jewry; a new path to the goal of entjudung was to be found after 1938.

ZIONIST RESPONSES TO CHANGING CONDITIONS

Under the circumstances it is clear why, despite deteriorating conditions in Europe, most Zionists retained the belief that rescue plans needed fine-tuning, not significant modification. Thus, a January 17, 1936, scheme for continued German Jewish aliya operated on the assumption that slightly more than half of the 430,000 Jews still in Germany were "emigrationsfähig" — that is, able to emigrate. This group would require a planned emigration program spread out over ten years. The author of the scheme assumed that 150,000 of the 230,000, including an anticipated 10,000 young people, would enter Palestine, while the remainder would be absorbed elsewhere. Those unable to emigrate, approximately 200,000 in number, "must be left out of our considerations — at any rate for the time being."[27]

Because of the continuing financial problems experienced by Haavara, the backlog in Paltreu payments grew even greater and capitalist aliya dropped in 1937, resulting in renewed efforts to extend Haavara sales to Middle Eastern countries. Some members of the JAE supported such efforts, but a plurality of the WZO Executive (citing the decisions made at the Nineteenth Zionist Congress), in addition to the London Executive and American Zionists, did not.[28] Discussion of expanding Haavara sales, or of arranging some similar agreement for Jewish emigrants to other destinations, continued until 1939 but never resulted in actual sales.

The Yishuv's financial difficulties also continued. The aforementioned immigration scheme assumed the availability of between £P637,500 and £P677,500 ($3,187,500 to $3,387,500), an astounding sum for the resettlement of 15,000 Jews per year.[29] Even so, proposals for independent fund-raising in America were strongly resisted by the JAE, since they "did not take into account the real needs of the country" and were made, presumably, without informing the JAE.[30] Eliezer Kaplan supported such fund-raising efforts, but he emphasized the need to "do everything possible to ensure that the plans and their execution be carried out through the channels of the Jewish Agency."[31] An identical position was enunciated by the JAE in a January 26, 1936, cable to Louis Lipsky and Morris Rothenberg in New York.[32]

This apparent continuity of plans should not be seen as implying that no one was aware of the changed circumstances. In 1936 the Reichsvertretung, the Nazi-imposed Jewish "self-government," reported on the difficulties created for refugees and emigrants by a new exit tax imposed by the Nazis.[33] Early in 1936, the Histadrut Executive discussed the situation in Germany resulting from the Nuremberg Laws, and the increasing desperation of German Jews seeking any haven.[34] Similarly, at a Histadrut-sponsored conference on the absorption of German olim, all the speakers emphasized that one period had passed and a new period had begun. Joseph Sprinzak's keynote address was therefore of special importance, since for the first time he discussed the need for mass evacuation of Jews from both Germany and Poland. Sprinzak did not offer any specific proposals as to how mass immigration would be accomplished — that was not the immediate task of the conference. But this was the first time that a Histadrut leader spoke explicitly of evacuation before a Histadrut forum. In his closing remarks, Berl Locker emphasized that the next step after the conference was to draw up specific plans for future aliya-related work.[35] The Histadrut did not, however, follow up with a specific plan, at least not immediately; in any case, Histadrut support for aliya plans already under consideration was probably more useful to the JAE than any new plan which would only muddy already unclear waters.

Within Ha-Zach, too, a new appreciation of the needs of the hour could be felt. An internal Ha-Zach memorandum discussing the need for a Jewish emigration bank to finance the Ten-Year Plan (as the Evacuation Plan was now known) spoke in terms that were reminiscent of the Haavara agreement.[36] Like Haavara, Ha-Zach's liquidation bank would operate on the basis of debentures to be repaid by the sale of products imported into the Yishuv. Unlike Haavara, however, no guarantee was made as to how much capital would ultimately be returned (Paltreu guaranteed a minimum of £P1,000).

It is unlikely that the authors of the Ha-Zach proposal knew how closely their proposal resembled the Haavara agreement. To be sure, the economic features of the evacuation scheme were set out quite clearly in 1935 by both Zeev Jabotinsky and Dr. Stefan Klinger. By 1937 the need to inject Jewish capital into Palestine reached such obvious dimensions as to force Ha-Zach's leadership to adopt the same type of agreement (albeit with the Poles, not the Nazis) for which the JA had long been pilloried by Jabotinsky.[37] While JAE members had been appropriating Jabotinsky's rhetoric regarding evacuation, this is the first (and apparently only) instance when the Revisionist leadership borrowed one of the JAE's ideas.

Interestingly, Jabotinsky never mentioned Haavara in any of his speeches after 1937. It also appears that Joint Committee to Boycott German Goods propaganda slackened. Although this is an argument from silence, it is clear that Jewish distress had reached such proportions by 1937 that few other alternatives to Haavara seemed reasonable.

It is clear that the controversy within the WZO over Haavara abated, if not in 1935 after the Nineteenth Zionist Congress, then certainly by the end of 1936. In seeking means to further increase German Jewish emigration, some German Zionists began another series of negotiations with the Nazi government relating to the transfer of Jewish wealth outside of Palestine. These negotiations led to the establishment of a new organization, the International Trade and Investment Agency (INTRIA), a London-based stock company for investing German Jewish capital outside Palestine, primarily in Latin America. INTRIA's purpose was to ease the plight of Jewish emigrants and refugees by financing their economic absorption in new host countries.[38] The leaders of INTRIA assumed that by converting Haavaramarks (the currency used by Paltreu for debentures) into Travelmarks, and with an initial investment of RM2,500,000 (£P20,000, or $100,000), emigration could be increased by 20 to 25 percent per year. Given that nearly 115,000 Jews had left Germany between 1933 and 1935, with more than 20,000 leaving in 1936, a 20 percent to 25 percent increase would translate to an average of 7,500 more Jews able to emigrate every year. The fact that RM90,000,000 (£P7,500,000) — or enough capital for 7,500 A-I certificates — still could not be transferred, owing to backlogs of orders in Palestine, seemed to confirm INTRIA's proposals.[39] The Jewish Central Information Office in Amsterdam also voiced its strong support for INTRIA's initiative, since there was a building movement to clear out as many refugees as possible from temporary havens in western Europe to permanent accommodations in Palestine or the Americas.[40]

There was also opposition to INTRIA. As with Haavara, INTRIA's main opponents were Jewish leaders supporting the anti-Nazi boycott, including especially Rabbi Stephen S. Wise of the United States. Wise and other

American Zionists harbored the same fears regarding INTRIA that they had harbored against Haavara in 1933: that it would destroy Jewish unity, damage the anti-Nazi boycott, and become a tool used by the Nazis to force Jewry to become Germany's export agents. Further, INTRIA's success would only encourage other countries (notably Poland and Romania) to assault Jews in the hope of gaining access to new markets. Finally, since INTRIA was not organized as an component of the WZO or JAE, and had no direct connection with Haavara, it could easily be manipulated by its directors and backers for their own purposes. Assurances that since INTRIA would use Haavara banking facilities in Germany it would fall under (indirect) WZO supervision appeared hollow.[41] Horace Kallen criticized the INTRIA proposal as irresponsible, condemning as blackmail this Nazi use of emigration as an incentive for Jews to help Germany's economy.[42] Still, even the Haavara Executive supported INTRIA as a means of encouraging emigration from Germany. Paltreu offered RM10,000,000 (£P800,000) as seed money, on the stipulation that INTRIA agree never to compete with Paltreu.[43]

However, INTRIA floundered from its inception, because few Latin American countries desired massive Jewish immigration. Not even the potential benefit from increased German imports changed the attitude in Latin America, since most countries there already maintained close economic relations with Nazi Germany and fascist Italy. Yet, INTRIA did briefly seem to offer another avenue of rescue for German Jewry, during the December 1938 talks between George Rublee and Reichsbank President Hjalmar Schacht.[44]

RESCUE ALIYA'S FINAL DAYS

The slowing rate of aliya remained the Yishuv's primary problem. As seen in Table 7.2, the gap between Labor schedule certificate requests and grants grew during the first schedule period of 1937, and then resumed the previous rate of 20 percent.

TABLE 7.2: Labor (C) Schedule Requests, 1937-1939

Schedule Period	Requests	Granted	Percent
April-Sept. 1937	11,250	770	6.8
Oct. 1937-March 1938	3,000	1,780	59.0
April-Sept. 1938	-----	1,000	----
Oct. 1938-April 1939	4,625	1,000	21.6

Source: D. Ofer, *Derech ba-Yam: Aliya Bet be-Tekufat ha-Mandat*, Jerusalem: Yad Yitzhak Ben-Zvi, 1988, p. 15.

At this rate, Palestine's role in furthering the rescue of European Jewry was fast becoming moot. The British continued to grant the few available certificates at an extremely slow pace. The London Council for German Jewry made a proposal to speed some certificate requests and increase the number of persons qualifying for capitalist certificates by granting long-term loans of £P1,000 to any middle-class German Jew requesting one. This proposal was met with strong silence by Edward Mills, director of the Palestine government's Department of Immigration and Statistics.[45]

As a direct result, aliya bet once again became a factor in Zionist immigration policy. Late in 1936, Ha-Zach established an organization code-named Af-Al-Pi (Despite All) to oversee independent immigration. Af-Al-Pi, which operated primarily from Austria and Greece sent two ships from Pireus to Palestine in 1937 with a total of 69 passengers, all of whom landed safely. Seven sailings in 1938 by ships associated with Af-Al-Pi brought a further 1,934 ma'apilim.[46] Shortly after Af-Al-Pi began its operations, the Polish branch of he-Halutz also pressed for a resumption of aliya bet, gaining the support of a majority of the Kibbutz ha-Meuchad Executive.[47]

The JAE remained adamantly opposed to aliya bet, fearing that illegal actions of this sort might jeopardize the partition scheme.[48] Yet the JAE did feel constrained to once again raise the issue of legalizing ma'apilim already in Palestine, especially after rumors of an impending amnesty for Arab terrorists surfaced in April 1937 — in honor of King George VI's coronation.[49] Chief Rabbi Isaac Halevy Herzog added his name to the list of prominent personalities who advocated action on behalf of ma'apilim. Responding to Herzog, Moshe Shertok commented: "As of now, we have not attained sovereignty; all we can do is turn to the government with our demands and then return with them repeatedly."[50] Shertok's words could be taken as a council of despair — which they were, to a degree — but when the British attitude toward aliya is considered, they ring true.

Despite the JAE's lack of support, he-Halutz and Kibbutz ha-Meuchad continued to lobby for the JAE approval of ha'apala, gaining the approval of Eliyahu Golomb and the Hagana. Finally, in late 1937, a compromise formula was worked out by the Histadrut Executive whereby the Yishuv's official agencies would not support aliya bet, but also would not oppose it.[51]

After the Histadrut Executive's decision, the Hagana created its own agency for illegal immigration, the Mossad le-Aliya Bet, operating mainly from Italy. The Mossad commenced operations in the autumn of 1937, and sent its first ship, the *Atarto A* with 300 passengers from Bari in November 1938. The ship successfully evaded the British, landing at Sheafyim. In comparison, Af-Al-Pi or individuals working with that organization sent eleven ships with 2,694 passengers in 1938. The difference in numbers may be explained by noting that Af-Al-Pi had been working on illegal immigration for four years and thus had built up a network that the Mossad initially lacked. Moreover, Af-Al-Pi was relatively more significant to Ha-Zach at this time than the Mossad was to the JAE (a situation that changed during World War II).[52]

A number of private parties, not all of them acting out of altruism, also arranged independent aliya.[53]   Nevertheless, considerable difficulties persisted in undertaking aliya bet.   Both the Mossad and Af-Al-Pi experienced problems in finding, buying, and crewing suitable ships.   British policy remained firm: when an illegal immigrant ship was captured, it was returned to Europe.   Such was the fate, for example, of the *Sandu*, a private ship that sailed from Varna, Bulgaria, on March 15, 1939, with 720 ma'apilim aboard. Seized, the ship, crew, and passengers were deported to Romania.[54]

NEW EFFORTS AT ZIONIST UNITY

With Ha-Zach and the WZO once again appearing to work independently toward the same goals, the time seemed ripe for a new effort to forge a united Zionist front.   When the Jewish State Party, the faction of HA-ZOHAR that did not leave the WZO in 1935, requested a small loan to defray aliya-related debts, the JAE approved, granting the loan by a vote of 4 to 1 (with one abstention).[55]   This decision was later modified.   In February, the loan request was transferred to the Va'ad ha-Poel ha-Zioni, since it was a Zionist matter, thus freeing non-Zionists such as Werner D. Senator from participating in the decision.[56]   On February 10, 1937, the Va'ad ha-Poel approved the loan, which was made shortly thereafter.[57] Agudas Israel as well sought a new relationship with the JA, and expressed its position in a series of talks held during Yitzhak Gruenbaum's March 1937 visit to Poland.[58]

After the abortive Ben-Gurion-Jabotinsky agreements of 1934/1935, the prospect of concluding an intra-Zionist peace seemed bleak. This negative impression grew in 1935 as a result of the Revisionist withdrawal from the WZO and the creation of Ha-Zach. In 1936 and 1937, however, a number of peace efforts were made, connected with the convening of a round-table conference to adjudicate still-outstanding disputes.[59] Although previous efforts to initiate a Zionist peace conference had foundered, Jabotinsky continued to propose negotiations as a means of reuniting the Zionist movement. Some encouraging signs appeared after Jabotinsky met Chaim Weizmann in London on May 26, 1936.[60] In May 1937, Ha-Zach renewed its conference proposal, adding that the Revisionists also sought to establish a unified rescue policy for eastern European Jewry. Ha-Zach, however, enumerated four preconditions that the WZO had to accept before the conference could actually take place: (1) all topics relating to Zionism, Palestine, and the fate of European Jewry would be openly discussed; (2) no "official" stenographic protocol would be published, to prevent its use for party propaganda; instead, each party would keep minutes of the meetings and would publish them as they saw fit; (3) any negotiations would be recorded as they took place; and (4) a neutral chairman, acceptable to both parties, would be appointed before the first session.[61]

It is not clear how serious the offer from Ha-Zach really was. Throughout, Ha-Zach's Executive saw the goal of the conference as limited to attaining a coordinated Zionist policy; it had no intention of returning to the WZO. The JAE, on the other hand, sought the reunification of the WZO as its exclusive goal, and would agree to coordinate activities only if reunification were part of the agenda.[62] From the JAE's perspective, negotiations for the round table conference were thus only a means to attain an end, while Ha-Zach saw the conference as an end in itself.[63]

It must be added that Jabotinsky even expressed doubts about the usefulness of a conference while he was still negotiating its details. He felt that the failure of partition would lead to the downfall of the WZO leadership and collapse of its organization and that a new international Jewish body would then be established to oversee creation of a Jewish state. In this new organization, Jabotinsky expected Ha-Zach to dominate.[64]

While the negotiations with the WZO and JAE remained in their infancy, the Nessiut of Ha-Zach issued a press release that summarized the correspondence regarding the conference. They hoped that the publicity would force the JAE to act on the conference proposal, despite the possibility that such publicity might frighten the JAE members away.[65] Simultaneously, Ha-Zach also undertook a series of negotiations with Agudas Israel. Officially, they related to the round-table conference, but their goals could be misinterpreted as an effort to undermine the JAE's authority.

The negotiations with Aguda culminated in the publication of a joint letter on July 22, 1937, demanding that Aguda and all parties interested in building a Jewish home in Palestine, be included in the round-table conference.[66] By the time the letter was published, Ha-Zach's Nessiut had concluded that negotiations with the JA had broken down irrevocably, because of the JAE refusal to accept a neutral chairman. The Nessiut suggested two avenues for continued political work: an effort to reach an agreement with the WZO groups who opposed partition, and another to force the democratization of the JA by a public petition campaign.[67] The Nessiut also accused the JAE of secretly conspiring to force partition on the WZO even if the Congress vetoed the idea, and called upon members "to raise before Jews and non-Jews a protest against the Jewish Agency as at present constituted."[68]

The question of JAE refusal to participate in the conference is perplexing. Perhaps it was fear of the same type of opposition among the Labor Zionist rank and file that had caused the scuttling of the Ben-Gurion-Jabotinsky agreements in 1934.[69] Paradoxically, contacts between the JAE and Ha-Zach continued. Of special importance were the negotiations between the

JAE and Betar concerning the issue of aliya certificates for Betar members. These talks also harked back to the abortive agreement between Ben-Gurion and Jabotinsky, and began on a successful note. Initial contacts was made in March 1937 in Warsaw, in the form of a discussion between Gruenbaum and the Polish Betar leader, Aron Zvi Propes. Central to these negotiations was Gruenbaum's suggestion that Betar's collective right to immigration certificates from the JAE could be resumed if Betar agreed to place its Aliya Department under the supervision of the Warsaw Palestine Office. Propes tentatively agreed to this, and the JAE unanimously approved the contacts.[70] Further approval for full-scale negotiations came from the Twentieth Zionist Congress, and the talks were then transferred to London.[71]

Believing that the Revisionists were negotiating from a position of weakness, the JAE seems not to have taken the negotiations seriously, and clearly did not intend to reach an agreement. It revived another long-standing demand: that Betar and Ha-Zach cease their propaganda campaign against the KKL, and their occasionally violent disruptions of KKL and KHY rallies.[72] One such disruption took place in Warsaw at the end of January 1937, resulting in sixty arrests. Although not as common as one might think, on the basis of the JAE's constant references to the subject, such disruptions were a sore point in relations with the Revisionists. At this stage the talks abruptly ceased, although they resumed again that autumn.

With the failure of a new round of talks, the ideological battle between the JAE and Ha-Zach resumed, with the JA leaders making special efforts to counter what they saw as Ha-Zach misrepresentations of Zionist goals at the League of Nations.[73]

ALIYA IN THE SHADOW OF A "POLITICAL MAXIMUM"

Despite these sundry political maneuvers, fund-raising and aliya — either legal or illegal — remained the priorities of both the JAE and Ha-Zach. Throughout 1937, the JAE continued to emphasize legal immigration, while Ha-Zach concentrated on aliya bet. Chief Rabbi Herzog, on his own initiative but with the blessings of the JAE, sought a ruling from the British regarding the possible legalization of ma'apilim, but he was refused. The chief secretary of the Palestine administration did, however, promise that some exceptional immigrant certificates would be granted to the JAE for illegals employed in Palestine, on condition that the illegal in question first return to his/her country of origin (or, in the case of a refugee, to a neighboring country).[74] Against this concession, the High Commissioner wrote to Herzog encouraging the rabbi's opposition to fictitious marriages as a means of aliya bet.[75]

In July 1937, another avenue for aiding ma'apilim surfaced, when members of the JA Aliya Department staff consulted Shertok regarding the possibility of using the courts as a means of legalizing illegal immigrants. Shertok thought it inadvisable for the JA as a body to become involved in such cases, but he did not oppose efforts by attorneys to approach the courts — even those associated with the JA, but acting independently. However, he did express considerable skepticism about possible results.[76]

The possibility of legalizing ma'apilim, combined with increasing aliya bet and further British efforts to uproot illegal immigration, brought the issue of ha'apala back to the JAE in the summer of 1937. Again, the overwhelming decision was to oppose aliya bet.[77] At the Twentieth Zionist Congress, numerous speakers opposed aliya bet, fearing that it would compromise the partition scheme, derail the Jewish state even before it was established, and drive an unnecessary wedge between Great Britain and the Zionist movement.[78] Opponents of aliya bet especially railed at Jabotinsky: it was easy for him to argue for aliya at any price, since he did not have to grapple with the possibility of the British halting legal immigration. The Revisionists could afford to behave irresponsibly, but the JAE, which was responsible for more than just aliya bet, could not. Nevertheless, both aliya bet and efforts to legalize ma'apilim continued.

In a renewed attempt to gain the legalization of ma'apilim, Bernard Joseph, assistant director of the JA Political Department, discussed one element of the Peel report that had not yet received sufficient attention in Zionist circles: in June 1937 the Royal Commission had suggested that a temporary "political maximum" be placed on aliya, as a means of appeasing the Arabs. Under this scheme a total of 8,000 olim per schedule period would be permitted into Palestine until the actual partition.[79] According to Joseph, the rate of aliya reflected in the political maximum could only be attained either by ignoring the residence of the 40,000 "illegals" that the Palestine administration claimed were already in the Yishuv, or by legalizing them. This held true since, according to an anonymous marginal note added to the letter, "they were [already] taken into account in fixing previous schedules."[80]

While the "political maximum" was fated (in 1938 and 1939) to become the touchstone of a major Zionist-British confrontation over aliya, for the time being the JA's finances appeared to be the greater threat to continued rescue operations. The Yishuv's generally weak financial situation has already been noted. Matters improved somewhat in 1935 and 1936, but fund-raising remained a major concern for the JAE. In response to Arab violence in 1936 the Palestine Jewish Colonization Association (PICA), the Palestine arm of the Territorialist Jewish Colonization Association (ICA; founded in 1891 by Baron Maurice de Hirsch to aid Jewish emigration from tsarist Russia), began cooperating with the WZO and JAE in settlement projects. This new collaboration, which lasted until PICA disbanded in 1948, eased but did not solve the Yishuv's financial distress.[81] In response to an increasingly difficult situation, the Histadrut suggested a massive increase in KHY fund-raising efforts to obtain the capital needed for new roads, new settlements, and grants to urban industrial plants that would help absorb thousands of olim from central and eastern Europe.[82]

As summer turned into autumn, a renewed struggle over aliya loomed. When negotiations over the new schedule began, covering the period between October 1937 and March 1938, the JAE requested only 3,000 certificates. This small request was based on financial and economic hardship, but it also appears to have been based on an unusually optimistic assumption that conditions in Europe had settled down for the foreseeable future.[83] Although the request was by no means outlandish — in fact, it was timid — the British granted only slightly more than half of it, some 1,780 certificates (see Table 7.2). Furthermore, the administration began to behave as though the "political maximum" already reflected a permanent policy, rather than a temporary expedient. The JAE understood British policy on the basis of the grant of only ninety-five Youth Aliya certificates, compared with the more generous allowance previously.[84]

When the JAE met to discuss the new developments, two heated arguments developed relating to aliya in general and Youth Aliya in particular. The first involved Henrietta Szold's proposal to use a number of Labor certificates to make up the shortfall in Youth Aliya certificates. Although unanimously approved by the JAE, this proposal touched off a protest by Rabbi Judah L. Fishman regarding the settlement of a number of religious youth in Degania, a non-religious kibbutz. Szold blamed the mistake on inattention to details in the Berlin offices, and assured Fishman that the religious preferences of parents were scrupulously observed by Youth Aliya.

A dispute over capitalist aliya then developed. Agreeing that Youth Aliya should obtain certificates from the Labor schedule, Eliezer Kaplan did so only on condition that the JAE accept a stipulation not to harm capitalist aliya. The Mapai leader then took his non-Socialist colleagues — Senator, Hexter, Fishman, and Gruenbaum — to task for their apathy toward capitalist aliya, which he characterized as "at least as important as labor aliya."[85] Taken together with Mapai's support for Haavara and other forms of Capitalist aliya, the statement indicates that Mapai's position on aliya priorities was not limited to the Labor schedule. Both arguments also reflected the growing frustrations within the Yishuv. Unable to control immigration and facing an impossible situation in Europe, the JAE members responded to powerlessness by arguing among themselves.

Another sign of Zionist frustration may be detected in the transcript of a meeting between Weizmann, Nahum Goldmann, and Polish Foreign Minister Jozef Beck. Beck, who had asked for the meeting, requested a briefing on the aliya situation. Reassuring the Zionist leaders of continued Polish support for "securing for the Jews the largest immigration possibilities in Palestine," Beck nonetheless emphasized that his government did not consider Palestine as the sole solution to the Jewish problem and considered itself free to explore other mass emigration schemes. Inter alia, Beck also mentioned that Poland was considering an agreement with France to open Madagascar for Jewish settlement.[86] What the document does not say is almost as important as what it does say: at the same time that he was telling the Zionist leaders that he did not think that Palestine could offer a complete solution to the emigration needs of Jews, Beck strongly encouraged Jabotinsky to continue advocating the evacuation scheme. Other Polish leaders also played this cruel, two-faced game with the Zionist leadership. Beck expressed his great delight when Weizmann informed him that the WZO was willing to guarantee an aliya rate of 34,000 Jews per year after partition. The conclusion that Jabotinsky was being used by the Poles, even while he saw them as his most reliable ally, cannot be avoided.

Toward the end of September 1937, the JAE members finally fully understood the meaning of the British machinations regarding the "political maximum." The British government clearly aimed to reduce aliya to a level below economic absorptive capacity, in order to slow the Yishuv's growth. On October 2, a deputation composed of Senator and Joseph met with Mills. The JA representatives protested the apparent fait accompli being presented by the administration, in contravention of the spirit, if not the terms of the Peel Plan and the Mandate. In addition, they demanded that 1,000 certificates that had been returned to British Passport Control officers in Europe be granted to the JAE. Neither the protest nor the demand succeeded; Mills flatly rejected the concept of carry-over from a previous schedule. In fact, he declared that he intended to investigate the legality of issuing immigrant certificates in the name of a specific bearer, thereby rendering them useless to anyone else.[87]

In an emergency session of the JAE held some three weeks later, Shertok summarized a newly proposed immigration law that would turn the "political maximum" into permanent policy. The new law, Shertok reported, had three components, and all of them would cause grievous harm to the Yishuv: (1) a limitation on the number and types of relatives who could qualify for class D certificates; (2) the "political maximum" capping all types of certificates, including all previously unregulated class A (capitalist) certificates; and (3) an even more severe decree punishing illegal immigration. Also distressing, in Shertok's view, was the fact that the law spoke of the Jews in racial, rather than national, terms.[88] The term "Jewish race" troubled Shertok, even though Zionists (notably Arthur Ruppin) had used similar terms in their writings since the turn of the century. It is plausible that Shertok was reacting to the rising tide of European antisemitism that had resulted from Nazi racial policy. None of the other JAE members were troubled by the usage. In fact, Gruenbaum and Eliyahu Dobkin opposed focusing on the racial aspects of the law, for fear of inciting antisemitism. Shertok completed his report with the call that the JAE "use every weapon to ensure the failure of this law."[89]

The new law represented the beginning of the end for the Zionist-British alliance, a fact that was clear to even the most pro-British elements of Mapai. On October 24, Dobkin reported to the Mapai Executive regarding the law. His report was as unequivocal as it was negative, since the new law clearly represented a breach of the Mandate. The JAE had already begun to take defensive action in June to prevent the political maximum from becoming a reality. According to Dobkin, the JAE's efforts concentrated on the League of Nations Permanent Mandates Committee and "won a moral victory." Although the Zionists assumed that they had in fact defeated the political maximum, the opposite was true. The moral victory proved to be an empty one, for it produced no practical results in halting British maneuvers to slow aliya. Nevertheless, Dobkin promised that the JAE would fight the new aliya law, and requested that Mapai members join "a vigorous campaign against it."[90]

Davar's editors entered the campaign as well, condemning the British in an October 22, 1937 editorial. Observing that the new law treated Jews as "foreign immigrants," Moshe Beilinson attacked the Palestine administration in no uncertain terms. In his view, the racial terminology of the new immigration law was not morally different from that in the antisemitic legislation of contemporary Romania, Poland, or Nazi Germany.[91] In retaliation for these strong words, the administration ordered *Davar* closed down for one week, beginning on October 25.[92] In what was clearly a disingenuous act, the British had now censorsed the Yishuv's Zionist press at a time when overtly Fascist and pro-Nazi literature, including an English translation of Hitler's *Mein Kampf*, was readily available in Palestine's bookstores.[93]

While the JAE implemented its planned protest strategy against the new immigration law, Rabbi Herzog suggested that the JAE grant ma'apilim already in Palestine any surplus Labor certificates that were available.[94] In response, Shertok stated that the JAE would do so if any certificates remained, although this prospect was unlikely, in view of the limited number of certificates available.[95] Undaunted, Herzog requested permission to attend the JAE's next meeting as an intermediary on behalf of the ma'apilim.[96] This meeting never took place, but the JAE understood Herzog's message, and offered to grant a small number of certificates to ma'apilim and their families. Following up on this offer, Herzog requested seventy certificates as a minimum, to aid some 200 to 250 persons. The JAE agreed to find certificates for seventy ma'apilim thus using about twenty certificates.[97] These discussions ultimately ended in a stalemate: the Irgun Olim Bilti Legali'im (Organization of Illegal Immigrants), the lobbying group established to protect the interests of the ma'apilim, refused to accept anything less than relief for its entire membership.[98] No one could deny the justice of this demand — not even opponents of aliya bet — but the JAE did not even have certificates for everyone who sought to immigrate legally.

Parallel to the issue of ma'apilim, the contacts regarding Betar aliya (begun in March 1937) were renewed in September. The Betar leadership expressed a new willingness to compromise, and reduced its request for certificates from 25 percent of all Labor certificates granted to 10 percent.[99] The reason for such a spirit of compromise is clear: if the new immigration bill became fact, Betar would be completely closed out of aliya unless the movement could once again obtain certificates from the JAE. The same held true for Agudas Israel, which began parallel negotiations with the JAE in October 1937 that resulted in a JAE promise to grant 6 percent of all certificates to Aguda.[100]

When the JAE met to discuss the agenda for negotiations with Betar, three positions were expressed. The first was that of Menahem M. Ussishkin, Gruenbaum, and Fishman, who all supported the agreement. They argued that since the JAE allowed many other groups (including Communists) to immigrate, punishment of Betar members — whose commitment to Zionist goals was unimpeachable — was not only unfair but also unwise. The second position was at the opposite extreme. Hexter and Senator, both non-Zionists, opposed any compromise with Betar. In Hexter's estimation, the JAE's purpose was to "make possible the immigration of those Jews suitable for conditions here and who possess a modicum of national discipline."[101] Even in 1937, both Hexter and Senator advocated selective aliya. Since their position continued to animate much of the JAE's policy, it became the crux of the disagreement with Jabotinsky and Ha-Zach.

Between these two positions stood Ben-Gurion, who admitted that he agreed with Hexter in theory: "Since we are unable to bring all Jews to Eretz Israel," he said, "we must choose the most appropriate ones for aliya." Under normal conditions, Ben-Gurion would likely have opposed granting certificates to Betar members. But, because contemporary circumstances required inter-Zionist peace, Ben-Gurion did not feel that a normal policy could be pursued. If inter-Zionist peace could be attained at the price of 10 percent of the Labor schedule, then he supported the grant to Betar. Ben-Gurion also felt that such a grant might induce the Revisionists to return to the WZO, an act that would strengthen the JA's hand in relation to the British, especially in negotiations regarding the new immigration law. He did, however, lay down one pre-condition to his support for compromise with Betar: that it had to end the propaganda against the KKL and KHY, and the occasional physical attacks on them.[102] His reasoning apparently convinced Ben-Gurion's colleagues, since the resolution to continue negotiations passed with his caveat. Only Hexter and Senator voted against the resolution.[103]

Ben-Gurion's position here appears to contradict other statements that he made regarding mass aliya. Three possibilities exist to explain the apparent contradiction. First, it is possible that this was a reflection of the real position that he adopted. If so, it indicates that Ben-Gurion continued to accept the premise of halutzic aliya, despite his statements to the contrary. Currently available evidence does not sustain this position, however. It seems highly unlikely that Ben-Gurion would negotiate with the British for mass aliya schemes if he did not believe that they were necessary or appropriate. Similarly, his statement implies that his true preference was to "bring all Jews to Eretz Israel," but he realized that such an eventuality was not likely in the immediate future. Second, it is possible that Ben-Gurion was merely being polite to Hexter, whom he held in high personal regard. In this case, Ben-Gurion would be using the appearance of agreement in theory as a rhetorical tool before arguing an opposite position. Third, Ben-Gurion's statement of agreement with Hexter related to the limited issue of Betar aliya only. As is well known, Ben-Gurion had no love lost for Betar; on a number of occasions he had, after all, described himself as being at war with the Revisionist movement (even while he appropriated some Revisionist arguments and policies). Furthermore, Ben-Gurion had also already stated his preference that Ha-Zach return to the WZO. Since the issue at hand was Betar aliya, Ben-Gurion could pose as a moderate while ultimately ensuring that no agreement was worked out with Ha-Zach unless it included their return to the fold.

The JAE's efforts to halt implementation of the new immigration law began in earnest in November. One early victory was scored: the racial definition clause of the new law was deleted because it represented too obvious a weapon in the hands of Nazi propagandists.[104] Despite this victory, however, more bad news awaited: the British announced their intention to further limit the maximum age for Youth Aliya candidates to 15 or under. Young people aged 16 or 17 could still immigrate, of course, but only under the Labor schedule. On the other hand, this change in the rules actually opened the possibility of a British concession on the issue of relatives, since youth olim could not apply for family reunion certificates (D schedule), whereas Labor class immigrants (C schedule) could.[105]

The sum total of these compromises was a new immigration ordinance that rendered the rescue aliya program virtually inoperative. Such few concessions as the British made were more than offset by the new restrictions and the miniscule schedules being offered. The British were clearly playing a game with the Zionists, one that the Jews could not possibly win.

In November, the JAE won another small victory when the League of Nations Permanent Mandates Committee condemned the new British immigration law as inconsistent with the Mandate.[106] Almost simultaneously, the British government announced the temporary postponement of the Peel partition plan in anticipation of the Woodhead Commission, which was sent to Palestine to report on the desirability of implementing the plan.[107] The JAE found these developments disturbing, and Shertok especially denounced the cynical attitude manifested by Harold F. Downie, the newly appointed Minister Resident in Cairo, toward the issue of Jewish immigration.[108]

Yet the British represented only part — although clearly the main part — of the problem. The Arab revolt that had begun in April 1936 continued, and caused much consternation for both the Zionists and the British. Despite efforts by the Palestine police, augmented by units of the Royal Army, Arab violence continued unabated. The revolt peaked on September 26, 1937, when Commissioner for the Galilee Louis Andrews was assassinated.[109] Violence also resulted in a continuation of the internal debate over havlaga. Purely defensive measures such as the use of barbed wire, the building of Tower and Stockade settlements, and the close cooperation between the Hagana and the Palestine police produced only temporary results, and overall did not lead to an abatement in the level of Arab terror. On November 5, 1937, Jabotinsky published an sarcastic article in *ha-Yarden* titled "The Easiest Line of Attack." In it, he stated that the Jews were placing too much reliance on the Royal Army, which he saw as an easier target owing to British prevarication and unwillingness to confront the Arab bands. Jabotinsky did not specifically mention havlaga, but his point — that the Hagana's defensive measures had worked "too" well (that is to say, not at all) — could easily be interpreted as a call for more active operations.[110] This was the meaning inferred by the commanders of the IZL, who began extensive retaliatory actions in 1937.[111] Moreover, havlaga was not popular within significant elements of the Yishuv. In addition to members of Betar and the IZL, many members of the Oriental Jewish Communities also found passivity distasteful and unwise.[112]

Opposition to havlaga took further strength from two sources: the November 13, 1937, announcement by the British that no further weapons would be given to Jews, out of fear that they would be used in retaliatory actions and the terms of a Syrian peace proposal dating to mid-November that offered Jews the right to settle in Syria, Lebanon, and Palestine if they relinquished the Zionist goals of a Jewish majority and national sovereignty.[113] The JA and the Va'ad Leumi leadership felt constrained to speak out in every forum, urging Jews to resist the temptation to retaliate.[114] Rabbi Herzog also supported havlaga, but opposed any form of enforcement by the JAE that involved the British, since he believed that such a policy would be equated in Jewish law with halshana (talebearing).[115]

The year 1937 ended in a deep crisis for the Yishuv, the Zionist movement, and European Jewry. The debate over partition continued, even though most Zionists realized that the Peel Plan was in doubt. Of special importance at a JAE meeting on December 19, was Berl Katznelson's report of his trip to America and England. In both places, he had sought to influence Jews and non-Jews alike to keep the gates of Palestine open.[116] Propaganda work continued, with the JAE and its supporters making extra efforts to convince the public of the propriety of their positions.[117] Arab terror also continued, and in December it gave impetus to a proposal to transfer Jewish neighborhoods of Jaffa to the authority of the Tel Aviv municipality.[118] Finally, negotiations to create a Zionist united front continued, although numerous obstacles produced more inertia than could be overcome at the time.[119]

8
The Decline of Rescue Aliya

INTRA-ZIONIST RELATIONS AT A BREAKING POINT

In January 1938, Ha-Zach launched a new offensive against the Jewish Agency, this time in the League of Nations. A petition, written by the Nessiut for the Permanent Mandates Commission, set out Ha-Zach's grievances and listed its suggestions for redress. The petition attacked the JA both for ideological partisanship in fulfilling its functions and for its undemocratic nature. In the latter claim, the petitioners were partially correct. Zionist members of the JAE were not elected by an open franchise, but one paid by WZO members. The non-Zionist members of the JAE were appointed by notables in America and Great Britain, although that meant that they were responsible to no one in particular.[1]

The petition concentrated on the non-Zionist members of the JA, condemning them as "plutocrats" who did not represent "a clearly defined electorate."[2] No less forcefully, the petition claimed that the WZO had ceased to represent Zionist Jewry, since more voters had participated in the elections for the first Ha-Zach Congress in September 1935 than for the Nineteenth Zionist Congress, one month earlier.[3] The authors of the petition also accused unnamed Zionist parties of electoral rigging. These parties, they claimed, sold immigrant certificates for Palestine and then used the profits of such sales to buy shekalim for distribution to supporters who otherwise could not afford to buy the shekel or were not willing to do so.[4] Finally, the petition again raised the issue of unfairness in the distribution of certificates, especially the deprivation of Betar aliya.[5] As a result, the petitioners claimed, the JA no longer fulfilled its purpose under Article 4 of the Mandate, and they suggested that it should be replaced with a World Jewish National Assembly.[6]

172

Interestingly, the Ha-Zach Nessiut never attacked a specific party, although the petition clearly implicated Mapai as the instigator of the JAE's anti-Betar policy. Instead, the petition placed all the blame for the organizational anomalies of the JA on the British authorities, since the latter had the real power in Palestine and should have been encouraging democracy.[7]

Ha-Zach, while participating in what can only be termed a frontal assault on the JA, also continued the intermittent efforts to attain an inter-Zionist truce. Negotiations were held in Warsaw in December 1937 and January 1938 between Joseph B. Schechtman and Moshe Kleinbaum (later Sneh), on the former's initiative. These negotiations elicited a strong response from the London Executive. Selig Brodetsky advocated using "all means" to attain inter-Zionist peace, with the ultimate goal of bringing Ha-Zach back into the WZO. In Brodetsky's view, if Ha-Zach accepted WZO discipline, then the WZO ought to concede on all other outstanding points, including the method of elections to the Zionist Congress.[8]

In December 1937, Brodetsky had the opportunity to test his ideas in negotiations with Dr. Benjamin Akzin, director of the NZO Political Department. Brodetsky again attempted to convince the NZO leadership to return to the WZO, offering membership in both the JAE and the Va'ad ha-Poel ha-Zioni. He reemphasized the need for Revisionists to accept WZO discipline, but he defined discipline as the acceptance of policies that had been decided upon by a democratically constituted majority. If the Revisionists did not agree with the majority, they could use every means to convince the delegates of the Revisionist point of view and thereby gain a majority. Akzin expressed interest, because of tensions between moderates and radicals within Ha-Zach, but he failed to follow up on Brodetsky's proposals.[9]

JA relations with Agudas Israel were also the subject of continuing negotiations.[10] After the initial contacts in January 1938, representatives of Aguda met with Moshe Shertok and Rabbi Judah L. Fishman on February 14. Aguda, in presenting its position, demanded that the JA and Va'ad Leumi take drastic measures to ensure stricter religious observance within the Yishuv. The JA representatives agreed to look into the matter, and proposed a joint committee to oversee religious issues. Shertok also briefed the Aguda representatives on political questions, including the fact that the JA would not accept any peace plan for Palestine that included a Jewish minority. Because of wide differences between Aguda and the JA on both religious and political issues, no firm agreement was worked out, although the two parties promised to coordinate activities in the future.[11]

While Ha-Zach's attack on the composition of the JA may be explained by reference to the joint Revisionist-Agudas Israel efforts to modify the JA in 1937, the peace negotiations must be placed in context. Throughout 1937 and 1938, efforts to create an inter-Zionist united front continued as a response to the rising antisemitic tide in eastern Europe.

This time, events in Romania provided the specific background for the renewed peace negotiations. On January 2, 1938, Hayim M. Shapira reported on the rising panic among Romanian Jews after Premier Octavian Goga's speech regarding the denationalization of most of Romanian Jewry. Because of the rising tide of persecution in Romania, Shapira reported, the Yishuv could expect more requests for certificates from middle-class Romanian Jews.[12] His words, of course, were irrelevant, since British policy by this time rendered the rescue aliya program almost inoperable.

As in Germany in 1933, the JAE did not believe that its sources in Romania provided sufficiently detailed information, and it decided to send a representative to assess conditions on the spot. The representative would also have a public relations mission for the JAE and WZO: he would, as it were, show the flag and bolster Jewish morale. That element of the mission should require the presence of a JAE member, but almost none of them were free to leave, since the JAE still had to attend to business relating to the Woodhead Commission. After a brief debate, a majority agreed that Gershon Agronsky, editor of the *Palestine Post*, would go.[13]

Agronsky reported his findings to the JAE (less Ben-Gurion, who was in London) and stated that the press had not exaggerated the severity of the Romanian Jewish problem. Whereas the Goga government had announced its intention to merely "revise" the citizenship status of all Romanian Jews outside the Regat (the territory of Romania before World War I), its actual intention was to annul their citizenship. Since most Romanian Jews lived outside the Regat, in Bukovina, Bessarabia, Transylvania, and Dobruja, this was not a minor persecution. The annulment, moreover, was planned as only a first step. Alexander Cuza, Goga's interior minister and one of the leaders of the Garda de Fier, advocated the expulsion of all Romanian Jews. Seeming more moderate, Cuza "only" advocated the creation of a special territory for Romanian Jewry, akin to the Indian reservations in the United States.[14]

While in Bucharest, Agronsky met with the American and British ambassadors, who assured him that the Goga government's "bark was worse that its bite," and that, at least as far as the United States was concerned, nothing would be done to extirpate Romanian Jewry or to seize their capital.[15] For the time being, the ambassador's comments were correct, insofar as the Romanians did not immediately follow up on their new antisemitic legislation. More broadly, however, United States policy toward European Jewry remained essentially static: empty expressions of sympathy, and pious regrets without any substantive action.

The initial Zionist response to the new conditions in Romania was for increased aliya. As in Germany in 1933 many Zionists did not believe that Palestine could solve the entire Jewish problem in the Danube basin. Nevertheless, they felt that aliya would place the government on notice that its antisemitic policies harmed the Romanian economy as much as it harmed the Jews, if not more so.[16] Since there had been no pogroms, Agronsky concluded, the situation did not warrant panic, but required the same immediate attention that Germany had received in 1933. Agronsky suggested that Romania be given an immediate grant of 100 certificates, half for capitalists and half for halutzim. He also passed on a Romanian Zionist request for 8,000 more certificates during 1938.[17]

Responding to Agronsky's report, Yitzhak Gruenbaum called for an anti-Romanian boycott, reasoning that unlike Germany, Romania would not be able to withstand that kind of pressure for very long. Gruenbaum also warned that failure to prevent Romania from carrying out this policy would further incite the Poles and would engulf all of eastern European Jewry in a new wave of antisemitism.[18]

Gruenbaum reiterated his warning at the JAE meeting of February 2, 1938, but few supported his call for a boycott. Shertok, for instance, advocated a transfer agreement to ease the aliya of Romanian Jewish capitalists. Shertok was not advocating a policy of inaction; the question was what action would be best for both Romanian Jewry and the Yishuv. The same was true for Gruenbaum. He opposed a Romanian transfer agreement as he had opposed Haavara from Germany, although his position carried little weight since he was engaged in "clearing" negotiations with the Poles.

Shertok also criticized the JAE's sense of propriety in a way reminiscent of the internal arguments in early 1933. He argued that the JAE's response to the crisis was too slow and that a JAE member, not Agronsky, should have gone on the fact-finding mission, if only for appearance' sake. Now the JAE had to act decisively on behalf of Romanian Jewry.

Despite Shertok's dramatic call for action, the JAE decided to bide its time and wait for further information concerning Romania.[19] The JAE's reluctance to act decisively, as compared to the decision made in 1933, cannot be fully explained. There does not seem to have been any specific reason not to act on behalf of Romanian Jewry; indeed, there may well have been a greater incentive not to act for German Jewry in 1933, since a much larger proportion of the community opposed Zionism. Continuing financial difficulties may explain part of the problem, although fiscal issues did not play a truly prominent role in the debate. While the monetary crisis even threatened continuation of the programs for the absorption of German Jews, if these difficulties were the main reason for hesitation, then the attractiveness of an anti-Romanain boycott would increase: no real investment would be needed to start a boycott, and the closing of Romanian imports would have strengthened tozeret ha-aretz (home production).[20] The only plausible explanation for this lack of decisive action is that fear of British noncooperation temporarily paralyzed the JAE.

Some tentative movement on behalf of Romanian Jewry began in March

1938. By then the Goga regime had fallen, although the new government had not yet (and in fact never would) completely restore the status quo ante. In mid-March Eliahu Dobkin visited Romania as a representative of the Histadrut. In addition to meetings with Jewish communal leaders, Dobkin explored the possibility of a clearing agreement with the Romanian government. Unlike the Haavara agreement, however, this agreement was not based on the transfer of Romanian goods. Instead, each emigrating Jew's investments would be transferred via the KKL and the new oleh received part of his capital (with a minimum guarantee of £P1,000) as a parcel of land which he could settle on or sell.[21] This clearing agreement continued as a topic of negotiations, but was not ratified before World War II broke out. Furthermore, by March events in Germany and Austria overtook the JAE, and the Romanian crisis had simmered down. Thereafter, the rescue aliya program expanded to include both Austria and Romania, despite the lack of a specific decision regarding the latter.

THE DECLINE OF RESCUE ALIYA

The entire series of aliya-related problems experienced in 1936 and 1937 continued and, in many cases, grew in 1938. This held true especially for Haavara. In January, the Anglo-Palestine Bank expressed a desire to withdraw its financial commitment to Haavara, and the bank's eighty-eight shares were transferred to the JAE, represented by Arthur Ruppin, Georg Landauer, and Werner D. Senator. The bank did, however, agree to continue to deal with Haavara debentures.[22] The smooth transition from the Bank to the JAE veiled significant financial difficulties. By the spring of 1938, Paltreu had fallen even farther behind in its payments; this process continued with each new group of immigrants. Thus, although in 1937 Paltreu transferred RM31,407,501.30 (£P2,512,600), or enough money for 2,500 immigrants, capitalist immigration for all countries in 1937 totaled only 2,558.[23] The actual Haavara immigration in 1938 totaled only 1,500, or 60 percent of the potential transfer, based on the amount transferred.[24]

Matters worsened in February 1938, when the Nazis announced their intention to curtail certain classes of Haavara exports, further limiting the transfer and reducing its effectiveness as a rescue tool.[25] As another example of the difficulties with rescue aliya, we may note the inconvenience experienced by capitalists who came to Palestine as tourists and then sought immigration certificates after they returned to Europe. Although such requests were accepted as legal in the immigration statutes, the British made certificates very difficult to obtain under these conditions.[26]

Capitalist aliya represented only one aspect of a general Zionist crisis that developed directly from British immigration policy. While in January 1938 it was still possible for Ben-Gurion (and other Zionists) to base their decisions on the premise that the British had no alternative but to carry out the partition plan, one month later this was no longer the case.[27] British policy now amounted to non-cooperation with Zionist goals and was intimately connected with the political maximum that had been placed on aliya. It will be recalled that the political maximum was initially enacted as a temporary measure until the partition scheme was carried out. As a result, even minute decisions on aliya policy emanated from London, a situation that neither the Zionists nor the British Palestine Administration desired. When, therefore, partition was put on hold the government decided to retain the political maximum pending future policies. In February 1938, the Colonial Office announced that henceforth London would publish only broad guidelines for aliya policy; details of number to be permitted to immigrate would again be in the High Commissioner's hands.[28] The Colonial Office was also very careful in its announcement of this return to the old system of setting quotas to declare that under no circumstances would the Mandatory government return to a policy of economic absorptive capacity as a criterion for aliya: the potential cost of such a policy, deriving from mass aliya schemes proposed independently by Ben-Gurion and Zeev Jabotinsky, was too dangerous from the British perspective.

Only in a few extraordinary cases did the British acquiesce to the rescue aliya program. One of these was the case involving the Jewish community of Rexingen, Germany, which relocated in its entirety to Palestine to found moshav Shavei Zion (near Nahariya).[29] More often, the British administration proved uncooperative, especially in the granting of D certificates (for relatives of Palestine residents). A mistake made by members of the JA Aliya Department left hundreds of capitalist certificates unused in December 1937 and January 1938 and did not help ease matters. The persons re-sponsible for the oversight were severely reprimanded, though not disciplined, and the mistake was not repeated.[30]

Shertok summarized the Yishuv's state of mind in a diary entry of March 1, 1938, in which he noted widespread fear concerning High Commissioner Sir Arthur Wauchope's replacement.[31] On March 6, 1938, the JAE received a telegram from the Reichsvertretung der deutschen Juden (Reich Representation of German Jews) regarding aid for aliya. The Reichsvertretung proposed a donation of £P33,000 ($165,000) to help absorb 1,000 olim. Successfully bringing this to fruition would require £P25,000 ($125,000) from the JAE, in adddition to £P90,000 ($450,000) from the Council for German Jewry in London. The JAE demurred at the financial commitment, since it did not have the money, but it established a subcommittee to study the proposal.[32] This subcommittee never reported; by the next JAE meeting, on April 3, 1938, the Anschluss (the Nazi annexation of Austria on March 11/12, 1938), created an entirely new situation for the Yishuv.

With the German takeover of Austria, another Jewish community had fallen under the Nazi sway. Almost immediately, the Nazis instituted the entire gamut of their antisemitic legislation, which operated with full force from the very beginning. Moreover, Austrian Nazis greeted the Anschluss with anti-Jewish violence, especially in Vienna, where they forced Jews to scrub the streets with their bare hands.[33] Albeit, Nazi policy still emphasized Jewish emigration and steps were taken to facilitate this goal. In particular, SS-Obersturmbannführer Adolf Eichmann became the chief planner and executor of Germany's anti-Jewish operations. Shortly after the Anschluss, Eichmann helped to evolve new methods of forced emigration. His efforts culminated in the creation of the Zentralstelle für Jüdische Auswanderung (Central Office for Jewish Emigration) in August 1938.[34]

The JAE reacted to the Anschluss by emphasizing aliya, but met with many significant difficulties in getting rescue operations started. On March 24 Zionist leaders met with High Commissioner Designate Harold MacMichael (who officially replaced Wauchope on April 1, 1938). Shertok, speaking on behalf of the JAE, requested that every available certificate be immediately granted to the JA for the rescue of Austrian Jews. MacMichael expressed sympathy with the Austrian Jews' plight but made no promises regarding open aliya. In the end only 200 certificates were made available.[35] Even direct requests for opening the gates of Palestine, on the premise that Jews had the financial wherewithal for mass migration but needed a safe destination, fell on deaf ears.[36]

On April 3, 1938, the JAE expanded the rescue aliya program to include Austria, placing it within the German Department's sphere of authority.[37] That same day, the British announced a new Labor schedule comprising 1,000 certificates. Of these, 430 were to be predesignated: 180 for individuals already in Palestine as "seasonal workers," and 250 for professionals (A-II, A-III, and A-IV certificates). After other, unspecified, deductions, the JAE calculated that 300 certificates remained, to be divided as needed.[38] As compensation for the small schedule, the High Commissioner agreed to use 100 certificates from the reserve to legalize 100 "illegal" immigrants. This announcement emboldened the JAE to request again that leftover certificates be granted to the JAE, to help in rescuing Austrian Jews.

A valid question may be asked regarding the financial conditions within the Yishuv and the Jewish world as a whole at this juncture. The Yishuv's financial situation was better in 1938 than it had been in 1933, but not by much. All Zionist activists realized that continued rescue work required secure finances in addition to the cooperation of British authorities. In this case, the latter was the more significant problem, but financial troubles still existed. In an undated letter (but one that clearly refers to events of 1938) to James G. McDonald, for example, Jabotinsky requested international financial support to resettle 500,000 Jews in Palestine in two years. A clear reference to the last version of Jabotinsky's evacuation scheme (originally framed around an exodus of 1,500,000 Jews in ten years) the plan could not even get off the ground without greater financial support than Ha-Zach could provide.[39]

Financial matters did not differ much for the WZO and JA. In March, Hitachdut Olei Austria (HOA) requested financing for a large, but very general, resettlement plan for Austrian Jews.[40] In response the Council for German Jewry agreed to provide £82,000 ($410,000) toward the resettlement of 1,000 Austrian Jews.[41] In June HOA requested aid for resettlement from Austria from the JAE.[42] Once again, money was an inhibition to rescue.

Ever more ominous news emanating from Austria and other east-central European states in early May fixed the Yishuv's attention on Europe. Within a period of three days there were reports of fresh pogroms in Poland, new antisemitic legislation in Hungary, and the Gestapo's closure of all Jewish institutions in Vienna.[43] The JAE sought 8,000 unused certificates for Austrian Jews from the administration. Although the British agreed in principle, by the time the JAE received the certificates they numbered only 300. In his report to the JAE, Shertok contrasted British policy in 1938 with the promises to liberalize immigration made in 1933.[44] Shertok also doubted that the British would grant even the promised 300 certificates, but he kept these doubts to himself.[45] As in the case of Romania in January, the JAE sought a representative to go to Vienna, in order to directly assess conditions and to demonstrate a Yishuv presence. The JAE was keenly aware that sending Agronsky might have been a mistake, since he might have been perceived as too unimportant a dignitary. Thus, it unanimously approved the choice of Rose Jacobs, the president of Hadassah (in Palestine as a member of the JAE).[46]

The plight of Austrian Jewry also evoked a response from the United States. President Franklin D. Roosevelt called for a conference on refugee affairs, inviting nearly three dozen countries to attend. On May 20, 1938, the *Palestine Post* responded to the American initiative by stressing the need to resettle 100,000 penniless Jews as an initial step toward rescue.[47] This represented a small number of the total in need of aid — Ha-Zach's contemporary memorandum called for the rescue of more than 6 million Jews — but it was a far cry from previous calls for limited emigration. Two days later, another editorial returned to the fate of Jews in the Grossreich, commenting that the new property laws and the almost complete Aryanization of the Austrian economy reflected an "open season" against Jews. According to Agronsky, "the present hour is to Israel a time of woe and disaster as well as consolation and hope, such as there has not been since the dispersion." By "woe and disaster" he clearly meant the fate of Jewry in central Europe, and by "consolation and hope," the prospect of emigration to Palestine.[48]

On June 7, 1938, the JAE met again to discuss the state of Austrian Jewry. Rabbi Fishman spoke first, emphasizing the urgency of speedy rescue. Seconding Fishman's appeal was Shapira, who, however, concentrated on the rescue of the Zionist officials incarcerated in Dachau.[49]   Agreeing to the overall approach, Eliezer Kaplan suggested a minimum aliya of 25,000 per year. This was clearly not enough, given the need at the time, but it still was beyond what the Yishuv was likely to attain. Kaplan, it should be noted, was proposing an aliya rate only one-half of that in Ben-Gurion's 1934 proposal, one-sixth of that in Jabotinsky's 1935 evacuation scheme, and one-twelfth of that in the 1938 NZO proposal on evacuation. Still, Kaplan's proposed rate was three times as large as the immigration rate instituted by the British when they inaugurated the so-called political maximum in 1937.

Even at this late date, however, not all members of the JAE accepted the need for evacuation. Senator, for example, suggested that an attempt be made to convince the Nazis that an orderly exodus was as much in their interests as it was in the Jews'.[50]   The target of JAE activity also called forth different proposals. In order to achieve a maximal aliya rate, Shapira urged, lobbying should be undertaken in Washington, DC, with the hope of convincing the Roosevelt administration to pressure the British to keep open the gates of Palestine. Ben-Gurion, in contrast, felt that the JAE's primary focus should be on London and Evian — the latter being the site chosen for President Roosevelt's international refugee conference. During the debate, the JAE tentatively approved a delegation of four to the Evian Conference: Menahem M. Ussishkin and Arthur Ruppin, representing the JAE; Nahum Goldmann, representing the London Executive and the American Zionists; and either Georg Landauer or Henrietta Szold, representing Youth Aliya.[51]

Other discussions centered on the need to protect Youth Aliya and to defeat the political maximum. According to Shertok, the latter goal transcended the specific needs of Austrian Jewry, and was vital for the continued growth of the Yishuv.[52]   Shertok placed political goals ahead of rescue, since he believed that rescue could not be accomplished without a secure Yishuv. Two other substantive decisions were taken at this meeting: to have the London Executive coordinate rescue and political work for Austrian Jewry, and to periodically send a member of either the Jerusalem or the London Executive to Vienna to hearten the Austrian Jews and oversee Zionist activities in Austria.[53]

All in all, the JAE response to the Anschluss must be seen as a further fine-tuning of the rescue aliya program. It is not difficult to see why the majority of the Yishuv opted for this policy, since the Zionists had few options and the impact of British policy was now clear for all to see. Thus, in July, the JAE requested 900 emergency Labor certificates, including 100 for Austria, and 1,000 certificates for Youth Aliya, to create the new category of "trainees." Trainees would be unmarried young people over 18 years of age with no previous vocational training; they would come to Palestine to study a trade, either in an agricultural training program or as apprentices in industrial firms.[54] This action was seen as a means to enlarge Youth Aliya; appropriate fund-raising and other arrangements were also discussed but never came to fruition.[55] The British response to this request was a swift and unequivocal refusal, soon followed by restrictions on Youth Aliya as well.[56]

INTRA-ZIONIST RELATIONS AT A NEW CROSSROAD

Under the circumstances, one would have expected a renewed effort to establish inter-Zionist peace. Instead, the dispute between the JAE and Ha-Zach, which had lain dormant in 1936 and 1937, returned with a passion. In May, the Organizational Department of the JA circulated an anonymous document purporting to be the transcript of speeches at a Betar meeting that took place on the evening of May 7, 1938. The purpose of the meeting was to announce the creation of an "Adult Betar" in the Holy Land for members between the ages of 20 and 50. Most of the speakers expressed nostalgia for Betar's "glory days" of the early 1930's. Two stood out among them. One was Dr. Julius Freulich, who said: "Betar members must close ranks and prepare for sacrifices and battle." The other was an anonymous speaker who called for Betar in the Holy Land to "go into the streets for the same type of operations we undertook in that [earlier] period and to use the same tactics we used then, with which we had so much success." In the remainder of this speaker's words, Mapai clearly was viewed as Adult Betar's prime enemy.[57]

The JAE inferred from this document and from a number of actions by Ha-Zach members in Europe that a new Revisionist attack was imminent, but this inference appears to have been incorrect.[58] On July 5, 1938, for example, the NZO Nessiut cabled the JAE to request funding from the Council for German Jewry for halutzim in Betar hachsharot in Germany and Austria.[59] This request was little more than an effort to get the JA to fund part of Betar's aliya bet program, thereby relieving Ha-Zach's Keren Tel Hai. The JA initially refused to help, citing the Council's "legal immigration" only policy.[60] Later that month, however, the JA reconsidered its refusal to help and agreed to transfer £P600 ($3,000) and ten immigrant certificates to Betar. This was only token aid, so Keren Tel Hai thus began fundraising in South Africa, Great Britain, and the United States.[61] Evidently, elements within the NZO sought an ad hoc accommodation with the JAE to cover refugee aid. However, the JAE did not trust Ha-Zach's motivations at this point, especially in view of NZO anti-JA propaganda activities in Australia, Hungary, and South Africa, and therefore an opportunity to reunite the Zionist movement was allowed to pass.[62]

Moreover, what the JAE classified as Betar's call to war was not by any means one-sided. In July 1938, Dr. Erich Breuer wrote Shertok a note stating that the JA had not done enough to defeat HA-Zach in Palestine. Breuer's specific suggestion related to anti-Revisionist propaganda primarily to the use of placards and more forceful slogans rather than violent means, but his letter is nevertheless of interest.[63] Shertok made a copy of it for Ben-Gurion, requesting his opinion. Although Ben-Gurion's response has not been preserved, there is little doubt that such a proposal interested him. Ever since his failed negotiations with Jabotinsky, he had pursued a policy of (at times) seeking negotiations to create a unified front, while (at other times) seeking an ideological victory over the Revisionists. Ben-Gurion seems to have been drawn to Jabotinsky on a personal level, but he could not bridge the political chasm that separated them. Within Ben-Gurion's mamlachti orientation, his position retained inconsistencies and even contradictions; these expressed themselves most clearly in relation to Ha-Zach, and they may be exemplified by two sets of negotiations held between the Revisionists and the JAE.[64]

In September 1938, Eliahu Golomb, representing the Hagana, undertook a series of negotiations with Jabotinsky in an effort to reunite the Hagana and IZL. The two soon worked out and initialed an agreement that regulated relations between the two undergrounds. Under its terms, the IZL would accept the overall command of the Hagana and would coordinate all of its operations with the Hagana's. Neither group would be compelled to change its policies (havlaga or retaliation), although if the IZL did do so, its members would be absorbed as a group into the legal segments of the Hagana that had been created as a result of the Arab revolt.[65]

Ben-Gurion, who was in London when the negotiations took place, saw no utility in the agreement, since it did not return Ha-Zach to the WZO. Initially, he responded to rumors of the agreement by requesting more information and by questioning Golomb's authority to sign an agreement in his absence.[66] In a further series of communications with Shertok and Ussishkin, Ben-Gurion uncategorically rejected the agreement, since Golomb did not have the proper authorization to negotiate an agreement behind the JAE chairman's back.[67] On September 30, 1938, he threatened to resign if the Histadrut ratified it.[68] Although the agreement had considerable support — from Shertok, among others — Ben-Gurion continued to attack it from London. In October the agreement was tabled, although that was not the end of all negotiations.

Clearly, another opportunity for Zionist unity was missed. Less clear, however, is Ben-Gurion's reasoning. In an October meeting with Shertok Ben-Gurion betrayed the real reason for his opposing this agreement: the same members of Mapai and the Histadrut who had negotiated this agreement and were its strongest advocates had been the first to attack his more encompassing agreement with Jabotinsky in 1934.[69] Interestingly, at the same time he instigated the failure of the Golomb-Jabotinsky agreement, Ben-Gurion undertook his own series of unauthorized negotiations with Shlomo Y. Jacobi, the head of Ha-Zach's political department. In reality, the initiative for the negotiations lay with Jacobi, who wrote Ben-Gurion on October 7, proposing negotiations to create a Zionist Emergency Committee, with its members appointed by both Weizmann and Jabotinsky. The Committee would prepare for elections for a Zionist Emergency Congress, based on a democratic, rather than a paid franchise. Jacobi sought the negotiations since, in his estimate, "the political aim of both our organizations has become essentially identical, namely, the whole of Palestine ultimately as the Jewish state."[70] Ben-Gurion wasted no time in responding that he supported the negotiations and expressing an interest in meeting with Jacobi.[71] The two men met on October 8, 1938.

No specific progress was made, although both Ben-Gurion and Jacobi aired their grievances and attitudes. Ben-Gurion rejected the idea of an Emergency Committee as likely "to produce chaos in the Zionist ranks, and to weaken the [World] Zionist Organization and the Jewish Agency both internally and externally."[72] This held true, in his estimation, despite the fact that the Emergency Committee would supersede the JA. Indeed, for precisely that reason, he felt this committee would create chaos, since the source of the new agency's legitimacy would be most open to question at the outset.

On the other hand, Ben-Gurion emphasized the unity of purpose of all Zionists, Revisionists and Mapai alike, concluding: "There is no justification whatsoever for your remaining outside the Zionist Organization."[73] Conceding that Ha-Zach had a valid grievance regarding the shekel, he proposed that the next Zionist Congress should settle the matter. Finally, Ben-Gurion offered to "endeavor, in case your party decided to discontinue separate action, and come back to the Zionist Organization, to secure the appointment of Revisionist representatives to the various organs of the organization even before the next Congress."[74] This was a concession on Ben-Gurion's part, designed to offer Ha-Zach a face-saving device that would allow Jabotinsky to declare victory while still returning to the WZO.

Disappointed that Ben-Gurion did not accept the Emergency Committee, Jacobi nevertheless viewed Ben-Gurion's position as a valid basis for negotiations, though not a sufficiently strong basis for an agreement. He promised to bring Ben-Gurion's proposals to Jabotinsky's attention.[75] Jabotinsky, however, failed to respond to the initiative, since he felt Ha-Zach's complete victory over the WZO was imminent.[76] Paradoxically, Jabotinsky was involved in other talks with Labor Zionists in Poland at the same time.[77]

One more initiative was started by the Histadrut Executive in late October. In a close vote, the Executive agreed to offer Ha-Zach members positions in the JAE as part of a united front if Ha-Zach agreed to return to the WZO.[78] At this point, the negotiations ceased and the contacts petered out, to be renewed intermittently in 1939.

Another opportunity to reunite the Zionist movement had clearly been lost, but this realization must be placed in context. Until November 1938, the JAE and WZO remained committed to partition, whereas Ha-Zach utterly opposed any proposal based on the Peel Plan. Even after the partition plan had collapsed and the two parties again began to work for similar goals, neither side could accommodate the other on substantive issues, and as a result, all such negotiations were doomed almost from the start. Therefore, the 1938 negotiations raise two questions. First, would a united Zionist movement have protected the rapidly disintegrating rescue aliya program? With the benefit of hindsight, the answer appears unequivocally negative. British immigration policy — always ambivalent to rescue aliya — had by mid-1938 become virtually opposed to further mass Jewish immigration. Zionist unity might have been able to defend the status quo, but it is not likely that a unified WZO could have returned the aliya rate to the levels of 1935 or 1936, unless it adopted a radical program of aliya bet. This was unlikely, in view of the continued opposition of the minimalist majority.

The second question relates to Ben-Gurion's behavior. To say the least, his dualistic policy regarding Ha-Zach requires clarification. From Ben-Gurion's public statements it appears that he was again gripped with fear that time was operating against the Zionist movement. Logically, a strong, unified Zionist movement would have been a major goal of Ben-Gurion's political activities. Given the failure of his earlier peacemaking effort, however, he now sought an agreement only on his own terms. Cooperation with Ha-Zach or its organs while maintaining Ha-Zach's independence was not acceptable; returning the Revisionists to the WZO and adherence to Zionist discipline was.

Although seeming to disagree with Ben-Gurion on making peace with the Revisionists, Shertok articulated a similar approach to the contemporary Jewish situation in a speech he made on September 6, 1938. Analyzing the Yishuv's strengths and weaknesses, he advised the Zionists to work for inter-party unity and "to do everything possible to exploit the various opportunities for strengthening our position."[79] A unified Yishuv, Shertok said, would offer considerable advantages, since the government could not easily abandon a united Zionist movement without the possibility of grave repercussions. The single most important weapon in the Yishuv's hands remained the suffering of European Jewry, which generated a positive public view of Zionism in Britain and the United States. Naturally, this propaganda weapon did not come cheaply; the fate of the diaspora was a weapon that most Zionists would willingly forgo. But since the tempest of persecution in central and eastern Europe had already been thrust upon the Yishuv, the Zionists had to do their utmost to rescue as much of European Jewry as possible.

In 1938 and 1939, the use of European Jewry's suffering for defensive purposes was not successful. The policies espoused by the Roosevelt administration and the Chamberlain government clearly did not take Jewish needs into account. It is not clear, however, whether the WZO could have made a greater impact if its public relations efforts had been undertaken in a different fashion. The same holds true regarding havlaga. A Jewish military effort designed to raise difficulties for the Palestine administration, as a counter to Arab terrorism, might have won concessions; alternatively, such a policy might have hastened the British swing toward the Arabs. Given the almost complete destruction that would result from the latter, the JAE was not willing to take such a risk to gain the small potential concessions held out by the former.

It was obvious to both Ben-Gurion and Shertok that the Jews could not achieve their goals and were not masters of their own fate — in other words, that Jewry was largely powerless. The continuation of the Arab revolt, which entered its twenty-eighth month in August 1938, added to the sense of powerlessness. Thus, for example, Shertok repeatedly emphasized that the entire Yishuv possessed only 3,700 rifles because the British were afraid to issue weapons that might be used for counterterrorism.[80] Shertok mentioned neither the Hagana nor the IZL, and he did not imply that weapons were un-available. Nevertheless, such a small proportion of legal firearms for a community of 400,000 in effect left the Yishuv unable to defend itself and forced it to rely on British bayonets to secure the situation. As a result, the JAE was left with only a narrow set of options, none of which included the possibility that the Jews could make the country safe by the force of their own arms. Signs of improvement, almost all of them related to joint British-Jewish units such as the Special Night Squads, founded by Captain Orde Charles Wingate, were few and far between.[81]

Ben-Gurion concentrated on security in an August 3, 1938, speech and the sense of powerlessness is perceptible on virtually every page. Thus, for example, Ben-Gurion did not defend the morality of havlaga, although he was convinced of the morality of not taking revenge. Instead, he advocated self-restraint because revenge would play into the Arabs' hands:[82]

> In America, for instance, there are four million Jews but
> the gates are closed to fresh immigration, while in
> Europe the Jews are being rendered destitute and are
> therefore anxious to emigrate. Imagine the American
> Jews trying to force America by means of terror to open
> the gates. Can you imagine that they could succeed?
> The opposite is conceivable. If the American masses
> opposed Jewish immigration and began terrorizing the
> Jews, they would succeed. But they had no need to do
> that. They had but to conduct propaganda to ensure the
> gates being closed. Among us this is forgotten by people
> eager to make false comparisons, not only morally false,
> but logically so. They say: "The Arabs succeed by
> murdering Jews and British, they commit sabotage and
> do damage to the English, and succeed in getting the
> English to make concessions; why should we not do the

same? Why should we not also employ terror so that
England will fear us as she fears them?" These Jews do
not ponder that if indeed Jewish terror were to achieve
its purpose, and England fear it, then there would be an
end to Zionism in this era, so long as England had any influence in Palestine.[83]

Thus, Ben-Gurion concluded that Jewish terrorism "means help for the Arab
movement."[84] Suggesting an alternative policy, he proposed the creation of
a Jewish military force — supported by Great Britain — to "engage in an
offensive to destroy the Arab terrorists."[85] Nevertheless, Ben-Gurion also
concluded that the Yishuv could not succeed on its own; the cooperation of
the Royal Army and the Palestine administration would be vital.[86] This
remained true primarily because the Jews lacked any other reliable ally: "Who
then will help us?" Ben-Gurion asked rhetorically, "[the] Germany of Hitler,
or the Russia of Stalin, or [the] Italy of Mussolini, or Poland, which would so
much like to see the Jews leave, wherever they may go to, or Romania? Not
even America."[87]

In reality, some of these countries did contribute to the building of the
Yishuv. The Poles, for example, assisted both the Hagana and the IZL in
procuring arms.[88] But none of them was willing to work publicly on Jewry's
behalf if that meant confronting Great Britain. Similarly, the Evian Conference, America's attempt to aid Jewry, turned out to be an empty gesture,
and proved that a policy of doing nothing was counterproductive. In sum,
only Great Britain — committed to the creation of a Jewish state in at least
part of Palestine — could help fulfill Zionism.[89]

Of course, not everyone shared Ben-Gurion's assessment of the Jewish and
Zionist condition. Jabotinsky, Ha-Zach, and the IZL all continued to oppose
havlaga, not only in words but in deeds. The IZL undertook its first
retaliatory operations as early as 1936. By 1938 such operations had become
regular, if not routine. They gained the support of some of the Yishuv's
intellectuals, especially the poet Uri Zvi Greenberg, who used stirring phrases
to praise the avengers and condemn havlaga.[90] But IZL operations did not
always succeed without a price. The clearest example of these operations and
their context is the case of Shlomo Ben-Yosef.

Ben-Yosef, a Betar member from Poland, arrived in Palestine as a ma'apil
in 1937. Living and working in Rosh Pinnah, Ben-Yosef, Sholom Zurabin,
and Avraham Shein attacked an Arab bus on April 21, 1938, in retaliation for
the murder of a number of local Jews by Arab terrorists. The three were
caught in the act. Ben-Yosef was tried before a British military court, and
was sentenced to death. Shein too was sentenced to death, but because of his
age the sentence was commuted to life in prison. Zurabim was also sentenced
to life in prison.[91] All of Jabotinsky's efforts to save Ben-Yosef failed.

Even proposing an official declaration of acceptance of havlaga in return for a stay of execution had no effect.[92]

The decision of the military court placed the majority of the Yishuv in a quandary. Although it was opposed to acts of retaliation, the JAE did not wish to see Ben-Yosef punished by a British court created to deal with Arab terrorism. The more so since, under other circumstances, Ben-Yosef's "crime" could be viewed as a legitimate form of self-defense. Ben-Yosef's hanging, quite apart from the issue of support or opposition to the IZL, could in the long run impact negatively on the Hagana.[93] Thus the JAE attempted to mobilize support for a reprieve, while also strongly urging a return to havlaga.

Prominent Zionist personalities who agreed to help Ben-Yosef's cause included Ashkenazi Chief Rabbi Isaac Halevi Herzog and Chaim Weizmann, who agreed to help despite his antipathy for the IZL and its actions.[94] Even the Polish consul general in Jerusalem, Witold Hulaniocki, inquired of the British administration whether Ben-Yosef's sentence could be commuted. His report that the British would consider a reprieve turned out to be false.[95] Here too, interparty animosities could not be avoided. Rabbi Herzog, for example, privately expressed his displeasure to Shertok at having to meet with government officials regarding Ben-Yosef at the same time that a delegation of Agudas Israel representatives made their pleas for Ben-Yosef's life.[96]

The pleas made for Ben-Yosef were ignored, and he was hanged on June 29, 1938.[97] Both havlaga and opposition to it continued unabated. Ha-Zach drew one conclusion from the hanging that was diametrically opposed to JAE policy: since the British had hanged Ben-Yosef, it was clear that their first priority was to appease the Arabs. Only Jewish militance, expressed by repudiating havlaga, could counter the British tilt toward the Arabs. Calling upon Jews to act, an IZL memorandum to the Va'ad Leumi struck at the core of havlaga. While self-restraint had won the Zionists considerable praise from the British at the Twentieth Zionist Congress in 1937, Arab terror had won concessions. "There can be no morality," wrote the commander of the Irgun, "[in a policy] that places difficulties in the path of rescuing the thousands of our brothers being persecuted by the government of the [Third] Reich and other countries, and in the path of our creation of a secure homeland."[98]

THE RETREAT FROM PARTITION

Besides havlaga, the issue of partition continued to divide the Zionist camp. The WZO continued to base its actions on the premise that partition would be carried through. Talks were begun with the British government at once, but hit a snag almost immediately. On January 4, 1938, Colonial Secretary William Ormsby-Gore announced inauguration of the Palestine Partition Commission (better known as the Woodhead Commission), and declared that the government was not necessarily committed to the Peel Plan. Ormsby-Gore charged the Woodhead Commission with considering the likelihood of a successful partition, drawing borders for the Jewish and Arab states, and creating the means by which Britain could fulfill its obligations under the terms of the Mandate.[99]

Unlike the Peel Commission, the Woodhead Commission held all its hearings in private, with a total of fifty-five sessions, including nine that took place in London. The first testimony came from the Palestine administration, in the form of a memorandum by outgoing High Commissioner Wauchope. Setting out his reservations about the Peel plan, Wauchope offered alternative borders for a more limited Jewish state. His proposal aroused strong indignation within Zionist circles. Weizmann, for example, accused Wauchope of insensitivity to Jewish needs.[100]

The first to give Zionist testimony to the Commission was Weizmann, who testified for three hours. Among other subjects, he touched on two primary themes: first, that support for Zionism weakened Britain's position in the Middle East, a mistaken notion that Weizmann sought to contradict, and, second, that Palestine represented Jewry's only hope for the future, a line of analysis he hoped would convince the commission members. "The awesome responsibility to decide the question of life or death for the Jewish people has fallen upon you," Weizmann told the Commission.[101]

Following Weizmann, the other members of the JAE testified, most of them during a single five-hour session on June 10. Ben-Gurion and Shertok closed the JA case, calling for British endorsement of mass Jewish immigration.[102] Shertok's impression, however, was that the fate of the Arabs living in the proposed Jewish state was of more concern to the commission's members than the ability of such a state to save Jewish lives.[103]

Other Jewish figures testified in late June and July. Agudas Israel's representatives supported the JA's positions on borders, economics, and security. However, they petitioned for guarantees of the status of halacha in the new state, in order to ensure its Jewish character.[104] Also testifying on religious grounds was Mizrachi. In tesimony that gained JAE clearance, though not approval, Mizrachi's representatives attacked partition as opposed to the historical principles and religious requirements of religious Zionism. Mizrachi therefore requested the Woodhead Commission to reconsider partition altogether, proposing a return to the original terms of the Mandate — the creation of a Jewish national home in an unpartitioned Palestine.[105]

Dr. Benjamin Akzin, testifying for Ha-Zach, also attacked partition. The Yishuv's daily press extensively reported Akzin's testimony, and summarized the contents of a memorandum submitted to the commission by Ha-Zach. The great need of world Jewry rendered partition untenable, said Akzin. He cited statistics showing that 5,450,000 Jews needed immediate rescue, 850,000 more lived in areas where antisemitism was rapidly spreading (but where

Nazi-inspired persecution had not yet begun), and another 484,000 lived in areas outside Europe to which antisemitism had spread. In all, the number of Jews who needed to migrate totaled 6,784,000.[106] Although a Jewish state would legally be able to establish its own immigration policy, the benefits of statehood in a partitioned territory were largely illusory, since the territory of the planned Jewish state already contained dense settlements.[107] Within the Jewish state, moreover, a large number of Arabs resided. While the Commission had suggested the possibility of transferring population, such transfers would be unfair if carried out, and unnecessary if Palestine remained unpartitioned.[108] Moreover, said Akzin, a sound alternative already existed in the form of the Ten-Year Plan.[109]

A number of other Jewish groups and interested parties, such as PICA, either testified or sent memoranda to the Commission. Ussishkin, after Jabotinsky the most prominent opponent of partition, had originally intended to testify, but did not; instead, he set out his positions in a detailed memorandum for the Commission.[110]

Its work in Palestine completed, the Woodhead Commission returned to London. There it heard testimony from British politicians on both sides of the issue, took further evidence from members of the Palestine administration, and then adjourned to consider its findings.

THE EVIAN CONFERENCE AND ITS AFTERMATH

The Anschluss animated an international response, with the United States government taking the lead in advocating an international conference to discuss the problem. In April, the Nessiut of Ha-Zach had responded to the American initiative with its own proposal for an international Jewish emigration conference. Beginning with an analysis of antisemitism in central and eastern Europe, the Nessiut estimated that refuge was needed for at least 6,780,000 Jews — 6,230,000 European Jews and 550,000 Jews in the Middle East, North Africa, and Asia.[111] Since there were no havens except for a few "scattered ghettos" (which existed in the abstract only), the memo proposed that mass resettlement in Palestine was the only realistic hope of Jewry and of humanity.[112] The Ha-Zach memorandum was nothing less than an attempt to side-step the increasing restrictions that the British were placing on aliya, by getting the United States government directly involved in opening up Palestine as a haven for Jewish refugees. Ha-Zach's justification for such activity, part and parcel of Jabotinsky's continuing efforts to find a stable ally if the Zionist-British rupture became unmendable, was the Anglo-American convention on Palestine, signed in 1924.[113] Ha-Zach's strategy appears to have hinged on the hope that the American-inspired initiative would discover that no viable haven existed for Jews outside of Palestine, thereby bringing pressure on the British to open the gates for mass migration. In reality, Jabotinsky and his opponents in the JAE almost completely misunderstood the conference's true purpose, which was to silence public pressure for a solution to the "refugee crisis" without actually doing anything for refugees.[114]

The Evian Conference thus actually represented a half-hearted attempt by the Roosevelt administration to find a solution. A *Palestine Post* editorial predicted the outcome of the conference before it even took place: Agronsky termed the response to Jewish suffering a conspiracy of silence, since nations willing to support the Spanish Republicans or the Chinese Nationalists shied away from helping Jewish victims of Nazism.[115]

The JA decided to send both a memorandum and a delegation to the Evian Conference.[116] Ha-Zach originally intended to follow suit, but was unable to meet the pressures of sending delegates to both the Woodhead Commission hearings and the Conference. Ha-Zach, therefore sent only a memorandum on the plight of Jewish refugees.[117]

Although it was skeptical about the likely outcome of the conference, the JAE nevertheless agreed that its participation was essential, because non-participation would silence the Zionist position.[118] The remote possibility that a territorialist resettlement scheme outside Palestine might be approved led Ussishkin and Gruenbaum to express the need for a strong delegation so that "Eretz Israel will remain a central destination for Jewish migration."[119] Ben-Gurion noted that the Conference might ultimately be the "opposite of the San Remo [Conference]."[120] The Zionists had few options, he said, since "neither Poland nor Romania will fight on our behalf."[121]

Zionist fears of a possible territorialist solution to the Jewish problem were confirmed by talks in London on the eve of the Conference between Lord Winterton, chief of the British delegation, and Weizmann. The latter emphasized the centrality of Palestine in any solution of the refugee crisis. Winterton, who professed to agree with Weizmann, took no pains to follow through.[122] The JAE memorandum and its hope of gaining support for the transfer of 1.2 million Jews to Palestine fared little better.[123] In the end, not even the limited proposals of diaspora Jewish organizations that requested the modest emigration of 200,000 German and Austrian Jews worldwide were given any serious consideration.[124]

Evian was a failure for the Zionists, at least from an organizational perspective. Weizmann, who might have swayed the conference with his oratorical skills, was absent, although he initially intended to attend. Present was Golda Meierson (Meir), who, by her own admission, spent too much time "sitting there hour after hour being disciplined and polite."[125] Arthur Ruppin, the only JAE member to attend, presented the Zionist case, but he was disheartened by the apathy of the delegates and left early.[126]

When Ruppin reported to the JAE, he held out one glimmer of hope concerning assistance to secure the status of elderly German Jews who were unable to emigrate.[127] If Ruppin's report at least ended on a positive note, the next speaker's words most likely returned JAE members to a pessimistic frame of mind. Shapira reported on his recent trip to Austria and concluded: "Actual conditions in Vienna are much worse than the reports in the press."[128] He observed that "in four months the government has managed to destroy Austrian Jewry both morally and financially."[129]

The rise of official racial antisemitism in Italy in August 1938 forced the JAE once again to seek measures to assist a Jewish community in distress, including a boycott Italian-registered shipping lines contracted to transport olim to Palestine.[130] When discussions with the Italian consul in Jerusalem proved futile, the JAE had no recourse but to follow through. As a result, it canceled all contracts with the Adriatic Shipping Line on September 4.[131] The JAE also requested that the Va'ad Leumi cancel the educational stipend for agricultural training provided by the Italian government. Henceforth, funds for this program would be provided by the JA.[132] Although both of these acts had symbolic importance, they had little impact on the Italians.

A more immediate problem was the increase in requests for certificates, primarily from German Jewish refugees who had found a temporary haven in Italy. As had happened so often, the unavailability of certificates slowed this rescue project. In this case, however, much of the fault lay with the JAE. Because of a small recession in the Yishuv during the final quarter of 1937 the JAE failed to request a schedule for the period between April and September 1938. When the British granted a schedule of 1,000 certificates anyway, this became the only schedule period in which the grant was larger than the request. On the other hand, it is not clear that a bigger request would have gained more certificates past this token schedule, for the British soon returned to their restrictive policies. In September, the JAE requested 4,625 certificates, but received only 1,000.[133]

With the rescue aliya program teetering, Haavara increased in importance as a means to maintain the aliya rate. This held true despite the Gestapo's reduction in the percentage of capital that Jews could take out of Germany.[134] Nevertheless, declining schedules meant that aliya could not keep pace with the growing need of European Jewry.

ZIONIST-BRITISH RELATIONS IN THE SHADOW OF MUNICH

The failure of the Evian Conference may be seen as a turning point in the development of Nazi policy toward Jews. That the conference had failed was realized almost immediately. A headline in the *Philadelphia Record*, for example, stated: "Humanitarianism suffers a new blow as Evian parley fails to provide system for aiding Europe's unhappy exiles."[135] More directly to the point, the *Munchner Nachrichten* wrote:

> Obviously Germany was not represented in this note-
> worthy conference. Nor are we concerned with the deci-
> sions that were reached there . . . If the Jews in Germany
> are so dear to their hearts, they can certainly have them.
> We are delighted to give them up, and we will not even
> ask any price for them.[136]

Moreover, the summer of 1938 represented a turning point for Europe as well. Previously, the Nazis had made a number of demands regarding territory that had been part of Germany but had been removed from German control by the Versailles Treaty. In 1935 and 1936 Nazi demands led to a plebiscite in the Saar and the unilateral German remilitarization of the Rhineland. In March, 1938, Hitler arranged the Anschluss of Germany and Austria, again with no response from the western allies. Now, in the summer of 1938, Hitler turned his attention to the Sudetenland, a heavily Volksdeutsch region of Czechoslovakia, with demands that this ethnically German territory be returned to the Reich.

Nazi agitation over the Sudetenland began with the meeting of the Sudeten German Party Congress on April 24, 1938. This agitation culminated in a series of demands made by Hitler in May 1938. The Czechs along with their British and French allies, initially resisted Hitler's demands. As a result, Hitler ordered plans for an attack on Czechoslovakia and war briefly threatened. By July, however, the allies backed down, refusing to consider military action on behalf of eastern Europe's only democracy. Instead British Prime Minister Neville Chamberlain announced the creation of an investigative commission led by Lord Runcinan. On September 16, 1938 the Runcinan Commission reported, recommending that Czechoslovakia cede the Sudeten territories to Germany. French prevarication over the terms of a mutual defense treaty with Czechoslovakia simply delayed the inevitable. At the Munich Conference of September 29, 1938, Britain and France surrendered Czechoslovakia. Two days later German troops marched into the Sudetenland; by the end of the week Slovakia gained extensive autonomy ending the Czech republic.

These events had a profound impact on the Jewish question and echoed strongly throughout the Yishuv and within the Zionist movement. As early as August 31, 1938, Ben-Gurion gave vent to intense fears about the future, both for Europe and particularly for European Jewry.[137] For Ben-Gurion, the implication of these fears was that time had virtually run out for European Jewry.[138] In a letter to his wife, Paula, Ben-Gurion stated: "we cannot rule out the possibility that they [the British] might abandon us, as they abandoned Ethiopia, China, Spain and now Czechoslovakia."[139] On September 29, Ben-Gurion addressed an Anglo-Jewish youth convention, calling upon his young charges to take up military training in order to form the basis of a

Jewish army.[140]   The Munich Conference simply reinforced Ben-Gurion's pessimism.   He confided to his diary that "it is likely that our turn is next."[141]   Ben-Gurion substantially repeated the same theme in letters to Yitzhak Ben-Zvi and members of the JAE.[142]   In his analysis, only immediate mass aliya would avert an imminent disaster.[143]   Ben-Gurion emphasized the pressing Jewish need in a talk with Conservative Party leader, Lord Lloyd: "We must have a Jewish state. But not **any** Jewish state. We must have a sufficiently lagre Jewish state, otherwise it will not be able to survive."[144]

Clearly, Ben-Gurion's endeavors had little impact.   The JAE met on September 28, 1938 to discuss preparations for emergency conditions if war broke out.   Fearing the worst, Shertok had approached members of the Palestine Administration with the intention of clarifying four issues: food, communications, defense against air or gas attacks, and aliya. In his report to the JAE, Shertok emphasized aliya, noting that the war scare came just as negotiations for the next schedule began.[145]   Asked by Chief Secretary Sydney Moody for an estimate of the number of certificates needed for a sufficient rate of immigration, Shertok replied that 10,000 Labor certificates would be a good starting point.   Under no circumstances, however, should 10,000 be considered a maximum so that the JAE could "retain the possibility of rescuing [Jews] as need be."[146]

In the aftermath of the Munich agreement, the JAE met to reassess the political situation.   Senator, the non-Zionist member, proposed a major shift in Jewish tactics, strongly advocating concessions to the Arabs on both aliya and the constitutional future of Palestine.   Senator reminded his colleagues that aliya had virtually ceased during World War I, and that much the same could be expected in a new war.   He proposed that the Yishuv sacrifice short-term growth in return for long-term security and agreement with the Arabs.[147]   In contrast, Ben-Gurion advocated mass aliya, including aliya bet, and a reassessment of the Zionist's exclusive reliance on Britain.[148] Unable to accept either position, the JAE decided to put the issue off until the next meeting of the Va'ad ha-Poel ha-Zioni.   Simultaneously, the Va'ad Leumi Executive sought closer cooperation with the JAE and advocated sending a delegation to London.[149]   The JAE also considered sending one of its own, since, in Kaplan's words, the Zionists needed to concentrate "all influential people in London."[150]   The JAE proposal to send Shertok to London was rejected though he was needed to spearhead the attack in the capital, he was also vitally needed in Palestine.[151]   Under the circumstances, the advocates of rescue aliya could do little besides pray that Palestine would remain open until the Woodhead Commission published its report.

Once again, Ha-Zach's posture on Zionist issues was parallel to the JAE's, but articulated independently.   As late as February 1938, Jabotinsky could not conceive of Great Britain abandoning an "honor bound promise."[152]   Sure that the allies would not back down, the Anglo-French surrender came as an unpleasant surprise. When his conclusion proved incorrect, Jabotinsky returned to his earlier analysis: only evacuation could save European Jewry.[153] Although Jabotinsky realized that the partition plan was virtually dead by the summer of 1938, most JA members continued to pin their hopes on it.[154] Jabotinsky proposed an end to concessions, including havlaga, and a return to a solution to the Jewish problem by evacuation.[155]

Ben-Gurion agreed with parts of this analysis, but he differed with Jabotinsky's conclusions. His agreement with the need to evacuate European Jewry helps, at least partially, to explain Ben-Gurion's proposal to Jacobi that Ha-Zach return to a reunited WZO in return for membership in the JAE, even though Ben-Gurion continued to reject cooperation with Ha-Zach. The JAE discussed the Ben-Gurion-Jacobi negotiations at length on October 18. Gruenbaum, Ussishkin, Shapira, Kaplan, and Shertok voted to approve Ben-Gurion's moves, while Senator, Dobkin, and Leo Lauterbach opposed Ben-Gurion's offer.[156] These negotiations ended with no agreement.

While efforts to create a united Zionist front foundered, ideological differences continued to play a role. Jabotinsky still urged the Zionists to adopt an independent policy in relation to the Mandatory government. Unlike Jabotinsky, Ben-Gurion felt that the Yishuv was too weak to attempt anything other than an "aliya war." With his new motto, "Not a war for aliya, but a war by means of aliya," he now changed his position and supported all forms of rescue aliya, including aliya bet, which he had previously opposed.[157]

Under the prevailing circumstances, only aliya bet seemed to offer the hope of a satisfactory aliya rate. From September 1938 onward, Ben-Gurion became a major supporter of the Mossad. Support for aliya by all means did not automatically translate into successful mass aliya, and aliya bet remained fraught with difficulties. Buying and outfitting ships, finding suitable crews, and running the gauntlet of British security forces remained crucial problems for the Mossad le-Aliya Bet and for its competitors from Af-Al-Pi.[158] Yet despite these difficulties, 2,865 passengers debarked from eleven ships.

Besides the technical difficulties connected with the trip, additional obstacles abounded for ma'apilim. As already noted, a Jewish immigrant in Palestine illegally was liable for arrest and summary deportation.[159] Efforts on behalf of ma'apilim continued throughout 1938, although with only limited success. On March 25, 1938, Rabbi Herzog wrote Shertok:

> I am writing to you to remind you of your promise to the
> illegal immigrants . . . again my heart is rent asunder in
> my body over the saddening plight of these unfortunate
> broken families. Please my friend do everything in your
> power — and you have the strength to do much — to
> repair the breakup of these families.[160]

Shertok responded that 10 percent of the next Labor schedule would be set aside for legalizing illegals, but even he realized that such aid would be minor

Call for a Hunger Strike in Defense of Aliya Bet
Courtesy of the Central Zionist Archives, Jerusalem

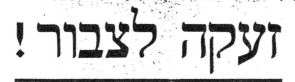

זעקה לצבור !

רצוצים ומדוכאים אנו קבוצת יהודים הבלתי לגליים הנמצאים בארץ

כבר שנים אחדות, פונים לצבור הרחב בזעקה גדולה ומרה, תקשיבו לזעקתנו

זעקת אנשים מיואשים, נרדפים ומעונים. אנו מנותקים מנשינו ויל־דינו

זה שנים. מכריזים שלא נוכל יותר לחיות בתנאים כאלה. עד מתי תמשך

הצרה הזאת של ענינו ?

זעקתנו היא זעקת אנשים מיואשים ואומללים, נשינו וילדינו סובלים

יסורי גיהנם – הילדים אינם מכירים ארת אבותיהם, משפחורת נשמדו

ונהרסו במשך השנים הללו.

יהודים !

הזדעזעו לשמע הצרה הגדולה והאיומה הזאת ותעזרו לנו. אנו

לא נוכל לשבת בחיבוק ידים. מצב כזה לא יוכל להמשך. ואנו הכרזנו

מהיום יום א׳ ל׳ ניסן (6 במאי) משע: 12

שביתת רעב

עד שינתן לנו רשיונות עליה

נפגין את אסוננו וידע הצבור כלו על עניינו.

compared with the actual need. One glimmer of hope existed in a British proposal to allow close relatives to enter Palestine on all immigrant certificates, rather than limiting that right to bearers of A-I certificates.[161]

On May 1, 1938, Irgun Olim Bilti Legali'im (the Organization of Illegal Immigrants) declared a one-day hunger strike to publicize the problem.[162] Herzog thereupon suggested to Shertok that an emergency meeting be held to discuss ways of helping the unfortunates.[163] As a result the JAE to sought certificates from the government reserve. Accepting the government regulations that recipients should first leave Palestine and then return legally, the JAE requested a minimum of 100 certificates.[164] Shortly thereafter, the JA Aliya Department received ten certificates for ma'apilim. The remainder could not be granted to the JAE, stated Edward Mills, since they were needed to help Austrian Jewish refugees.[165]

In addition to the direct pressure of police sweeps to find illegals, the British applied indirect pressure, with the intention of halting the flow. Thus, by the end of July 1938, British pressure on the Greek government resulted in strict regulations regarding Jewish transmigration. The Greeks announced that they would no longer permit Jews to board ships in Piraeus. Unfortunately for Zionists, the decree included both legal and illegal immigrants, thus in effect closing a point of legal embarkation while having little real impact on the flow of illegal immigrants.[166]

Although the British policy on illegals affected both the Mossad and Af-Al-Pi in equal measure, the two organizations remained competitors. On June 28, Mossad agents cabled Tel Aviv regarding rumors that Betar members in Vienna had succeeded in preparing ships and supplies for 1,000 ma'apilim; the Mossad agents called for immediate action.[167] One day later, the estimated number of Betar ma'apilim was reduced to 400, but that still represented twice as many as the Mossad could care for at one time.[168] The group, which actually numbered 350, landed near Herzliya. Their exit had been aided by the Gestapo, although travel, provision, and other arrangements had to be made independently. Each had paid between 200 and 300 Austrian Schillings and had been told to bring enough food to last five days. Once ashore, the ma'apilim were brought to residences in Tel Aviv, whence they spread throughout the city.

Indicative of the Jewish desperation to leave Vienna was the fact that only fifty or sixty of the ma'apilim were actually Betar members.[169] This fact also focuses on a fundamental element in the operational methods of Af-Al-Pi, and of the Mossad as well: despite party sponsorship, neither organization operated on an exclusive basis, and as a result, many nonaffiliated Jews (including many who had previously identified themselves as non-Zionists) were saved. Yet despite their similar policy regarding whom to save, Af-Al-Pi and the Mossad remained competitors throughout the 1930s. Only in 1944, did the two organizations begin to cooperate.[170]

Given the enormous sums required for ha'apala, Ha-Zach turned to the Council for German Jewry in London, seeking financial aid for the emigration of 380 Austrian Jews. The Council, committed to a policy of legality, refused to support this case of independent immigration.[171] Abraham Abrahams responded with "astonishment and intense indignation." Denying that the application was for ma'apilim, he reminded the council of its obligation to "assist in ensuring the welfare of the emigrants and the proper organization of their departure."[172] For now, the matter remained at an impasse. So, too, did the attempt by Rabbi Herzog to approach the British independently of the JA in the hope of legalizing ma'apilim on humanitarian grounds.[173] Although the JAE approved Herzog's approach, most members were skeptical about the likely results.[174] Since the British made no concessions, the JAE's skepticism appears to have been well founded.

9
Toward the Abandonment of the Jews

KRISTALLNACHT AND ITS AFTERMATH

Within Zionist circles, the realization of the need for organizational unity to save the rescue aliya program grew during the autumn of 1938, but ideological and personal considerations made unity less attainable than previously. On November 6, the JAE discussed the negotiations regarding relations between the IZL and the Hagana that derived from the October 1938 meetings between Eliahu Golomb and Zeev Jabotinsky. Although most of the JAE, including Moshe Shertok, and virtually the entire Executive of the Va'ad Leumi supported the agreement, David Ben-Gurion adamantly opposed it.[1] Bringing most of the London Executive to his point of view, Ben-Gurion was able to overturn the tentative agreement initialed by Golomb and Jabotinsky.[2] Almost all attention returned to Europe by the following week, as a result of the Kristallnacht pogroms. Kristallnacht — presented by the Nazis as a spontaneous eruption by an indignant German people inflamed by the assassination of the third secretary of the German embassy in Paris, Ernst vom Rath, by a seventeen-year-old Polish Jew, Herschel Grynszpan — was actually the culmination of a new and harsher Nazi policy regarding Jews. In particular, Nazi authorities increasingly took to coercing Jews to emigrate, despite the new barriers facing potential migrants after the Evian Conference. More and more individual Jews and entire groups were forcibly expelled from Germany.

On October 28, 1938, after a Polish attempt to deprive Polish Jews of the right of return from countries under German rule, the Nazis ordered the deportation of 17,000 Polish Jews. They were driven into no-man's-land near the border town of Zbaszyn. Grynszpan's parents were part of this group, and news of their plight drove him to his act of revenge on November 7.

On the afternoon of November 9, vom Rath died. That night, orders were conveyed to police and security forces throughout Germany. In accordance with these orders, crowds were encouraged by members of the SA and SS to participate in the atmosphere of outrage. Mass frenzy resulted: synagogues were desecrated and burned, windows of Jewish-owned stores and homes were shattered, and Jewish shops were looted. In many places Jews were physically attacked. Ninety-one Jews were killed during the pogrom, and more than 900 synagogues were destroyed. After the pogrom 30,000 Jews were seized by the SS and were placed under "protective custody" in concentration camps. A new series of administrative and legal orders followed; these completed Aryanization, isolated the Jews from the rest of the population, and placed the Jewish community under police control. Kristallnacht was, thus, a turning point in the history of the Holocaust: it was the Nazis' first experience of large-scale anti-Jewish violence, and opened the way to the complete eradication of the Jews' position in Germany.[3]

The Yishuv expressed an intense desire to aid German Jewry, concentrating on a plan to facilitate the evacuation of 100,000 German and Austrian Jews, but it lacked the ability to do so.[4] Again, the prime cause for the failure to rescue appears to have been the British: tragically, on the day before the pogrom (November 9), the Woodhead Commission published its report and cancelled the Peel partition plan.[5] Though divided into majority and minority opinions, members of the Woodhead Commission did concur on two points: that partition was not technically feasible, and that the government should make a new effort to achieve peace in Palestine.[6]

Not surprisingly, many in the Yishuv viewed both the Woodhead Commission report and Kristallnacht as closely connected, despite British attempts to distinguish between Palestine and rescue as independent issues.[7] The autumn meeting of the Va'ad ha-Poel ha-Zioni in Jerusalem from November 11 to 16 concentrated on these two events.[8] All of Palestine's major dailies devoted considerable print space to the pogroms. Coverage by the *Palestine Post* was most extensive, and as late as November 22, 1938, it continued to publish detailed eyewitness accounts of the horrors in Germany, culled from reports filed by the correspondents of the *London Times*.[9] The *Post* also devoted much attention to efforts to find refuge for Jews from central and eastern Europe, a subject that it had extensively covered even before Kristallnacht.[10] Agronsky saw no contradiction between aliya and havens for Jews elsewhere, especially under the emergency conditions. In an editorial on November 14, 1938, he wrote:

> The provision of facilities for the refugees elsewhere
> than in Palestine should not be an excuse, even were
> those facilities anything like adequate, for barring the
> Jews' entry into this country.[11]

On the other hand, both the *Post* and *ha-Aretz* had harsh words for Herschel Grynszpan: though recognizing that his attack was used by the Nazis as an excuse, the *Post* still characterized it as "insane and criminal," while *ha-Aretz* concluded that he had acted irresponsibly.[12]   *Ha-Aretz* did concede that Grynszpan was an "unfortunate youth."[13]   Only *Davar's* editorial writer, Moshe Beilinson, viewed Grynszpan sympathetically, casting him as a tragic youth who sought to avenge his parents' suffering and in that way kindle public opinion to save German Jewry.[14]   *Ha-Aretz* concentrated on the implications of the pogroms, and especially stressed the critical role that the Yishuv had to play if German Jewry were to be rescued. In one editorial, *ha-Aretz* argued that it was not enough for members of the Yishuv to do the minimum necessary and then return to a smug sense of apathy. Rather, the Yishuv should seek to move heaven and earth to rescue threatened Jewry — if even unsuccessfully. Otherwise, the paper warned, Jews would conclude that the Zionists had "failed the test of our generation."[15]

Davar followed a similar editorial policy, calling upon humanity to rescue German Jewry, but concentrating on Palestine's role in the process.[16] In an editorial marking the meeting of the Va'ad ha-Poel ha-Zioni, *ha-Aretz* took the conclusion one step further, calling for the creation of a united Zionist front (including Ha-Zach). The editors saw unification of all youth groups in Tel Aviv behind a joint banner as an encouraging sign, and hoped that adults would behave in a spirit similar to that of their young counterparts.[17]

The Kristallnacht pogrom also had a profound personal impact on the Yishuv's leaders. In a note to Werner Senator, Henrietta Szold bared her fears about "Who has gone mad — we or Germany? We — since we do nothing, and the world still says it can't (sic) interfere with the domestic concerns of a country."[18] The pogrom also had a profound impact on Ben-Gurion, although he did not always show his feelings in public.[19] Albeit, it is important to remember that after Kristallnacht Ben-Gurion began to talk of a new Zionism, which he dubbed "fighting Zionism."[20]

The JAE met in London on November 13, 1938, to discuss Kristallnacht. Felix Rosenblueth, newly appointed to membership in the Jerusalem JAE, stated forcefully that the JA had to take the initiative in all aid or be swept aside.[21] As before, discussion focused primarily on how best to aid German Jews by assuring their immigration to Palestine. Moshe Shertok said that although the JA had requested a schedule of 4,500 (750 certificates a month for six months), an emergency grant of 2,000 would be needed immediately. Thousands more would follow if certificates could be found.[22]   Shertok observed, however, that only Youth Aliya was unaffected by the recent government decisions relating to immigration. Consequently, he and Chaim Weizmann expressed considerable skepticism about the likelihood of government aid. Weizmann thought that an approach to Prime Minister Neville Chamberlain would be futile, saying: "In both France and England they say we are responsible for creating bad relations with Germany."[23] Selig Adler-Rudel, a respected German Jewish communal leader invited to attend this JAE meeting, suggested a twofold approach: a protest by the JAE against Nazi use of violence, combined with constructive work. At this point, Ben-Gurion, who had remained silent during the entire deliberation, proposed the creation of two subcommittees, one political and the other administrative, to carry out Adler-Rudel's suggestion. The resolution passed unanimously.[24]

The denouement of these proposals came on November 22, 1938. The JAE published a statement requesting the immediate entry into Palestine of 100,000 German, Austrian, and Czech Jews. "This would be the first installment," read the statement, "of what is necessary. Bigger schemes could be realized if friendly governments would help by guaranteeing a loan for this purpose."[25] To finance this project, the Va'ad ha-Poel ha-Zioni proposed changing the Yishuv's defense fund (Kofer ha-Yishuv) into a rescue and resettlement fund, to be called Kofer ha-Am (the National Fund).[26]

As a direct result of Kristallnacht, even the most minimalist members of the JAE came to accept some form of evacuation scheme, nearly four years after Jabotinsky had first proposed it. However, evacuation was not so simple. In planning for their relief programs, most American and British philanthropic agencies appeared to ignore Palestine, again raising fears within the JAE of a territorialist solution to the Jewish problem.[27] These fears had a basis. On November 18, 1938, Rosenblueth wrote to Ben-Gurion that the Council for German Jewry "will approve plans which, though constructive, will have nothing to do with Palestine, at any rate not to begin with." Rosenblueth thus called upon the JAE to reevaluate relations with the council and to respond forcefully to these plans.[28]

For his part, Jabotinsky claimed not to fear mass resettlement outside of Palestine as a temporary refuge, since it would remove Jews from harm's way without prejudicing long-term Zionist goals. Jabotinsky's supposed territorialist phase, which lasted from late 1938 until his death, has been used ex-post-facto as a major source for crititcism of the Yishuv's leadership. The critics claim that Jabotinsky was the only Zionist leader to agree that salvation had to take second place to the immediate Jewish need for rescue. While there is some truth to these claims, they also ignore the fact that Jabotinsky's "territorialism" was always tactical. Jabotinsky never surrendered the ultimate goal of a Jewish state on both banks of the Jordan River. Insofar as short-term Jewish needs might be fulfilled by accepting mass exodus to a territory other than Palestine, Jabotinsky accepted the reality and acted accordingly. Two caveats must be noted, however, and they prove the tactical nature of Jabotinsky's attitude. First, he insisted that all Ha-Zach representatives who discussed non-Palestine rescue schemes do so only in private. Second, when they did discuss such schemes they were to emphasize that the proposals were personal initiatives and not the responsibility of Ha-Zach.[29] Obviously, there was a method to such discussions: since Jabotinsky did not honestly believe that any rescue scheme could succeed without Palestine, he hoped to play on interest in exploring alternate havens. He expected all such schemes to collapse, after which no alternative but Palestine would remain thereby bringing pressure to bear on the British to acquiesce to Ha-Zach's Ten Year Plan. Further evidence that Jabotinsky's "territorialism" was little more than a tactical ploy may be adduced from the fact that just when Bernard Baruch suggested sending Jewish refugees to Angola, Jabotinsky sent one of his closest advisors, Robert Briscoe, to Washington to test the Roosevelt administration's interest in a new evacuation plan designed to bring 1,000,000 Jews to Palestine in three years rather than the ten years originally planned.[30]

THE END OF RESCUE ALIYA

Regardless of which propoasl is emphasized, the reality was that the British represented the principle obstruction to rescue. A few days after the JAE meeting in London, Weizmann met with Prime Minister Chamberlain and Jewish members of the House of Lords to request an emergency grant of 10,000 certificates above the schedule. Though outwardly sympathetic to the Jews' plight, Chamberlain refused to commit his government to any specific action in response to Weizmann's request.[31] When Weizmann further proposed the immediate entry of between 75,000 and 100,000 German Jews into Palestine, Chamberlain did not reject the proposal, but rather brushed it off casually. He stated that since such an aliya rate would require an extraordinary number of certificates, he would approve any quantity that Colonial Secretary Malcolm MacDonald approved of. Chamberlain did reject any direct action against Germany, as "likely to do more harm than good."[32]

Weizmann hoped to convince the government to increase the aliya rate beyond the political maximum of 12,000, although he was unsure of the extent of the potential increase.[33] He reported to the JAE that his immediate goal was an aliya rate of 30,000 Jews per year for at least five years. Weizmann believed that privately, MacDonald would support such a rate, even if he opposed it publicly.[34]

On November 23, 1938, the JA made a formal request for 24,000 certificates, divided as follows: 7,500 for halutzim from disbanded hachsharot (many of whom were incarcerated in concentration camps); 2,500 for youth olim between ages 15 and 17; 10,000 for youth olim between ages 6 and 14; 2,000 A-category certificates; and 2,000 D-category certificates.

Of these, the 2,000 A-category certificates and 600 of the D-category certificates had already been granted. The JAE also requested that 600 A-I certificates be converted to categories A-II, A-III, and A-IV, since the Berlin Palestine Office had only 1,400 requests for A-I certificates.[35]

The British responded to the JA request without enthusiasm. Bernard Joseph cabled Shertok:

> Apparently, H.M.G. only concerned [to] please [the] Arabs to [the] extent [of] unwillingness [to] show elementary humanitarian consideration [for the] calamity [of] Jews [in] Germany . . . we evidently have nothing [to] hope for from negotiations . . . and must exert what little influence we can through public opinion which will condemn [the] government's refusal [to support] immigration. If we are to be treated as [a] negligible quantity we have little to lose by adopting [a more] aggressive attitude. Perhaps fear [of] upsetting negotiations may move them.[36]

In response to the British demurral, the JAE decided to concentrate only on the Youth Aliya request. Although in effect admitting defeat and capitulating to the British refusal to rescue German Jewry, the JAE had no options other than aliya bet, which many still opposed. In turn, the original plan was whittled down to only 5,000 certificates.

Concentration on Youth Aliya raised three questions among rescue activists. First, would enough parents be willing to work with the Youth Aliya offices in Berlin to allow the creation of a group of 5,000 youth? Second, did the Yishuv have the financial resources to settle the olim? Third, did the Yishuv have sufficient settlement space to absorb the 5,000 youth? The urgent nature of these questions, none of which had been properly addressed before, led Georg Landauer to warn: "This project is so large that we cannot consider the possibility that, because of it, other rescue projects will also succeed."[37] Nevertheless, initial planning began, since the JAE needed to find foster parents for at least some of the youth. The haste with which the plan developed originated from the British demands that they receive specific details about resettlement before they would grant approval in principle.[38]

The project, though curtailed, excited the entire Yishuv even before approval, and rejuvenated the advocates of rescue aliya. *Ha-Aretz* reported that the largest rally to be held since the rise of the Nazis took place in defense of the plan in Tel Aviv on November 13, 1938.[39] Three days later, the Palestine Writers' Federation joined in, with a biting anti-Nazi protest.[40] On November 19 the Va'ad Leumi brought a new organization into existence, Pidyon Shevuyim. Its purpose was to serve as a primary rescue agency for German, Austrian, and Czechoslovak Jewish youth.[41]

Although the *Palestine Post* did not initially connect Pidyon Shevuyim with the Youth Aliya scheme, Agronsky expressed support for both.[42] On November 20 he wrote a strongly worded editorial, saying that "not a minute should be lost in saving the children." Agronsky also warned, though, against using the children to "pry open the doors for the admission of extra Jewish immigrants."[43] He opposed the idea of politicizing Youth Aliya in so blatant a fashion, hoping that the rescue program could remain purely humanitarian in nature. The German Zionists, however, had no such qualms; indeed, many of them desperately sought certificates from relatives already living in the Holy Land.[44] A majority of the Yishuv agreed with Agronsky and opposed politicizing the humanitarian aid program.[45]

In December 1938, the JA submitted an official request for 2,500 B-III certificates and 2,500 D certificates, to accommodate the 5,000 youth olim.[46] High Commissioner Harold MacMichael decided not to deal with the request, and referred the matter directly to the Colonial Office in London.[47] The JA leadership felt betrayed by this decision, al-though MacMichael framed it in "routine" terms. Some JAE members said that the British had reneged on their promises to help in humanitarian rescue work.[48] Weizmann, for one, went so far as to suggest non-participation in the upcoming St. James Conference unless the British made the Youth Aliya certificates available.[49]

Because the issue had become an emotional one, the JAE reiterated the re-quest in December 1938, justifying the clamor for more certificates on two grounds. The first was the unqualified success of Youth Aliya, and the second, the great need of German Jewish youth for immediate rescue.[50] By then, the British had granted 630 certificates. The JAE sought a further immediate grant to settle 970 youth in twenty-three settlements, and also assurances that 900 more certificates would be granted as new opportunities arose.[51] In January 1939, the JAE requested certificates for 10,000 children, in addition to help in freeing 300 veteran Zionists still incarcerated in Nazi concentration camps.[52] Meanwhile, the JAE also considered requesting 300 immigrant visas to send hachshara graduates to England in order to evacuate them from Germany without using scarce certificates.[53]

Clearly, the JAE intended to use Youth Aliya as a means of opening Palestine. If public opinion in Great Britain and America would not permit the Palestine administration to actively oppose the humanitarian request to rescue Jewish youth, especially after Kristallnacht, the JAE hoped to use the rescue of children as a means to rescue their parents and families as well. While Henrietta Szold opposed such tactics, calling them "emotional black-mail," she too had plans for a massive expansion of Youth Aliya. In Szold's scheme, Youth Aliya would include Germany and Austria, Czechoslovakia, Poland, and other eastern European countries.[54] Further plans for Youth Aliya expansion continued until the eve of World War II, and concerned the rescue of 30,000 young people, many of whom would be transferred to England, western Europe, or Scandinavia before aliya. Despite progress, the program remained incomplete before the outbreak of the war, and must be considered only partially successful.[55]

In addition to Youth Aliya, the JAE presented other rescue proposals to the British. Weizmann and Ben-Gurion met with Chamberlain on November 19. The latter responded coolly to Weizmann's request for 20,000 emergency certificates.[56] Between October 1938 and September 1939, the British granted a total of only 2,600 certificates. At this point, exasperation gave way to despair, even among the Zionists.

THE SEARCH FOR A SAFE HAVEN

The British refusal to continue helping the rescue aliya program received considerable attention within the Yishuv and in Jewish communities worldwide. The WJC protested the new restrictions on Jewish immigration and called on the Mandatory government to take the necessary steps to rescue threatened Jews.[57] Public protests in America, Argentina, and Great Britain reinforced this message.[58] The JA and Va'ad Leumi sponsored a one-day strike in defense of aliya on October 31, 1938. When Parliament debated the refugee problem, *ha-Aretz* joined the chorus in an editorial demanding that the British match their words with deeds.[59]

In January 1939, Ben-Gurion traveled to America to secure American Jewish support in four areas: preparations for the upcoming Twentieth World Zionist Congress, Zionist participation in the United Jewish Appeal for Refugees and Overseas Needs, aliya bet (especially money to buy ships), and Ben-Gurion's plan for a world Jewish conference to meet in America concurrently with the planned Arab-Jewish-British peace talks planned for February.[60] Although somewhat frightened by Ben-Gurion's forthright and tough language, American Labor Zionists supported him at a meeting on January 11. In particular, Ben-Gurion's explicit statements regarding the need to rescue both European Jewry and the Zionist movement won the day.[61] Ben-Gurion met with many Zionist and non-Zionist leaders during the rest of his one-month stay, but, although he gained much verbal support for his ideas, the American Zionists simply were not prepared to come to the Yishuv's assistance in any real way and the conference never took place.[62]

All of these protests had two elements in common: they all concentrated on legal immigration, and they all failed to sway the British government. As a result, aliya bet returned to the JA agenda. Though many JAE members still opposed ha'apala, a critical number supported getting Jews into Palestine by whatever means. Thus, although aliya bet still did not play as central a role in JA activity as it did for Ha-Zach, the JAE recognized the need to maintain the Mossad, to expand its activities, and to aid ma'apilim before they arrived at the coast — a major change in JA policy. In order to assist ships in avoiding the British blockade (the only blockade in history undertaken during peacetime by a country over a coastal territory under its own control), the

Hagana high command created a special communications unit.[63] Ten radio operators were recruited and trained; from then on at least one of them joined the crew of every Mossad ship that sailed.[64]

Willingness to undertake this arduous journey was a reflection of the Jewish desperation to escape Europe. The Jewish problem had now expanded to include not only Germany, but also Austria, the Sudetenland (granted to Germany at the Munich conference), Slovakia, and those parts of Slovakia seized by Hungary.[65] Initially, the Slovak Jews requested only financial aid. Soon, however, requests for aid turned into appeals to the Yishuv or friendly governments to help find a haven. By the spring of 1939, desperation increasingly animated these requests. In the interim, Slovakia had become an independent republic, although it was actually a puppet state under Nazi control. The new Slovakian government enacted racial legislation modeled on the Nuremberg Laws. "The blood of our brothers, which is being spilled daily, calls to us for rescue action," wrote one rescue advocate.[66]

Despite persisting Zionist fears of a territorialist solution that would ignore Palestine, many members of the JAE realized that, for the time being at least, the Yishuv could offer little or no actual assistance to European Jewry. The constructive aid program, begun so auspiciously in 1933, had, in effect, come to a crashing end. As a result, Zionist leaders sought any means of rescue, even outside Palestine. Thus, Arthur Ruppin cabled the London Executive to "suggest for your consideration that the German Council should appeal to [President] Roosevelt [to] grant 100,000 visas [on] account [of the] next five years' quotas."[67] Ben-Gurion, witnessing from London the demise of rescue aliya, reluctantly supported Ruppin's suggestion.[68]

Although the United States overtook Palestine as a refugee destination in 1938, this rescue proposal never came to fruition. Because of immigration laws enacted in 1924, America remained a highly equivocal haven for Jews throughout the 1930s and 1940s. Despite calls for liberalizing immigration policy, especially after Kristallnacht, the isolationist atmosphere both in Congress and among the American public underwent little change. Yet, by some estimates, the United States government had granted 1,000,000 too few entry visas in the years between 1933 and 1939. In other words, virtually all of the German and Austrian Jews could have been rescued without any changes to America's immigration quotas — had the will to do so existed. Instead, the State Department obstructed refugee immigration, while the Roosevelt administration took no effective steps to remedy the situation.[69]

THE LONDON (ST. JAMES PALACE) CONFERENCE

After the Woodhead Commission report was published, many Jews feared that the government intended to impose an arbitrary policy on Palestine that would surrender British promises to the Jews in order to win Arab quiescence. These fears were soon confirmed. On October 24, 1938, the Chamberlain government announced its intention to convene a round-table conference on Palestine, to include Jewish and Arab representatives, members of the government, and the ambassadors of Transjordan, Iraq, Egypt, and Saudi Arabia. The conference soon turned into two sets of negotiations when the Arab delegation declared their unwillingness even to sit at the same table as the Jews, meaning that the British would act as intermediaries throughout the talks.[70]

As before the Peel Commission hearings, the Zionists disagreed on the issue of participation or nonparticipation. In this case, however, advocacy of non-participation did not necessarily translate into advocacy of a maximalist counterposition. Thus, for example, Weizmann proposed that the JAE not participate in the talks unless the British released the 2,000 extra Youth Aliya certificates that they had promised.[71] Yitzhak Gruenbaum supported this position, advocating cooperation while threatening noncooperation to gain leverage for aliya demands, as he had done during discussions regarding the Legislative Council.[72] Mizrachi, which had opposed partition, went on record as the first party to oppose participating in the conference.[73]

Eliezer Kaplan opposed both Weizmann and Gruenbaum, since such a Jewish ultimatum had no potency: all the British had to do was to promise the certificates (intending to renege on the promise later), in so doing calling the JAE's bluff to force Jewish participation.[74]

Most members of the JAE agreed with Kaplan, to a greater or lesser degree. Although recognizing the great peril of participation — that a Jewish presence would lend an air of legitimacy to the British-imposed solution — they saw no alternative. As framed by Shertok, this position had two bases: that nonparticipation offered no means of defending Zionist interests before the government, and that threatening not to attend would be perceived as a hollow threat, leaving the government free to impose its own solution.[75] In his analysis, Shertok also touched on the Jews' weakness: "If only [the press] was completely at our disposal," he ruminated.[76]

Assuming participation, therefore, most JAE members felt the need to analyze the overall situation. Ben-Gurion's analysis is the most important, since it reflects the changes in his orientation during the preceding three or four years. Basing himself on his recent talks with government members in London, he predicted "a new departure in our relations with the mandatory power," adding: "If the conference concludes not in our favor — and the chances of a successful result are miniscule — we must be prepared to adopt a new tactic in our political struggle."[77]

Ben-Gurion based this pessimistic assessment on two factors: (1) the international situation, especially the threat of German expansion, which required Great Britain to buy Arab neutrality in case of war, and (2) the new situation faced by the Jews.[78] "What is now being done to Jews in Germany," he flatly stated, "is not an end, but a beginning." Ben-Gurion predicted that Poland and Romania would soon learn from the Nazis' example.[79] The upshot of an ever-expanding antisemitic threat and of the increasingly internationalized refugee crisis was a grave danger to Zionism which arose from the largely futile attempt to find other havens for Jewish refugees. The British had blocked further large-scale aliya and sought to separate the rescue issue from the Palestine problem.[80] For public relations reasons Ha-Zach agreed with the British that rescue could be detached from the Palestine problem, arguing only that large-scale resettlement was not possible outside the Yishuv, except as a temporary measure.[81]

Ben-Gurion predicted that the British would severely limit aliya and land acquisition, though in both cases they would not completely ban Zionist work. "We still have some favorable public opinion in England," he noted "the British still must consider America, and would never break a solemn pledge in such a shameless and conspicuous manner."[82] This was a total misreading of the situation, one that Ben-Gurion shared with Jabotinsky, since neither believed that the British would repudiate their promises to the Jews. Therefore, according to Ben-Gurion, Zionists had to be prepared for a new policy:

> We shall have to inform the government of our inability
> to continue cooperation. Publicly, the Executive will have
> to resign, we shall have to convene a world Jewish
> conference in America and we will have to declare and
> carry out an aliya war: we shall organize aliya on our
> authority — and we shall place before the British the
> alternative of combating this aliya by force . . . Let the
> British fleet fight against the tens of thousands of our
> youth who will set sail from the ports of Europe (and
> perhaps America as well) for the coast of Eretz-Israel
> and its ports. We shall organize this aliya in public. This
> will be the centerpiece of the political struggle for our
> homeland. In this operation we will unify the entire Jew-
> ish people, the Yishuv, public opinion in America and all
> of Europe, and even public opinion in England.[83]

Ben-Gurion now agreed with Jabotinsky that only the public pressure of an aliya war could bring about victory. Other tactics would not move the government, since Arab pressure was too great. Only an aliya war, to be carried out by "The Committee to Rescue the People and Land of Israel," had a chance to succeed, but only if the leadership represented the entire Jewish people.[84] For the short term, Ben-Gurion proposed attending the London Conference and airing a three-part Jewish stance: (1) Eretz Israel as a Jewish state; (2) transfer of the Arabs in Palestine to other Arab states; and (3) mass aliya.[85]

Ben-Gurion's position immediately gained Menachem M. Ussishkin's backing. Ussishkin also scored the JA's twenty-year policy of compromise, which, he said, had gained nothing and must cease. As against Ussishkin, a General Zionist, Eliyahu Dobkin of Mapai differed with Ben-Gurion for three reasons. First, Dobkin believed that Ben-Gurion's prognosis was too pessimistic. Second, he felt that the JAE could wait until after the conference to make substantive decisions regarding policy. Third, he did not believe that the JA, or world Jewry, possessed sufficient resources to prosecute successfully Ben-Gurion's "aliya war." Nevertheless, Dobkin supported Ben-Gurion on two points: that the JAE's minimum demand in London be mass aliya (with British consent), and that an international Jewish conference for the defense of aliya be called immediately.[86]

Unlike the circumstances in late 1934 when Ben-Gurion made his first call for mass aliya, the JAE now supported his demand for an "aliya war," which Ben-Gurion defined as "not a war for aliya, but a war by means of aliya, an aliya rebellion."[87] Over the objections of Gruenbaum and Rabbi Judah L. Fishman the JAE also approved participation in the London talks and set out to prepare its delegation.[88] Ben-Gurion reiterated his position at a meeting of the Va'ad ha-Poel ha-Zioni on December 17, 1938.[89]

During its next three meetings (December 18 and 25, 1938, and January 1, 1939), the JAE prepared the makeup of its delegation. Afterward, two features of the Zionist position became clear: that the delegation should be as large and as representative as possible, and that the policy of compromise was no longer an option. For the time being, the aliya war would be put on hold. The JAE did not forget the proposal, but it concentrated on the slim possibility of gaining British approval for legal mass aliya as a reward for attending the conference. As some JAE members realized, convincing the British to accede was never very likely.

Commitment to aliya at all costs was the crux of the disagreement between the JA and Ha-Zach in 1939. In talks held between Eri Jabotinsky and Ben-Gurion in 1937, the former proposed that Ha-Zach accept Mapai's socio-economic policy in return for Mapai's acceptance of Ha-Zach's political program.[90] In 1937 Ben-Gurion did not yet accept the need for aliya bet, and thus no agreement was reached; by 1939, he did. Many members of the JAE such as Dobkin still did not share Ben-Gurion's sentiments, even though they used his rhetoric because of its popular appeal.

In other words, significant areas of disagreement remained within the Zionist camp. Although he was still reluctant about Mizrachi participation, Rabbi Fishman demanded an additional representative besides himself (since he was a member of the JAE), so as to balance the deputation of Agudas Israel.[91] Eventually, the JAE decided to add Rabbi Yitzhak Halevy Herzog, thus satisfying Mizrachi's demands. The JAE also met demands for representation made by the Yishuv's Sephardi and Yemenite parties.[92] By mid-January 1939, even ha-Shomer ha-Zair, long a critic of Mapai's leadership and ideology, had requested a representative. The Jerusalem JAE, however, placed the decision on this matter exclusively in the London Executive's hands.[93] The Jewish delegation was completed by representatives of the diaspora communities, primarily deleagations of eastern European and American Zionists.[94]

Paradoxically, only the Jerusalem JAE had committed itself to participation by the end of January 1939. On December 16, 1938, the London Executive initially voted not to participate.[95] However, the London JAE voted to create a political advisory committee. The twenty-two-member panel was to be comprised of representatives of all JA member organizations and Agudas Israel. Planned to last the conference's duration, the panel possessed advisory powers only.[96] Even so, its creation appeared to contradict the policy of non-participation in the conference, and the London Executive eventually reversed itself.

The position of the Va'ad Leumi was more problematic. Initially, the Va'ad Leumi Executive agreed to participate.[97] Early in January 1939, it unofficially announced its intention not to participate. It appears that the Va'ad Leumi's underlying motivation was a serious question regarding its role in the Yishuv, and especially its relation to the JA.[98] Friction existed even though both the JA and the Va'ad Leumi were dominated by Mapai and derived from both agencies' electoral sources. The JA drew its power from the assent of the WZO and from the non-Zionists who chose their representatives. The Va'ad Leumi, on the other hand, answered to Assefat ha-Nivharim, and, in theory at least, represented all Jews in Palestine. The question of whose authority to govern the Yishuv predominated had never been resolved clearly. Since neither ultimately ruled Palestine, such lack of precision had not generally been a problem. The January 1939 JAE request that the Va'ad Leumi Executive postpone any official decision regarding the conference ended the dispute.[99] Just before the conference, the Va'ad Leumi reversed course again and agreed to participate. Thereafter, relations between it and the JAE were regulated by a system of invitations extended to the Va'ad Leumi leaders to attend JAE meetings. American Zionists also agreed to participate, despite the initial hesitation of Justice Louis D. Brandeis, Rabbi Stephen S. Wise, and other leaders.[100]

By the end of January 1939, only Ha-Zach had been left out of the Jewish delegation by the JAE. Although this was never justified, it appears that the continuing ideological struggle between the WZO and the NZO explains this blatant negligence. Antagonism continued unabated, despite the obvious danger posed by disunity. Thus, for example, the JA Administrative Department wrote to the Executive regarding the need to counter Ha-Zach propaganda in Argentina as late as December 5, 1938.[101] Despite the now popular get tough rhetoric used by members of the JAE, the years of struggle with the Revisionists had left too many petty hatreds that could not be overcome. Though both sides in the dispute were now working for the same goals, they had to do so independently.[102]

With the decision on participation made and the makeup of the delegation almost settled, the JAE turned its attention to the content of its arguments. Immediately, Dr. Werner D. Senator suggested that the JAE request a one-for-one rebate of certificates granted to olim who later left Palestine, in order to supplement the "political maximum." This quite original way of using yerida to open up Palestine was never pursued by the JAE.[103]   Moreover, some JAE members attempted to silence Senator by restrictin his contact with American non-Zionists by forcing him to obtain prior approval for all such contacts.[104]   This action, sponsored by Kaplan and Gruenbaum, stemmed from Senator's attitude toward the Jewish position at the conference.

After a month of preparation, the JAE delegation arrived in London, and on February 7, 1939, the talks began. The conference opened with speeches by Chamberlain, Weizmann, Ben-Zvi, Wise, and Lord Reading. Weizmann presented the Jewish case on February 8, citing Jewish rights in Palestine as recognized by the Balfour Declaration and the Mandate, and stressing the urgent need of Jewry for a safe haven.[105]   Colonial Secretary MacDonald responded, expressing "a great deal of sympathy with the Jewish people" but, nevertheless, exclusively presenting the Arab case.[106]   Ben-Gurion spoke next, saying that he did not regard the problem "as a case between Arabs and Jews: it was a case between the Jews and the world." He referred repeatedly to Jewish homelessness and suffering, concluding that the Jews' return to Palestine was "a restitution of the civilized world for 2,000 years of persecution."[107]   MacDonald interjected that he would "not admit for one minute that 16 million Jews had the right to go back to Palestine."[108]   To this, the JA leaders responded that they did not anticipate the immigration of all Jews, but that they considered consultation with diaspora Jewry on issues affecting the Jewish national home at least as legitimate as the interference in Palestine's affairs by neighboring Arab states.[109]

Sessions held between February 13 and 15 and on February 17 and 20, repeated this pattern. At every meeting the British took the Arabs' side on all issues, especially on immigration. Throughout, the British offered no concessions; in effect, they operated as intermediaries for the Arab delegation that refused to meet with the Jewish leaders. On February 16, the JA delegation decided to make one last effort to reach an agreement. The Zionists proposed direct negotiations with the Arab delegation on all issues except immigration.[110]   Again, the Arabs refused to sit with the Jewish delegation. As a result, the conference rapidly approached a deadlock.

Under these circumstances, cracks began to appear in the Jewish delegation. The position of the non-Zionists, reflected in Senator's private letters, and of the Zionists began to diverge greatly. Senator commented:

"The fundamental problem we have to face is the Arab problem."[111] Since the British needed peace in the Middle East to secure their empire, he said, they sought a modification of the situation in Palestine. Given that they had abandoned partition, they now had two options. Senator weighed and rejected the possibility of decisive British support for either the Jews or the Arabs. He did consider an alternative, however: connecting Palestine with Syria or Iraq in a Middle Eastern federation.[112] This would alleviate Arab fears of Jewish domination. Furthermore, Senator argued, the JA should agree to a mora-torium on mass aliya for ten to twelve years. During this period the Yishuv's population would not rise above 40 percent of Palestine's total popula-tion.[113] As a quid pro quo, Senator suggested the creation of a legislative council for Palestine, based on parity between the communities, so that aliya could not be completely halted, though it would be voluntarily restricted.[114]

Senator seems to have misread the situation in Europe, and especially the mood among governing circles in Britain. Calculating that war would ulti-mately result, he did not fully take into account the changes in Nazi policy toward Jews after Kristallnacht. These spelled doom for European Jewry un-less a haven could be found for them. Equally significant in the debate over Senator's proposed policy was the fact that the Jewish public was not to be consulted in this vital matter, since his letter was never meant to be published.

To be fair, Senator was not alone in misunderstanding Nazi goals. Only a handful of Zionists — including Jabotinsky (to whom virtually none were listening in any case) and Ben-Gurion — realized the implications of the new situation. Even among them, no one recognized that war, and systematic extermination of European Jewry, was imminent. In practice, therefore, the Zionists' analysis differed little from that of Senator, although they did differ in their appreciation of the imminence of war. Both were aware that Britain's interest in Arab rights arose more from considerations of strategy than from a concern with justice. More importantly, the Zionists rejected the possibility of stopping immigration, realizing that the situation boded ill for European Jewry. Thus, the distress of European Jewry became the centerpiece of the Zionist argument. Shertok, for instance, stressed Jewish needs in a speech he made on February 13, 1939. All Zionists, he stated, had one goal: "to settle Jews in Palestine — the largest number of Jews."[115] He continued:

> Two months ago we had on our hands 2,000 applications of
> would-be capitalist immigrants, and all we could offer was
> 250 permits. The remainder of the quota had all been
> taken up . . . The whole world is discussing the problem
> of refugees . . . And here, Jewish capital is being frittered
> away because people are not allowed to save it, before it
> is too late, by taking it with them to Palestine.[116]

As already noted, the British ignored the Zionist arguments. On February 20, 1939, formal sessions ended. Six days later the JAE publicly set out a list of actions that, if carried out by the government or the Arabs, would cause the JAE's withdrawal from the conference.[117]

Meanwhile, nothing had come of the aliya war. Obviously, the JA could not wait any longer. If the JA actions did not begin to match its rhetoric quickly, its authority would be severely damaged. On February 27, the JA delegation followed through on the threat and announced its withdrawal.[118] Mapai's delegates later explained: "The time has come for us to tell the government that, if there is a need for concessions, then they should be given to the Jews and not demanded from them."[119] In effect, the JAE told the government that it would not silently accept the policy about to be imposed on the Yishuv.

ALIYA BET AND ELEVENTH HOUR RESCUE

While the JAE involved itself in fruitless negotiations with the British, Jabotinsky and Ha-Zach continued operations that concentrated on aliya bet. On November 29, 1938, Jabotinsky had appointed Joseph Katznelson, Berl's cousin, to a senior position on the Betar Aliya Committee in Warsaw. Acting as Jabotinsky's personal representative, Katzenelson was responsible for all aliya-related matters and helped Eri Jabotinsky.[120] Upon his arrival, Katznelson plunged directly into independent immigration activities. By early February 1939, three new convoys were being prepared: from Danzig, from Poland, and from France and Switzerland (a joint convoy). To keep operations running smoothly, Betar established four subcommittees, for (1) organization of convoys; (2) land transportation (also responsible for visas and provisions); (3) sea transportation (also responsible for buying and crewing ships); and (4) finances. The first and second subcommittees were chaired by Eri Jabotinsky (using the nom de guerre B. Schwarz), the third by Katznelson (using the non de guerre Ben-Menachem), and the last by G. Cohen.[121] Despite intense difficulties, primarily financial, the operation was a relative success, thanks to the tacit cooperation of the Polish authorities.[122] Financial problems derived from the fact that the Jewish establishment, including the JAE, refused to finance Af-Al-Pi's activities directly.

In 1939 Af-Al-Pi expanded its activities to include Romania. Because of limited funds, each ma'apil had to pay for transportation, a point often exploited by Ha-Zach's opponents. Af-Al-Pi planned its initial operations in Romania around a total of 5,000 emigrants per year at a cost of 350,000,000 lei (£P500,000 or $2,500,000). Part of this sum already existed, in the form of a £P100,000 ($500,000) bank account in London. The remainder would come from the surplus of Palestine-Romania transfer agreement exports, from donations by local Jewish communities, and from the emigrants.[123] Once the financing became available, Af-Al-Pi reorganized itself as a public corporation, Rompalia (the Association for Organizing Jewish Emigration from Romania).[124] It was constituted "to facilitate and to organize a Jewish emigration from Romania to Palestine and other countries."[125]

At least part of this Revisionist aliya was supposed to be funded by the JAE. In January 1939, for example, Dobkin promised a considerable contribution for refugee migration (i.e., ha'apala), but Ha-Zach received only £P600 ($3,000), covering the expenses for ten legal immigrants.[126] As a result, Ha-Zach representative David Bookspan wrote to the JAE to protest the lack of financing. Landauer responded that no financing could be granted for olim already in Palestine, although he did promise that in the future, Ha-Zach would be assisted with its financial obligations for all forms of aliya in the same way that all other parties were.[127] Bookspan was happy to accept Landauer's promises regarding the future, but he expressed great disappointment for the present, since at the time Dobkin had promised to help, the olim were en route.[128] It is not clear whether the JAE actually transferred the money; the commitment to do so, however, presages the wartime cooperation between Af-Al-Pi and the Mossad le-Aliya Bet.

THE COLLAPSE OF CAPITALIST ALIYA

The new situation may be most easily exemplified by the virtual collapse of capitalist aliya. Until 1939, immigration by Jews possessing independent financial resources was the least limited form of aliya. That condition changed radically in anticipation of the London Conference. The JAE requested 600 Capitalist (A-I) certificates from the British in January 1939.[129] The government offered 65 certificates, provided that none were used before March 31, 1939.[130] As a result, the JAE felt compelled to take over their distribution directly (until then, it had only divided Labor certificates).[131] Bernard Joseph proposed that the JAE use the letter of British immigration law for Palestine as a means to undermine the restrictive policy and revive the rescue aliya program. He suggested that the JA request a carry-over of authorized certificates from previous schedules that were not used (because the potential oleh had received more tangible results by emigrating elsewhere).[132] Although Joseph's premise clearly was that many more Jews could be rescued if only certificates could be found, his proposal does not contain any broad aliya goals: it appears the JAE could not plan for long-term goals at a time when short-term aliya could not be guaranteed. Some perspective on the problem may be gained from Table 9.1.

Other countries accounted for twenty-five certificates, while sixty-five remained available but were held by the administration. Fifty-five additional certificates had been granted in other capitalist classes (A-III or A-IV), or had

TABLE 9.1: A-I Certificates Granted, October 1938-January 1939[133]

Country	Certificates	Country	Certificates
Grossreich	951	Switzerland*	282
Czechoslovakia	184	Poland	101
Holland*	78	England*	66
Italy	64	Belgium*	38
France*	23	Romania	21
Danzig	14	Hungary	10
Yugoslavia	9	Lithuania	5
Denmark*	3	Greece	2
Sweden*	2	Latvia	1
Estonia	1	TOTAL	1,855

Source: Y. Becher, "Division of A-I Certifictaes October 1938-March 1939," CZA S25/2512.

been converted to B-III certificates for Youth Aliya. This brought capitalist and related aliya to the inadequate total of 2,000 certificates, at the decisive turning point in German Jewish history.[134]

Joseph unsuccessfully attempted to put his proposal to a test by writing to Edward Mills, the government secretary for immigration. Joseph hoped to retrieve 361 certificates: 65 authorized but never granted, 222 granted but never issued, and 74 of unknown status.[135] When his first attempt failed, he tried again with Mills's replacement, William Battershill. Joseph argued on humanitarian and juridical grounds, pointing out that British immigration law required the issuance of a certificate that had been allotted when suitable candidates could be found.[136] In denying the request, Battershill came full circle to the British explanations for bouncing schedules: he explained the withdrawal of the 361 certificates as punishment for aliya bet.[137]

By March 1939, even the Haavara agreement no longer represented an effective means of rescue. Due to new restrictions at both ends of the process, but especially the latest German tax and property registration laws, the agreement helped only a small number of German Jews. Moreover, because of the increasing difficulties in transferring German goods for sale in Palestine, Paltreu was in dire financial straights.[138]

JAE efforts to help veteran Zionists also failed. In February 1939, for example, the Jewish State Party requested financial assistance to rescue Robert Stricker, a well-known Jewish State Party member from Austria and a close associate of Jabotinsky's. Stricker had been imprisoned in Dachau after Kristallnacht, but he could be rescued for £P300 ($1,500). The Jewish State Party requested and was granted a £P100 ($500) JAE donation. By so doing, the JAE showed its concern for the rescue of a veteran Zionist and proved its ability, on occasion, to rise above petty partisanship.[139] Unfortunately, the rescue plan failed: Stricker was deported to other concentration camps and was murdered in Auschwitz in 1944.[140]

In March 1939 the British made a proposal: a few veteran Zionists would be permitted to enter Britain, in return for a commitment from the JAE to dedicate 300 certificates from the forthcoming schedule, covering April to September 1939. Sensing that it had no choice, the JAE reluctantly accepted, pending the size of that schedule.[141] By that time, the JAE was attempting to balance a variety of Jewish needs against increasing British intransigence and the indifference of other countries. At a JAE meeting on March 5, the failure of the negotiations with the Polish government over a clearing agreement was patently obvious.[142] After much soul-searching, the JAE voted not to break off negotiations. They decided instead to order the Warsaw Palestine Office to inquire about a loan for future development.[143]

NEW TALKS WITH THE ADMINISTRATION; NEW PROTESTS

After the Zionists left the London conference the resumption of unofficial talks with the British elicited some hope, but did not change the JAE members' somber mood.[144] During a conversation with Weizmann and Ben-Gurion, Lord Halifax, the British foreign minister, suggested that the Zionists ought to announce a voluntary suspension of aliya in order to win a feeling of "friendliness from the Arabs." The Zionist leaders rejected this suggestion out of hand as it failed to consider the pressing Jewish need for a safe haven.[145] The Zionist leaders, however, did not view their conversation with Halifax as presaging any specific changes in long-term British policy.

Yet, despair did not result in a change in overall Yishuv policy. The Va'ad Leumi declared, but failed to publicize, a one-day general strike for March 20, 1939, to protest British actions against immigration. After lengthy meetings with the JAE, the Va'ad Leumi Executive agreed to postpone the strike, since the lack of publicity almost guaranteed failure. Realizing that a poorly attended protest would do more harm than a postponed one, both the JAE and the Va'ad Leumi proved the waste and inefficiency of having two organizations govern one society. However, the postponement forced the JAE to consider offering an explanation for its actions.[146]

In reality, two disparate groups opposed the general strike. Weizmann and Shertok opposed it for political reasons, since they saw it as unlikely to change the British attitude toward aliya, while causing disruptions in Anglo-Jewish cooperation. Members of the Farmers' Association (Hitahdut ha-Ikkarim, the organization that represented the Yishuv's private smallholders), opposed the strike for economic reasons, even though they supported a somewhat more radical political position. Still, the actual reason for the postponement was organizational. The Va'ad Leumi Executive admitted that insufficient publicity left the Yishuv unprepared for the strike. Thus, although the postponement was announced in the press, the strike originally was not.[147] Still, the onus of explaining the postponement fell on the JAE, with contradictory opinions leading to a deadlock. Senator, Dobkin, and Gruenbaum supported an announcement that would emphasize the role played by recent events in causing the postponement. Ussishkin, Ruppin, and Kaplan opposed the idea and succeeded in getting the issue tabled until the return of the JA delegation from London.[148]

An interesting sidelight to the debate on the general strike is the debate within the JAE regarding the future. Both Senator and Hayim M. Shapira cited elements of the White Paper that the government was planning to publish on May 17, 1939. Here too, differences existed. Senator opposed the limitations placed on the Jewish national home, but expected them to be temporary, and he optimistically concluded: "While the Arab delegation will return from London hopeless, the Jewish delegation will return unsatisfied."[149] Both Shapira and Va'ad Leumi representative Eliayu Berlin castigated Senator for undue optimism — the more so, considering the planned government declara-tion that would limit aliya to 75,000 persons over the next five years.[150] We may thus conclude that the JAE already knew the broad parameters of British plans for Palestine. The JAE took the precaution of drawing up plans for an emergency period by creating a joint committee with the Va'ad Leumi.[151]

GERMAN JEWRY IN THE THROES OF DESTRUCTION

On the evening of March 19, Dobkin reported on his trip to Germany and Austria. "The state of the Jews there is so bad," he began, "that he doubt[ed] that his report would give an adequate picture." He then elaborated: 11,000 Jews were still in concentration camps, Jews had lost all sources of income and Aryanization continued apace. Dobkin estimated that since 1933, Jewish enterprises worth RM6,000,000,000 ($500,000) had been seized.[152] As a result, he added, "every Jew in Germany and Austria thinks of escape."[153] Unfortunately, Dobkin reported, no havens existed other than Palestine, England, and the United States. The government of the Dominican Republic had offered to settle some Jews in Santo Domingo, but it demanded a $500 entry fee for each refugee.[154] Dobkin also spoke of the continuing process of "graying" within German Jewry: as younger individuals and some families escaped, the average age of the Jews remaining in Germany continued to increase.[155] In sum, his report was sobering, and the JAE meeting ended in silence.

Meanwhile, another Jewish community fell under the Nazi heel, further increasing the need for rescue. On March 15, 1939, the Wehrmacht began the occupation of Czechoslovakia, in direct contravention of Hitler's promises at Munich in September 1938.[156] Just before the invasion, Slovakia, already a center of intense antisemitic agitation, declared its independence.[157] As in Austria, the Nazis began to institute their new order immediately upon entering Prague.[158] In response, the two Chief Rabbis of Palestine, Isaac Halevy Herzog and Jacob Meir, declared a one-day fast to symbolize the solidarity of the Yishuv with European Jewry.[159]

When Britain and France announced that they had abandoned their policy of appeasement for one of confrontation with the Nazis, they elicited a dual response within the Yishuv: support for the new policy, mixed with fear over the fate of Jewry in an impending war. A *ha-Aretz* editorial, entitled "Politics and Human Morality — A Single Chain," summarized the feeling. Praising Prime Minister Chamberlain for his newfound resolve to stop Hitler, the editorialist said that such action should have been undertaken in 1933:

> Did the nations really need to wait six years in order to
> recognize the nature of this regime? Was not the persecu-
> tion of the Jews, which began a few days after Hitler
> seized power, sufficient to warn them of the danger: that
> if they gave this devil a small finger, in the end he would
> seize the entire hand?[160]

Yet as in 1933, fear for the safety of the Jews coming under Nazi domination muted much of the Yishuv's public response.

As had held true in 1933, the struggle to increase aliya became the JA's primary response to the persecution of Czech Jewry. Thus, when the Nazis closed down all the Jewish institutions in Prague, the staff of the Palestine Office either continued to work at the British Consulate or worked at home. Shortly after the German takeover, the JA sought to send a representative to Prague in order to obtain a firsthand report on the situation, an effort which initially failed. The JA also tried to involve the British in the rescue effort by seeking to procure transit visas to England for dozens of Czech Zionists.[161]

While the JAE was trying to send a representative into Prague, Af-Al-Pi already had a significant operation there, and in Vienna as well. Ha-Zach's Vienna and Prague emigration offices were active in organizing ha'apala ventures, both by land (to Greece, and then by ship to Palestine) and by sea (down the Danube River to the Black Sea).[162] The Revisionists' organiza-tion in the Balkans even won the grudging admiration of Ehud Avriel, the Mossad's chief operative in Vienna.[163]

With Jewish distress reaching immense proportions, finances again became a crucial problem. On April 20, 1939, Felix Zeidman, of Hitachdut Olei

Czechoslovakia, wrote two letters to the JAE requesting aid. In his second letter, Zeidman raised the issue of creating a new fund for Czech Jewry.[164] That same day, individuals in London proposed a rescue and relief scheme to aid Jewish students and academicians from Slovakia. The authors of the proposal hoped that Hebrew University could take in seventy students, the newly opened Haifa Technion another twenty, and universities in England, Norway, and Switzerland a further fifty. They estimated that £20,800 would cover all expenses for the emigrating students and for those remaining in Slovakia.[165] As in Germany in 1933, the contemporary planners operated with the assumption that some form of modus vivendi was possible with the Slovak leadership, and that as a result a Jewish community would be able to survive there.

The JA helped as much as it could, but by April it needed an infusion of outside capital. Again, it turned to Jewish philanthropic organizations in London for assistance.[166] On May 17, 1939, the day the White Paper was published (and, ironically, the day the Nazis completed the occupation of Bohemia and Moravia), Hitachdut Olei Czechoslovakia announced the start of its own effort to finance a self-help and rescue agency.[167] At almost the same time, the Czechoslovakian transfer agreement finally began to operate. In April 1939, the JA and the Czech government signed a transfer agreement assuring the aliya of an initial 80 persons.[168] A first transport of 408 Czech Jews left shortly after that, and the Czechs approved a total transfer of £5,000,000 ($25,000,000).[169] The Nazi takeover did not immediately cause any change in plans. As late as May 17, Leo Hermann, chairman of the KHY, could cable Jerusalem: "Transfer of whole account [from the] Transfer Office [in] Prague approved, expect payment [in the] next days."[170]

Actually, only a few more families succeeded in escaping. In May, £P20,000 ($100,000) was transferred for twenty families.[171] By then, the British White Paper had totally undermined rescue aliya, and no further certificates were made available to the JAE for Czech capitalists. As a result, the total number of Jews rescued through the Czech transfer agreement was only 1,000. Nevertheless, the failure of rescue programs in the early months of 1939 cannot be blamed on the JA. Again, the primary culprits resided in the government house in Jerusalem, in Whitehall, and at 10 Downing Street.

THE CASE OF PIDYON SHEVUYIM

As will be recalled, the JAE had called for a major expansion of Youth Aliya in the aftermath of Kristallnacht.[172] Even before the pogroms, the Yishuv had begun to gear up for a further expansion of the rescue aliya program. A new fund, parallel to the Joint Committee established in 1933, began to operate in September 1938. Called Pidyon Shevuyim (Rescue of Captives), the fund operated under the dual authority of the Va'ad Leumi and the JA. The fund itself was organized along conventional lines, with a board of overseers that included Arthur Ruppin, Henrietta Szold, Aharon Barth, and Israel Rokach. In announcing the beginning of the campaign, the fundraisers emphasized the needs of the hour. A fund-raising letter read, in part:

Pidyon Shevuyim Fund-raising Letter
Courtesy of the Central Zionist Archives, Jerusalem

מפעל ה י ש ו ב ל מ ע ן ע ו ל י א ו ס ט ר י ה

תל־אביב.
שד. רוטשילד 33, ט.ד. 4060

לכבוד

העם היהודי נתון במצב של מלחמה לחיים ולמוח.
יהודי מזרח אירופה הולכים ונחרבים. מלחמתהשמד בגרמניה
ובאיטליה מתנהלת בכל תקפה. ועכשיו עברה הכוס על אחינו
באוסטריה.

על אף סיוט הדמים הרובץ על הישוב ולמרות המשבר
הקשה — מטמשת ארץ ישראל קרן־אור יחידה לכל אחינו בגיהנום
האוסטרי, המגיעים הנה למאותיהם בעירום ובחסר כל.

אנו מצווים לדאג לסדורם הראשון של העולים האלה
ולשמש דוגמא לעולם כולו במאמצינו להקל עליהם את יסורי הק־
לטה והשתרשותם בארץ.

המוסדות הלאומיים והישוביים הכריזו על מפעל של
טעת חרום להצלת עולי אוסטריה   והישוב מצווה לקיים את מצות
* פדיון שבויים * ולהושים יד אחים לעולי אוסטריה.

המצב הבלתי רגיל דורש אמצעים בלתי רגילים.

אנו פונים בזה לכב' בבקשה חמה להשתתף במפעל
האנושי והלאומי הזה ע"י תרומה שחנתן בעין יפה וביד רחבה
ואנו מקוים שכב' יסביר פנים לבאי־כחנו שיבקרו אצלו בימים
הקרובים.

ועד הנאמנים של המפעל " פדיון שבויי אוסטריה "

הנריסה סאלד, אהרן ברט, יטראל רוקח, ארכור רופין

> The Jewish people is currently engaged in a war for
> survival. The Jews of eastern Europe are rapidly being
> destroyed. The war of extermination continues in full
> force in Germany and Italy. Now Austrian Jewry faces
> its turn. The National Institutions have declared an
> emergency fund to aid Austrian olim. We command the
> entire Yishuv to carry out the order of Pidyon Shevuyim
> and extend a brotherly hand to Austrian Jews.[173]

Originally created to aid Austrian olim, Pidyon Shevuyim initially set a goal that baffled even its supporters: the immigration of 1,000 Austrian Jewish youth.[174] In three months the fund-raisers collected £P1,616 ($8,080), in addition to £P1,208 ($6,040) gained from the sale of lottery tickets. Pledges totaled £P6,535 ($32,675); this means that only one-fourth of all donations were defrayed.[175] Expenses for the office alone came to £P1,427 ($7,135) — almost half the entire income. Moreover, expenses when added to the commitments, amounted to a grand total of only £P8,500 ($42,500). In other words, the fund began its existence with a deficit. Ruppin, head of the JA German Department, strongly questioned the logic of such practices, but he was unable to effect any changes in the methods of operation.[176]

By May 15, 1939, Pidyon Shevuyim had received pledges for £P21,645 ($108,225). Of this sum, only £P4,650 ($23,250) had actually been collected. Despite high hopes, the fund helped only 147 children. The last group of them, 40 in all, received their certificates in April 1939.[177] The failure to gain adequate funding cannot be attributed to a lack of publicity or to insufficient press support. Pidyon Shevuyim advertised a great deal, publishing notices regarding mass fund-raising rallies such as the one held in Tel Aviv on December 24, 1938.[178] The organization's failure to finance projects correctly, and hence its failure to become a force on behalf of rescue aliya, was the direct result of institutional inefficiency.

Pidyon Shevuyim can be considered an unequivocal success in only one sphere: gaining the unified support of all segments of the Yishuv. Supporters of the fund included both Chief Rabbis, Agudas Israel, most of the Yishuv's political parties, and the Histadrut.[179] Pidyon Shevuyim also brokered the agreement of confederation between Hitachdut Olei Germania and Hitachdut Olei Austria, that resulted in the creation of Hitachdut Olei Germania ve-Olei Austria (HOGOA).[180] Despite this wide range of support, however, Pidyon Shevuyim failed to become a major financial factor in the Yishuv.

What caused this long-term failure? Two factors must be considered: the failure of most Zionists to work for mass aliya in the early 1930s, and the British refusal to assist rescue during the last crucial months of 1938 and the first five months of 1939. These two factors cannot, however, be evaluated in equal measure. Even if all Zionists had adopted mass aliya as early as 1933

or 1934 — adopting Ben-Gurion's proposals, for example — there is no
evidence that the British would have cooperated. The severe curtailment of
Youth Aliya in 1939 implies a consistent British attempt to halt aliya
altogether. Nowhere is Britain's role in the collapse of rescue aliya more
apparent than in the fall of Youth Aliya.

An indication of the difficulties that the British administration placed in the
path of Youth Aliya in 1939 is reflected in Szold's correspondence. The
earliest of her letters, written on January 1, 1939, requested 2,500 Youth Aliya
certificates for 1939. Included in this amount were 970 certificates needed
immediately. Szold noted the increasingly severe financial and personal
requirements imposed by the government in order to limit Youth Aliya.[181]
In a second letter, written on January 9, she reminded Kaplan about the
JAE's decision to finance Youth Aliya to the extent of £P20,000 ($100,000).
She mentioned, among other matters, that the British had demanded written
guarantees regarding care for the children. They had also requested the
Youth Aliya office to sign a contract setting out its obligations toward each
group of immigrants and listing all sources of financing.[182]

The financial considerations of Youth Aliya became moot, however, when
the British rejected the request for 2,500 certificates.[183] Youth Aliya
advocates called for strong protests, including a general strike by the Yishuv,
to pressure the government to increase all forms of aliya.[184] Despite the
protests, the British continued to limit aliya. Thus, total Youth Aliya for 1938
barely exceeded 1,200.[185] A letter from Szold to Joseph paints a similar
picture. Szold enquired about the wisdom of obtaining passports for each
child, instead of the collective passports used until that time. Her purpose
was to outflank the bureaucratic tactics used by the Palestine administration
to slow Youth Aliya.[186]

The proposal to transfer 10,000 Jewish children to Palestine became the
cornerstone of the Yishuv's response to Kristallnacht. British demurral
rapidly whittled down the proposal until, by the time of the St. James Conference, only 2,500 youth were actually transferred. The Va'ad Leumi
continued to advocate the rescue of all 10,000 young people. Since the British
refused to make certificates available, only two alternatives existed: either give
up the plan or find some interim refuge. In February 1939, the Va'ad Leumi
Executive proposed that 6,000 German and Austrian Jewish youth be
transferred to England, to remain there until certificates for Palestine became
available. Once transferred to Palestine, they would be followed by a second
group, numbering 4,000. Others would follow as conditions permitted.[187]

Some JAE members opposed the idea of temporary refuge in England.
They feared both the financial burden of maintaining the children in England
and the implications of such a rescue project for long-term Zionist aliya plans.
Especially irksome in this regard was the fact that the JA would have to
secure B-III certificates for the children, although they could not immigrate

to Palestine directly. Such a policy, many feared, would deplete much-needed certificates. Landauer, for example, maintained that if enough certificates existed to undertake the transfer to England, then the direct aliya of 2,500 youth would be preferable.[188]

The first of the so-called kindertransporte left Germany in March 1939. By September, some 10,000 refugee children had been brought to England, of whom 7,500 were Jews.[189] But despite the success of the British side of the project, Youth Aliya continued to experience severe difficulties. In mid-June 1939 — a month after the publication of the White Paper — the Palestine administration issued 1,400 certificates, to be used between the months of July and September. Three limitations were placed on the certificates: (1) they could be used only for Jewish youth in Nazi-occupied countries (or for refugee youth from those countries); (2) they could not be used to reunite families of ma'apilim; and (3) the olim were limited to the ages of 13, 14, and 15.[190] In transmitting this decision, the British did unofficially promise to consider further certificates for youth below the age of 13 at an indeterminate future date.[191] On the other hand, they rejected outright a request for 500 certificates for youth aged 16 and 17.[192]

As late as August 1939, the Palestine administration continued to find new means to restrict Youth Aliya, using taxation to keep olim, both young and old, out of Palestine.[193] The British introduced legislation taxing clothing, virtually the only possession most olim were able to bring with them. This was done precisely because most individuals coming to Passport Control Offices to request a certificate would be unable to put up a sufficient bond to cover the tax and could therefore be legitimately rejected.[194]

The reasoning behind such tactics was clear: Imperial interests required that the Arabs be appeased by placing limitations on Jewish immigration. Youth Aliya most clearly reppresented the humanitarian element of rescue aliya; it also retained considerable support in both Britain and America. A direct assault on Youth Aliya thus seemed politically inexpedient. Instead, other means existed to slow it, without halting it altogether. The Palestine administration exploited all these means, to the detriment of rescue.

For the Zionists, therefore, only one other option existed to continue a rescue program: that of aliya bet. Aliya bet, if it had been adopted as official Zionist policy earlier, might have taken up some of the slack. But here too, it is difficult to state unequivocally that Zionist policy was incorrect: why, the Zionists had asked in the early 1930's, act illegally when legal immigration could accomplish so much more? Only in 1939, when it had become clear that no recourse to legal means remained, was consideration given to the possibility of a program of mass aliya bet. By then, the Yishuv's resources would be stretched to their limit in one last attempt to save rescue aliya.

10
The White Paper

On April 16, 1939, *ha-Aretz* reported that German Jews would no longer be permitted to emigrate. Instead, they were to be registered by the Nazi authorities for use as slave laborers in the event of war.[1] War seemed imminent to the Yishuv and to many Europeans, especially in view of Hitler's newest series of threats against Lithuania (regarding Memel) and Poland (regarding Danzig and the "corridor").[2] By mid-April, two other facts had become clear: that the British government would soon announce its new Palestine policy, and that this policy would be inimical to the growth of the Yishuv. Ominous reports on the publication of a new White Paper that had emerged soon after the collapse of the London talks were coming true.

The Zionists had good cause for fear. On April 12, 1939, the British government published a new law granting the High Commissioner the right to set immigration schedules without regard to either political or economic conditions. Ben-Gurion saw the new law as the first step toward the White Paper, and he wrote to High Commissioner Harold MacMichael to protest it.[3] Simultaneously, the JAE constituted itself as a "Defense Committee" and began meeting in secret to consider contingency plans to be undertaken when the White Paper was published.

During these discussions, Ben-Gurion again strongly advocated a massive aliya program to be keyed with protests by the Yishuv. "I was very moved," he said, "when I heard the news of the government sending a shipload of Jews away from the coast of Palestine, and the Yishuv was silent. I felt embarrassment and shame."[4] He went on to note that British gunboats had fired on ma'apilim. Ben-Gurion was not merely posturing; his words betrayed a fear that some elements in the Yishuv would make their peace with the government, accepting the severe restrictions on aliya and land purchase.[5] In fairness, what Ben-Gurion did not say must also be kept in mind. An Af-AL-Pi ship, the SS *Ostia*, was intercepted before reaching Palestine and was forced by British warships to turn around. The lack of public protest actually worked to the ship's advantage, for once out of the range of British patrol boats, the *Ostia* changed course again, returned to its original destination, and landed safely near Herzliya.[6]

Against potential advocates of surrender, Ben-Gurion called for a "war" on behalf of Zionism, but he did not, at this stage, define how that war was to be carried out. Anticipating casualties, he advocated "a new regime within the Zionist movement and the Yishuv."[7] Ben-Gurion received support from Menachem M. Ussishkin.[8] In contrast, both Yitzhak Gruenbaum and Eliezer Kaplan questioned the implications of Ben-Gurion's policy, especially in view of Zionist dependence on British goodwill.[9] Thus, the JAE divided into two factions. One faction, composed of Ben-Gurion, Ussishkin, and Yitzhak Ben-Zvi, advocated public Jewish noncompliance even before publication of the White Paper. The other faction opposed Zionist "provocations" before publication.[10] The only immediate decision taken related to the building of new settlements in the near future: a unanimous resolution, proposed by Kaplan, called for the continuation of settlement activity, even without British permission.[11] Aliya bet was not mentioned in the discussions at this stage.

At the next meeting, April 18, 1939, Ben-Gurion emphasized the need to guarantee the failure of the new British policy, since "that is the only way to save Zionism."[12] "Noncooperation" had, by this time, become the rallying cry of all Zionists and even of such non-Zionist JAE members as Dr. Werner D. Senator. But noncooperation also had nuances. Senator, for example, accepted passive resistance but rejected any form of active noncooperation. Instead, he emphasized the need to continue operating as ususal — even if only in a limited fashion and in an unfriendly atmosphere.[13]

Chaim Weizmann vacillated between Ben-Gurion's forceful position and Senator's call for passivity. Although he supported an active policy, Weizmann cautioned JAE members to consider the fate of the diaspora before issuing what was, in effect, only a symbolic declaration of war on Great Britain.[14] Weizmann feared that if the Yishuv acted hastily, the suffering of Jews in the diaspora would not be alleviated, and their only hope — of emigration to Eretz Israel — would evaporate altogether. What Weizmann failed to consider was that doing nothing also did not ease diaspora Jewry's plight.

To Weizmann's words, Ben-Gurion replied with another stirring call for resistance. Recognizing that diaspora Jewry lacked the resources for "war" with the British Empire, he nevertheless advocated "a brave and wise battle to defend our rights and the rights of the entire Jewish people."[15] Two practical policies emerged from this debate: a proposal on independent settlements and a proposal to turn to American Zionists, requesting them to ask the Roosevelt administration to place pressure on the British.[16] The upshot of these decisions was that cooperation was no longer desirable and, to an extent, an admission that the minimalist policies advocated from 1931 onward had failed.

These decisions may seem timid, but in the days before publication of the White Paper, the JAE saw itself as possessing only limited options. The JAE and the entire Yishuv remained divided as to the best course of action for the near term. Daniel Auster, for example, argued against a public policy of non-cooperation on two grounds: that it could backfire, creating an Anglo-Arab alliance, and that a permanent policy of noncooperation would rapidly sap the Yishuv's resources. Auster advocated instead a dualistic policy in an attempt to undermine the White Paper: continuation of overt collaboration, coupled with covert resistance. Auster did not specify the means of resistance, but he did suggest that the operation be supervised by a committee of three who would act in the name of the entire Jewish people. Only in recommending that all Jewish officials tender their resignations from the Mandatory government on the day the White Paper was published did Auster suggest open noncooperation.[17]

Even the JA Political Subcommittee, which suggested more extensive resistance than Auster, did not really propose much more. The subcommittee made three proposals: (1) a census of all adults in the Yishuv; (2) an independent economic policy based on the removal of Arab labor and a boy-cott on all British imports; and (3) reduced involvement with the government, combined with the creation of parallel Jewish institutions. Specifically, the subcommittee suggested non-use of the railroad, the postal system, and the courts, as well as a complete refusal by Jews to pay any taxes. The last move, in the subcommittee's estimation, would reduce government revenues by 20 percent (approximately £P800,000 or nearly $4,000,000) per year.[18] Although confiscation of possession to pay for taxes owed could not be avoided, a total tax boycott by the Yishuv would force the British to use a considerable pro-portion of the police for tax enforcement purposes and might render them unavailable for other anti-Yishuv actions.

While considering its contingencies, the JA also undertook a public cam-paign to delay or overturn the White Paper. Protesting the new immigration statute, the JA took the opportunity to attack continuation of the very concept of a political maximum.[19] The JAE also continued to lend its tacit approval, though not its outright support, to the efforts of the Mossad le-Aliya Bet. Three ships arrived in Palestine within days of one another in mid-April. The first to arrive was the *Assimi* (organized by Mizrachi's Polish branch), with approximately 470 passengers. Following it were the *Katina*, carrying 750 passengers from the Af-Al-Pi ship *Gepo II* (which had sunk), and the Mossad ship *Atrato VII*, with almost 400 aboard.[20] Both the *Assimi* and the *Atrato* were seized before landing. The *Katina's* ma'apilim landed successfully, but most were captured and incarcerated in military barracks before deportation.

The Yishuv's response to this was swift but unsuccessful. The Va'ad Leumi called a one-day general strike to protest the deportation of Jewish refugees from their homeland. A Hagana attempt to free the *Assimi* ma'apilim on April 21, apparently undertaken under Ben-Gurion's direct orders, also failed.[21] In view of the failure to free the *Assimi*, there seemed to be nothing the Hagana could do for the *Katina* passengers, especially since they were being held in Royal Army's barracks at Sarafand under military (not police) guard. Ben-Gurion attempted to intercede with the government on their behalf, but this too failed.[22]

The JAE met on April 23, 1939, and discussed the plight of the ma'apilim in light of its previous discussions. From the outset, the members agreed that all efforts should be made to prevent their deportation. The only argument available appeared to be that the ships were unseaworthy and that deportation would endanger lives.[23] That the entire JAE agreed on this matter may be seen from statements by Senator, who opposed ha'apala and advocated Jewish concessions. Here, he supported calls for a general strike, and said that from the JAE's perspective, the indefinite incarceration of the ma'apilim was preferable to their deportation.[24]

Once again, Ben-Gurion articulated the broadest position on the issues involved in. Viewing efforts at ha'apala as the first broadsides in his aliya war, he strongly advocated using aliya as a weapon to defeat the White Paper. In practice, Ben-Gurion called for the utilization of Palestine's coastal lands as illegal immigration reception centers. To do so, dozens of new settlements would be needed. To lend an air of credibility to their purpose, he suggested creating fishing villages. These would require small boats, which could later be used to unload the ma'apilim. More immediately, he advocated buying a ship and equipping it with a wireless radio so as to ensure unfettered communications with the Mossad's blockade runners.[25]

Despite the Yishuv's protests, the British deported almost all of the ma'apilim, beginning with those from the *Assimi*, which was towed out of the Haifa harbor on April 23, 1939.[26] On April 24, the British forced the *Atrato* out to sea. The *Katina* refugees followed shortly afterward.[27] These deportations renewed Jewish protests against British immigration policy. The Yishuv's three major dailies — *ha-Aretz, Davar,* and the *Palestine Post* — all published scathing editorials against the British action. *Ha-Aretz* concentrated on the shame that Prime Minister Neville Chamberlain and Colonial Secretary Malcolm MacDonald had brought upon themselves. In one particularly bitter editorial, *ha-Aretz* wrote that the ma'apilim had received the same amount of "sympathy" that Jewish refugees were receiving throughout the world: none.[28] Gershon Agronsky echoed similar sentiments in a *Palestine Post* editorial entitled "Humanity Adrift":

> When one country after another forces out its Jewish
> citizens by violence and persecution which no legal enact-
> ment can justify, and these unfortunate people are
> compelled to wander abroad, are subjects to untold
> misery for no fault but that they are Jews, and are finally
> washed up on the shore of a country where their
> brethren would welcome them, is it just to invoke law in
> order to throw them back into the sea, is it merciful?[29]

Davar's editorials followed a similar line. Berl Katznelson and the editorial staff added a uniquely Laborite twist to the rescue agitation. Thus, *Davar's* April 30 banner headline read: "On this May first the labor public will display its will for unity, defense, upbuilding, ha'apala — for the freedom of the nation and the individual!"[30] The headline referred to a series of Histadrut resolutions calling on Jews and Socialists throughout the world to fight fascism and Nazism in order to save threatened European Jewry. Within the Yishuv, the Histadrut called for protests against the deportation of the ma'apilim. Publicly, Ha-Zach adopted a similar protest strategy, although the Af-Al-Pi activists had a better response. Shortly after the *Katina* was towed out of Palestine's territorial waters, three more ships were sent to run the blockade: the SS *Aghia Dzioni*, with 600 ma'apilim from Fiume; the SS *Panagai Conasteriu*, sailing form Corinth with 80 aboard; and the SS *Liesel*, a joint Maccabi ha-Zair-Af-Al-Pi operation that sailed from Tulcea, Romania, on the day the White Paper was published.[31]

Within the JAE, desperation turned to recrimination. Rabbi Judah L. Fishman of Mizrachi quoted anonymous sources to the effect that the *Assimi* refugees had been deported because of JAE negligence, thus implying that someone might have tipped off the police. While Rabbi Fishman admitted that he doubted the veracity of these accusations, he declared that their impli-cations were clear: the JAE should eschew partisanship and should aid all efforts at aliya bet.[32] Senator also raised the issue of aliya bet, suggesting that the JAE had to decide its priorities: "mass legal immigration and a small number of illegal immigrants, or massive illegal immigration and the termi-nation of legal immigration."[33] Senator's suggestion was not realistic, since it did not consider the possibility that neither might be available. His proposal, to submit the aliya question to a committee of three nonparty representatives, touched off yet another debate regarding the best response to the upcoming White Paper. In this case, all of the participants used Ben-Gurion's ideas of an aliya war as their starting position. The actual decisions made by the JAE, however, barely reflected the serious nature of the problem. The JAE decided to create a three member subcommittee (Fishman, Ben-Zvi, and Kaplan) to investigate the *Assimi* issue, and called for a reorganization of the Yishuv's defense arrangements hoping that an intra-Zionist agreement on aliya would be reached.[34] This resolution did not specifically mention an attempt to bring Ha-Zach back into the WZO, but it implied such a goal. During an open session on April 30, 1939, the JAE decided to meet more often and to return to the pre-1933 aliya key, by which Poland received half of all available Labor certificates.[35]

These decisions raise a question of perspective. The JAE's decisions during April and May did not advance any form of aliya. On the one hand, the JAE members — and their colleagues in Mapai's coalition — continually referred to the incipient emergency. In all of their statements, they used rousing terms to call for action — but in the abstract. On the other hand, in almost every case, their concrete actions seem to have been out of proportion with the rhetoric used. Jabotinsky sensed this dichotomy and repeatedly hammered at the JAE for it. In a speech he delivered in Warsaw shortly after the White Paper was issued, he asked pointedly: "What will the leftist youth do?"[36]

In contrast, Jabotinsky had a plan, and he at least thought that it could succeed: a renewed and expanded Ten-Year Plan to rescue European Jewry and save the Yishuv from destruction. The first step would be the emigration of 1 million Jews from eastern and central Europe, along with their capital. Following this first group, additional waves of emigrants would leave, until the bulk of eastern European Jewry was out of harm's way — either in Palestine or in temporary havens elsewhere. Carrying out this plan, however, required massive financial arrangements, as well as Zionist unity.[37] The plan did not include specific ideas about how to achieve unity, nor did Jabotinsky move to mend fences within the Zionist movement. The realism of Jabotinsky's plan may also be called into question, since he assumed, even at this late date, that the British or other European powers would assist in carrying out the plan.

THE EVE OF BETRAYAL

With the White Paper expected at any time, the JAE met to discuss its response. In his report, Ben-Gurion emphasized that the Yishuv's response had to be immediate: anything else would result in the loss of JA authority. He particularly emphasized the need to publish a detailed legal refutation of the White Paper.[38] The JAE also voted unanimously to coordinate any actions with the Va'ad Leumi and with American Zionists.[39]

It was Moshe Shertok who raised a divisive question of principles: despite the stated JA policy of noncooperation, the government was likely to retain the White Paper for some time. In that case, the JAE had to decide on a policy regarding immigration certificates, in order to protect any unused ones. Shertok suggested approaching the government for assurances that some form of "carry-over" would be permitted. He justified his position by calling on the Executive to "save what can be saved."

Senator and Kaplan both supported Shertok's position. Ben-Gurion and Ussishkin opposed it, since it seemed incongruous for the JAE to haggle with the British over a policy that it sought to overthrow. Here, the JAE adopted a compromise position. Shertok's suggestion would be followed. The JAE, however, would not make the representations. Instead, British Jews friendly to the Zionist endeavor, but not directly connected with the WZO, would approach the government.[40]

When the JAE heard an unsubstantiated report of the imminent publication of the White Paper, renewed calls for Zionist unity were made, though the JAE did not take any substantive decisions in that regard. Rather, the Va'ad ha-Poel ha-Zioni took up the question.[41] The Va'ad ha-Poel considered all possible actions available and resolved to: (1) withdraw all Jewish employees in government agencies charged with carrying out the new policy; (2) advocate nonrespect for "all laws designed to stop or slow our growth"; (3) establish priorities for further settlements and investment; and (4) hold a census of all Jews between the ages of 18 and 35, for conscription into the Hagana.[42]

On May 8, 1939, the JAE decided that Weizmann should travel to London to attempt to cancel or delay the White Paper. He would then travel to the United States to confer with the American Zionists on a joint plan to overturn the new British policy if his mission in England proved to be a failure.[43]

As the planned publication inexorably went ahead, the Yishuv's press devoted considerable attention to the march of events. *Ha-Aretz* reported on May 11 that the White Paper would be published as a "command paper." This same item also mentioned the debate in Parliament on the *Assimi* refugees, but it concluded on a pessimistic note.[44] The *Palestine Post* also drew pessimistic conclusions regarding the White Paper, but it mentioned the possibility of a refugee haven opening in British Guiana.[45] Meanwhile, Weizmann arrived in London and began two days of talks with Chamberlain and MacDonald.[46] Weizmann attempted to obtain the cancelation of the White Paper, or at least to delay its issuance until the international situation could clarify, saying that war was not imminent and that the British should therefore not make a hasty decision on Palestine's future.

Weizmann's statement that war was not imminent could not have been more ill-timed: even as these statements were being made, the Germans were massing troops in the east. Although most of the Yishuv incorrectly assumed that the immediate target was Poland (at this time, the Nazis occupied Bohemia and Moravia), the reports of imminent Nazi aggression proved correct. Ironically, Jabotinsky proclaimed his belief that war was not imminent in a speech in Warsaw at almost the same time.[47] This led to the rather discordant reality of advocates of two diametrically opposed Zionist strategies both basically maintaining that Jews need not act, literally at the last moment when action might still have been possible to save European Jewry.

THE WHITE PAPER

In light of the tense diplomatic situation, the government rejected Weizmann's position unequivocally and announced that the White Paper would be published by the end of the week.[48]

The text of the White Paper was completed on May 15, 1939. Although the official text remained secret, *ha-Aretz* published a summary of the contents on May 16.[49] By then the JAE already possessed a copy of the White Paper, and was prepared to respond. To finance its actions the JAE requested a £P25,000 ($125,000) loan from the Anglo-Palestine Bank.[50]

The White Paper, Command 6019, officially published on May 17, 1939, contained three elements. First, was the limitation of Jewish immigration to 15,000 persons a year (including 5,000 refugees), for a period of five years. Further aliya would be contingent upon Arab approval. Since such approval remained unlikely, the White Paper guaranteed Jews a permanent minority status, at approximately one-third of Palestine's population. Second, the White Paper severely restricted Jewish land acquisition in those areas where Jews did not already represent the majority population. Finally, the White Paper's "constitutional clause" promised the creation of an Arab Palestinian state in 1949 with vague guarantees for Jewish minority rights.[51]

The White Paper was a watershed. As the adopted policy of the Mandatory power in Palestine, it meant the irrevocable British repudiation of both the Balfour Declaration and the League of Nations Mandate. As such, it also represented the elimination of rescue aliya as a policy. Ironically, on the same day that the White Paper gained final Cabinet approval, the Nazis occupied Prague. The suffering of European Jewry had again increased immeasurably, with the Yishuv unable to offer any realistic help. On October 29, 1938, Labour Member of Parliament Stafford Cripps had written in the *Tribune*: "At a time of persecution like the present it would indeed be criminal to snatch from the Jewish race the hope of having even a tiny territory that they may call their own."[52] Yet, that is exactly what the government had done.

Chamberlain's Middle Eastern policy was based on the percieved need to mollify the Arabs and to "buy" their support (or at least their neutrality) in any upcoming European war. On the other hand, Jewish support in such a war was considered virtually guaranteed, since the Jews would be unlikely to support the Nazis. Stubbornly refusing to modify its approach, even after events in Syria and Iraq showed appeasement of the Arabs to be unsuccessful, the White Paper remained official British policy on Palestine until the matter was turned over to the United Nations after World War II.[53]

The Yishuv's press responded almost immediately. Condemning the White Paper as an act of betrayal, the *Palestine Post* sought to place it in context. An editorial Agronsky wrote declared: "The Jewish people will be called upon to face the most challenging act in the history of their martyrdom."[54] In a rare front-page editorial on May 17, Agronsky refined his position. Although his opinion did not officially reflect Mapai's position, it remained very close to Mapai's view and is thus significant. His argument may be summarized thus: by issuing the White Paper, the British government had not only betrayed its sacred promise, but had also forced a parting of the ways between Jews and the British Empire. All Jews were duty bound, therefore, to resist the new policy. Agronsky did not specify the tactics to be used, but he cautioned against hatred toward either the British or the Arabs: "In saying 'No' to the policy which the Government . . . is today promulgating, the Jews must not give up all legitimate attempts to bring the British people back to their promises."[55] In another editorial, Agronsky scored the cynical British attempt to pass off the White Paper as a reinterpretation of the Mandate.[56]

Ha-Aretz pursued a similar line. On May 16, an editorial emphasized the need for unity within the Yishuv, and juxtaposed news of the issuance of the White Paper with information about the enactment of the latest antisemitic legislation in Hungary.[57] One day later, *ha-Aretz* called on the entire Yishuv to "assemble like a wall" in order to defeat the White Paper. The editorial was juxtaposed with information about the introduction of the Nuremberg Laws into the newly created Nazi protectorate of Bohemia and Moravia. Even a casual reader could neither miss the close connection made between an attack on the White Paper and advocacy of rescue nor the use of Jabotinsky-like rhetoric.[58]

Davar, too, based its editorials on an unequivocal rejection of the White Paper, although differences in approach may be discerned. Whereas *ha-Aretz* advocated resistance, the *Palestine Post* advocated cautious opposition. *Davar* also advocated resistance, calling on Jews to use all weapons at their disposal to defeat the White Paper.[59] Even so, *Davar*'s editorials seem much more optimistic than those in either *ha-Aretz* or the *Palestine Post*. The lead editorial of May 16, for example, noted that the Yishuv had many allies in its struggle for justice.[60]

The JAE knew the contents of the White Paper well before its actual publication, since Mizrachi member Hayim M. Shapiro had discussed them at a March 1939 meeting. Thus, the devastating British blow to the Yishuv came as no surprise, but it did catch the Yishuv unprepared. The JAE had prepared its responses as a series of pronouncements advocating noncooperation. As had been the case in previous undertakings, the JAE was outwardly united but inwardly divided. When it reviewed a draft of the proposed JA manifesto on the White Paper, some members resented the use of the term "ghetto" to describe post-White Paper Palestine. Dr. Emil Schmorak, a General Zionist, proposed replacing the term with "Pale of Settlement" (a reference to restrictions on Jewish residency rights in tsarist Russia), or simply with "territorial restrictions."[61] Disagreements over wording did not necessarily reflect a willingness to accept the White Paper, however. Schmorak especially felt that the draft did not sufficiently emphasize the Jews' intentions to continue developing their national home, and did not give Jewish youth a sufficiently strong foundation for the forthcoming struggle.[62]

It must be emphasized that the JAE did approve the draft, despite the dissenting opinions. In its final form, the JA manifesto condemned the White Paper as a breach of faith and declared that the Yishuv was not willing to cooperate in its own liquidation. The last section of the text referred to events in Europe:

> In this hour of unprecedented danger for the Jewish
> people, the English Government announces its intention
> to cut off Jewry's last hope and to seal off the road to
> its homeland.
>
> This is a cruel blow. It is an especially hard blow be-
> cause it comes from the government of a great power
> which had offered its hand to help the Jewish people and
> whose power rests on moral prestige and loyalty to inter-
> national obligations.
>
> This blow will not make the Jewish people surrender. The
> historical connection between Jewry and its homeland
> will not be cut. The Jewish people will never accept the
> closure of the gates of the homeland in the faces of its
> sons and will not allow the national home to be converted
> into a ghetto.[63]

The manifesto appeared in *ha-Aretz*, *Davar*, and the *Palestine Post*.[64] The JA manifesto also appeared as a two-page broadsheet, handed out on city streets or plastered on walls.[65] *Ha-Aretz* also published a manifesto issued by the Va'ad Leumi that called on the Yishuv to wage war on the new government policy: "Know, that only with the power of unity, responsibility, and discipline will we be able to succeed in this campaign."[66] Jews paid attention to the call for noncooperation, but the British government, convinced that only Arab neutrality could avert disaster in the upcoming war, and that the Arabs could be bought at the Jews' expense without fear of reprisal, was not influenced by either manifesto. Other elements of the JA's anti-White Paper policy included publication of a detailed analysis and refutation of the key elements contained in the command paper. This refutation, written by Ben-Gurion, was serialized in all three of Palestine's main dailies.[67]

Thursday, May 18, 1939, also witnessed a one-day general strike throughout the Yishuv. In its aftermath, the JA implemented its protest strategy, in a significantly modified form. The JAE, which had announced its intention to resign upon the White Paper's publication, did not do so, fearing that such a move would create chaos. That decision cost the JAE more in the long term, since both its unwillingness to follow the precedent set by Weizmann in 1930 and its apparent sloth in protesting the White Paper were widely interpreted within the Yishuv as cowardice, collaboration, or both. Behind the scenes, a different reality existed. On May 20, 1939, the Yishuv held its first internal census of military-age men, carried out with the full cooperation of Ha-Zach. The next day, the JAE approved a staged plan of action by a vote of 4 to 2: three new settlements were to be created immediately, and the Mossad budget would be increased. Diplomatic action in Geneva and London would be combined with these acts of defiance. If the White Paper was not cancelled by the autumn of 1939, a prospect that Ben-Gurion alone doubted, then the Hagana would begin to undertake military operations.[68]

Ben-Gurion expected that military operations would be needed, and he instructed the Hagana high command to draw up a contingency plan, code-named "Plan Avner," which was completed in late May.[69] He also attempted to mobilize wide elements of the Yishuv, especially amongst organized youth movements. For example, on May 31, Ben-Gurion met with representatives of the religious Zionist Bnai Akiva movement. In his plan all youth groups would create new sports clubs as a cover for anti-government activities including aliya bet, collection of underground taxes, weapons training, illegal settlement building, and self-defense.[70]

Not everyone agreed with this strategy. Within the JAE, two members — Senator and Arthur Ruppin — opposed any talk of military operations on grounds of utility. Neither of them thought that a revolt could succeed, and both posited that it would not be needed, since they saw the White Paper as a British response to increasing tension in Europe. Since neither Senator nor Ruppin expected a war to break out, both considered it likely that British policy would turn from its pro-Arab tilt as soon as matters calmed down.[71]

The other opposition to JA policy took three different forms, although the position articulated by Ha-Zach and the IZL must be reviewed independently. Agudas Israel, the orthodox anti-Zionist party, declared its opposition to any protest strategy that included illegal acts or the advocacy of illegal acts, such as aliya bet.[72] Aguda joined the Yishuv's protest, but limited itself to a demand that the British fulfill the promises expressed in the Mandate.[73]

Within the Zionist camp, some figures expressed intense discomfort with the policy of noncooperation. In late May, Ya'acov Thon suggested that Jews should resist the White Paper in the same quiet ways in which they had resisted Ottoman immigration restrictions. Thon, a former member of Brit Shalom, the party that had worked for the creation of a binational Palestine, doubted the efficacy of Ben-Gurion's plans for public protest and active measures. In particular, he doubted the Yishuv's staying power, especially since the British could marshal so many possible countermeasures. Thon also disagreed with two fundamental elements of Ben-Gurion's analysis, the first being Ben-Gurion's hope of arousing sympathy in Europe and using it to pressure the British. Thon argued that European public opinion could play no role, or virtually no role, in lessening the impact of the White Paper. Similarly, he believed that Ben-Gurion's plan to convince the British public to oppose this blatant abandonment of its solemn commitments was unlikely to succeed. Given the imminence of war, Thon predicted, British public opinion would invariably support the government.[74]

On these two points, Thon proved correct. Parliament did approve the White Paper with no modifications — although by only a small majority — and the protests of most European countries were muted. Thon did not, however, offer a fully articulated alternative strategy, and he failed to consider the Yishuv's need to act in order to improve the increasingly untenable condition of European Jewry, as well as the Yishuv's own self-image.

Indeed, the precarious conditions in which the Polish Zionists found themselves impelled them to make protests that were anything but muted. On May 18, 1939, they declared a one-day sympathy strike. Since that same day witnessed the Yishuv's general strike, the linkage was important and cemented a sense of solidarity between the Yishuv and diaspora Jewry. Because of the significant contribution to morale that derived from the knowledge of world Jewish solidarity with the Yishuv, the Polish Jewish protests enjoyed considerable coverage in Palestine's Jewish press.[75] On the other hand, diaspora Jews also became more desperate to leave Europe by any means available. This, in turn, led to a rise in the number of potential ma'apilim seeking transit from Af-Al-Pi (and from the Mossad as well).[76]

FINAL EFFORTS AT INTRA-ZIONIST UNITY

Not surprisingly, efforts to establish a Zionist united front resumed, having been rejuvenated by the emergency conditions. Initial efforts centered on the general strike and met with many ideological and institutional differences. The Histadrut Executive succeeded in obtaining support for the strike from all the Socialist Zionist groups, but only after protracted negotiations. As late as the evening of May 17, 1939, the eve of the great rally, Poale Zion Smol's youth wing, ha-Noar ha-Borochovisti, demanded the right to march under the red Communist banner rather than the blue-and-white flag.[77] Although the Histadrut Executive did not view the red banner as an anathema, it did consider the banner's use, under the circumstances, to be inappropriate, since this was to be a national — not a class — protest. Ha-Noar ha-Borochovisti marched under the red banner anyway.

Less embarrassing, but still reflecting intense ideological differences among Socialist Zionists, was Poale Zion Smol's independent anti-White Paper manifesto. In concert with the JA manifesto, Poale Zion Smol condemned the White Paper and called for unity. Unlike the former, the latter framed its call in Marxist and anti-imperialist terminology. In addition, the manifesto called for marches under the red banner, described as "the nationalist and socialist liberation flag."[78] Nevertheless, Poale Zion Smol and ha-Shomer ha-Zair did agree to cooperate with the Histadrut for the time being, thus, in effect, accepting the JA's policy against the White Paper. Neither party viewed the contemporary events as a struggle with Arab nationalism; indeed, both parties were continuing to call for the creation of a binational state in Palestine as late as 1946.[79]

Relations with Ha-Zach represented an entirely different problem for the JA, because the Revisionists demanded more active protests. In late April, the Histadrut Executive began negotiations with Ha-Zach through the offices of the Tel Aviv municipality. Although the talks began badly, by May 17 an agreement was worked out according to which the Revisionists agreed not to disrupt JA-sponsored marches. On the other hand, the Revisionists refused to join the JA marches, preferring their own independent protests.[80] Ha-Zach leaders explained their unwillingness to join the JA protests by noting that the Histadrut had already considerably weakened its impact by first requesting permits for the march from the government. Since the government had issued the permits, Ha-Zach representatives said, it clearly expected the Yishuv's protest to be of little long-term consequence.[81]

Ha-Zach's leaders also considered the JA's plans to be both too moderate and too amorphous. In late May, an IZL flyer asked Hagana members about the future and claimed that "nothing remains of the [JAE's] promise to fight to the end."[82] A poster dated May 23, 1939, called on workers and students to join the war against the White Paper. This poster disingenuously accused the JAE of using the census to turn the Yishuv "away from the war against our real enemies and toward a wasteful civil war."[83] In mid-June 1939, the IZL called on students to strike against the JA in order to protest its lack of effective action.[84] This was the crux of the ideological battle between Ha-Zach and the JAE, since the latter appeared to be doing little or nothing.

Further complicating relations among the Zionist parties was the fact that the JA's policy did not yet call for active resistance measures. In contrast, Jabotinsky's tentative plans called for immediate revolt. In the earliest phase of this plan, the IZL intended to increase ha'apala massively. Hoping to swamp British defenses, the plan presumed that the road to victory lay in rendering the White Paper untenable.[85] Further operations, if needed, would concentrate on small-scale guerrilla warfare, supplemented by sabotage of government installations.

Jabotinsky may have prepared a more extensive plan. Abraham Stern, a member of the IZL high command who split from the Irgun in 1940 to create Lohame Herut Israel, claimed that in two coded letters he received from

Jabotinsky, the latter had discussed plans for a seaborne invasion of Palestine by armed ma'apilim from Poland. Although a few historians have taken these letters at face value, more recent researchers doubt their authenticity.[86] The skeptics note that whereas Jabotinsky signed and dated all his letters in one form or another, these are unsigned and undated. Moreover, the wording (which details the travails of setting up a perfume shop) does not lend itself to interpretation by internal evidence. There are no references to anything specific that could otherwise be identified with Jabotinsky. Finally, Stern had a vested interest in claiming that he — and not his rivals in the IZL high command — represented Jabotinsky's true wishes after the latter's death. Thus, it is not clear that such a plan did in fact exist. If it did, it may not have been meant as a realistic plan of operations; it could have been a plant created to draw the British police off the trail of an actual plan.

Within the context of its plan for revolt, the IZL projected its operations in such a way as to avoid unnecessary casualties. A commitment to avoid harming innocent civilians was needed by Ha-Zach, which remained a legal political party even when the IZL received the appellation of "terrorists." Given the nature of the IZL's plans, such a commitment seemed reasonable and the IZL high command consented to it.[87]

Clearly, the IZL devised its war of liberation to be significantly different from the JA's program of noncooperation. It viewed the protest strategy of the WZO, JA, and the Va'ad Leumi as comprising little more than "economic pressure and physical fitness." In view of this, Ha-Zach again called for the dissolution of the JA and Va'ad Leumi and fusing them into an "Emergency Committee."[88] In that way, they hoped to attain a more activist policy for the Yishuv.

In a one-time publication entitled *Emor la-Am*, which appeared in July 1939, the IZL accused the JAE of causing the White Paper. Its argument was that by accepting havlaga, the JAE had accepted a policy of concession to the Arabs; logically, complete concession should follow from "self-restraint." The result of JA policy, therefore, was a virtual ghetto in the Jewish national home. The IZL high command's reasoning was simple. In the forthcoming international struggle, the British would need to maintain peace in Palestine. Since the Jews had not responded properly to the initial Arab attacks, they had only proved that they were not a factor to be considered in Britain's Middle Eastern strategy. More devastating was the criticism that the JA, despite its knowledge of the emergency, had done nothing to overturn the White Paper. To the contrary the IZL accused the JA of having behaved as though nothing had changed with their "business as usual" policy.[89] Even the May 18 general strike was viewed as a fiasco. According to *Emor la-Am*'s editors, the Histadrut had succeeded in maintaining decorum to such an extent that the anti-British rallies were barely distinguishable from pro-British rallies.[90] *Emor la-Am*, however, saved its most scathing criticism for Weizmann. A cartoon portrayed him as "the Arabs' Pillar of Smoke," and compared him to Prime Minister Chamberlain, "the Arabs' Pillar of Fire."[91] The cartoon's obvious conclusion — that Weizmann was guilty of collaboration with the enemy — vividly shows just how far apart the JAE and the IZL, with their respective political blocs, remained.

Yet, when all is said and done, the real differences between the IZL's approach and the JA's are more apparent than real. For one thing, Ha-Zach also placed heavy reliance on a diplomatic campaign aimed at the League of Nations and designed to either cancel the White Paper or replace Britain as the mandatory power for Palestine.[92] Furthermore, for all their criticism, the IZL leaders were hardly privy to the Hagana's plans for revolt.

Still, the rift between Zionist parties should not be underestimated. The extent of the rift may also be seen in the failure to establish an official united front of all Zionist parties. At a meeting of the JAE on May 21, 1939, Rabbi Fishman spoke of the need to act more forcefully. "Let us not act like slaves," he declared, "let us not be afraid of the British hooligans just as we did not fear the Russian hooligans."[93] Fishman may have been venting the frustrations of elements within the JA and the Yishuv that sought more forceful anti-White Paper action. Ben-Gurion also spoke of the need to act, although he said that at the time only the JA seemed ready for action.[94]

Yet for all the rhetoric about the need for immediate action, the JAE actually discussed only one minor matter: a proposal to enlarge the Executive by seven members. The JAE made no decision at this meeting; instead, the issue was referred to a subcommittee and then to the authority of the World Zionist Congress, slated to meet that August.[95]

Inherent in the enlargement proposal was the idea that all Zionist parties should be included in the new Executive on the basis of parity.[96] Despite occasional acts of cooperation, as during the national census, Ha-Zach still remained outside the JAE's authority, and acted in ways that the JA leadership felt were counterproductive. Unity, on the other hand, could strengthen the Yishuv in its struggle against the British. In order to attain such unity, the Revisionists had to return to the WZO and enter the JAE. This line of negotiations had been tried before, notably in the 1934 Ben-Gurion-Jabotinsky negotiations and in the 1938 talks between Ben-Gurion and Shlomo Y. Jacobi. But it had stalled because of irreconcilable differences over the issues of responsibility and discipline. Plainly, the Revisionists feared that the JA leadership was using the term unity as a means of silencing them, while the JAE uncategorically demanded that Ha-Zach desist from acts that the JAE considered irresponsible. Despite the emergency situation, the mutual mistrust between both parties continued.

Hoping to reinforce the trend toward unity, a delegation of veteran Zionists approached the JAE on May 28, 1939, to request the creation of a unified rescue agency for the entire Yishuv. Led by the highly respected professor

David Yellin, the delegation claimed to represent fifty Jewish groups of all political orientations.[97] The delegation hoped to obtain JAE approval for the creation of a five-member body to undertake the rescue program. Of the five, three would be "key people within the Zionist movement," and Agudas Israel and Ha-Zach would have one representative each.[98] Alternatively, one member of the delegation suggested, the JAE could simply be reorganized to consist of five members: David Ben-Gurion, Zeev Jabotinsky, Pinhas Rutenberg, Rabbi Meir Berlin, and Yitzhak Rokach.

In response to Ben-Gurion's questions concerning the authority of the new body and its program, Yellin answered that the new agency would derive its authority from the entire Yishuv, although in reality it would be an outgrowth of the JA and Va'ad Leumi. Ben-Gurion's question was not merely technical, and it cannot be used to prove anything about his political emphasis in May 1939. He truly doubted the delegates' sense of reality, and viewed their plan as mere utopianism; although it contained a sincere desire to be helpful, it was also tinged with a wish to advance personal agendas. Ben-Gurion repeatedly questioned Yellin if any of the other members of the proposed committee had already been contacted and had agreed to serve. As Ben-Gurion anticipated, the answer was that none of them had been contacted and none had agreed to the proposal.[99] The same held true regarding the authority of the new agency. Ben-Gurion saw the delegates as traditional Jewish luftmenschen (dreamers), who created vast plans out of thin air and believed in them with an almost messianic fervor. The issue of authority, Ben-Gurion believed, was vital. If the new body were created and then collapsed — because the members had no means of enforcing agreement on a common policy — the harm to the Yishuv would be greater than any possible benefit to be derived from the new body. Such a commitment, he felt, was not worth the risk.[100]

As to a program, the delegation maintained the JA and Va'ad Leumi position of resistance to the White Paper — since ultimately the goal of the rescue agency was to overturn the White Paper — but with greater activism. Although one member of the delegation distinguished between a policy of "get up and go" and a policy of "sit down and do nothing," the delegation did not suggest any specific plans for resistance to the White Paper.[101]

If the members of the delegation thought that the JAE would immediately approve their proposal, they were sorely disappointed. Ben-Gurion, speaking for most of the JAE members, completely rejected the establishment of a new body that, he said, would create anarchy in the Yishuv and the Zionist movement. Although he expressed some sympathy for the delegates' fears that the Yishuv had not yet acted forcefully to overturn the White Paper, he did not see how the creation of a new agency would help. Nor did he see how the proposed organization would fit into the the Yishuv's quasi-government. As it was, two agencies were competing to do the same job (the JAE and Va'ad Leumi). Adding one more center of authority would only make matters worse.

On the other hand, Ben-Gurion did not reject the implicit idea of cooperation with organizations that were not JAE members. He noted that the JAE
already cooperated with Aguda, and reiterated his long-held position that Ha-
Zach would be welcomed back into the WZO. He did not, however, make
any promises regarding Revisionist membership on either the JAE or the
Va'ad ha-Poel ha-Zioni, presumably because he did not wish to make concessions before he knew whether negotiations were actually going to begin.[102]

At this point, the meeting turned into pandemonium, with much mutual recrimination. Yellin accused Ben-Gurion of not letting all members of the
delegation speak. Denying this, Ben-Gurion declared that the JAE had nothing further to discuss with the delegation, and emphasized that its proposal
had been rejected. He also strongly rejected the implied threat in the words
of several delegates that unless their demands were met, the Yishuv would
lose its trust in the JA.[103] Tempers flared further, and the delegation
stormed out unsatisfied.

Within the JAE itself, two opinions reigned. Rabbi Fishman said that the
JAE had handled the delegation poorly and should have allowed all members
to speak. Gruenbaum, on the other hand, claimed that the JAE should not
have met the delegation at all; and it should not repudiate its responsibilities
toward either the White Paper or rescue issues, since its authority derived
from the WZO and the World Zionist Organization.[104] The entire matter
might have ended there, except that one of the delegates, Shlomo Jacobi —
the same Revisionist who had unsuccessfully attempted to negotiate with Ben-
Gurion over replacement of the JA by a "World Jewish National Assembly"
in October 1938 — released a one-sided summary of the meeting to the press.
Jacobi accused Ben-Gurion of threatening the delegation with violence, and
distorted what had been said in the meeting.[105] *Ha-Aretz* published the
item as front-page news, apparently without first contacting either Yellin or
the JAE.[106] *Ha-Aretz* also published a scathing editorial that accepted Ben-
Gurion's arguments against the creation of a new body, but criticized both the
JA and the Va'ad Leumi for their inability to unify the Yishuv behind one
banner. The editorialist also demanded that the JAE be more forthright regarding the actual situation and the options available for future action.[107]
Other Yishuv newspapers published the same item, as well as editorials on it,
embarrassing the Executive even more.[108]

The adverse publicity generated by the article and the editorials led to a
further meeting between Ben-Gurion and Bernard Joseph, reprsenting the JA,
and Yellin and Shalom Schwartz (another member of the delegation). Yellin
admitted that Jacobi's article contained inaccuracies, but he repeated his statements on the need for unity. After a lengthy dialogue during which both sides
expressed themselves on both significant issues and picayune details, an agreement emerged. No action would be taken on replacing the JAE unless the
upcoming World Zionist Congress agreed to it and the various organizations

would follow Ben-Gurion's lead regarding the campaign to overturn the White Paper. Although no Revisionist representative was present at this second meeting, the agreement implied that both Ha-Zach and the IZL would at least coordinate their activities with the JAE (an eventuality that did not occur even during the war).

Throughout, Yellin and Schwartz continued to emphasize that their position was not based on opposition to Ben-Gurion's leadership. Indeed, in their original plan the entire delegation had hoped to convince Ben-Gurion and Ussishkin to agree to represent the JA at the "Emergency Committee."[109] Yellin and Schwartz did, however, express much apprehension regarding the ability of the rest of the JAE to take any effective decisions. They said that Zionism required rescue, and to carry it out required dramatic action. The JA, however, had not yet acted, and along with the Va'ad Leumi, it seemed unable to do so. As noted, a verbal agreement to persist and to prepare for action at the appropriate time was finally worked out at this meeting.[110] Yet, advocates of immediate rescue action for European Jewry had to wait three more years, for only in January 1943 did the JA establish its Joint Rescue Committee.[111]

To say that the JAE had been inactive is not quite accurate. In May the JA undertook a number of preliminary steps related to the protest strategy. A census, ordered by the JA and the Va'ad Leumi, did take place.[112] All males between the ages of 18 and 35 were counted, with the understanding that they would be liable for national duty at some point. On May 24, 1939, Ben-Gurion presented his plan of action in a meeting with representatives of non-Socialist youth groups (including Betar).[113] Since the British Parliament had approved the White Paper by only a small majority, Ben-Gurion felt that Jewish pressure could result in its cancellation.[114]

Although concerted political pressure might have achieved Ben-Gurion's goal, conditions in Europe militated against the plan. His strategy was not based only on political pressure. Distinguishing three stages of Zionism, he declared that the stage of "fighting Zionism" had arrived. Fighting Zionism was at war with the White Paper policy on behalf of diaspora Jewry. Ben-Gurion specifically rejected a war against the British, since they had not declared war on the Jews. Instead, he suggested, the enemy of the Zionists was the White Paper policy of the British government. Insofar as fighting Zionism had a goal, that goal was overturning the White Paper. Similarly, Ben-Gurion rejected the notion that the goal of the war was independence. Independence, which he defined as defending the rights of the Yishuv, would be a goal only if it furthered prospects for aliya. Throughout this war aliya, not independence, was the main goal.[115] Thus, Ben-Gurion's position was based on the need to defend Zionism. The aliya war and fighting Zionism were primarily defensive in nature; they did not necessarily seek to remove Great Britain from Palestine.[116]

In practice, Ben-Gurion identified eight areas of operation: (1) aliya, without reference to any British legislation or external criteria, including economic absorptive capacity; (2) land settlement, again without reference to any British legislation; (3) defense, by which Ben-Gurion meant the creation of a power base sufficient to defend aliya and settlements; (4) toppling the new British policy and bringing about the end of the Anglo-Arab alliance; (5) strengthening economic independence; (6) creating a unified and disciplined Yishuv for the purpose of resistance; (7) maintaining morale and Jewish pride; and (8) preparing for mobilization.[117]

Ben-Gurion believed that not only was this a realistic line of operation, it was the only one. To carry out this plan, he sought the aliya of 1,000 Jews per week.[118] This would compel the British to either abandon the White Paper or to use force against the ma'apilim. In either case, the moral foundations of British control over Palestine would be weakened, permitting the renewed growth of the Yishuv. Ben-Gurion, however, did not take all factors into account. His plan assumed the ready availability of the financial resources needed to carry out the program: he himself noted that the JAE would need £P7,000 ($35,000) per week, or £P364,000 ($1,820,000) for the first year alone. His plan also assumed the continued existence of a vibrant Jewish diaspora, especially in Poland and eastern Europe. Without this core of Jews there could be no aliya war, and the Yishuv would wither on the vine.[119]

Ben-Gurion's plan received enthusiastic support from all the youth organizations, since they sought action. Clearly, however, the plan represented only an outline of operations, and Ben-Gurion offered no further details. Thus, when it seemed that weeks were passing without any action from the JAE, many of the young activists became disenchanted. What the militants did not know was that Ben-Gurion had taken the next step, moving from rhetoric to action. In order to begin the aliya war, he ordered the creation of a new arm of the Hagana, to be called Peulot Meyuhadot (Special Operations; POM). POM was created in early June 1939 and undertook its first anti-British operation, sinking the coastal patrol boat HMS *Sinbad II*, on August 9.[120]

Considering the differences in approach between the JA and the IZL, it is clear that a de jure united front could not be attained. The Hagana (which still preferred defensive to offensive operations) and the IZL could not even agree on a common basis for future cooperative policies. An example of the rift in attitudes was the May 30, 1939, assassination of Arye Polonski. A member of the Palestine police and the Hagana, Polonski was accused of informing on IZL operations to the British. After an in camera IZL court-martial, he was killed.[121] In a letter to Louis D. Brandeis, Ben-Gurion responded to the assassination, saying that Polonski was innocent and expressing fear that this incident could spark renewed internecine violence.[122]

Similarly, a small minority of Zionists still sought a confrontation with Ha-Zach. The JA leadership, and Ben-Gurion in particular, continued to hear much criticism for the policy of nonconfrontation. One irate correspondent opposed any compromise with the IZL and wrote Ben-Gurion:[123]

> You and the other members of the Executive of the Jewish Agency should receive many thanks — Above all from the New Zionist Organization for the cordial reception of seven thousand members or friends of this organization, instead of modest trained Zionists. And then from all the orderly candidates for certificates who are now allowed to wait because the gentlemen of the Agency prefer illegals.
> Oh the lip service against terror. The terror will destroy the Jewish work in the Holy Land. The terror will destroy all goodwill the world still has for the Jewish People. Alas! Herzl lives no more! Herzl would have protected his work against terror![124]

Such hostile positions had become increasingly rare by 1939. Therefore, although de jure cooperation never became the official policy of either the JA or Ha-Zach, de facto both worked to overturn the White Paper. The pattern established in 1939 — working independently for the same goal, side by side with competition and conflict — continued to be the hallmark of inter-Zionist politics until the establishment of the state of Israel, and beyond. Good examples of both cooperation and conflict abound: cooperation may be exemplified by the 1944 pooling of resources by Af-Al-Pi and the Mossad le-Aliya Bet, while conflict may be exemplified by the simultaneous Hagana effort (under JAE orders) to uproot the IZL in the so-called hunting season. Neither policy completely replaced the other, however, since personal and ideological factors continued to animate the Zionist parties and their leaders.

IMMIGRATION UNDER THE WHITE PAPER REGIME

Although the White Paper appeared to seal the fate of the Yishuv, immigration, both legal and illegal, remained the premier issue facing the Zionists until September 1939. Even Zionist minimalists were caught up in the newfound emphasis on aliya at all costs. Weizmann, for instance, suggested that all 25,000 refugees permitted by the White Paper should be brought over at once. He predicted that such an act would present the Palestine administration with a fait accompli. The British could not, after all, turn back refugees whose immigration was accepted by the White Paper. When more refugees arrived after the quota was used up, public opinion would force the British to let them in, making a shambles of the new immigration policy.[125]

Under the prevailing circumstances, however, illegal immigration became the primary focus of continuing rescue aliya activities. As a result, both Af-Al-Pi and the Mossad le-Aliya Bet expanded their operations. Shaul Avigur, one of the Mossad's key agents, wrote that expansion had finally become realistic, since "the legal restrictions that stood in our way have been lifted." Financial difficulties remained, however, although they had eased considerably.[126] The new situation meant that more operations could be planned and carried out, a fact that was reflected in the communications received by Hagana headquarters from Mossad agents throughout Europe.[127] The ex-pansion of operations did not, of course, always guarantee success. For ex-ample, a group of Czech ma'apilim organized by the Mossad was stopped by police authorities at the Yugoslav border and could not make the rendezvous with the ship that would have run the blockade to Palestine.[128]

Despite setbacks, the Mossad succeeded in transporting 4,788 people during the first eight months of 1939. Af-Al-Pi contributed another 9,245 ma'apilim, and private organizers a further 1,725 in the same period. Though the British caught and deported many of these ma'apilim, some succeeded in evading the police and struck roots in the Yishuv.[129] Af-Al-Pi's operatives gained several spectacular successes during this period. Of special importance was the agreement between Rompalia — Af-Al-Pi's cover in Romania — and the Romanian Official Commercial Society for Tourism.[130]

Nevertheless, ha'apala continued to be a source of tension between the JA and Ha-Zach. Its specific cause was the sailing of the Af-Al-Pi ship SS *Astir* and accusations by some ma'apilim that they had been mistreated by the IZL crewmembers.[131] When contacted by representatives of the Va'ad Leumi Health Department in the Sarafand Prison, all 400 of the ma'apilim from the *Astir* hurled bitter accusations at the crew. Fifty refugees even demanded to be returned to Europe, saying that in view of the treatment they had received, they did not desire to remain in a Jewish national home.[132] The IZL also investigated these reports, and found them to be substantially true. As a result, the IZL commander and his entire crew were court-martialed and punished severely.[133]

Since these complaints gained wide attention within the Yishuv, it appears that the JA sought an opportunity to draw Ha-Zach supporters away from the IZL by selectively leaking more such "horror" stories.[134] In June, Shertok used one of these press releases as the centerpiece of a letter he sent to Josiah Wedgwood, one of Jabotinsky's strongest supporters. While accepting that the poor sanitary and living conditions aboard such ships were sometimes unavoidable, Shertok claimed that "other transports are quite differently organized: they are not run on such bestial lines and are free from totalitarian 'discipline.'"[135] Wedgwood remained unimpressed. In April, when the story first surfaced, he wrote a note supporting Revisionist ha'apala and rejecting partisanship.[136] The reason Wedgwood was not convinced was that cases of premeditated mistreatment of passengers were rare, and were punished when reported. For the most part, living conditions aboard ship were poor because of insufficient funds and bad planning, rather than disdain for the refugees.[137] Wedgwood continued to staunchly support Jabotinsky and Af-Al-Pi, despite the pressure from Shertok and other Zionists.[138] The same could not be said for American Jewish refugee relief agencies such as the JDC, which refused to help aliya bet because all the organizations involved did not care properly for the refugees.[139]

The JA's charges of mistreatment did not go unanswered. In April 1939, an article in *Yediot Le'umiyot* (an underground weekly published by the IZL) accused the JA of unwillingness to provide food for 280 starving ma'apilim. Forced to remain aboard their ship before being returned to Europe, the ma'apilim were refused supplies by the British. However, their pleas to the JA went unnswered as well.[140] This article, which referred to the experience of the Af-Al-Pi ship SS *Sandu*, was only partially correct. The British seized the ship in late April and slated it to return to Europe. While awaiting their fate, the ma'apilim were kept prisoners on board the ship. The JAE did not refuse to aid them — what it did refuse was to aid them as long as they were to be kept aboard ship. The JAE adopted this policy hoping to make the British allow the passengers to disembark, after which their release might have been secured.[141] The result was failure.

The IZL accused the Va'ad Leumi of insensitivity and cowardice as well: although the Va'ad Leumi Executive called for a general strike in the Yishuv to protest the treatment of the ma'apilim, the strike was called off, according to *Yediot Le'umiyot*, after the British threatened to disarm the Jewish Supernumerary Police.[142] If the events had taken place as described, this would have indeed been a powerful indictment. The press makes no mention of it, however: if a general strike had been planned and then canceled, some announcement would have been made in the major dailies. The only thing remotely similar was the decision to delay a meeting of the Va'ad ha-Poel ha-Zioni from April 8 to April 25, 1939.[143]

Betar also categorically denied all accusations of cruel behavior, and claimed that the JA's concern for the safety of ma'apilim was only a facade. The JA actually opposed ha'apala, but out of fear for public opinion it could not admit to its opposition in principle. Instead, the JA sought another means to oppose aliya bet. Hoping to sway Jewish public opinion against aliya bet, the JA released these horror stories. When public opinion was convinced, the JA would show its true face.[144] If Betar's evaluation was correct, it is clear that the JA attempts to discredit aliya bet had failed. As Jews became increasingly more desperate to escape the Nazis, they turned to whatever means were available, including the dangerous trip across the Mediterranean.

The IZL also had strong words for the British. One entire issue of the *Sentinel*, an IZL English-language publication for British troops stationed in

Palestine, was dedicated to ha'apala. Calling for the opening of Palestine to desperate Jewish refugees, the *Sentinel* combined sophisticated propaganda techniques with an attempt to engage the soldiers' emotions. The issue ended with these words: "Shame on those who turn their guns on Jewish refugees and allow the Arab terror to ravage the country."[145]

Efforts to convince the British to ignore illegal Jewish immigration largely failed. IZL-supported acts of resistance by ma'apilim, whose purpose was to convince the British that opposition to Jewish demands would be too costly in moral terms were not successful. The ma'apilim of the SS *Liesel*, for example, refused to disembark when ordered to do so, and were removed by force.[146] The need to use force did not deter the British — they already were using force against Jews to break up JA-sponsored rallies — but it did compel the JAE to act on behalf of the *Liesel* refugees, in this case by the use of enough certificates to legalize the entire group and thereby prevent their deportation.[147] A July hunger strike by some eighty ma'apilim who were still in detention after their prison sentences had ended, did not conclude so happily: they were deported just before the outbreak of World War II.[148]

As with the attempts to coordinate political policy, the attempts to unify aliya bet activities failed. Af-Al-Pi and the IZL viewed the JA and WZO as weak-willed and irresolute; the JA leadership viewed the IZL as undisciplined and dangerous.[149] Both characterizations have a grain of truth to them, but both also overgeneralize. While the two main Zionist blocs continued to fight, both operated against the White Paper. Even if the JA and Ha-Zach had co-operated, it is not certain that a greater portion of European Jewry could have been rescued. More individuals might have been rescued, compared with the slightly more than 18,000 who were rescued by means of aliya bet during the war, but mass rescue proposals required considerable financial and political support.[150] British appeasement of the Arabs and the increasingly violent nature of Nazi antisemitism left European Jewry in mortal danger. The Yishuv, numbering slightly more than 400,000 souls, with no army, navy, or air force, could hardly offer any real assistance. World Jewry had reached the nadir of its influence.

THE BITTER END

With the White Paper policy in place, the abandonment of European Jewry by the free world was virtually complete. Zionist efforts to delay the inevitable had failed, and Great Britain had repudiated its commitments. In June, the League of Nations Permanent Mandates Commission met to discuss the White Paper. Both the JA and Ha-Zach representatives in Geneva attempted to convince members of the League that the White Paper contravened the terms of the Mandate.[151] Although they operated independently, both used similar arguments and hoped to attain the same goals. To a limited degree, they did succeed. The League of Nations debated the White Paper and condemned it as inconsistent with the Mandate.[152] The League planned further action, but any decision was permanently delayed by World War II.

The Va'ad ha-Poel ha-Zioni met on June 27, 1939, and approved the JAE's plans to continue the policy of noncooperation with the Palestine administration as long as the White Paper remained in force. The Va'ad ha-Poel, however, also condemned blind retaliation, and called for Zionist unity in face of the crisis.[153] This in itself was not an adequate response, but it also was not the whole response. During the summer, the Hagana continued preparations to put "Plan Avner" into operation, with a target date of early September.

On the political front, noncooperation became the hallmark of JA policy. Most Zionists agreed that noncooperation had only limited chances for success, unless it became a systematic policy carried out on all levels. Anything else would be viewed by the British as a short-duration protest, after which the Jews would make their peace with the new situation.[154] In practice, therefore, the Yishuv had to strengthen its autonomous institutions. Actions such as establishing an internal postal service and an independent court system — hallmarks of noncooperation — would be only minor irritants in the short run, but in the long run they could make a difference. Strengthening local industry could also offer long-term security, and could be attained by an anti-British boycott.[155] A Central Office for the Economic Defense of the Yishuv opened under the auspices of the JA on June 8, 1939, in order to oversee the boycott.[156]

The outbreak of World War II on September 1, 1939, altered the entire situation. Successful noncooperation under wartime conditions was viewed as more likely to help the Nazis than to harm the British. The all-out struggle against the White Paper would have to be delayed, but it would not be canceled. Ben-Gurion framed this new policy in a statement of September 3, 1939: "We shall fight Hitler as though there were no White Paper, and we shall fight the White Paper as though there was no Hitler."[157]

Conclusion

On September 3, 1939, Great Britain declared war on Nazi Germany. That afternoon, British gunboats intercepted the Mossad blockade runner the SS *Tiger Hill*. As the *Tiger Hill* ran aground and began to unload, the British commenced firing. Two ma'apilim were killed and the remaining 1,415 were captured. Thus the first casualties of British arms on the first day of World War II were not Nazis, but Jewish refugees fleeing the Nazis.[1]

Four questions were posed at the beginning of this book: (1) Did differing party ideologies reflect clear divergences in rescue-related issues? (2) Were the policies advocated by the Yishuv's leaders and their opponents reasonable responses to the perceived threat? (3) Were these policies pursued creatively and energetically? (4) To what extent did the Yishuv's disunity impact on the success or failure to rescue European Jewry? Before we can offer a tentative answer to these questions, we ought to consider Shimon Golan's conundrum on activism in a study comparing the actions of the Zionist Left and Right during the years between 1945 and 1947. Activism, Golan writes, "is a policy distinguished by the active struggle on behalf of a set of goals, undertaken by a body which adopts measures to overcome those factors inhibiting the goals' achievement."[2] Framed in terms that relate to our subject, Golan's point is an apt reminder that ex-post-facto criticisms notwithstanding, the Yishuv faced serious objective and subjective hindrances to accomplishing a goal that was essentially acceptable to all but a small, fringe, minority within the Zionist movement, i.e. the rescue of European Jewry.

On the basis of the information reviewed, it is possible to offer a tentative conclusion and to suggest further avenues for research. One point must be emphasized: the Endlösung did not develop at once. Since Nazi policy began slowly, and developed its murderous content only later, many Jews both inside

248

and outside Germany presumed that a modus vivendi was possible and that evacuation was not necessary. We now know that this presumption was incorrect; Jews did not realize that cruel reality until it was too late.

Moreover, Jews possessed only a narrow range of alternative options. Lack of sovereignty and the absence of any strong-willed allies meant that effective diplomatic action against Nazi Germany was impossible. Economic pressure also failed, because because world Jewry could not mobilize sufficient financial resources to develop a successful boycott. Disunity among Jewish groups also hindered the boycott. As it was, the boycott caused little more than minor ripples in a German economy that was increasingly geared to a military build-up rather than to exports.

Only refugee aid remained a realistic approach to the Nazi threat. Here, however, at least four severe limitations existed. First, German Jews were not willing to emigrate in the early years of the Third Reich, when flight was still relatively simple. Second, financial realities meant that sufficient funds for mass resettlement projects did not exist. Third, there were few havens for Jewish refugees. Besides the Yishuv, no country actively sought the immigration of Jewish refugees. To the contrary, the eastern European countries actively sought to rid themselves of Jews. Finally, even Palestine was only a limited haven because of British efforts to keep Jews out of the territory.

Mapai and Ha-Zohar differed on many fundamental issues, but rescue aliya as a policy was *not* an issue of contention. Both parties sought to direct the flow of Jewish refugees toward the Yishuv. Yet there were serious differences between the parties on both the means and the ends of such aims. Mapai (and the Mapai-dominated JAE) initially rejected both mass evacuation and immediate creation of a Jewish majority that would lead logically to statehood. Ha-Zohar, on the other hand, supported both, seeing the persecution of German Jewry as an unprecedented proof of the needs of the hour, and the last chance to achieve positive goals before catastrophe struck. From 1933 on, the Revisionists perceived the threat as more serious, and argued for the immediate evacuation of European Jewry so as to fulfill the Zionist goal of statehood. Initially, Mapai and the JAE did not support mass aliya, did not see the need for immediate action, and did not link rescue aliya with the call for sovereignty. As the Nazi menace unfolded, however, the JAE's policy changed. This transformation may be seen most clearly in the attitude of the JAE toward aliya bet: from opposition in 1933, to tacit support in 1937, and to active patronage after Kristallnacht.

Similarly, Mapai and Ha-Zohar disagreed noticeably on the issue of the anti-Nazi boycott. While the idea of a boycott was not completely consistent with the idea of evacuation, Ha-Zohar strongly supported a public declaration of economic war by Jewry. In contrast, Mapai opposed a boycott, publicly because of fear that the Nazis would retaliate against German Jewry. In reality, Mapai's position was more complex. Individual Mapai members supported and participated in the Yishuv's anti-Nazi boycott while the party supported the Haavara agreement, which sought the orderly transfer of part of German Jewish capital. Unlike Jabotinsky, the JA leaders saw their dilemma as a Hobson's choice, and chose what they felt represented the lesser of two evils.

Previous historians have viewed both of these cases, aliya and Haavara, as examples of the clash between two monolithic political blocs over the definition of Zionism. The position holding that the choices made by both parties were fixed and immutable is untenable, however. Mapai, as already noted, ultimately came to adopt a form of evacuation and statehood as immediate goals of Zionism. For Mapai and the Mapai-led JAE coalition, this statement of goals was formulated explicitly in the Biltmore Resolution of 1942. The groundwork for Biltmore was, however, laid in the late 1930s. On the other hand, by the second half of the 1930s, Jabotinsky came to realize that evacuation could only be financed by the export of diaspora Jewish capital, and he eventually advocated Haavara-like agreements with the antisemitic regimes of Poland and Romania. Thus, the supposedly fixed and immutable ideological positions of Mapai and Ha-Zohar thus turn out to have been both porous and flexible.

As against these areas of agreement that developed during the 1930s, considerable differences continued to exist, primarily on social and economic issues. For example, disagreements also existed on tactics — the hows and whys of rescue — in addition to disagreement over questions of activism or passivity, in the face of Arab and British opposition to rescue aliya. Mapai and the JA adopted a purely defensive approach, exemplified by havlaga, while Ha-Zohar advocated an end to defensive tactics and the adoption of an offensive plan. These disagreements prevented cooperation between the competing Zionist blocs, except on a few ad hoc occasions. The external threat posed by the Nazis slowed the inter-Zionist rivalry, the opening rounds of which were fought between 1931 and 1933, but it did not prevent violent clashes from breaking out in earnest near the end of World War II.

Still, it cannot be said that a unified Zionist movement could have achieved a more successful rescue program. Three factorc guaranteed the ultimate downfall of rescue aliya: (1) the lack of financial resources, which meant that only small numbers of olim could be absorbed at any one time; (2) the seeming improvement of conditions in Germany in 1936 and 1937, which deterred mass flight; and, primarily, (3) the unwillingness of the British government to cooperate with the rescue scheme. The British withdrawal from the commitments that had been made to Jews in 1937 and 1938, such as the partition plan, impacted negatively on aliya and boded ill for any mass rescue scheme. While Zionist unity might have permitted a more forceful approach to the government, it is not clear what would have resulted. A more strongly stated Zionist case could not have convinced the British to aid rescue, since it is clear that by the late 1930s the Palestine administration, the Colonial Office, and the Prime Minister had concluded that helping Jews no longer coincided with British Imperial interests.

In this regard, Great Britain's policy of appeasement must be placed in context. Between 1933 and 1938, the British sought to appease Hitler and thus did not support forceful actions on behalf of threatened European Jewry. In 1939, however, Britain's decision to confront Hitler did not reverse British policy regarding the Jews. To the contrary, preparations for war seemed to require a new policy of appeasement — in this case, of the Arabs — that meant Britain's final and irrevocable abandonment of the Jews.

Like the Endlösung, the abandonment of the Jews took place in stages. In 1933 it still seemed possible that the British might cooperate in the rescue of German Jewry. Despite some difficulties, this hope did not seem far-fetched. Indeed, in 1934 and 1935, aliya reached unprecedented proportions. Subsequently, however, the British returned to a policy of limiting Jewish immigration. What is of greater consequence is that the British retrenchment took place at precisely the time when Jewish needs were greatest. As Jewish needs increased, British policy grew even harsher. From 1937 to 1939 the British experimented with three policies: partition, cantonization, and appeasement of the Arabs. Only the first two maintained any semblance of the promises made in the Balfour Declaration. The Zionists were cognizant of Britain's turn toward the Arabs, but were powerless to prevent it.

Clearly, Jabotinsky disagreed with the other Zionist leaders over how to respond to British betrayal. Again, it must be recalled that neither party had the power or influence to change the reality. In general, Jabotinsky appears to have understood the threat to Jewry earlier than his colleagues (by 1933 he had been predicting an imminent catastrophe for nearly two decades), but he had even less power to affect the outcome of events. At the time, his dire predictions seemed wildly exaggerated. No one living in 1933 — or in 1939, for that matter — could have predicted the depths of depravity to which the Nazis would descend in their efforts to attain Entjudung.

One fact is clear: not enough was done to rescue European Jewry. Given the reality of six million murdered, even rescue aliya, which accounted for the aliya of nearly 250,000 Jews between 1933 and 1939, must be considered a failure. The program that began in 1933 still seems, when viewed in context, the only reasonable response to the Nazi threat. Given the Jews' lack of options and the overall weakness of Jewish defenses, Zionists cannot be damned for this failure. Compared to states with greater resources, the Yishuv accounted for half of all the Jews rescued from the Nazis' clutches. The example of the United States is apt: the Yishuv saved more than twice as many refugees as the United States did, despite the latter's obviously superior resources. Small consolation may be taken from that fact, and there appears to be only one lesson that can be drawn from the events in Palestine between 1933 and 1939: powerlessness is a dangerous state of being for small, beleaguered groups.

Appendix
Aliya Bet Ships

The following table, previously published in Abraham J. Edelheit and Hershel Edelheit, *History of the Holocaust: A Handbook and Dictionary*, Boulder: Westview Press, 1994, is based on a list prepared in the mid-1960s by the Israel State Archives. Versions of the same list have appeared in a variety of secondary sources on Aliya Bet: most recently in Dalia Ofer, *Escaping the Holocaust: Illegal Immigration to the Land of Israel, 1939-1944*, New York: Oxford University Press, 1990.

Ship	Party	No. of *Olim*	Sailed From	Date	Result[1]
Prewar					
Velos I	H	350	Pireaus	7/34	Landed Tel Aviv
Union	R	117	Pireaus	8/34	Landed Tel Aviv
Velos II	H	350	Varna	9/34	Captured/Returned
Af-Al-Pi	R	15	Pireaus	4/37	Landed Herzliya
Af-Al-Pi II	R	54	Dorado	9/37	Landed Binyamina
Poseidon A	H	65	Lorion	1/38	Landed Mizpe ha-Yam
Af-Al-Pi III	R	96	Fiume	3/38	Landed Tantura
Artemisia A	R	128	Pireaus	4/38	Landed Tantura
Poseidon B	R	65	Pireaus	5/38	Landed Tantura
Artemisia B	R	157	Pireaus	7/38	Landed Tantura
Af-Al-Pi IV	R	156	Pireaus	8/38	Landed Binyamina
Af-Al-Pi V	R	38	Pireaus	9/38	

253

Draga A	R	180	Shusak	10/38	Landed Tantura
Atarto A	M	300	Bari	11/38	Landed Shefayim
Draga B	R	550	Constantsa	12/38	Landed Netanya
Ely	R	340	Galatz	12/38	Landed Netanya
Gepo A	R	734	Tulcea	12/38	Landed Netanya
Delphi	R	250	Constantsa	12/38	
Atarto B	M	300	Ancona	1/39	Landed Shefayim
Katina	R	800	Baltzec	2/39	Landed Netanya
Atarto C	M	300	Naples	2/39	Landed Tel Aviv
Atarto D	M	378	Shusak	3/39	Landed Tel Aviv
Sandu	P	270	Constanta	3/39	Captured/Returned
Assimi	Mi	470	Constanta	3/39	Captured/Returned
Gepo B	R	750		4/39	Sank, olim rescued
Aghia Dezioni	R	400	Fiume	4/39	Landed Nebi Ruben
Atarto E	M	408	Shusak	4/39	Landed Herzliya
Atarto F	M	337	Brindisi	4/39	Landed Herzliya
Ostia	R	699	Italy	4/39	Landed Herzliya
Agia Nicolaus	P	800	Burgas	5/39	Landed Netanya
Karliza Maria	P	350		5/39	
Atarto G	M	400	Constantsa	5/39	Captured/Detained
Demetrius	M	244	Greece	6/39	Captured
Liesel	R	921	Constantsa	6/39	Captured/Detained
Colorado I	M	379	Constantsa	6/39	
Astir	R	724	Rani	6/39	Landed Majdal
Los Perlos	R	370	Constantsa	7/39	
Nikko	R	560	Fiume	7/39	Landed Netanya
Colorado II	M	377	Constantsa	7/39	Captured/Returned
Rudnichar A	P	305	Varna	8/39	Landed Netanya
Dora	M	480	Flisingen	8/39	
Rim	R	600	Constantsa	8/39	Sank, olim rescued
Agia Nicolaus B	R	745	Constantsa	8/39	Landed Netanya
Parita	R	850	Constantsa	8/39	Captured/Detained
Osiris	R	650	Varna	8/39	
Cartova	R	650	Varna	8/39	
Tripoli	R	700	Varna	8/39	

Wartime

Prosola	P	654	Varna	9/39	Trans. to *Tiger Hill*
Tiger Hill	M	1,417	Constantsa	9/39	Landed Tel Aviv[2]
Rudnichar B	P	371	Varna	9/39	Landed Herzliya
Naomi Julia	R	1,130	Constantsa	9/39	Captured/Returned

Rudnichar C	P	457	Varna	11/39	Landed Tel Aviv
Hilda	M	728	Baltzec	1/40	Captured/Detained
Sakarya	R	2,400	Constantsa	2/40	Captured/Detained
Pentcho	R	500	Bratislava	5/40	Sank[3]
Libertad	P	700	Varna	7/40	Landed Zichron Yaacov
Pacific	M	1,100	Tulcea	11/40	⌐ Captured and
Milos	M	671	Tulcea	11/40	⌐ transfered to *Patria*[4]
Atlantic	M	1,880	Tulcea	11/40	Captured/Returned
Salvador	P	327	Varna	12/40	Sank[5]
Darien II	M	800	Constantsa	3/41	Captured/Detained
Struma	P	769	Constantsa	2/42	Sank[6]
Vitorul	P	120	Constantsa	9/42	Sank
Milka A	M	239	Constantsa	3/44	Landed Turkey[7]
Marissa A	M	224	Constantsa	4/44	Landed Turkey
Milka B	M	517	Constantsa	5/44	Landed Turkey
Marissa B	M	318	Constantsa	5/44	Landed Turkey
Kazbek	M	735	Constantsa	7/44	
Bulbul	M	410	Constantsa	8/44	Landed Turkey
Mefkurie	M	344	Constantsa	8/44	Sank[8]
Salah-al-Din	M	547	Constantsa	11/44	
Taurus	M	948	Constantsa	12/44	

Postwar

Dahlin	M	35	Barletta	8/45	Landed Caesarea
Netuna I	M	79	Bari	9/45	Landed Caesarea
Pietro I	M	168	Chiatone	9/45	Landed Shefayim
Netuna II	M	73	Bari	10/45	Landed Shefayim
Pietro II	M	171	Chiatone	10/45	Landed Shefayim
Berl Katznelson	M	211	Greece	11/45	Captured after landing
Hanna Szenesh	M	252	Savona	12/45	Landed Nahariya
Enzo Sereni	M	900	Vado	1/46	Interned in Atlit
Orde Wingate	M	238	Palestrina	3/46	Interned in Atlit
Tel-Hai	M	736	France	3/46	Interned in Atlit
Max Nordau	M	1,666	Constantsa	5/46	Interned in Atlit
Eliahu Golomb	M	1,014	⌐ La Spezia	5/46	⌐ Ships seized by
Dov Hoz	M		⌐		⌐ Italians[9]
Haviva Reich	M	462	Greece	6/46	Interned in Atlit
J. Wedgewood	M	1,257	Vado	6/46	Interned in Atlit
Biriya	M	999	France	7/46	Interned in Atlit

Hagana	M	2,678	Yugoslavia	7/46	Interned in Atlit
Hayal ha-Ivri	M	510	Belgium	7/46	Interned in Atlit
Yagur	M	754	France	8/46	Interned on Cyprus
H. Szold	M	536	Greece	8/46	Interned on Cyprus
Katriel Jaffe	M	604	Bocca di Magra	8/46	Interned on Cyprus
23 Yorde haSira	M	790	Bocca di Magra	8/46	Interned on Cyprus
A. Shochat	M	183	Bocca di Magra	8/46	Landed Caesarea
Arba Heruyot	M	1,024	Bocca di Magra	9/46	Interned on Cyprus
Palmach	M	611	Bocca di Magra	9/46	Interned on Cyprus
Bracha Fuld	M	806	Bocca di Magra	10/46	Interned on Cyprus
Latrun	M	1,275	France	11/46	Interned on Cyprus
Knesset Israel	M	3,845	Yugoslavia	11/46	Interned on Cyprus
Rafiah	M	785	Yugoslavia	12/46	Sank
La-Negev	M	647	France	2/47	Interned on Cyprus
Maapil Almoni	M	746	France	2/47	Interned on Cyprus
H. Arlosoroff	M	1,348	Trelleborg	2/47	Landed Bat Galim
Ben Hecht	R	600	Port-de-Bouc	3/47	Interned on Cyprus
S. Lewinski	R	823	Metaponto	3/47	Landed Nizzanim
Moledet	M	1,563	Metaponto	3/47	Interned on Cyprus
T. Herzl	M	2,641	France	4/47	Interned on Cyprus
She'ar Yashuv	M	768	Boliasco	4/47	Interned on Cyprus
Hatikva	M	1,414	Boliasco	5/47	Interned on Cyprus
Morde haGetaot	M	1,457	Mola di Bari	5/47	Interned on Cyprus
Yehuda haLevi	M	399	Algiers	5/47	Interned on Cyprus
Exodus 1947	M	4,530	Marseilles	7/47	Returned to Germany
Gesher A-Ziv	M	685	Milliarino	7/47	Interned on Cyprus
Shivat Zion	M	411	Algiers	7/47	Interned on Cyprus
Af-Al-Pi-Chen	M	434	Formia	9/47	Interned on Cyprus
Geula	M	1,388	Burgas	10/47	Interned on Cyprus
Jewish State	M	2,664	Burgas	10/47	Interned on Cyprus
Kadima	M	794	Palestrina	11/47	Interned on Cyprus
Aliya	M	182	France	11/47	Landed Nahariya
HaPorzim	M	167	France	12/47	Landed Tel Aviv
Lo Tafhidenu	M	850	Civitavecchia	12/47	Interned on Cyprus
29 November	M	680	Girolata	12/47	Interned on Cyprus
The U.N.	M	537	Civitavecchia	1/48	Interned on Cyprus
Pan York	M	7,623	Burgas	1/48	⎤ Agreed to
Pan Crescent	M	7,616	Burgas	1/48	⎦ sail to Cyprus[10]
HaLamed Heh	M	274	Palestrina	1/48	Interned on Cyprus
Yerushalayim	M	670	Civitavecchia	2/48	Interned on Cyprus
La Komemiyut	M	699	France	2/48	Interned on Cyprus
Bonim	M	1,002	Yugoslavia	2/48	Interned on Cyprus

Yehiam	M	769	Gaeta	3/48	Interned on Cyprus
Tirat Zvi	M	798	Italy	4/48	Interned on Cyprus
Mishmar Emek	M	782	France	4/48	Interned on Cyprus
Nachson	M	550	France	4/48	Interned on Cyprus
LaNizahon	M	189	Brindisi	5/48	Landed Tel Aviv[11]
Medinat Israel	M	243	Brindisi	5/48	Landed Tel Aviv
Emek Ayalon	M	706	Brindisi	5/48	Landed Tel Aviv

Notes

[1] The following abbreviations are used to designate parties: H = he-Halutz (Mapai's youth division in the diaspora); M = Mossad le-Aliya Bet; Mi = Mizrachi; P = Private; R = Revisionist Zionists (ha-Zohar or ha-Zach). Details of journey, such as port of departure and result, given when known.

[2] As the *Tiger Hill* unloaded, it was fired upon by British gunboats; two olim were killed.

[3] The *Pentcho* passengers were picked up by the Italian Navy and were interned on Rhodes; many were later deported to death camps in Poland.

[4] After the British announced that the *Patria* was to be sailed to the Mauritius Islands the Hagana attempted to sabotage the ship. The *Patria* sank in Haifa harbor as a result of the explosion with 260 olim killed.

[5] The *Salvador* sank in the Dardanelles and 120 *olim* drowned; the remainder later transferred to the *Darien*.

[6] The *Struma* sank under mysterious circumstances in the Black Sea; there were no survivors.

[7] The *olim* from all ships that landed in Turkey were permitted into Palestine legally.

[8] The *Mefkurie* was torpedoed by a German U-Boat that surfaced to machine-gun the survivors; only five passengers survived.

[9] The *Eliahu Golomb* and the *Dov Hoz* were impounded by the Italian police at the instigation of the British before either could sail. The international crisis that followed forced the British to permit all 1,014 of the olim (who would have sailed aboard the two ships) to enter Palestine legally.

[10] Given the large number of olim, especially out of concern that resistance would be met with deadly force, the Mossad agreed to sail the ships directly to Cyprus.

[11] The last three ships arrived after the State of Israel had become independent.

Notes

Introduction

1. Yeshayhu Klinov, "Adolf Hitler: His Life, His War, His Movement," *ha-Aretz*, Part I, July 3, 1932, p. 2; Pt. II, July 5, 1932, p. 2; Pt. III, July 8, 1932, p. 2; Pt. IV, July 11, 1932, p. 2; Pt. V, July 12, 1932, pp. 2-3; Pt. VI, July 18, 1932, pp. 2-3.

2. Moshe Brachman, "On the Question of Aliya from Germany," *Davar*, July 5, 1932, pp. 2-3.

3. See the front page articles in the January 30, 1933, issues of *ha-Aretz, Davar,* and *The Palestine Post*.

4. For example, the reports in *ha-Aretz* on Febraury 1, and February 5, 1933 both proved to be false.

5. *Ha-Aretz*, February 7, 19233, p. 1. *Davar* and *The Palestine Post* published similarly inaccurate reports on that date.

6. Cf. Ezra Mendelsohn, *The Jews of East Central Europe Between the Two World Wars*, Bloomington: Indiana University Press, 1983.

7. Minutes of a Conversation with the High Commissioner, October 17, 1933, Central Zionist Archive (hereafter CZA) S25/17/1, p. 4.

8. Abraham G. Duker, *The Situation of the Jews in Poland*, New York: American Jewish Congress, 1936, p. 35.

9. Cf. M. B. Lepecki, *Madagaskar, Kraj, Ludzie, Kolonizacja*, Warsaw: Polonia, 1938.

10. Laski and Montefiore to Under-Secretary of State for Foreign Affairs, January 3, 1938, in Jean Ancel (ed.), *Documents Concerning the Fate of Romanian Jewry*, New York: The Beate Klarsfeld Foundation, 1986, vol. 1, pp. 186-187.

11. Nathaniel Katzburg, *Hungary and the Jews, 1920-1943*, Ramat Gan: Bar-Ilan University Press, 1981, ch. 5-7.

12. Weizmann to MacDonald, June 11, 1933, in *The Letters and Papers of Chaim Weizmann, Series A: Letters*, New Brunswick, NJ: Transaction Books, 1973, vol. 15, pp. 447-448 (hereafter cited as Weizmann: *Letters*).

13. Abaraham J. Edelheit and Hershel Edelheit, *History of the Holocaust: A Handbook and Dictionary*, Boulder, CO: Westview Press, 1994, pp. 41-42.

14. "The Jewish Population of Palestine — Census of 1931," *American Jewish Yearbook* (hereafter cited as *AJYB*), vol. 34 (1933/1934), pp. 272-278.

Chapter 1

1. Abraham J. Edelheit and Hershel Edelheit, *History of the Holocaust: A Handbook and Dictionary*, Boulder, CO: Westview Press, 1994, pp. 299-310.

2. *The Palestine Post*, February 9, 1933, p. 1; *ha-Aretz*, February 10, 1933, p. 1; *AJYB*, vol. 35 (1934/1935), pp. 29-31.

3. *AJYB*, vol. 35, pp. 31-32.

4. Ibid., pp. 32-34.

5. Cf. Karl A. Schleunes, *The Twisted Road to Auschwitz*, Urbana: University of Illinois Press, 1970, pp. 77-91.

6. *Reichsgesetzblatt*, vol. 1 #100 (September 1935), pp. 1146-1147.

7. Schleunes, *Twisted Road*, ch. 5.

8. Edelheit and Edelheit, *History of the Holocaust*, pp. 46-49.

9. Herbert A. Straus, "The Drive for War and the Pogrom of November 1938: Testing Explanatory Models," *Leo Baeck Institute Yearbook* (hereafter: *LBIYB*), vol. 35 (1990), pp. 268-278.

10. Robert Weltsch, "Traght ihn mit Stolz, den gelben Fleck!" *Jüdische Rundschau*, April 4, 1933, p. 1.

11. Cf. Abraham Barkai, *From Boycott to Annihilation: The Economic Struggle of German Jews, 1933-1943*, Hanover, NH: University Press of New England, 1989, pp. 37-38.

12. Ibid., pp. 47-54.

13. As late as September 1935 the German Zionist Federation published a plan calling for an orderly exodus. Cf. *Jüdische Rundschau*, September 24, 1935, p. 1.

14. Yitzhak Arad et al (eds.), *Documents on the Holocaust*, New York: Ktav for Yad Vashem and the Anti-Defamation League, 1981, p. 69.

15. *Centralverein Zeitung*, April 27, 1933, p. 1.

16. Abraham Margaliot, "The Problem of Rescue of German Jews during the Years 1933-1939: The Reasons for the Delay in their Emigration from the Third Reich," in *Rescue Attempts During the Holocaust*, edited by Israel Gutman and Efraim Zuroff, Jerusalem: Yad Vashem, 1977, pp. 256-259.

17. Ibid., p. 263.

18. Cf. Bernard D. Weinryb, *Jewish Emancipation under Attack*, New York: American Jewish Committee, 1942, ch. 2-4.

19. Cf. David Frankfurter, *Rishon Lohame ha-Nazim*, Tel Aviv: Reshafim Press, 1984.

20. On the American Press see Deborah Lipstadt, *Beyond Belief: The American Press and the Coming of the Holocaust, 1933-1945*, New York: Free Press, 1986, and, more generally, Walter Laqueur, *The Terrible Secret: Suppression of the Truth About Hitler's Final Solution*, Boston: Little Brown, 1980, pp. 214-219.

21. The *New York Times*, for example, buried the December 12, 1942, report that 2,000,000 Jews had already been murdered by the Nazis on page 31. Other newspapers refused to even publish the report. Lipstadt, *Beyond Belief*, pp. 162-176.

22. Leonard Dinnerstein, *America and the Survivors of the Holocaust*, New York: Columbia University Press, 1982, pp. 1-8.

23. In addition to Laqueur, *The Terrible Secret*, see: Andrew Sharf, *The British Press and Jews Under Nazi Rule*, London: Oxford University Press, 1964, and Bernard Wasserstein, *Britain and the Jews of Europe, 1939-1945*, Oxford: Clarendon Press for the Institute of Jewish Affairs, 1979.

24. Oscar I. Janowksy, *The Jews and Minority Rights*, New York: Columbia University Press, 1933, pp. 379-382 and Nathan Feinberg, *ha-Agudot ha-Yehudiot le-Ma'an Hever ha-Leumim*, Jerusalem: Magnes Press, 1967, ch. 4.

25. Nathan Feinberg, *ha-Maavak ha-Yehudi Neged Hitler be-Hever ha-Leumim*, Jerusalem: Magnes Press, 1957, pp. 31-32, 35.

26. "The Bernheim Petition to the League of Nations," *AJYB*, vol. 35 (1934/1935), p. 74.

27. *Ha-Aretz*, May 18, 1933, p. 1.

28. Ibid., June 1, 1933, p. 1.

29. Feinberg, *ha-Maavak*, p. 43; Weizmann to Weiss, May 7, 1933, Weizmann: *Letters*, vol. 15, p. 415.

30. Feinberg, *ha-Maavak*, p. 27.

31. Yehuda Bauer, "Jewish Foriegn Policy during the Holocaust," *Midstream*, vol. 30 # 10 (December, 1984), pp. 22-25.

32. Protocols of the JAE, April 9, 1933, CZA S100/14, pp. 5/3651-6/3652; *ha-Aretz*, March 23, 1933, p. 1, March 26, 1933, p. 1, March 27, 1933, p. 1; March 28, 1933, p. 1.

33. Cf. Abba Hillel Silver, "Why We Boycott Germany," *Anti-Nazi Economic Bulletin*, vol. 1 # 4 (May, 1934), p. 4 and Walter Citrine, "Boycott Most Useful Weapon Against Dangers of Nazism," Ibid., vol. 3 # 7 (October, 1936), p. 1.

34. There had been a number of highly publicized successful boycotts which could serve as an example to the boycotters, but none had been against a foreign government. For one example of a successful, but very limited, boycott

see Edwin Black, "The Anti-Ford Boycott," *Midstream*, vol. 32 # 1 (January, 1986), pp. 39-41.

35. Joseph Tenenbaum, Review of Three Years of the Anti-Nazi Boycott, 1936, CZA A209/139, pp. 7-9.

36. Cf. *Twenty-Seventh Annual Report of the American Jewish Committee*, New York: The Committee, 1934, pp. 43-44.

37. Nana Sagi, Teguvat ha-Ziburiut ha-Yehudit be-Britania le-Redifat ha-Yehudim ba-Reich ha-Shlishi ba-Shanim 1930-1939, Unpublished Doctoral Disseration: Hebrew University, 1982, pp. 98-115.

38. Sagi, Teguvat, pp. 432-437 and Naomi W. Cohen, *Not Free to Desist*, Philadelphia: Jewish Publication Society, 1972, pp. 162-166.

39. Charles Higham, *Trading With the Enemy*, New York: Delacorte Press, 1983.

40. "Healing Hatred," *Christian Science Monitor*, April 4, 1933, cited in *Dimensions: A Journal of Holocaust Studies*, vol. 4 # 3 (1989), p. 11.

41. Interview with R. Zorach Warhaftig, July 30, 1991, notes in the author's possession. Although Warhaftig prepared a history of the anti-Nazi boycott for the American Jewish Congress in 1943 it was never published. Warhaftig's files on the boycott are held in the Yad Vashem and Israel State Archives (hereafter cited as YVA and ISA).

42. On non-cooperation by consumers see Minutes of a Meeting of the Boycott Committee of the American Jewish Congress, February 22, 1924, ISA GL8586/1; on retailers see Minutes of a Meeting of the Boycott Committee of the American Jewish Congress, February 15, 1934, Ibid.

43. Minutes of a Meeting of the Boycott Committee of the American Jewish Congress, March 1, 1933, ISA GL8586/1.

44. Cf. Abraham Barkai, *Nazi Economics: Ideology, Theory, Policy*, Oxford: Berg Publishers, 1990, p. 250.

45. Ibid., pp. 254-255.

46. Tenenbaum, Review of Three Years, pp. 3-5.

47. Dan Michman, "The Committee for Jewish Refugees in Holland (1933-1940)," *Yad Vashem Studies*, vol. 14 (1981): 205-232.

48. Westerbork was eventually taken over by the Nazis and became a transit camp for the deportation of Dutch Jewry. Jacob Boas, *Boulevard des Miseries: The Stroty of Transit Camp Westerbork*, Hamden, CT: Archon Books, 1985.

49. Cf. Irving Abella and Harold Troper, *None is Too Many: Canada and the Jews of Europe, 1933-1948*, New York: Random House, 1982.

50. Ibid., p. 46. Cf. Lois Foster, "No Northern Option: Canada and Refugees from Nazism Before the Second World War," in Paul R. Bartrop (ed.), *False Havens: The British Empire and the Holocaust*, Lanham, MD: University Press of America, 1995, pp. 79-98.

51. Michael R. Marrus, *The Unwanted: A History of Refugees in the Twentieth Century*, New York: Oxford University Press, 1985, pp. 135-141.

52. Bruno Blau, *Das Ausnahmerecht für die Juden in deutschland, 1933-1945*, Third Edition, Dusseldorf: Verlag Allgemeine Wochenzeitung der Juden in deutschland, 1965, p. 117.

53. Yehuda Bauer, *American Jewry and the Holocaust: The American Jewish Joint Distribution Committee, 1939-1945*, Detroit: Wayne State University Press, 1981, ch. 1.

54. Weizmann to American Jewish Joint Distribution Committee, November 3, 1933, Weizmann: *Letters*, vol. 16, pp. 111-112.

55. Bericht Über die Lage der Jüdischen Flüchtlinge aus Deutschland in den verscheidenen Länder, die Tätigkeit verscheidener Hilfs-Comites, etc., No Date, CZA J14/1/IV.

56. Weizmann to Ehrenpreis, February 8, 1934, CZA L18/117; Weizmann to Braunschweig, May 8, 1934, CZA L13/35.

57. Tschernowitz to Szold, July 29, 1933, CZA J14/1/III; Weizmann to Nahon, October 4, 1933, Weizmann: *Letters*, vol. 16, pp. 61-62.

58. Bulgarian Jewish Community to Joint Committee, July 25, 1933, CZA J14/1/III.

59. Cf. Melvin I. Urofsky, *American Zionism From Herzl to the Holocaust*, Second Edition, Lincoln: University of Nebraska Press, 1995, ch. 4.

60. *Jewish Agency Bulletin*, vol. 1 #6 (April 28, 1931), p. 8, vol. 2 #2 (November 4, 1931), p. 6.

61. Weizmann to Lipsky, November 5, 1933, Weizmann: *Letters*, vol. 16, p. 118; Weizmann to Rothenberg, October 4, 1934, Ibid., pp. 377-383; Weizmann to Beck, January 9, 1936, CZA S53/331/II.

62. Joan Steibel, "The Central British Fund for World Jewish Relief," *Transactions of the Jewish Historical Society of England*, vol. 27 (1978/1980): 51-60.

63. Weizmann to Laski, October 20, 1933 and October 24, 1933, Weizmann: *Letters*, vol. 15, pp. 84, 99.

64. Peretz Merhav, *The Israeli Left*, San Diego: Barnes, 1980, pp. 20-35.

65. See the selection of documents charting developments in General Zionist ideology during the 1930s and 1940s cited in Baruch Ben-Avram (ed.), *Miflagot u-Zeramim Politiim be-Tekufat ha-Bayit ha-Leumi, 1918-1948*, Jerusalem: The Zalman Shazar Institute, 1978, pp. 173-179.

66. On Mizrachi's ideology, see the selections from Rav Kook and Rabbi Berlin in Arthur Hertzberg (ed.), *The Zionist Idea*, New York: Atheneum, 1976, pp. 416-431 and 546-555.

67. Zeev Jabotinsky, *The War and the Jew*, New York: Dial Press, 1942, ch. 6-8.

68. Ibid., p. 68.

69. Ha-Zohar was a member of the World Zionist Organization until 1935 when it seceeded to found the Histadrut ha-Zionit ha-Hadasha (Ha-Zach).

70. The figures do not add up to 100 percent because of unaffiliated individuals who attended the congresses.

71. Merhav, *Israeli Left*, ch. 2-5.

72. "The Mapai Program," in Ben-Avram, *Miflagot*, p. 95.

73. For positive evaluations of Ben-Gurion's ideology see Avraham Avihai, *Ben-Gurion State-Builder*, Jerusalem: Israel Universities Press, 1974, pp. 1-7 and Nathan Yanai, "Ben-Gurion's Concept of Mamlahtiut and the Forming Reality of the State of Israel," *Jewish Political Studies Review*, vol. 1 #1/2 (Spring, 1989): 151-177; for a negative assessment see Mitchell Cohen, *Zion and State*, New York: Basil Blackwell, 1987.

74. David Ben-Gurion, *Mi-Maamad le-Am*, Tel Aviv: Am Oved, 1938, p. 302.

75. Chaim Arlosoroff, *Der Jüdische Volkssozialismus*, cited in Shlomo Avineri, *Arlosoroff*, New York: Grove Weidenfeld, 1989, p. 25. Compare Arlosoroff's words with those of Shmuel Hugo Bergmann, cited in Ben-Avram, *Miflagot*, pp. 55-56: "What is our Socialism and what isn't it? . . . Our Socialism aspires, contrary to Marxism, to fulfillment from the bottom up and not the opposite . . . For that reason, we oppose virtually every form that Socialism has taken in Europe."

76. *Davar*, Wednesday, January 8, 1930, p. 2.

77. Merhav, *Israeli Left*, pp. 102-103.

78. Cf. Yael Yishai, *Siyyot be-Tenuat ha-Avoda: Siya Bet be-Mapai*, Tel Aviv: Am Oved, 1978, p. 31.

79. Ibid., pp. 63-69.

80. Ha-Shomer ha-Zair and Poale Zion Smol were diaspora parties with long roots. The Palestinian branches continued to exist independently until the late 1940s when the two, along with Ahdut ha-Avoda, merged to form Miflaga Poalim Meuhedet (Mapam). Cf. Merhav, *Israeli Left*, ch. 8-10.

81. Sondra M. Rubenstein, *The Communist Movement in Palestine and Israel, 1919-1984*, Boulder, CO: Westview Press, 1985.

82. Joseph B. Schechtman and Y. Benari, *The History of the Revisionist Movement*, Tel Aviv: Hadar Publishing, 1970, vol. 1.

83. Yaacov Shavit, *Jabotinsky and the Revisionist Movement, 1925-1948*, London: Frank Cass, 1988, p, 126.

84. Zeev Jabotinsky, *Raayon Betar*, cited in Joseph B. Schechtman, *The Life and Times of Vladimir Jabotinsky*, New York: Thomas Yoseloff, 1961, vol. 2, p. 416.

85. Cf. Zvi Adiv, "Iyunim be-Hashkafato ha-Zionit shel Zeev Jabotinsky," in Ben-Zion Yehoshua and Aaron Kedar (eds.), *Ideologia u-Mediniut Zionit*, Jerusalem: The Zalman Shazar Institute, 1978, p. 119.

86. Shavit, *Jabotinsky*, p. 115.

87. Zeev Jabotinsky, *Autobiographia*, Jerusalem: Eri Jabotinsky, 1948, p. 27.

88. Cf. Shlomo Avineri, *The Making of Modern Zionism*, New York: Basic Books, 1981, ch. 5 and Cohen, *Zion and State*, pp. 170-174 for two examples of the continuing effort to portary Jabotinsky as a fascist.

89. Weizmann to Landsberg, December 30, 1931, Weizmann: *Letters*, vol. 15, p. 246.

90. Jabotinsky to Jacobi, October 4, 1933, JIA A1/2/23/2.

91. Zeev Jabotinsky, "Militarizm: Psycho-Historia," in *Umma ve-Hevra*, Jerusalem: Eri Jabotinsky, 1950, p. 43.

92. Cf. Ezra Mendelsohn, *On Modern Jewish Politics*, New York: Oxford University Press, 1993, pp. 34-35.

93. Yosef Heller, *LEHI: Ideologia u-Politika, 1940-1949*, Jerusalem: The Zalman Shazar Institute, 1989, ch. 1.

94. Shavit, *Jabotinsky*, p. 366.

95. Jabotinsky to Yeivin, cited in Schechtman, *Lifa and Times*, vol. 2, p. 216.

96. Cf. Jabotinsky's foreword to Stefan Klinger, *The Ten Year for Palestine*, London: New Zionist Press, 1938, pp. 5-6.

97. For differing views on the General Zionist collapse see, Ben-Avram, *Miflagot*, pp. 175-179 (on the Yishuv), Urofsky, *American Zionism*, ch. 7-9 (on the United States), and Mendelsohn, *Jewish Politics*, pp. 67-71 (on Poland).

98. Cf. Yosef Goldstein, "Mapai and the Seventeenth Zionist Congress (1931)," *Studies in Zionism*, vol. 10 #1 (Spring, 1989): 19-30.

99. Schechtman, *Life and Times*, vol. 2, pp. 151-153; for a very different view of these events, see Cohen, *Zions and State*, pp. 149-152.

100. *Verhandlungen der 17 Zionistische Kongress*, London: The World Zionist Orgaization, 1931, pp. 164-194, 475. The tumult that resulted in Jabotinsky tearing up his delegate card is described in Schechtman, *Life and Times*, vol. 2, pp. 152-154.

101. Cf. Meir Avizohar, *be-Rei Saduk: Idealim Hevratiim ve-Leumiim ve-Histakfutam be-Olama shel Mapai*, Tel Aviv: Am Oved, 1990, ch. 4-5.

102. In addition to Avizohar, *Rei Saduk*, ch. 5, see Anita Shapira, *Berl: The Biography of a Socialist Zionist*, New York: Cambridge University Press, 1984, pp. 189-191.

103. *Davar*, Tuesday, April 18, 1933, p. 1; Protocol of the Jewish Agency Executive, May 14, 1933, CZA S100/14, p. 2/3717.

104. Howard Rosenblum, A Political History of Revisionist Zionism, 1925-1938, Unpublished Doctoral Dissertation: Columbia University, 1986, p. 140.

105. Zeev Jabotinsky, "Matok me-Dvash," in *Ba-Sa'ar*, Jerusalem: Eri Jabotinsky, 1948, pp. 77-82. Sha'atnez is a halachicly impermissable mixture.

106. Rosenblum, Political History, pp. 143-145.

107. Zeev Jabotinsky, "Ken Lishbor," *Ba-Sa'ar*, op cit, p. 45.

Chapter 2

1. Minutes of a Meeting of the Zionist Executive, London, April 5, 1933, CZA Z4/302/21.

2. Cf. Abraham Schwadron's article on the petition in *ha-Aretz*, Monday, December 4, 1933, p. 2 and Nathan Feinberg's response thereto on Tuesday, December 19, 1933, p. 2.

3. Zioniburo, London, to Jevagency, Jerusalem, March 29, 1933, CZA S49/381.

4. Minutes of a Meeting of the Zionist Executive, loc cit.

5. Cf. *Ha-Aretz*, Friday, May 19, 1933, p. 1, *Hazit ha-Am*, Friday, May 19, 1933, p. 1, and Joseph Heller, "'ha-Monism shel ha-Matara' oh 'ha-Monism shel ha-Emzaim?' ha-Mahloket ha-Raayonit veha-Politit ben Zeev Jabotinsky le-ben Ab'a Ahimeir, 1928-1933," *Zion*, vol. 52 #3 (1987): 315-369.

6. Threats by Nazi leaders were repeatedly reported in the Yishuv's press. For example see, *ha-Aretz*, Tuesday, February, 21, 1933, p. 2, on a speech by Hitler, Friday, February 24, 1933, p. 1, on a statement by Ernst Röhm, and Sunday, April 2, 1933, p. 1, for a comprehensive statement by Josef Goebbels.

7. Intentionalists hold that the Final Solution was preplanned and that it derived from Hitler's ideological fixation with Jews. Functionalists hold that no central plan existed and ideology played little or no role in its development. Cf. Abraham J. Edelheit and Hershel Edelheit, *History of the Holocaust: A Handbook and Dictionary*, Boulder, CO: Westview Press, 1994, pp. 41-42.

8. Anita Shapira, "Did the Zionist Leadership Foresee the Holocaust?" in Jehuda Reinharz (ed.), *Living With Antisemitism: Modern Jewish Responses*, Hanover, NH: University Press of New England, 1987, p. 412.

9. Cf. Philip Friedman, "The Lublin Reservation and the Madagascar Plan: Two Aspects of Nazi Jewish Policy during the Second World War," *YIVO Annual*, vol. 8 (1953): 151-177.

10. Ruth Zariz, "Officially Approved Emigration from Germany after 1941: A Case Study," *Yad Vashem Studies*, vol. 18 (1987): 275-291.

11. Accusations about the Yishuv's alleged guilt during the Holocaust have been raised from time to time and has been most strongly identified with non-historians with an axe to grind. The most recent such a book is Tom Segev, *The Seventh Million: The Israelis and the Holocaust*, New York: Hill and Wang, 1993. Previous attempts to tar the Yishuv's leadership include: Ben Hecht, *Perfidy*, New York: Robert Speller, 1961, Shabbetai B. Bet-Zvi, *Ha-Zionut ha-Post Ugandit ba-Mashber ha-Shoa*, Tel Aviv: Bronfmann's Agency, 1977, Lenni Brenner, *Zionism in an Age of Dictators*, London: Croom Helm, 1983, and Idith Zertal, "The Poisoned Heart: The Jews of Palestine and the Holocaust," *Tikkun*, vol. 2 #1 (1987): 79-83. Critical reviews of these books have not stopped writers with an axe to grind from reviving the myth periodically, despite its tenuous historical foundations. Cf. Tuvia Friling, *"Ha-Million ha-Shvi'i* ke-Mizad ha-Avelut veha-Rishut shel ha-Tenua ha-Zionit," *Iyyunim be-Tekmat Israel*, vol. 2 (1992): 317-367.

12. Dina Porat, *The Blue and Yellow Stars of David*, Cambridge, MA: Harvard University Press, 1990, p. 262.

13. Protocol of the Va'ad Leumi, March 30, 1933, CZA J1/7235. The German version of the manifesto is contained in CZA S49/381. The Hebrew version was published in M. Atias (ed.), *Sefer ha-Teudot shel Vaad ha-Leumi le-Knesset Israel*, Jerusalem: The Zionist Library 1963, p. 195.

14. Protocol of the Va'ad Leumi, op cit, pp. 3-5.

15. Ibid., p.3.

16. Protocols of the Vaa'd Leumi, April 27, 1933, CZA J1/7235.

17. Va'ad Leumi to Sokolow, no date, CZA S75/9809.

18. Weizmann to Sieff, April 23, 1933, Weizmann: *Letters*, v. 15, p.403.

19. Cf. Arthur Ruppin's diary entry for May 12, 1933, in *Arthur Ruppin: Memoirs, Diaries, Letters*, edited by Alex Bein, Jerusalem/London: Weidenfeld and Nicolson, 1971, p. 264.

20. Atias, *Sefer ha-Teudot*, p. 196.

21. Protocol of the Histadrut Executive, April 13, 1933, HIS M20, pp. 2-4.

22. Landauer to Senator, March 3, 1933, CZA S49/381.

23. Nahum Goldmann, "The Jewish People Facing the Nazi Danger," *From the Danger of Annihilation to the Dawn of Redemption: Four Speeches*, Jerusalem: The World Zionist Organization, 1958, p.9.

24. Senator to Locker, March 19, 1933, CZA S49/381.

25. Zioniburo, London, to Jevagency, Jerusalem, March 21, 1933, CZA S49/381.

26. Senator to Jewish Agency Employees, March 17, 1933, CZA S49/381.

27. Landauer to Senator, March 24, 1933, CZA S49/381.

28. Zioniburo, London, to Arlosoroff, March 29, 1933, CZA S49/381.

29. Cf. Michael Marrus, *The Unwanted: European Refugees in the Twentieth Century*, New York: Oxford University Press, 1985, p. 68.

30. HICEM to Jevagency, March 29, 1933, CZA S49/381.

31. Jevagency to HICEM, March 30, 1933, CZA S49/381.

32. HOG to Jewish Agency Executive, March 31, 1933, CZA S25/9713.

33. Senator to HOG, April 6, 1933, CZA S49/381.

34. Arlosoroff to Landauer, June 16, 1933, CZA S25/9809. A Handwritten note at the bottom of the telegram records that this was Arlosoroff's last communique before leaving the office on that fateful Friday.

35. Frumkin to Arlosoroff, June 16, 1933, HIS IV/1/104/3.

36. Idem.

37. The memorandum is contained in CZA S25/980.

38. Ibid., p. 1.

39. Ibid., pp. 1-2.

40. Ibid., p. 2.

41. Idem.

42. Ibid., pp. 3-4.

43. Ibid., p. 4.

44. Ibid., p. 5.

45. Senator to HICEM, April 9, 1933, CZA S49/381.

46. Zioniburo, London, to Jevagency, Jerusalem, April 7, 1933, CZA S25/9713.

47. Conversation between Berl Locker, Harry Sacher, and Israel Sieff, April 10, 1933, CZA S25/9809.

48. Va'ad Leumi to Sokolow, cited in note 13. See also statement by Pinner (representing HOG) in the Protocols of the Jewish Agency Executive, April 9, 1933, CZA S100/14 p.5/3651.

49. Weizmann to Sieff, April 23, 1933 in Weizmann: *Letters*, vol. 15, p. 403.

50. Protocols of the JAE, April 9, 1933, CZA S100/14, p. 5/3651-6/3652.

51. Ibid., p. 6/3652.

52. Cf. the statement by E. Neumann in Ibid. pp. 7/3653-8/3654.

53. Weizmann to Lipsky, May 5-7, 1933 in Weizmann: *Letters*, vol. 15, pp. 409-410.

54. Weizmann to Arlosoroff, April 25, 1933 in Weizmann: *Letters*, vol. 15, p. 404: "Telegrams received; regret their unsatisfactory contents."

55. This suggestion, by Dr. Maurice G. Hexter, was accepted. Protocols of the Jewish Agency Executive, April 9, 1933, CZA S100/14 p. 8/3654.

56. Ibid., p. 9/3655.

57. Jevagency, Jerusalem, to Zioniburo, London, April 11, 1933, CZA S25/9809.

58. Protocol of the Mapai Executive, April 11, 1933, ILPA 2/23/33, p. 4.

59. Medzini to Executive, April 13, 1933, CZA S25/9809.

60. See Pinner's statement as cited in the Protocols of the Jewish Agency Executive, April 14, 1933, CZA S100/14, p. 1/3658.

61. Idem.

62. Senator to Kahn, April 6, 1933, CZA S49/381.

63. Jevagency, Jerusalem, to Zioniburo, London, April 24, 1933, CZA S25/9809.

64. Sokolow to Rutenberg, no date, CZA S25/9809.

65. Senator's report, Protocols of the Jewish Agency Executive, April 16, 1933, CZA S100/14, p. 1/3663.

66. Idem.

67. Ibid., p. 2/3664.

68. Protocols of the JAE, April 19, 1933, CZA S100/14, p. 2/3668-3/3669.

69. Cf. Protocols of the Mapai Executive, April 23, 1933, ILPA 2/23/33, pp. 2-3.

70. Ibid., p.3.

71. Protocols of the JAE, April 19, 1933, CZA S100/14, p. 3/3674.

72. Protocols of the JAE, April 23, 1933, CZA S100/14, pp. 2/3679-10/3687.

73. Protocols of the JAE, April 30, 1933, CZA S100/14, pp.6/3704-7/3705.

74. See Weizmann to Warburg, May 19, 1933, in Weizmann: *Letters*, vol. 15, pp. 413-414, 429-430.

75. The final draft of the manifesto, which was delayed for a day because of last minute changes in style, is contained in CZA S25/9809. The English version was published in *New Judea*, vol. 9, No. 7 (April 1933), pp. 93-95.

76. Zioniburo, London, to Jevagency, Jerusalem, May 29, 1933, CZA S25/9809.

77. Zeev Tzahor, "Chaim Arlosoroff and His Attitude Toward the Rise of the Nazis," *Jewish Social Studies*, vol. 46, No. 3/4 (Summer/Fall 1984) pp. 321-330.

78. Shapira, "Did the Zionist Leadership," pp. 397-400.

79. David Ben-Gurion, *Zichronot*, Tel Aviv: Am Oved, 1976, vol. 2, p. 11.

80. Protocol of the Mapai Executive, April 11, 1933, ILPA 2/23/33, p. 3.

81. Manifesto to all Branches and Members [of Ha-Zohar], May 4, 1933, JIA T14/5.

82. Zeev Jabotinsky, "Al Kishlono shel ha-Kongress ha-Yod-Het" in *Neumin, 1927-1940*, Jerusalem: Eri Jabotinsky, 1948, pp. 161-163.

83. Jabotinsky to Jacobi, October 13, 1933, JIA A1/2/23/2.

84. Jabotinsky to Brit Ha-Zohar Branches, October 30, 1933, JIA A1/2/23/2.

85. Protocols of the JAE, April 9, 1933, CZA S100/14, p. 5/3651.

86. Outline of My Opinion on mattters of the German Boycott, June 1, 1933, CZA L51/402, p. 1.

87. Ibid., pp. 2-3.

88. Ibid., p.3.

89. Protocols of the Va'ad Leumi, April 27, 1933, CZA J1/7235, pp. 7-8.

90. Frumkin to Neumann, May 12, 1933, CZA J14/1/II.

91. *ha-Aretz*, Friday, May 19, 1933, p. 1.

92. *ha-Aretz*, Monday, May 29, 1933, p.1.

93. Anonymous note to Rozenboim, June 2, 1933, CZA J14/6/I; Kook to Joint Committee, June 6, 1933, CZA J14/1/II.

94. Protocol of the Joint Committee Executive, June 8, 1933, CZA J14/18, pp. 6-7.

95. Ibid., pp. 1-4.

96. Ibid., p. 5.

97. Summary report of the Joint Committee to Resettle German Jews in Eretz-Israel, CZA J14/16, pp. 1-4.

98. Horowitz to Szold, June 16, 1933, CZA J14/6/II.

99. Cf. Jordan to Agronsky, June 6, 1933; Agronsky to Szold, June 7, 21933; and Szold to Jordan, June 15, 1933, CZA J14/6/I.

100. Protocol of the Urban Settlement Committee, June 25, 1933, CZA J14/18.

101. Minutes of meeting of the Joint Committee Executive with Representatives of the Va'ad Leumi, June 6, 1933, CZA J14/1/I.

102. Wallach to Joint Committee, June 27, 1933, CZA J14/6/I.

103. CZA J14/6/II. Notwithstanding different titles, the contents are identical. Undated they are also identical to the original draft contained in Wallach to Joint Committee, loc cit, and were published in early July 1933.

104. Undated circular letter, CZA J14/6/I.

105. Respectively, *ha-Aretz*, Thursday, June 1, 1933, p. 3 and Sunday, June 4, 1933, p.4.

106. *ha-Aretz*, Friday, June 9, 1933 p. 3

107. Ibid., Thursday, June 22, 1933 p. 3

108. Protocol of the Joint Committee Executive, July 9, 1933, CZA J14/18, pp. 4-6

109. Institute to Educate the Children of Olim to Joint Committee, no date, CZA J14/1/III.

110. Memo on Executive meeting, July 2, 1933, CZA J14/18, p.3

111. Goldmann to Szold, July 11, 1933, CZA J14/1/I.

112. Szold to Goldmann, July 20, 1933, CZA J14/1/III.

113. Bericht Über die Lage der Jüdischen Flüchtlinge aus Deutschland in den verscheidenen Länder, die Tätigkeit verscheidener Hilfs-Comites, etc., No Date, CZA J14/1/IV, pp. 4-5.

114. General Secretary to Klinov, July 31, 1933; General Secretary to Davar, July 31, 1933, CZA J4/1/IV.

115. Aliya Committee Report, *ha-Aretz*, Thursday, Agust 1, 1933 p. 3.

116. Minute of meeting of the Joint Committee Executive with Representatives of the Va'ad Leumi, June 6, 1933, CZA J14/1/I.

117. Bachman to Szold, July 25, 1933, CZA J14/1/I; Levi to Joint Committee Executive, August 9, 1933, CZA J14/4/1.

118. Szold to HOG, September, 8, 1933, CZA J14/1/IV.

119. Form letter by Joint Committee to editors, with press release attached, September 8, 1933, CZA J14/1/IV.

120. Szold to Ronfo, September 14, 1933, CZA J14/6/I.

121. Summary report, op cit, p. 5.

122. Rozenboim to Szold, October 2, 1933, CZA J14/1/IV, p. 1.

123. Ibid, pp. 2-4.

124. Joint Committee Financial Records, 1933-1934, CZA J14/20. This record book covers outlays only; the parallel volume (CZA J14/21) covering income, is unreadable due to water damage.

125. Szold to Ronfo, December 7, 1933 and Szold to Clark, December 7, 1933 (actually two versions of the same form letter), CZA J14/6/1.

126. Rozenboim to Szold, op cit, pp. 5-6.

127. Margulies to Szold, September 5, 1933; Szold to Union Internationale de Secours aux Enfants, September 25, 1933, CZA J14/1/III.

128. Form letters signed Szold and Rokah, August 17, 1933 (with tear-off) and August 23, 1933 (without tear-off), CZA J14/6/I. Except for the tear-off and dates the letters are identical.

129. Szold to Karpf, June 4, 1933, CZA J14/1/II. In his response, Karpf noted that American Jewish relief efforts were beset by the same problems. Karpf to to Szold, July 19, 1933, CZA J14/1/II.

130. Szold to Rabinoff, September 10, 1993, CZA J14/1/IV

131. Joan Dash, *Summoned to Jerusalem*, Philadelphia: Jewish Publication Society, 1979, pp. 191-192, 197.

132. On Tel Aviv: Rozenboim to Szold, October 6, 1933, CZA J14/1/IV; on Haifa: Zunzigel to Rozenhoim, July 23, 1933, CZA 14/1/III.

133. Zunzigel to Rozenboim, August 1, 1933, CZA J14/1/III. Wilensky was the Joint Committee office manager in Haifa.

134. Rivlin and Yellin to Ben-Zvi, May 29, 1933, CZA J14/1/I; Hantkey to Rozenboim, June 12, 1933, CZA J14/1/II.

135. Summary Report, op cit, p.2; Levi to Joint Committee Executive, December 15, 1933, CZA J14/3/I.

136. HOG to Joint Committee Executive, no date, CZA J14/1/II.

137. Levinson and Levi (HOG) to Joint Committee Executive, July 6, 1933, CZA J14/3/I.

138. Levinsohn and Levi to Joint Committee Executive, August 9, 1933. CZA J14/3/I. Other examples are contained here and in CZA J14/3/II.

139. Levinsohn and Levi to Szold, October 20, 1933, CZA J14/3/I.

140. HOG to Joint Committee Executive, January 1, 1934; HOG to Joint Committee Executive, March 4, 1934, CZA J14/3/I.

141. Protocol of the Joint Committee Executive, June 26, 1933, CZA J14/18, p.6; Protocol of the Mapai Executive, June 26, 1933, ILPA 2/23/33, pp.8-9.

142. Protocol of the Mapai Executive, June 20, 1933, ILPA 2/23/33; Protocol of the Histadrut Executive, July 18, 1933, HIS M21, p.3.

143. Protocol of the Joint Committee Executive, July 9, 1933, CZA J14/18, pp. 7-9.

144. Proposed agreement, July 12, 1933, CZA J14/1/III.

145. Protocol of the Joint Committee Executive, July 13, 1933, CZA J14/18, p.3.

146. The statement is preserved in both the English original and Hebrew translation in CZA J14/1/I.

147. Joint Committee to the Arlosoroff Fund, July 21, 1933, CZA J14/1/III.

148. Arlosoroff Fund to Joint Committee, July 27, 1933, CZA J14/1/III.

149. Baratz to Local Committees and Representative, July 27, 1933, CZA J14/1/IV.

150. Krupnik ro Joint Committee, July 31, 1933, CZA J14/1/IV.

151. Baratz to Joint Committee, August 2, 1933, CZA J14/1/III.

152. Memo on Executive meeting, August 6, 1933, CZA J14/18, p.2.

153. Szold to Arlosoroff Fund, August 6, 1933; Joint Committee to Arlosoroff Fund, August 8, 1933, CZA J14/1/IV.

154. Protocol of the Joint Committee Executive, August 13, 1933, CZA J14/18, p.1.

155. Taubman to Szold, September 6, 1933, CZA J14/1/III.

156. In October, the Histadrut decided that instead of providing the £P1,500 at one time, three installments should be made. Baratz to Joint Committee, October 3, 1933; Szold to Arlosoroff Fund, October 18, 1933, CZA J14/1/III.

157. Protocols of the Jewish Agency Executive, September 1, 1933, CZA S100/14, p.1/3736.

158. KKL to Joint Committee, September 25, 1933, CZA J14/1/IV.

159. Protocol of the Joint Committee Executive, September 17, 1933, CZA J14/18; Levi to Joint Committee Executive, September 25, 1933, CZA J14/4/I.

160. Memo on Joint Meeting, October 17, 1933; Memo on Joint Committee Executive meeting, October 17, 1933, CZA J14/18.

161. Summary Report, op cit, pp. 4-5.

162. Report by Joint Committee Aliya Committee, no date, P. 2; Report by HOG labor office, no date; CZA J14/4/I.

163. Summary Report, op cit, pp. 8-9.

Chapter 3

1. This statistical abstraction is based on the index to CZA S25/17/1.

2. Michael R. Marrus, *The Unwanted: European Refugees in the Twentieth Century*, New York: Oxford University Press, 1985, pp. 129-131.

3. Zioniburo, London, to Arlosoroff, April 7, 1933, CZA S25/9713.

4. Wauchope to Arlosoroff, April 4, 1933, CZA S25/9713.

5. Wauchope to Arlosoroff, April 6, 1933, CZA S25/9713; Hyamson to Arlosoroff, April 6, 1933, CZA S49/381; Arlosoroff to Wauchope, April 7, 1933, CZA S49/9713.

6. Protocols of the JAE, May 18, 1933, CZA S100/14, p.2/3719.

7. Wauchope to Arlosoroff, April 4, 1933, loc. cit.

8. Protocols of the Jewish Agency Executive, February 5, 1933, CZA S100/14, pp. 1/3647-3/3649. Only a few illegals were caught at this time, most of whom had enterred Palestine during the Maccabiah games of 1932. Cf. *ha-Aretz*, Monday, April 3, 1933, p.1.

9. Foley, Berlin, to Central Department, London, March 29, 1933, PRO/FO 371/16721.

10. Senator to Locker, March 1933, CZA S49/381.

11. Schiff to Zionist Organization, London, June 14, 1934, CZA S25/9713.

12. Hyamson to Chief Secretary, May 12, 1933; Passport Control Officer, Paris, to Hyamson, October 27, 1933, ISA M1176/22.

13. Hyamson to Chief Secretary, October 26, 1933, ISA M238.

14. Minute by Attorney General dated November 23, 1933 and attached to Hyamson to Chief Secretary, op cit; Hyamson to Passport Control Officer, Paris, December 5, 1933, ISA M1176/22.

15. Hyamson to HOG, October or November, 1933, ISA M1176/22.

16. Levy (HOG) to JAE, July 3, 1933, CZA S25/9713.

17. Assistance in Setting Up German Immigrants in Moshavot, no date, CZA S49/381.

18. Memorandum of Hitachdut Olei Germania to the Delegates of the 18th Zionist Congress, no date, CZA S25/9707, pp.2-3.

19. Histadrut Executive to Shertok, July 10, 1933, CZA S25/9707; Frumkin to Locker, July 11, 1933, CZA S49/460.

20. Jevagency to Zioniburo, London, July 6, 1933, CZA S25/9809.

21. Memorandum of HOG, loc cit. Weizman set out a similar plan for action in a letter to Osmond E. d'Avigdor Goldsmid, the president of the Board of Deputies of Anglo-Jewry. Cf. Weizmann: *Letters*, v. 16, pp. 25-28.

22. Arthur to Hanna Ruppin, September 4, 1933, in *Arthur Ruppin: Memoirs, Diaries, Letters*, edited by Alex Bein, Jerusalem/London: Weidenfeld and Nicolson, 1971, p. 264; Chaim to Vera Weizman, September 9, 1933, in Weizmann: *Letters*, vol. 16, PP. 46-47.

23. The speech is published in the original German in the stenographic protocol of the Congress, *Stenographiches Protokol der Verhandlungen des 18 Zionistische Congress*, London: Executive of the World Zionist Organization, 1933, pp. 174-185, and in Hebrew in *ha-Olam*, the Zionist Congress's daily newspaper, issue for August 22, 1933. All quotes of Sokolow's speech are from the Hebrew version.

24. *ha-Olam*, p.6.

25. Idem.

26. Ruppin's speech is in *Stenographiches Protokol*, pp. 185-196.

27. *Stenographisches Protokol*, pp. 198-199.

28. Ibid., p. 198. Emphasis in original.

29. Ibid., pp. 239-244 and 260-266.

30. Ibid., pp. 211-226, 270-274, 283-287.

31. Ibid., pp. 314-316.

32. Ibid., pp. 197-198; *ha-Olam*, August 28, 1933, pp. 2-3.

33. Ben-Gurion was coopted to the JAE in 1933, without any specific area of responsibility. He was listed as chairman of the JAE as early as July 10, 1934 (CZA S100/15, p.1/3961), although he officially became chairman in late 1935 and remained in that position until 1948. Cf. Avraham Avi-Hai, *Ben Gurion, State Builder*, Jerusalem: Keter, 1974, p.30.

34. Protocols of the JAE, September 27, 1933, CZA S100/15, pp. 7/3740-8/3741.

35. Senator to Central British Fund, October 3, 1933, CZA S25/9809, p.1.

36. Idem.

37. Protocols of the JAE, October 15, 1933, CZA S100/15, p. 1/3748.

38. Senator to Weizmann, November 2, 1933, CZA S25/9713; Rothschild to Weizmann, October 3, 1933; Weizmann to Wauchope, October 6, 1933; Weizmann to Ben-Gurion, October 24, 1933; Zionburo to Jevagency, October 24, 1933, CZA S25/2519; Weizmann to Ben-Gurion, October 7, 1933, Weizmann: *Letters*, vol. 16, p.65.

39. Report by Y. Reizer, March 1, 1934, CZA S25/9809.

40. Report of the Central Office for the Settlement of German Jewry in Eretz Israel (the German Department) to the Zionist Actions Committee, March 1934, CZA S25/9707, p.2.

41. Ibid., pp. 2-4,5,7.

42. Yosef Heller (ed.), *ba-Maavak la-Medina: ha-Mediniut ha-Zionit, 1936-1948*, Jerusalem: The Zalman Shazar Center, 1984, pp.15-16.

43. Tourists and ma'apilim are not included in this table. Cf. Yoav Gelber, *Moledet Hadasha: Aliyat Yehudei Merkaz Europa ve-Klitatam, 1933-1948*, Jerusalem: Yad Yitzhak Ben-Zvi, 1990, ch.2.

44. Max Gruenwald, "About the Reichsvertretung der Deutschen Juden," in *Imposed Jewish Governing Bodies Under Nazi Rule*, New York: YIVO, 1972, p. 43.

45. Abraham Margaliot, "The Problem of the Rescue of German Jewry during the Years 1933-1939: The Reasons for the Delay in Their Emigration from the Third Reich," in *Rescue Attempts During the Holocaust*, edited by Y. Gutman and E. Zuroff, Jerusalem: Yad Vashem, 1977, pp. 247-265.

46. Liebenstein to Mapai Executive, April 28, 1933 and Liebenstein to Mapai Executive, May 14, 1933, ILPA 2/101/33.

47. Protocol of the Mapai Executive, June 15, 1933, ILPA 2/23/33.

48. Protocol of the Mapai Executive, November 21, 1933, ILPA 2/23/33, pp. 6-10.

49. Minutes of a Conversation with the High Commissioner, February 22, 1934, CZA S25/17/1.

50. Both Weizmann's letter (dated May 31, 1934) and the report are contained in CZA S25/9809. Weizmann's talk of doubling Palestine's Jewish population loses much of its impact when the small proportion of Jews to Arabs is kept in mind — had this been the Zionists' final goal, Jews would have comprised only one-third of the total Palestinian population.

51. Protocols of the JAE, March 30, 1934, CZA S100/15, p. 1/3873; Minutes of a Conversation with the High Commissioner, April 25, 1934, CZA S25/17/1.

52. Protocols of the JAE, March 30, 1934, loc cit.

53. Barlas to Aliya Offices, March 19, 1934, HIS IV/208/1/367A.

54. Protocol of a Meeting between Chaim Weizmann and Signior Mussolini, February 23, 1934, BGA Protocols.

55. Protocols of the JAE, October 21, 1934, CZA S100/16, p. 4/4027.

56. Protocol of the Mapai Executive, October 10, 1934, ILPA 2/23/32, pp. 7-8.

57. Weizmann to Lipsky, November 5, 1933, Weizmann: *Letters*, vol. 16, p. 118.

58. Protocols of the JAE, June 10, 1934, CZA S100/15, p. 3/3928; November 11, 1934, CZA S100/16, p. 1/4042.

59. Moshe Shertok's Office Diary, Sunday, October 7, 1934, CZA A245/1, p. 3.

60. Ibid., Monday, November 5, 1934, CZA A245/1, p. 2.

61. Ibid., Monday, November 5, 1934, CZA A245/1, p. 14.

62. Ibid., Monday, October 15, 1934, CZA A245/1, p. 9.

63. Bakstansky to Hantke, July 31, 1934, CZA S25/9809.

64. Protocols of the JAE, April 30, 1935, CZA S100/16, pp. 1/4180-3/4182.

65. Protocols of the JAE, May 5, 1935, CZA S100/16, p. 4/4186.

66. See Weizmann to Ruppin, July 3, 1933, Weizmann: *Letters*, vol. 16, pp. 462-466; Weizmann to Marks, December 15, 1933, Ibid., vol. 17, pp. 87-91.

67. Protocols of the JAE, June 30, 1935, CZA S100/16, p. 2/4219.

68. Protocols of the JAE, September 27, 1935, CZA S100/17, pp. 2/4289-3/4290.

69. Protocol of a Meeting with Mr. Samuel, October 17, 1935, BGA Protocols.

70. Protocols of the JAE, October 9, 1935, CZA S100/17, p. 1/4293; Protocol of the Mapai Political Committee, October 27, 1935, ILPA 2/23/35, pp. 1, 6-7.

71. Protocol of the Mapai Political Committee, op. cit, p. 2.

72. *Protokolim shel ha-Congress ha-Zioni ha-19*, Jerusalem: The World Zionist Organization, 1935, pp. 15-35.

73. Ibid., p. 46.

74. Ibid., pp. 123-127.

75. Ibid., p. 127.

76. Marminksy to A. Katznelson, December 9, 1935, HIS IV/208/1/649.

77. Landauer to JAE, November 22, 1935, CZA S25/9809.

78. Frumowitz to Ben-Gurion, February 16, 1936, CZA S25/9713.

79. Protocol of the Mapai Political Committee, March 30, 1936, ILPA 2/23/36, p.1.

80. Protocol of the Mapai Political Committee, April 16, 1936, ILPA 2/23/35, pp. 2-3.

81. *JA Report*, 1937, pp. 26-32.

Chapter 4

1. *JA Report*, 1933, p.8.

2. Levi, Aliya Committee, to Joint Committee Executive, October 31, 1933, CZA J14/4/I.

3. Histadrut Executive to JAE, 8 Iyyar 5693 (= May 8, 1933), CZA S25/977.

4. Protocols of the JAE, July 14, 1933, CZA S100/14, p. 2/3721.

5. Zeev Tsur, *ha-Kibbutz ha-Meuchad be-Binyan Eretz-Israel*, Tel Aviv: Yad Yitzhak Tabenkin, 1979, pp. 113-114.

6. Ibid., p. 115.

7. Joseph Sprinzak's speech at the Nineteenth Zionist Congress, as quoted in M. Braslavsky, *Tnuat ha-Poalim ha-Aretz Yisraelit*, Tel Aviv: ha-Kibbutz ha-Meuchad, 1956, vol. 2, pp.399-400.

8. Braslavsky, *Tnuat ha-Poalim*, p. 404.

9. Cf. Meir Avizohar, *be-Rei Saduk: Idealim Hevratiim ve-Leumiim ve-Histakfutam be-Olama shel Mapai*, Tel Aviv: Am Oved, 1990, pp. 113-116, and Anita Shapira, *Berl: The Biography of a Socialist Zionist*, New York: Cambridge University Press, 1984, pp. 168, 188.

10. David Ben-Gurion, *Zichronot*, Tel Aviv: Am Oved, 1976, vol. 2, p. 12.

11. Kreutzberger to JAE, November 11, 1935, CZA J18/2.

12. Ben-Zvi to Hyamson, August 14, 1933, ISA M1179/5.

13. Foley to Hyamson, September 9, 1933, ISA M1179/5.

14. Protocols of the JAE, May 6, 1934, CZA S100/15, pp. 2/3897-4/3899.

15. Protocols of the JAE, December 12, 1934, CZA S100/16, pp. 4/4064-5/4065.

16. Protocols of the JAE, May 19, 1935, CZA S100/16, p.3/4193.

17. Protocols of the JAE, May 28, 1935, CZA S100/16, p.3/4201.

18. Protocols of the JAE, June 23, 1935, CZA S100/16, p. 1/4212.

19. Cf. Shertok's statement in the Protocol of a Meeting with the High Commissioner, January 10, 1934, BGA Protocols, p.2.

20. Cf. Abraham Margaliot, "The Problem of the Rescue of German Jewry During the years 1933-1939: the Reason for the delay in their Emigration from the Third Reich," in *Rescue Attempts During the Holocaust* edited by Y. Gutman and E. Zuroff, Jerusalem: Yad Vashem, 1977, pp. 247-265.

21. This line of analysis was not limited to the Zionist left and center, but, at least in 1933, appeared to be the correct line of analysis. Cf. A. Kalisher, "Our Enemy," part I, *Betar*, #8 (November, 1933), pp. 206-218; part II, Ibid., #9 (December, 1933), pp. 304-321.

22. Ben-Gurion's Diary, May 3, 1935, p.4, BGA. It should be noted that Ben-Gurion did not accept the premise of such limited aliya. In response to German Zionist complaints, he argued that the JAE had to devise a rescue plan for six million Jews — all of German Jewry, plus the Jews of Poland, the Baltic Republics, Romania, Hungary, and Austria.

23. "German Jewry: A Plan for Emigration", November 3, 1935, CZA S25/9819.

24. All pamphlets may be found in JIA G4/12.

25. Zeev Jabotinsky, "Tochnit Ha-Evacuatzia", *Neumim, 1927-1940,* Jerusalem: Eri Jabotinsky, 1948, pp. 197-212, and Stefan Klinger, *The Ten Year Plan for Palestine*, London: The New Zionist Organization, 1938.

26. Klinger, *Ten Year Plan*, p.3.

27. Jabotinsky, "Tochnit," p. 203.

28. Jabotinsky, "Tochnit," pp.197-199.

29. "Jabotinsky's 4 Points," extract from *Die Stimme*, November 29, 1936, CZA S44/69B.

30. Jabotinsky, "Tochnit," p. 198.

31. Idem. Cf. Joseph Goldstein, "Jabotinsky and Jewish Autonomy in the Diaspora," *Studies in Zionism*, vol. 7 #2 (Autumn, 1986), pp.219-232.

32. Jabotinsky, "Tochnit", p. 197.

33. The letters are reproduced verbatim in Ben-Gurion, *Zichronot*, vol. 2, pp. 410-415.

34. Protocols of the JAE, January 7, 1934, CZA S100/15, P.1/3782.

35. Both Poland and Rumania exemplified the rising tide of ultra-nationalist antisemitism in the 1930s. In both countries antisemitic parties advocated the removal of Jewish influence on the economy and sought to pressure the Jews to emigrate. Violence played a major role in the antisemitic campaign in Poland, but, during the 1930s, was almost completely absent from Romania. Cf. Ezra Mendelsohn, *The Jews of East Central Europe Between the World Wars*, Bloomington: Indiana University Press, 1983, ch.1, 4.

36. Joan Dash, *Summoned to Jerusalem*, Philadelphia: JPS, 1979, pp. 229-284, reviews Youth Aliya through Szold's perspective; Yoav Gelber, "The Origins of Youth Aliya," *Studies in Zionism*, vol.9 #2 (Autumn, 1988), pp. 147-172, offers a broader historical review. Considerable archival material on Youth Aliya is held in the CZA and in the Hadassah Archives (New York).

37. In addition to Youth Aliya, a movement existed to save German Jewish children by sending them west European countries (i.e. Great Britain). This element of the rescue story still requires further elucidation, but is outside the scope of the present work. Cf. Mary Ford, "The Arrival of Jewish Refugee Children in England, 1938-1939," *Immigrants and Minorities*, vol. 2 #2 (July, 1983), pp. 135-151.

38. Dash, *Summoned*, pp. 255-256. Dash notes that Szold always saw Youth Aliya as a means of promoting family aliya.

39. Becker to Szold, July 16, 1933, CZA J14/1/III.

40. Note on a conversation with Mr. Hyamson, July 25, 1933, CZA J14/1/III.

41. Szold to Hyamson, August 9, 1933, CZA J14/1/III.

42. Hyamson to Szold, September 10, 1933, CZA J14/1/III. Gelber, "Origins", p. 159, correctly cites this letter as evidence of British attempts to limit the size of Youth Aliya from its inception.

43. Protocol of the Joint Committee Executive, August 17, 1933, CZA J14/18, pp. 1-2.

44. Joint Committee to Settle German Jews in Eretz Israel to the Histadrut Executive, August 9, 1933; Histadrut Executive to the Joint Committee Executive, August 25, 1933, HIS IV/208/1/369.

45. Senator to Director of the Department of Immigration, October 25, 1933; Jacobs to JAE, November 22, 1933, CZA S25/9809.

46. Lubinski and Rau, Arbeitgemeinschaft, Berlin, to JAE, Jerusalem, September 29, 1933, CZA S25/9705.

47. Report on Youth Aliya, by Szold, May 1934, CZA S25/9705, pp. 5-7. Gelber, "Origins", p. 157 notes the arrival of the first group of 43 and discusses 18 more youngsters who arrived, in his terms, "a few weeks later."

48. Histadrut Aliya Committee to JA German Department, February 8, 1934; Szold to Histadrut Cultural Committee, January 22, 1934, HIS IV/208/1/491A.

49. A copy of the bulletin is contained in CZA S25/9705.

50. Copies of the questionnaire are contained in CZA J14/4/II.

51. Szold to Landauer, February 4, 1934, CZA S25/2519.

52. Szold to Landauer, February 19, 1934, CZA S25/2519.

53. Landauer to JA Political Department, February 21, 1934, CZA S25/2519.

54. Szold to Senator, November 7, 1934, CZA S25/9705.

55. Report on Youth Aliya, February 12, 1936, CZA S25/9809.

56. Landauer to Shertok, Ruppin, and Kaplan, August 16, 1936, CZA S25/9705, p.2.

57. Shertok to Mills, July 16, 1936; Mills to Shertok, August 4, 1936, CZA S25/2499.

58. Szold to Shertok, December 17, 1936, CZA S25/9705.

59. The full exchange of telegrams is contained in Chedash to Senator, December 29, 1936, CZA S25/9705.

60. An especially obvious case of polemic is Edwin Black, *The Transfer Agreement*, New York: Macmillan, 1984. Two relevant scholarly studies are Shaul Esh, *Iyunim ba-Shoa ve-Yahadut Zemanenu*, Jerusalem: The Leo Baeck Institute, 1976, and Francis R. Nicosia, *The Third Reich and the Palestine Question*, Austin: Texas University Press, 1985.

61. Manifesto to all branches and members of Brit Ha-Zohar, signed Z. Jabotinsky, May 4, 1933, JIA T14/5.

62. A copy of the document is contained in CZA S25/9706.

63. *ha-Olam*, June 22, 1933, as cited in Yitzhak Arad et al (eds.), *Documents on the Holocaust*, New York: Ktav, 1981, p. 53.

64. Cf. Bruno Blau (ed.), *Das Ausenahmerecht für die Juden in deutschland, 1933-1945*, Third edition, Dusseldorf: Verlag Allgemeine Wochenzeitung der Juden in deutschland, 1965, p. 117.

65. Werner D. Senator, Memorandum on the Transfer of Jewish Capital from Germany, July 24, 1933, CZA S25/9706, p.1.

66. Margalit to JAE, July 28, 1933, CZA S25/9706; Senator to Zioniburo, London, August 4, 1933, CZA L9/441. Cf. Abraham Barkai, "German Interests in the Haavara-Transfer Agreement, 1933-1938," *LBIYB*, vol. 35 (1990), pp. 254-256.

67. Abraham Barkai, *Nazi Economics*, New York: Berg Publishers, 1990, pp. 174-183.

68. Barkai, "German Interests", p. 252.

69. W. Hecker, "Retung des Vermoegens Deutscher Juden und Seine Fruchtbenachung fur Palaestina oder Boykott mit Zweifelhaften Erfolg," CZA S25/9706, see also the unsigned, undated, letter to Joseph Sprinzak in HIS IV/208/1/491B.

70. *The Palestine Post*, Thursday, March 30, 1933, P.8.

71. Weizmann to Rothenberg, October 19, 1933; Weizmann to Lipsky, October 19, 1933, Weizmann: *Letters*, vol. 16, pp.76-79.

72. *Stenographiches Protokol der Verhandlungen des 18 Zionistische Congress*, London: Executive of the World Zionist Organization, 1933, pp. 446-447; *ha-Aretz*, Thursday, August 24, 1933, p. 1; Ibid., Friday, August 25, 1933, p.1.

73. Shertok to Nurock, October 4, 1933, CZA S25/9706.

74. Esh, *Iyunim*, p. 87.

75. Shenkar to Palestine Trust Company, July 11, 1933, CZA S25/9706.

76. *ha-Aretz*, Thursday, September 7, 1933, p.1.

77. Haavara Fact Sheet #1, CZA L57/124.

78. Even as strident a critic as Black cannot avoid a glowing description of the ultimate results that Haavara had for the Yishuv. Cf. *The Transfer Agreement*, p. 373.

79. Hantke to Alexander, May 2, 1934, CZA S7/86, p.2.

80. On November 12, 1933 the JAE passed a resolution requesting that the British expand the number of banks permitted to deal with capitalist immigration. Although Haavara is nowhere stipulated in the resolution, it is implied. Protocols of the JAE, November 12, 1933, CZA S100/15, p.

81. *ha-Aretz*, Thursday, September 14, 1933, p.1.

82. Zionists, New York, to Zioniburo, London, October 19, 1934; Alexander (South African Zionist Federation) to JA, October 16, 1934; Alexander to Keren ha-Yesod, April 17, 1934, CZA S25/9706.

83. Protocol of the Haavara Executive, May 27, 1934, CZA L57/1, pp. 2-4.

84. Hantke to Alexander, op cit, p.1.

85. Haavara to Goldman, August 7, 1934; Goldman to Weiss, August 14, 1934, CZA L57/63.

86. Goldmann to Haavara, August 20, 1934, CZA L57/63.

87. Landauer to Sprinzak, September 27, 1934, CZA S25/9706. This version is actually a draft which was sent, for comments, to Moshe Shertok.

Shertok's marginal queries and Landauer's responses thereto are of special interest and are reflected in this paragraph.

88. Levi to JAE, October 14, 1934, CZA S25/9706.

89. Statistical summary of Haavara to 1936, ISA 67/1253.

90. *Palestine Tourist Annual*, #1 (1935), p. 67.

91. Landauer to Ruppin, October 7, 1934; Senator to Haavara, September 25, 1934, CZA S25/9706.

92. Nicosia, *Third Reich*, chapter 5.

93. Kaplan to Senator, April 25, 1934; Senator to JAE, April 30, 1934, CZA S25/9706.

94. Protocol of the Haavara Executive, May 27, 1934, CZA L57/1.

95. Protocol of the Haavara Executive, August 26, 1934, CZA L57/1, p.8.

96. Protocols of the JAE, April 21, 1935, CZA S100/16, pp. 1/4176-2/4177.

97. Ulrich, Auswartigesamt, to German Consul General, Beirut, December 14, 1934; M. Liwni, "Bericht Über Meine Reise nach Syrien" and "Bericht Über Meine Reise nach Aegypten"; van Meetern to Wolff, February 22, 1935; Wohltat to PALTREU, March 7, 1935; "Bericht an die Reichsstell für Devisenbewirtschaftung Über die Arbeit der Trust and Transfer Office Haavara," October 12, 1936, ISA 67/1246. The idea of expansion fell through, however, primarily because of the oppostion of German merchants, who feared for their profits. Protocols of the JAE, June 30, 1935. CZA S100/16, p. 3/4220.

98. Protocols of the Histadrut Executive, November 8, 1934, HIS M24, pp. 4-6. The citrus deal with Germany was approved by a margin of five to two, but was apparently never carried out.

99. Protocols of the JAE, May 28, 1935, CZA S100/16, p. 2/4200.

100. Transferbesprechung im Luzern, 1935, CZA L57/42.

101. Protocol of a Meeting with Mr. Mills, June 5, 1935, BGA Protocols.

102. Transfer Resolution (short version), 1935, CZA L57/73; Statement of the Executive of the Jewish Agency on the Subject of the "Haavara," December 10, 1935, CZA S53/1626/A, pp. 5-6

103. Transfer Resolution (long version), September 18, 1935, JIA T14/16.

104. Statement of the Executive of the Jewish Agency, p. 1.

105. Protocols of the JAE, October 9, 1935, CZA S100/17, p. 4/4296.

106. Clippings of the two letters, which are identical except for language, and drafts of a response to Kisch are contained in CZA L57/296.

107. Ze'ev Jabotinsky, "Al Kishlono shel ha-Kongress ha-Yod-Het," *Neumim*, p. 161.

108. Both posters are undated, but probably date to late 1935, since the plebescite took place in December 1935. The cited billfolds are in JIA T14/5.

109. Example in JIA T14/2.

110. Circular letter #1, November 6, 1935, JIA T14/2; Circular letter #3, December 3, 1935, JIA T14/4.

111. Results of the Plebiscite on the Haavara and the Boycott, no date, JIA T14/2.

112. Protocol of the Histadrut Executive, November 4, 1935, HIS M27, p. 8.

113. What is the Transfer? 1935, CZA S25/9810, pp. 8-10.

114. *Palestine Tourist Annual*, #2 (1936), p. 52.

115. See the undated poster citing anti-Haavara articles from the Hebrew press, JIA T14/5.

116. Cf. Yoav Gelber, *Moledet Hadasha: Aliyat Yehudei Merkaz Europa ve-Klitatam, 1933-1948*, Jerusalem: Yad Yitzhak Ben-Zvi, 1990, p. 79.

117. "Numbers on the Transfer", November 17, 1935, CZA S25/9754.

118. Professor Francis Nicosia of St. Michael's College has kindly made two letters he received on this subject from Werner Feilchenfeld (the Haavara Ltd. accountant) available to me. Both discuss the difficulties Haavara experienced in selling goods in the Yishuv.

119. Protocols of the JAE, October 29, 1935, CZA S100/17, pp. 3/4313-5/4315; Haavara to Kaplen, November 27, 1935, CZA S25/9810. Against this plan, Landauer proposed to limit the amount of capital to be transferred to £P1,000, which was the de facto limit of payments at the time. "Proposal Regarding the Division of [currency] Redemption Through the Transfer," November 11, 1935, CZA S25/9810.

120. Protocols of the JAE, November 3, 1935, CZA S100/17, pp. 2/4317-5/4320.

121. Protocols of the JAE, November 10, 1935, CZA S100/17, pp. 2/4323-3/4324.

122. David, Haavara, to Ben-Gurion, November 22, 1935, CZA S44/158B.

123. Protocols of the JAE, November 27, 1935, CZA S100/17, p. 2/4354.

124. Vitkovsky "The Haavara" (circa December 1935), JIA T14/3.

125. Jevagency, Jerusalem, to Karpf, New York, 1935, CZA S25/9755.

126. David to Magnes, December 19, 1935, CAHJP P3/2322.

127. My dating of the speech is based on the other items in the file. CAHJP P3/2322.

128. *Haavara Newsletter*, #1 (December 22, 1935), p. 4, CZA S25/9754. In a letter to Ben-Gurion, the Haavara Directorate thanked him effusively for his support. Margalit to Ben-Gurion, December 24, 1935, CZA S25/9755.

129. Ben-Zvi to Austrian Consul, Jerusalem, March 15, 1937, BZA 1/4/21/54.

130. List of invitations to the Press Conference, no date, CZA S25/9754; Vitkovsky, "The Haavara", p. 1.

131. Compare the speech of Leo David, the director of Haavara Ltd., at the press conference, CZA S25/9754 with Vitkovsky, loc. cit.

132. Jabotinsky to Haskel, August 17, 1934, JIA A1/2/24/34.

133. Examples filed in JIA T14/1.

134. Financial statement for period of August 15 to November 1, 1935, JIA T14/1.

135. Hillel Kook to JCB, August 19, 1935, JIA T14/1.

136. Kook to Motor Trading Corporation; Kook to Benziman, August 21, 1935, JIA T14/1.

137. Cf. Senator's comments in Protocols of the JAE, May 28, 1935, CZA S100/16, p. 2/4200. A number of similar statments have been cited above.

138. *Palestine Tourist Annual*, #2, p. 52. Cf. Nicosia, *Third Reich*, p. 130.

139. JCB to Ben-Zvi, September 20, 1935, JIA T14/1.

140. Summons against HOG by the Joint Committee to Boycott German Goods, September 20, 1935, JIA T14/1.

141. JCB to Ben-Zvi, October 2, 1935, JIA T14/1.

142. Boycott Committees of Haifa and Jerusalem to Va'ad Leumi Executive, March 21, 1936, JIA T14/1.

143. Boycott Committees of Haifa and Jerusalem to Va'ad Leumi Executive, March 29, 1936, JIA T14/1. The conference took place in London on April 19, 1936.

144. Jerusalem Boycott Committee to Mapai Executive, March 24, 1936, JIA T14/1. From the letter it appears that representatives of the Mapai's Jerusalem branch did continue to attend JCB meetings.

145. Haavara to JCB, March 14, 1937, HIS IV/208/1/1476.

146. Nir to Goldmann, August 3, 1934, HIS IV/208/1/942.

147. A fuller analysis of the economic situation in Jewish Palestine is offered in Avizohar, *Rei Saduk*, pp. 293-295, which focuses on the rise of unemployment in the Yishuv in 1934 and 1935, a spiral that continued until the mobilization of resources for war in 1939.

148. *JA Report*, 1937, pp. 26-32.

149. Skolnik to Ben-Gurion and Hoz, no date, CZA S44/158B.

150. Rosenberg to Gruenbaum, November 10, 1935, CZA S46/302.

151. Granowski to Landauer, September 7, 1938, CZA S46/302. Cf. F. Brada, "Emigration to Palestine" *The Jews of Czechoslovakia*, Philadelphia: JPS, 1971, vol 2, pp. 595-597.

152. *AJYB*, vol. 38 (1936/1937), p. 290.

153. Idem.

154. Rottenstreich to JAE, May 8, 1936, CZA S7/212.

155. Protocols of the JAE, November 22, 1936, CZA S100/20, p. 1/5051-9/5059; Gruenbaum to Polish Foreign Ministry, November 24, 1936; Gruenbaum to Polish Consul-General, Tel Aviv, November 25,1937, CZA S46/289.

156. All told, 18 files in the Gruenbaum papers deal with the clearing negotiations with the Poles: CZA S46/285-299 and 303-305. To these must be added files in other record groups, including those of the German Department (S7), the Political Department (S25), and the papers of Ben-Gurion

(S44) and Landauer (S49). These files cry out for a systematic review.

157. Report on the Results of the Haavara Transfer, no date, CZA L57/242.

158. Bericht an die Reichstelle fur Devisenwirtschaftung über die Arbeit der Trust and Transfer Office, Haavara Ltd, Tel Aviv, No date, ISA 67/1253.

159. Arab Chamber of Commerce to German vice-Counsul, Jerusalem, September 17, 1936, ISA 67/1253.

160. See the relevant files from the Politisches Archiv des Auswartigen Amt, the Geheime Staatspolizei Archiv, and the Bundsarchiv vited in Nicosia, *Third Reich*, pp. 140-144.

161. Haavara, Ltd. to Goldmann, August 16, 1936, CZA L57/63.

162. Weizmann to Marks, January 7, 1936, , vol. Weizmann: *Letters*, vol. 17, pp. 120-123.

163. Walter Schevenells, "The Sydicalist International and the Problem of German Refugees," no date, CZA S44/158BB, pp. 2-3.

164. Cf. Yitzhak Avneri, ha-Histadrut ha-Zionit ve-he-Aliya ha-Bilti Legalit le-Eretz Israel, Unpublished Doctoral Dissertation: Tel Aviv University, 1981 and Dalia Ofer, *Escaping the Holocaust: Illegal immigration to the Land of Israel, 1939-1944*, New York: Oxford University Press, 1990.

165. Dalia Ofer, "The Hitoriography of Aliyah Bet," in *The Historiography of the Holocaust Period*, edited by Y. Gutman and G. Greif, Jerusalem: Yad Vashem, 1988, pp. 594-595.

166. Ibid., pp. 595-596.

167. Ofer, *Escaping*, p. 72.

168. Avneri, ha-Histadrut ha-Zionit, p. 72.

169. Avneri, ha-Histadrut ha-Zionit, Appendix I (vol. 2, p. 1.).

170. Moshe Shertok's Office Diary, Sunday, November 26, 1933, CZA A245/1. p. 3; Minute of a Conversation with the High Commissioner, October 17, 1933, CZA S25/17/I; German Department to Senator, December 12, 1935, CZA S25/2651.

171. For example, in September 1933, Adolf Grinberg sought entry into Palestine as a refugee, but without a certificate or a tourist visa. The JAE sought unsuccessfully to gain his entry into the country on grounds that he had already been attacked by Nazis and had fled Germany without proper papers to gain a visa. Cf. Ben-Zvi to Hyamson, September 1, 1933, ISA M1179/5.

172. Moshe Shertok's Office Diary, Monday, November 5, 1934, CZA A245/1, pp. 5-6; Avneri, ha-Histadrut ha-Zionit, pp. 113-114.

173. Draft by Bernard Joseph, April 1, 1936, CZA S25/2651.

174. Avneri, ha-Histadrut ha-Zionit, pp. 113-114.

175. Yael Yishai, *Siyyot be-Tenuat ha-Avoda: Siya Bet be-Mapai*, Tel Aviv: Am Oved, 1978, pp. 52-57.

176. Shapira, *Berl*, p. 274.

177. Davar, November 25, 1934, Evening Supllement, p. 1.

178. Sokolow's statement is cited supra, p. 58; Sprinzak and Ben-Gurion are quoted in Avneri, ha-Histadrut ha-Zionit, pp. 94, 99 and 112.

179. Ibid., pp. 116-117.

180. Shertok to Wauchope, March 12, 1936, CZA S25/2651, p. 3.

181. Ibid., pp. 1-2.

182. Haim Lazar-Litai, *Af-Al-Pi*, Tel Aviv: Hadar, 1972, passim.

Chapter 5

1. Protocols of the JAE, November 12, 1933, CZA S100/15, p. 2/3758.

2. Includes lawyers, teachers, and other free professionals.

3. A. Viest, *Idedtiat und Integration: Dargestellt am Beispiel Mittel-europaeschier Einwanderer in Israel*, Frankfurt A/M: P. Lang, 1977, pp. 81-91.

4. Zeev Tsur, *ha-Kbbutz ha-Meuchad be-Binyan Eretz-Israel*, Tel Aviv: Yad Yitzhak Tabenkin, 1979, p. 219.

5. Ibid., pp. 218-219.

6. E. Beling, *Die gesellschaftliche Eingliederung der deutschen Einwanderer in Israel*, Frankfurt A/M: P. Lang, 1967, p. 36.

7. Jaski to Brodetsky, November 23, 1933, CZA S25/9707.

8. Dobkin to JA German Department, January 30, 1934, HIS IV/208/I/520.

9. Feldstein to JA German Department, May 31, 1934; Protocol of the Vocational Sub-Committee of the JA German Department, June 4, 1934, HIS V/208/l/491-A.

10. Beling, *Die gesellschaftliche Eingliederung*, p. 39.

11. Idem. The 1936 figures break down as follows: under 20 = 31%; 21-40 42%; 41-50 = 10%; 50 and above = 17%.

12. Stern to HOG, June 2, 1934, HIS IV/208/l/491B.

13. Bader to JA German Department, September 4, 1934, HIS IV/208/I/369.

14. Beling, *Die gesellschaftliche Eingliederung*, p. 126.

15. Stenographic Protocol of the HOG Annual Convention, 1936, CZA J18/2, p. 6.

16. Levinsohn to Histadrut Executive, September 4, 1933, HIS IV/208/l/369.

17. Protocol of a meeting with HOG Representatives, November 24, 1934, HIS IV/208/l/369.

18. Viest, *Idedtiat und Integration*, pp. 19-32.

19. Stenographic Protocol of the HOG Annual Convention, 1936, CZA J18/2, p. 5.

20. Gedud Meginei ha-Safa to Szold, October 7, 1933. CZA J14/1/III

21. Protocol of an Employees meeting, May 15, 1935, HIS IV/208/l/656, pp. 3-4.

22. *Palestine Illustrated News*, Friday, March 10, 1939, p. 10 and Friday, March 17, 1939, pp. 2-3. Ironically, two of the papers most adamantly opposed to *JWR* were published in English.

23. *Palestine Illustrated News*, Friday, March 24, 1939, p. 15, Friday, April 14, 1939, p. 1.

24. *Jüdische Welt-Rundschau*, Friday, March 10, 1939, pp. 1-2, 5-6.

25. Note by Robert Weltsch, August 1978, LBI (NY) AR-7185/2/17.

26. Ben-Gurion's Diary, May 3, 1935, BGA, p. 4.

27. Hans Rubin, Memorandum on work with German Olim in Tel Aviv, September 9, 1935, HIS IV/208/l/656, p. 9. Emphasis in original.

28. Rubin to Sprinzak, June 6, 1935, HIS IV/208/l/656.

29. Protocol of the West European Aliya Committee, November 17, 1935, HIS IV/208/l/656, p. 1; West European Aliya Committee to Landauer, August 18, 1936; HIS IV/208/l/756; Mapai Secretariat Diary, August 28, 1936, HIS IV/406/l/13, p. 1.

30. Minutes of a Conversation with the High Commissioner, January 18/19, 1934, CZA S25/17/1.

31. Minutes of a Conversation with the High Commissioner, February 22, 1934, CZA S25/17/1.

32. Zelzion to Histadrut Executive, August 19, 1934, HIS IV/208/t/369.

33. Yerida to Germany is documented in ISA 67/1236 and 67/1237, which contain requests for return visas to Germany by German Jews living in Palestine. The Nazis also permitted a small amount of re-immigration from other countries, mostly for propaganda purposes, in 1933 and 1934. Cf. Doron Niderland, "Back to the Lion's Jaws: A Note on Jewish Return Migration to Nazi Germany," *Studies in Contemporary Jewry*, vol. 9 (1993), pp. 174-180.

34. Cf. W. Preuss "Histadrut und Alija aus Deutschland" *Die Mitteilungsblatt*, # 14-15 (April, 1973) p. 27 and the manuscripts in the 40th anniversary of German emigration collection, LBI(J) file 627/1.

35. Stenographic Protocol of the HOG Annual Convention, 1936, CZA J/18/2, p. 2.

36. Beling, *Die gesellschaftliche Eingliederung*, pp. 273-274.

37. HOG Annual Convention, p. 4.

38. Weizmann's address is filed separately from the stenographic protocol of the conference, in CZA J18/2.

39. HOG Annual Convention, pp.24-26.

40. General Zionist Alliance to Moses, May 29, 1939, LBI(J) #469.

41. S. Moses, Welche Grundtendenz Können Jetzt Verhandlungen mit der englischen Regierung Haben? no date, LBI(J) #469.

42. Ahdut Ha'am to JAE, December 28, 1938; Memo by the League for Jewish Arab Cooperation, June 18, 1939, LBI(J) #469.

43. Susan L. Hattis, *The Binational Idea in Palestine During Mandatory Times*, Haifa: Shikmona Press, 1970, passim.

44. Yoav Gelber, *Moledet Hadasha: Aliyat Yehudei Merkaz Europa ve-Klitatam, 1933-1948*, Jerusalem: Yad Yitzhak Ben-Zvi, 1990, pp. 491, 511.

45. Hattis, *Binational Idea*, pp. 57, 81.

46. Stephen Poppel, *Zionism in Germany*, Philadelphia: Jewish Publication Society, 1976, pp. 144-157.

47. Manifesto of the Confederation of General Zionists and the 21st Zionist Congress, 1939, LBI(J) #469.

48. Gelber, *Moledet Hadasha*, p. 240.

49. For examples of HOA activities, see: Zweig to Samuel, March 15, 1938 and Bernay and Zweig to MacMichael, June 15, 1938, CZA S7/513.

50. HOA to JAE, June 10, 1938, CZA S7/513.

51. Landauer to HOA, August 16, 1938, CZA S7/513. The two month delay between HOA's original request and the JA's rejection of a financial grant are not clear from the documents I have seen.

52. Fuller documentation of the HOA office in Tel Aviv is contained in CZA S7/1415 and Jl/4392.

53. "Olei Austria," poster of July 1938 explaining the agreement, CZA S7/513.

54. Gelber, *Moledet Hadasha*, pp. 515-516.

55. Pinkus to David, August 3, 1938; HOA to JAE, August 4, 1938, CZA S7/513.

56. For examples of this attitude see Steven E. Aschheim, *Brothers and Strangers: The East European Jew in German and German Jewish Consciousness, 1800-1923*, Madison: University of Wisconsin Press, 1982.

57. Landauer to Dobkin, August 14, 1938, CZA S6/1414.

58. Gelber, *Moledet Hadasha*, p. 244. IOME still exists and remains active as a landsmannschaft for Central European Jews.

59. David Bechor et al, *Din ve-Heshbon shel Ve'idat ha-Hakira le-Hakirat Rezah Dr. Chaim Arlosoroff*, Jerusalem: The Committee/Israel Government Printing Office, 1985.

60. Shabbetai Teveth, *Rezach Arlosoroff*, Jerusalem: Schocken, 1982, pp. 10-12. As against Teveth's reconstruction of events, see: C. Ben-Yerocham, *Alilat ha-Dam*, Tel Aviv: The Jabotinsky Institute, 1982. All relevant material on the affair held by the CZA is closed until 2017.

61. David Ben-Gurion, *Letters to Paula*, Pittsburgh: University of Pittsburgh Press, 1968, pp. 63-65. Ben-Gurion was in Riga at the time.

62. Protocols of the JAE, July 1, 1934, CZA S100/15, p. 1/3943. *ha-Aretz*, Monday, April 23, 1934, p. 1; AJYB, vol. 36 (1934/1935), p. 216.

63. Protocol of the Histadnit Executive, October 16, 1933, HIS M21, pp. 4-6. Intersetingly, the only one who spoke up for Pa'amoni was Ben-Gurion who otherwise was in the forefront of Mapai's anti-Revisionist battle. In this case, however, he distinguished between a worker fired without just cause and a justified battle against an (in Ben-Gurion's mind) inplacable foe.

64. Teveth, *Rezach Arlosoroff*, pp. 155-156. The term used, "malshin," has connotations that go beyond merely being disloyal: in the Amida services for weekdays an execratory prayer against informers is repeated, since informers undermine the very security of the Jewish community.

65. Joseph Schechtman, *The Life and Times of Vladimir Jabotinsky*, New York: Thomas Yoseloff, 1961, vol. 2, pp. 190-191.

66. Ibid., p. 193.

67. Numerous examples of the internecine violence may be found in the daily press, especially during the spring of 1933. Cf. Howard I. Rosenblum, A Political History of Revisionist Zionism, Unpublished Doctoral Dissertation: Columbia University, 1986, pp. 139-146.

68. Protocol of the JAE Meeting with the Va'ad ha-Poel ha-Zioni, August 6, 1934, CZA S100/15, pp. 1/3969-2/3970.

69. Jabotinsky to Ginsburg, September 9, 1933, JIA A1/2/23/2.

70. Betar Circular # 60, no date, CZA S44/69B.

71. Lauterbach to Betar, November 29,1933, CZA S44/69B. Cf. David Ben-Gurion, *Zichronot*, Tel Aviv: Am Oved, 1976, vol. 2, pp. 127-128.

72. Lubotzky to WZO, December 12,1933; Lubotzky to WZO, December 22, 1933, CZA S44/69B.

73. WZO to Betar, January 29, 1934, CZA S44/69B.

74. The World-Wide Jewish Petition to the Crown and Parliament and Governments Abroad, May 15, 1934, JIA G3/4/1.

75. Ibid., pp. 11-12.

76. Ibid., p. 11.

77. Zioniburo, London, to Jevagency, Jerusalem, January 17, 1934; Statements Issued by the Central Office of the Zionist Organization and the Jewish Agency for Palestine, January 23, 1934, CZA S25/2092; Protocols of the JAE, May 13,1934, CZA S100/15, p. 1/3901.

78. Protocols of the JAE, May 13, 1934, CZA S100/15, p. 1/3901.

79. Landauer to Ben-Gurion, April 15, 1934, CZA S44/69B.

80. Protocol of a Special JAE Meeting with South African Zionists, March 21, 1935, CZA S100/15, pp. 8/3855-11/3858.

81. Zeev Jabotinsky, "Ken Lishbor," *Ba-Saar*, Jerusalem: Eri Jabotinsky, 1953, p, 45-53.

82. Protocol of Special Meeting, op cit, p. 24/3871. Emphasis added.

83. Ibid., p.25/3878.

84. Protocol of Special JAE Meeting with Members of the Va'ad ha-Poel ha-Zioni, August 6, 1934, CZA S100/15, pp. 1/3969-6/6974.

85. The standard biography of Rutenberg, a veteran Zionist who claimed to be above intra-party struggles, is: Eli Shaltiel, Pinhas Rutenberg: *Aliyato u-Nefilato shel Ish Hazak be-Eretz Israel, 1879-1942*, Tel Aviv: Am Oved, 1990.

86. Protocol of a Meeting between Rutenberg and leaders of the Histadrut and Betar, September 18, 1934, BGA Protocols.

87. Protocols of the JAE, November 2, 1934, CZA S100/16, p. 1/4034.

88. Protocols of the JAE, November 4, 1934, CZA S100/16, pp. 2/4036, 4/4038.

89. Protocols of the JAE, November 7, 1934, CZA S100/16, p. 1/4041.

90. Ben-Gurion-Jabotinsky Agreement, JIA Al/432; Protocols of the JAE, November 20, 1934, CZA S100/16, pp. 1/4049-3/4051; Protocol of the Mapai Executive, October 31, 1934, ILPA 2/23/34, pp. 5-8.

91. Protocols of the JAE, November 25, 1934, CZA S100/16, p. 3/4054. Kaplan's vote is not recorded even though he is listed as attending.

92. Protocols of the JAE, November 25, 1934, CZA S100/16, pp. 1/4052-2/4053.

93. Protocols of the JAE, December 16, 1934, CZA S100/16, p. 3/4070.

94. Zeev Jabotinsky, "Likrat Koalitzia Zionit?" *Ketuvim, 1927-1940*, Jerusalem: Eri Jabotinsky, 1947, pp. 167-174; *Davar*, Evening Supplement, December 1, 1934, p. 1; Schechtman, *Life and Times*, vol. 2, pp. 251-252.

95. *Davar*, November 6, 1934, p. 1.

96. *Davar*, Wednesday, November 21, 1934, p. 3.

97. *Davar*, November 21, 1934, p. 2.

98. *Davar*, Sunday, November 25, 1934, p. 1.

99. "On Ben-Gurion's Return," No date, HIS IV/406/1/6. Emphasis in original.

100. Moshe Shertok, for example, called news of the agreements, which he strongly supported, "sensational." Cf. Moshe Shertok's Office Diary, October 27, 1934, CZA A245/1, p. 6.

101. Protocol of the Mapai Executive, October 31, 1934, ILPA 2/23/34, pp. 9-33.

102. Ben-Gurion to the Mapai Executive, October 27, 1934, BGA Correspondence

103. Protocol of the Mapai Executive, op cit, p. 34.

104. Protocol of the Mapai Executive, November 20, 1934, ILPA 2/23/34, p. 17.

105. Originally skeptical, Katznelson came to support the agreements. Cf. Anita Shapira, *Berl the Biography of a Socialist Zionist*, New York: Cambridge University Press, 1984, pp. 204-205. For Tabenkin's view, see Tsur, *ha-Kibbutz ha-Meuchad*, pp. 133-136.

106. Protocol of the Mapai Executive, November 24, 1934, ILPA 2/23/34.

107. Protocols of the Histadrut Executive, January 31, 1935, HIS M 25, pp. 1-3.

108. Ibid., pp. 8-10.

109. *ha-Zioni ha-Klali*, December 11, 1934, p. 17.

110. Melchett to JAE, October 29, 1934, BGA Correspondence.

111. Shabbetai Teveth, *David Ben-Gurion: The Burning Ground*, Boston: Houghton Mifflin Company, 1987, pp. 486-489; Shapira, *Berl*, p. 203-206.

112. M. Erem, *Ba'ad oh Neged ha-Heskem im ha-Fascism ha-Revisionisti?* Tel Aviv: The Action Committee of Opponents of the Agreement, No Date.

113. Ibid., pp. 7-8.

114. Brodetsky to Zionist Federations, March 1, 1935, CZA S25/2092.

115. Jabotinsky had proposed a moderately worded resolution stating that the Congress affirmed that the final goal (Endziel) of Zionism was the creation of a sovereign Jewish state. When the resolution was rejected by a vote of 121 to 57, pandemonium reigned. Ha-Zohar delegate Meir Grossman attempted to speak, but was shouted down. At this point Jabotinsky stood on his chair and in a symbolic gesture tore up his delegate card declaring that "this is not a Zionist Congress any more." Cf. Schechtman, *Life and Times*, vol. 2, p. 152.

116. Jabotinsky, *Ba-Saar*, pp. 117-142.

117. Zeev Jabotinsky, "Zionut Romema," in *Neumim*, p. 180.

118. Ibid., pp. 191-193.

119. One example, dated July 21, 1935, is contained in CZA S44/69C.

120. *ha-Protocol ha-Stenografi shel ha-Congress ha-Zioni ha-Tesha-Esrei*, Jerusalem: The World Zionist Organization, 1935 pp. 27-28, 43-56.

121. Undated examples of the posters are contained in CZA S44/69B.

122. Ha-Zoahar Poland, circular # 13, December 7, 1935, CZA S44/69A.

123. Rotenstreich to Ben-Gurion, April 14, 1936, CZA S44/69B.

124. Palestine Office, Trieste, to JAE, May 13, 1936, CZA S44/69B.

125. Presidency of the NZO, February 12, 1936, JIA G4/2/1, p. 1.

126. NZO Palestine Executive to Wauchope, January 1, 1936, CZA S44/69A; Presidency of the NZO, Circular to South African Revisionists, April 30, 1936, JIA G4/2/1.

127. Rotenstreich to Ben-Gurion, September 14, 1936, CZA S44/69A.

128. Jerzy Tomaszewski, "Vladimir Jabotinsky's Talks With Representatives of the Polish Government," *Polin*, Vol. 2 (1988), pp. 276-293.

129. Thomas to Weizmann, April 8, 1936, CZA S44/275

130. Lourie to Shertok, May 29, 1936, CZA S25/2072.

131. Rotenstreich to Ben-Gurion, September 30, 1936, CZA S44/69B.

132. Auszug aus *der Stimme*: Jabotinsky's Vier Punkte, November 20, 1936, CZA S44/69B.

133. Rosenblum, Political History, pp. 414-420.

134. Ibid., Chap. 6.

135. In his memoirs Emanuel Neumann, an American General Zionist who chaired the JAE in 1933 and 1934 (see supra, p. 30), had the following to say about Ben-Gurion's transformation: "Quite unconsciously, I am sure, he gradually came to share some of the most important of Jabotinsky's positions and slogans." Cf. *In the Arena: An Antibiographical Memoir*, New York: Herzl Press, 1976, p. 109.

Chapter 6

1. Moshe Shertok's Office Diary, November 27, 1933, p. 1.

2. *The Churchill White Paper, Command 1700, 1922*, London: HMSO, 1923.

3. "Immigration Ordinance of 1925, Article 2," cited in Aharon S. Kleiman (ed.), *Practical Zionism, 1920-1939*, New York: Garland, 1987, pp. 167-168.

4. *Palnews Economic Annual of Palestine*, vol. 2 (1936), pp. 77-78; Memorandum on the Development of the Jewish National Home, June 1936. CZA S7/212, pp. 3-4.

5. *Palnews Economic Annual of Palestine*, vol. 5 (1939), pp.141-143.

6. *ha-Aretz*, Monday, October 14, 1933, p.1

7. Protocols of the JAE, July 14, 1933, CZA S100/14, p. 1/3720.

8. Minute of a Conversation with the High Commissioner, October 20, 1933, CZA S25/17/1, p.3.

9. Minute of a Conversation with the High Commissioner, Noveber 1, 1933, CZA S25/17/1, pp. 1-3.

10. Ibid., pp. 4-5.

11. Ibid., pp. 5-7.

12. E. Beling, *Die gesellschaftliche Eingliederung der deutschen Einwanderer in Israel*, Frankfurt A/M: P. Lang, 1967, p. 39.

13. Minute of a Conversation with the High Commissioner, November 10, 1933, CZA S25/17/1. It must be noted that Arab illegal immigration was not a new problem: even the British admitted that "the number of Arabs who entered Palestine illegally from Syria and Trans-Jordan is unknown but probably considerable." Cf. *Great Britain and Palestine, 1915-1945*, London: Royal Institute of International Affairs, 1946, p. 64.

14. Moshe Shertok's Office Diary, Sunday, November 26, 1933, CZA A245/1, pp. 2-3.

15. Protocols of the JAE, January 7, 1934, CZA SIOO/15, p. 1/3782.

16. Ibid., p. 2/3873.

17. David Ben-Gurion's Diary, Thursday, October 27, 1934, BGA.

18. Protocols of the JAE, February 11, 1934, CZA SIOO/15, p. 3/3816.

19. Ben-Gurion's Diary, May 1, 1934, BGA.

20. Idem.

21. Minute of a Conversation with the High Commissioner, February 22, 1934, CZA S25/17/1, pp.1-4.

22. Minute of a Conversation with the High Commissioner, April 25, 1934, CZA S25/17/1.

23. Protocols of the JAE, May 2, 1934, CZA S100/15, p. 1/3891.

24. Ibid., p. 3/3893.

25. Protocols of the JAE, May 6, 1934, CZA S100/15, pp. 1/3896-2/3897.

26. Minutes of a Conversation with the High Commissioner, May 15, 1934, CZA S25/17/1.

27. Shertok to Commissioner for Migration and Statistics, June 15, 1934, CZA S25/2519.

28. Protocol of a Meeting with Mr. Hall, signed Ruppin, October 16, 1934, BGA Protocols.

29. Minutes of a Conversation with the High Commissioner, June 19, 1934, CZA S25/17/1.

30. Minutes of a Conversation with the High Commissioner, June 21, 1934, CZA S25/17/1.

31. Susan L. Hattis: *The Bi-National Idea in Palestine During Mandatory Times*, Haifa: Shikmona Publishing, 1970, pp. 52, 105-114.

32. Moshe Shertok's Office Diary, Sunday, October 7, 1934, CZA A245/1, p. 3.

31 Protocols of the JAE Meeting with Representatives of the Va'ad ha-Poel ha-Zioizi, October 3, 1934, CZA S100/16, p. 6/4005.

34. Protocol of a Meeting between Representatives of the Jewish Agency, the Vaad Leumi, and Agudas Israel, November 20, 1935, BGA Protocols.

35. Joseph B. Schectman: *The Life and Times of Vladimir Jabotinsky*, New York: Thomas Yoseloff, 1961, vol. 2, pp. 292, 300.

36. Protocol of a Meeting between Jewish Representatvies and the High Commissioner, December 22, 1935, BGA Protocols.

37. On Transjordan: Melchett to Erleigh, No Date, CZA S25/9707; and Moshe Shertok's Office Diary, Tuesday, October 16, 1934, CZA A245/1, p. 10; on the Negev: Moshe Shertok's Office Diary, Wednesday, October 10, 1934, CZA A245/1, p. 10.

38. This figure is based on the topic headings in each of the JAE protocols. The breakdown is: February to September 1933 six meetings; September 1933 to September 1934 six meetings; September to December 1934 two meetings.

39. Moshe Shertok's Office Diary, Friday, October 19, 1934, CZA A245/1, p. 14.

40. Ibid., Wednesday, October 17, 1934, CZA A245/1, p. 13.

41. Rosenblueth to Jevagency, Jerusalem, May 23, 1935, CZA S25/2519.

42. Minutes of a Converation with the Head of the Immigration Department, June 15, 1935, CZA S25/2519, pp. 1-2.

43. Arnett to Blitzstein, July 1, 1935, CZA S25/2519.

44. Minutes of a Conversation, op cit, p. 1; Protocols of the JAE, June 11, 1935, CZA S100/16, p. 1/4207.

45. Protocols of the JAE, June 23, 1935, CZA S100/16, p. 1/4213.

46. Samuel to JAE, February 23, 1935, CZA S25/2512.

47. Minute of a Conversation with Mr. Hall, October 16, 1935, CZA S25/19, p. 1.

48. Protocols of the JAE, December 25, 1935, CZA S100/17, p. 2/4389.

49. Moshe Shertok's Office Diary, Sunday, December 10, 1933, CZA A245/1, P. 9.

50. A frank statement of Britain's position in Palestine is contained in: Hugh A. Wyndham et al, *Political and Military Interests of the United Kingdom: An Outline*, London: Oxford University Press for the RIIA, 1939, pp. 142-144.

51. Schechtman, *Life and Times*, vol. 2, pp. 292-295.

52. Chaim Weizmann: *The Jewish People and Palestine*, Jerusalem: The Jewish Agency, 1939, pp. 1-4.

53. Anita Shapiro, *Berl: The Biography of a Socialist Zionist*, New York: Cambridge University Press, 1984, pp. 99-101.

54. Protocols of the Mapai Central Committee, April 16, 1936, ILPA 2/23/36, PP. 1-2.

55. Schechtman, *Life and Times*, v. 2, pp. 434-441.

56. Cf. Yaacov Shavit, *Jabotinsky and the Revisionist Movement*, London: Frank Cass, 1988, pp. 182-184.

57. Wedgwood was a prominent gentile Zionist and Member of Parliament who set out his scheme in a work entitled *The Seventh Dominion* (1927). For a more detailed analysis of the proposal see Joshua B. Stein: "Josiah Wedgwood and the Seventh Dominion Scheme," *Studies in Zionism*, vol. 11 # 2 (Autumn, 1990): 141-155.

58. Cf. Mitchell Cohen, *Zion and State*, New York: Basil Blackwell, 1987, chapters 11-12.

59. Ben-Gurion's Diary, January 16, 1936, BGA.

60. Ibid., February 12, 1936, BGA.

61. Ben-Gurion, *Zichronot*, Tel Aviv: Am Oved, 1976, vol. 3, pp. 238-240. The proposal's context also must be kept in mind. In early June 1936, Dov Joseph held talks with the Arab statesman Mussa Alami, and sparked Ben-Gurion with a renewed sense of urgency.

62. Moshe Sharett: *Yoman Medini*, Tel Aviv: Am Oved, 1968, v. 1, pp. 21-23.

63. Ibid., pp. 38-41.

61. Shlomo Lev-Ami: *ba-Maavak u-ba-Mered*, Tel Aviv: Maarachot/IDF Press, N.D., p. 65.

65. Protocols of the JAE, May 3, 1936, CZA S100/19, P.1/4578.

66. Sondra M. Rubenstein: *The Communist Movement in Palestine and Israel, 1919-1984*, Boulder, CO: Westview Press, 1985, ch. 9-10.

67. Proclamation of the Central Committee of the PCP, June, 1936, CZA S7/212.

68. Rubenstein, *Communist Movement*, pp. 221-238.

69. Ben-Gurion's Diary, Sunday, June 21, 1936, BGA.

70. Cf. Yaakov Shavit (ed.), *"Havlaga" oh Teguva?* Ramat Gan: Bar-Ilan University Press, 1983, pp. 7-9 and Anita Shapira, *Land and Power: The Zionist Resort to Force, 1881-1948*, New York: Oxfrod University Press, 1992, ch. 6.

71. Memorandum on the Defense of Palestine, 1936, JIA G4/1/5.

72. Lev-Ami, *ba-Maavak*, pp. 39-40, 47-49. The Hagana's official history presents the events leading up to the schism in a different light, blaming the dissidents for a lack of "discipline." Cf. Yehuda Slutsky et al, *Kitzur Toldot ha-Hagana*, Tel Aviv: Maarachot/IDF Press, 1978, pp.147-149, 158-165.

73. Shavit, *"Havlaga"*, pp. 20-23.

74. The changes in Hagana operational policy are described in Slutsky, *Kitzur Toldot*, chapters 11-14.

75. Slutsky, *Kitzur Toldot*, p. 188.

76. Cf. the analysis of havlaga by Shaul Avigur, one of the founders of the Mossad le-Aliya Bet and a member of the Hagana High Command, cited in Shavit, *"Havlaga"*, p. 11.

77. Ibid., pp. 10-19.

78. Ibid., p. 18.

79. The four editorials were published in *Davar*, respectively on Tuesday, June 9, 1936, p.1; Monday, August 17, 1936, p. 1; Friday, August 28, 1936, p. 1; and Sunday, September 13, 1936, p. 1.

80. Cf. Katznelson's comments at a Va'ad ha-Poel ha-Zioni meeting on Havlaga, in Bracha Habas (ed): *Meoraot Tarzu*, Tel Aviv: Davar Publications, 1937, pp. 359-360.

81. Ze'ev Jabotinsky, "Havlagat ha-Yishuv - Ad Matai?" *ha-Yarden*, Sunday, July 12, 1936, p. 1.

82. B. Lubotzky, "Mamlehet Kohanim ve-Goy Kadosh," Cited in Shavit, *"Havlaga"*, pp. 75-79.

83. Ben-Gurion's Diary, Saturday, July 11, 1936, BGA.

84. Shavit, *"Havlaga"*, pp. 55-66.

85. Cf. Howard Rosenblum, "The New Zionist Organization's Diplomatic Battle Against Partition, 1936-1937," *Studies in Zionism*, vol. 11 #2 (Autumn, 1990), pp. 154-181. Rosenblum points out that Ha-Zach policy was ultimately a failure, but I think he is too critical of Jabotinsky's motivations. Under prevailing circumstances, few alternate policies existed for those opposed to partition as long as the British remained committed to the Peel plan.

86. Ben-Gurion's Diary, September 14, 1936, BGA. The version of this entry contained in Ben-Gurion, *Zichronot*, vol. 3, p. 432, is much more strongly worded than the original diary entry and may reflect Ben-Gurion's feelings about the Irgun after the forcible integration of the underground movements into the Israeli Army in May and June 1948.

87. The broader issues raised by the abortive Hagan-Irgun agreement are fascinating but, have little direct relevance to the subject at hand. The matter is extensively documented in the Hagana and Jabotinsky Institute Archives and in Ben-Gurion's diary at the Ben-Gurion Research Center. Cf. Lev-Ami, *ba-Maavak*, pp. 73-76.

88. David Ben-Gurion, "Likrat ha-Vaada ha-Malhuti," Statement before the Va'ad ha-Poel ha-Zioni, November 10, 1936, CZA G33242, p. 1.

89. Minutes of a Conversation with the High Commissioner, July 9, 1936, CZA S25/19, p. 1.

90. Ibid., p. 2.

91. Ibid., p. 3.

92. Ben-Gurion to Ussishkin, July 20, 1936, BGA Letters.

93. Ben-Gurion to Shertok, August 16, 1936, BGA Letters.

94. Ben-Gurion to Shertok, August 24, 1936, BGA Letters.

95. Ben-Gurion, "Likrat ha-Vaada ha-Malhuti," p. 2.

96. Protocols of the JAE, October 29, 1936, CZA S100/20, p. 2/4965.

97. Ibid., p.6/4969.

98. Ben-Gurion, "Likrat ha-Vaada ha-Malhuti," pp. 3-4.

99. Ibid., p. 4.

100. Ibid., pp. 4-5.

101. Weizmann, *The Jewish People and Palestine*, p. 7.

102. Ibid., p. 10.

103. Ibid., pp. 17-19.

104. Ibid., p. 19. On a number of occasions Weizmann argued that the Jewish National Home should "be as Jewish as England is English."

105. Ibid., p. 25.

106. *Minutes of Evidence Heard at Public Sessions of the Palestine Royal Commission*, London: HMSO, 1937, p. 32.

107. Ibid., p. 38.

108. Ibid., p. 39.

109. Cf. Shabetai Teveth, *David Ben-Gurion: The Burning Ground*, Boston: Houghton, Mifflin Company, 1987, pp. 526, 531-534.

110. *Minutes*, pp. 58-59. The commission members uncategorically denied the validity of enlarging aliya solely on the basis of Jewish needs. Cf. David Ben-Gurion's Diary, Wednesday, December 9, 1936, BGA.

111. *Minutes*, p. 62.

112. Ibid., p. 54.

113. Ibid., pp. 93-101.

114. Ibid., p. 272.

115. Ibid., pp. 279-280.

116. Ibid., pp. 288-289.

117. Ibid., pp. 290-291.

118. Ibid., pp. 557-558.

119. David Ben-Gurion: *The Peel Report and the Jewish State*, London: The Palestine Labour Studies Group, 1938, pp. 3, 14-18. Cf. Yosef Heller, "Weizmann, Jabotinsky, ve-She'elat ha-Aravim — Veidat Peel," *Eighth World Congress for Jewish Studies: Papers*, Jerusalem: WCJS, 1982, vol. 2, pp. 175-176.

120. Ben-Gurion, *Jewish State*, pp. 6-8.

121. *Minutes*, p. 369.

122. Idem.

123. Ibid., p. 370.

124. Idem. Jabotinsky's choice of words in this case is certainly interesting, when one considers that critics have long attacked the Zionist establishment for its supposed concentration on "salvation" as opposed to "rescue."

125. Idem.

126. Idem.

127. Ibid., pp. 372-373.

128. Ibid., p. 395.

129. Ibid., p. 369.

130. B. Akzin: *me-Riga li-Yerushalayim — Pirke Zichronot*, Jerusalem: The Zionist Library, 1989, pp. 276-277. Heller, "Veidat Peel," pp. 177-178, accepts Akzin's testimony and makes the center of his comparative analysis of the positions of Weizmann and Jabotinsky regarding the Arab issue. In a review of Akzin's memoir in *Studies in Zionism*, vol. 11 #1 (Spring, 1990), p. 97, Yaakov Shavit questions the veracity of Akzin's report as it is based on a letter whose origianl contents Shavit claims cannot be confirmed. On the basis of Akzin's well-known reputation for exactitude, however, I have followed Akzin (and Heller) in this paragraph.

131. *Minutes*, p. 376.

132. Idem.

133. Idem.

134. Ibid., p.377

135. Ibid., pp. 380-389.

136. Moshe Shertok, "Al ha-Matzav ha-Politi," Report to the Va'ad ha-Poel ha-Zioni, 1937, CZA G33244, p. 3.

137. Minutes of a Conversation with the High Commissioner, May 13, 1937, CZA S25/19, p, 1-7.

138. Ibid., pp. 7-9.

139. M. Shertok's Office Diary, Sunday, May 23, 1937, CZA A245/6, p. 4.

140. Protocol of the JAE, February 21, 1937, CZA S100/21, p. 1/5248; Moshe Shertok's Office Diary, Saturday, May 29, 1937, CZA A245/6, p. 31; Slutsky, *Kitzur Toldot*, ch. 16.

141. Moshe Shertok's Office Diary, Thursday, May 27,1937. CZA A245/6, pp. 5-6.

142. Protocols of the JAE, March 23, 1937. CZA S100/21, p. 2/5297.

143. Moshe Shertok's Office Diary, Monday, May 31 and Tuesday, June 1, 1937, CZA A245/6, pp. 33, 36.

144. Shavit, *"Havlaga"*, pp. 97-102.

145. Moshe Shertok's Office Diary, Saturday, June 12,1937, CZA A245/6, pp. 58-59.

146. Ibid., Thursday, June 10, and Saturday, June 13, 1937, CZA A245/6, pp. 55, 59-60.

147. Ibid., Monday, June 21, 1937, CZA A245/6, p. 70.

148. *Palestine Royal Commission: Report, 1937*, London: HMSO, 1937, pp. 4042, 394-396.

149. Shmuel Dothan: *Pulmus ha-Haluka be-Tekufat ha-Mandat*, Jerusalem: Yad Yitzhak Ben-Zvi, 1979, chapters 2-3.

150. Statement by the Presidency of the NZO on Partiton, no date, JIA G4/14, p. 2.

151. Memorandum on the Partiton of Palestine Submitted to the Permanent Mandates Commission on Behalf of the New Zionist Organization, July, 1937, JIA G4/l/5, pp. 1-9.

152. Ibid., pp. 15-16.

153. Ibid., p. 21.

154. Zeev Jabotinsky, *Al ha-Haluka*, Jerusalem: Ha-Zohar, no date, p. 7. The same item is held in JIA G4/14 where it is cited as a speech Jabotinsky gave on Partition in 1937.

155. Zeev Jabotinsky, "Mul Tochnit ha-Haluka — Tochnit ha-Asor," in Zeev Jabotinsky, *Neumim, 1927-1940*, Jerusalem: Eri Jabotinsky, 1948, p. 293.

156. Ibid., pp. 299-300.

157. Ibid., pp. 292, 294.

158. Schechtman, *Life and Times*, vol. 2, pp. 323-328. Schechtman's un-equivocal evaluation of Jabotinsky's impact on the partition issue is, I believe, accurate only for the period between July 1937 and April 1938. From that point onward, Britain's repudiation of the Mandate — and the consequent collapse of rescue aliya became virtually inevitable. Cf. Aharon Kleiman, *Hipared oh Mishol — Mediniut Britania ve-Halukat Eretz Israel, 1936-1939*, Jerusalem: Yad Yitzhak Ben-Zvi, 1983, pp. 102-105 and Rosenblum, "The New Zionist Organization's Diplomatic Battle," pp. 177-181.

159. *The State of Doom or a Jewish State*, Tel Aviv: Tnuat Bnei Chorin, 1938, pp. 12-14.

160. Ibid., p. 14.

161. *A New Deal for Palestine*, Tel Aviv: Tnuat Bnei Chorin, 1938, Chap. 3.

162. Ibid., pp. 3-5.

163. Ben-Gurion, *Zihronot*, vol. 4, p. 388.

164. Ibid., p. 294. Cf. Yaacov Shavit, "Realism and Messianism in Zionism and the Yishuv," *Studies in Contemporary Jewry*, vol. 7 (1991), p. 112 and Dvorah Hacohen, "Ben-Gurion and the Second World War: Plans for Mass Immigration to Palestine," Ibid., pp. 247-268.

165. Ben-Gurion's Diary, June 7, 1937, BGA.

166. Ibid., June 15, 1937, BGA.

167. A list of the relative demerits and merits of the plan is included in Ben-Gurion's diary entry for July 17, 1937, BGA.

168. Ben-Gurion, *Jewish State*, pp. 37-42.

169. Ibid, p. 3.

170. Cf. Dothan, *Pulmus ha-Haluka*, pp. 59-87.

171. Ben-Gurion's diary, July 10, 1937, BGA. Specifically, the commission considered the possiblity of limiting all aliya to only 12,000 Jews per year for an indefinite period.

172. Moshe Shertok's Office Diary, Tuesday, June 22, 1937, CZA A245/6, p. 71.

173. *Protokolim shel ha-Kongress ha-Zioni ha-Olami ha-Esrim*, Jerusalem: The World Zionist Organization, 1937, p. 1.

174. Ibid., p. 6.

175. Ibid., p. 33.

176. *Three Congress Addresses: XXth Zionist Congress, Zurich*, New York: Zionist Organization of America, 1937, Stencilled copy #34, NYPL, Ben-Gurion, p. 1.

177. Ibid., p. 2.

178. David Ben-Gurion's Diary, Sunday, July 11, 1937, BGA.

179. *Three Congress Addresses*, Ben-Gurion, p. 8. Ben-Gurion here appears to have reversed the terms of Jabotinsky's 1921 "Iron Wall" speech. Therein, Jabotinsky had predicted the unequivocal enmity of the Arabs to the Zionist cause unless Jews, with British assistance, built an "iron wall" (i.e., a defense of sufficient strength) to force the Arabs to accept the Yishuv and a Jewish state. Zeev Jabotinsky, "Homat ha-Barzel," *Neumim, 1905-1927*, Jerusalem: Eri Jabotinsky, 1957.

180. *Protokolim*, p. 35.

181. Ibid., p. 36.

182. *Three Congress Addresses*, Katznelson, pp. 1-2.

183. Idem.

184. *Eretz-Israel ha-Shlema*, Tel Aviv, no publisher, 1938, p. 7. Brodetsky's use of Jabotinsky's terms, even as only a rhetorical flourish, is striking.

185. *Arthur Ruppin: Memoirs, Diaries, Letters*, edited by Alex Bein, Jerusalem/London: Weidenfeld and Nicolson, 1971, pp. 283-286.

186. On the first meeting cf Protocol of a Secret Meeting with Representatives of the Yishuv's Parties, October 25, 1933, BGA. The press conference is cited verbatim in David Ben-Gurion, *Zihronot*, v. 1, p. 708.

187. Cf. Anita Shapiro: "The Concept of Time in the Partition Controversy of 1937," *Studies in Zionism*, vol. 6 #2 (Autumn, 1985), pp. 211-228.

Chapter 7

1. Shmuel Dothan: *Pulmus ha-Haluka be-Tekufat ha-Mandat*, Jerusalem: Yad Yitzhak Ben-Zvi, 1979, pp. 156-158.

2. Moshe Shertok's Office Diary, Friday, November 5, 1937, CZA A245/4, p. 5.

3. *AJYB* vol. 38 (1936/1937), pp. 324-345 and vol. 39 (1937/1938), pp. 393-397.

4. *AJYB*, vol. 39 (1937/1938), pp. 328 and 446-447.

5. *ha-Aretz*, Sunday, January 12, 1936, p. 1.

6. *AJYB*, vol. 39 (1937/1938), pp. 416-425.

7. While all the reports are too numerous to mention here, the items on antisemitism in Greece and Austria in *ha-Aretz*, (respectively) Wednesday, January 1, and Sunday, February 9, 1936 are fairly typical.

8. Rotenstreich to JAE, May 8, 1936, CZA S7/212.

9. Protocols of the JAE, February 7, 1937, CZA S100/21, p. 9/5232.

10. Protocols of the JAE, March 7, 1937, CZA S100/21, p. 8/5271.

11. Protocols of the JAE, March 23, 1937, CZA S100/21, pp. 3/5298-4/5299.

12. Cf. Jacob Lestchinsky, "The Anti-Jewish Program: Tsarist Russia, the Third Reich, and Independent Poland," *Jewish Social Studies*, vol. 3 #2 (April, 1941), pp. 141-158.

13. Lauterbach to Landauer, February 7, 1938, CZA S7/499.

14. Report on the Situation in Hungary, no date, CZA S7/212.

15. Nathaniel Katzburg, *Hungary and the Jews, 1920-1943*, Ramat Gan: Bar-Ilan University Press, 1981.

16. Cf. Ezra Mendelsohn, *On Modern Jewish Politics*, New York: Oxford University Press, 1994.

17. Cf. Robert M. Shapiro, *The Polish Kehile Elections of 1936: A Revolution Re-Examined*, Working Papers in Holocaust Studies #1, New York: Yeshiva University, 1988.

18. B. Johnpoll, *The Politics of Futility: The General Jewish Workers Bund of Poland, 1917-1939*, Ithaca, NY: Cornell University Press, 1967, pp. 216-220.

19. Simon Dubnow, *Nationalism and History*, edited by Koppel S. Pinson, Philadelphia, PA: JPS, 1958, pp. 155-191.

20. Ibid., pp. 354-360.

21. Shimon Huberband, *Kiddush Hashem: Jewish Religious and Cultural Life in Poland During the Holocaust*, Hoboken, NJ: Ktav, 1987, pp. 235-236. While it is possible that Huberband exaggerated the extent of wealth among orthodox Polish Jews, the exitsence of hundreds, not thousands, of wealthy orthodox Jews does not appreciably alter his observation, which is fundamentally correct. Rabbinic authorities (except those connected with Mizrachi) consistently opposed aliya. Cf. Gershon Greenberg: "Orthodox Theological Responses to Kristallnacht: Chayyim Ozer Grodzensky (Achiezer) and Elchonon Wassermann," *Holocaust and Genocide Studies*, vol. 3 #4 (1988): 431-441.

22. Karl Schleunes, *The Twisted Road to Auschwitz*, Urbana: University of Illinois Press, 1970, pp. 126-127.

23. Avraham Barkai, *From Boycott to Annihilation*, Waltham, MA: Brandeis University Press, 1990. pp. 122-123.

Notes

24. Karl A. Schleunes, *The Twisted Road to Auschwitz*, Urbana: University of Illinois Press, 1970, ch. 3-5.

25. See the documents and statistics cited in Jeremy Noakes and Geoffrey Pridham (eds.), *Documents on Nazism, 1919-1945*, New York: Viking, 1974, pp. 376-383.

26. D. Hart-Davis, *Hitler's Games: The 1936 Olympics*, New York: Harper and Row, 1986.

27. Scheme for Immigration of German Jews to Palestine, January 17, 1936, CZA S7/1068.

28. Brodetsky to JAE, January 2, 1936, CZA S44/158A; Statement by Mr. Lipsky, February 26, 1936, CZA S53/1589. Lipsky, however, expressed strong support for continuing Haavara, since (in his opinion) its impact on the anti-Nazi boycott movement in America was minimal.

29. Scheme for Immigration, p. 8.

30. Kaplan to Lipsky, January 9, 1936, CZA S44/158A, p. 2.

31. Ibid., p. 4.

32. Jevagency, Jerusalem, to Zionists, New York, January 26, 1936, CZA S44/460.

33. Report by the Reichsvertretung, 1936, CZA S25/9810.

34. Protocol of the Histadrut Executive, January 23, 1936, HIS M28.

35. Protocol of the Conference on the German Aliya, April 12, 1936, HIS IV/406/l/151, pp. 1-3.

36. Memorandum on the Jewish Emigration Bank, 1937, JIA G4/4/12/1.

37. Yaacov Shavit, *Jabotinsky and the Revisionist Movement*, London: Frank Cass, 1988, pp. 199-200. Shavit argues that some form of capital transfer was inherent to the evacuation plan from its inception. Given the nature of the documentation, however, such a hypothesis cannot presently be fully sustained.

38. Landauer to Wise, November 8, 1936, CZA S25/9810.

39. Proposal by INTRIA, January 12, 1937, CZA S49/378.

40. Circular from the Jewish Central Information Office, December 4, 1937, YVS P/20.

41. Landauer to Wise, loc cit; "Some Arguments Against the Support of the Plan for the Transfer of Jews from Germany," no date, YVS P/20. Though unsigned this document appears to have been written by Horace Kallen.

42. Undated draft for a speech on the Transfer Proposal, YVS P/20.

43. Feilchenfeld and Moses to Senator, March 18, 1937, CZA S49/378.

44. In December 1938 Schacht began a series of negotiations with George Rublee, a representative of the Inter-Governmental Committee on Refugees over the orderly transfer of German Jewry after a large financial payment by American- and Anglo-Jewish financiers. Despite intense opposition by American Jewish organizations the talks continued until June 1939, when an agreement was signed by Helmut Wohlthat (who replaced Schacht) and Hugh Wilson (who replaced Rublee), but the outbreak of World War II prevented

the agreement from ever being carried out. Cf. Henry L. Feingold, *The Politics of Rescue*, Rutgers, NJ: Rutgers University Press, 1970, pp. 49-64.

45. Senator to Mills, May 24, 1937, CZA S25/2512.

46. William Perl, *The Four Front War*, New York: Crown, 1979. ch. 1; Chaim Lazar (Litai), *Af-Al-Pi*, Tel Aviv: Hadar Publications, 1957, ch 10-14.

47. Yitzhak Avneri, ha-Histadrut ha-Zionit ve-ha-Aliya ha-Bilti Legalit le-Eretz Israel, Unpublished Doctoral Dissertation: Tel Aviv University, 1981, pp. 157-160.

48. Ibid., p. 161.

49. Ben-Nahum to Political Department, April 16, 1937, CZA S25/2651. Ben-Nahum was one of the code names used by Shaul Avigur, the founder of the Mossad le-Aliya Bet.

50. Shertok to Herzog, no date, CZA S25/2651.

51. Avneri, ha-Histadrut ha-Zionit, pp. 161-164.

52. Ehud Avriel, *Open the Gates!* New York: Atheneum, 1970, Part 1; Dalia Ofer, *Escaping the Holocaust*, New York: Oxford University Press, 1990, pp. 11-20. The statistical data is cited from Abraham J. Edelheit and Hershel Edelheit, *History of the Holocaust: A Handbook and Dictionary*, Boulder, CO: Westview Press, 1994, p. 181.

53. Avriel, *Open the Gates*, p. 31. Not all of the private haapala organizers were Zionists; in fact, not all were Jews. They were, however, united by a desire to reap massive profits from the suffering of hapless Jewish refugees.

54. Ofer, *Escaping the Holocaust*, p. 73.

55. Protocols of the JAE, February 7, 1937, CZA S100/21, pp. 10/5233-12/5235.

56. Protocols of the JAE, March 23, 1937, CZA S100/21, p. 2/5297.

57. *ha-Aretz*, Friday, February 12, 1937, p. 1. No complete study exists on the Jewish State Party, as of this writing, but the party's orientation may be summarized thus: opposition to partition, limited support for havlaga. Insofar as the JSP remained a Revisionist party, it viewed its role in the WZO as that of a "loyal opposition." Cf. Baruch Ben-Avram (ed.), *Miflegot u-Zramim Politiim be-Tekufat ha-Bayit he-Leumi, 1918-1948*, Jerusalem: The Zalman Shazar Center Press, 1978, p. 160.

58. Protocols of the JAE, op cit, pp. 5/5300-8/5303.

59. Joseph Scechtman, *The Life and Times of Vladimir Jabotinsky*, New York: Thomas Yoseloff, 1961, vol. 2, pp. 276-277.

60. Ibid., pp. 374-376.

61. Protocol of the NZO Political Department, May 29, 1937, JIA G4/1/2.

62. Benjamin Akzin, *me-Riga li-Yerushalayim — Pirke Zichronot*, Jerusalem: The Zionist Library, 1989, pp. 286-287.

63. Ben-Gurion's Diary, July 16, 1937, BGA.

64. Jabotinsky to Haskel, August 9, 1938; Jabotinsky to Jacobi, August 22, 1938, JIA A1/2/28/1

65. Press Release, Presidency of the NZO, June 29, 1937, JIA G4/3/1.

66. Joint Letter by the NZO and Agudas Israel, July 22, 1937, JIA G4/3/1.

67. Ha-Zach Nessiut Resolutions, July 21, 1937, JIA G4/l/2, pp. 1-3.

68. Ibid., p. 4.

69. Howard I. Rosenblum, A Political History of Revisionist Zionism, 1925-1938, Unpublished Doctoral Dissertation: Columbia University, 1986, pp. 358, 369.

70. Protocols of the JAE, March 25, 1937, CZA S100/21, pp. 3/5307-7/5311.

71. "On Aliya Questions," Mapai Central Committee Newsletter, November 2, 1937, HIS IV/406/1/157, p. 6.

72. Idem. Cf. David Ben-Gurion, *Zichronot*, Tel Aviv: Am Oved, 1976, vol 4, p. 181

73. M. Sharett, *Yoman Medini*, Tel Aviv: Am Oved, 1971, vol. 2, pp. 55, 329.

74. Chief Secretary to Herzog, June 11, 1937, CZA S25/2651.

75. Wauchope to Herzog, June 12, 1937, CZA S25/2651.

76. Shertok to Aliya Department, July 16, 1937, CZA S25/2651.

77. Protocols of the JAE, August 8, 1937, CZA S100/22, p. 1/5484.

78. Avneri, ha-Histadrut ha-Zionit, p. 168.

79. Becher to Joseph, August 16, 1937, CZA S25/2651.

80. Idem. Based on the handwriting, I believe that this minute was written by Shertok.

81. T. Norman, *An Outstretched Arm: A History of the Jewish Colonization Association*, London: Routledge and Kegan Paul, 1985, pp. 152-154.

82. Histadrut Executive to Ben-Gurion, August 8, 1937, HIS IV/208/l/368A.

83. Protocols of the Temporary JAE, September 8, 1937, CZA S100/22, pp. 1/5489-2/5490. Although the Executive was considered "temporary" (for the duration of the twentieth World Zionist Congress) it was empowered to act in the JAE's name. Shertok and Kaplan — two members of the JAE — attended its meetings. Regarding Zionist assessments of the European Jewish situation in the summer of 1937, see Anita Shapira: "Did the Zionist Leadership Foresee the Holocaust?" in J. Reinharz (ed.), *Living with Antisemitism: Modem Jewish Responses*, Hanover, NH: University Presses of New England, 1987, pp. 397-412.

84. Protocols of the JAE, September 25, 1937, CZA S100/22, p. 3/5496.

85. Ibid., pp. 4/5497-5/5498.

86. Report of a Conversation with the Polish Foreign Minister, Colonel Beck, September 12, 1937, CZA L22/390.

87. Protocols of the JAE, October 3, 1937, CZA S100/22, pp. 4/5503-5/5504.

88. Protocols of the JAE, October 20, 1937, CZA S100/22, pp. 1/5528-3/5530.

89. Ibid., p. 2/5529.

90. "On Aliya Ouestions," loc cit.

91. *Davar*, Friday, October 22, 1937, p. 1.

92. Moshe Shertok's Office Diary, Monday October 25, 1937, CZA A245/4, P. 1.

93. William Ziff, *The Rape of Palestine*, New York: Longman, Green and Company, 1938, pp. 336-337.

94. Herzog to Shertok, Heshvan 13, 5698 (= October 18, 1937), CZA S25/2651.

95. Shertok to Herzog, October 24, 1937, CZA S25/2651.

96. Herzog to Shertok, Heshvan 29, 5698 (= November 3, 1937), CZA S25/2651.

97. Herzog to Shertok, Kislev 13, 5698 (= November 17, 1937), CZA S25/2651.

98. Irgun Olim Bilti Legaliim to JA Aliya Department, November 18, 1937; Irgun Olim Bilti Legaliim to JAE, November 18, 1937, CZA S25/2651.

99. "On Aliya Questions," p. 7.

100. Protocols of the JAE, October 31, 1937, CZA S100/22, p.4/5541.

101. Ibid., pp. 5/5542-6/5543.

102. Ibid., p. 7/5544.

103. Ibid., p. 8/5545.

104. Note of a Conversation with Mills, November 5, 1937, CZA A245/4, pp. 1-2.

105. Ibid., p. 4.

106. Protocols of the JAE, November 14, 1937, CZA S100/22, p. 1/5565.

107. Aharon Kleiman, *Hipared oh Mishol — Mediniut Btitania ve-Halukat Eretz Israel, 1936-1939*, Jerusalem: Yad Yitzhak Ben-Zvi, 1983, pp. 106-109.

108. Protocols of the JAE, November 14, 1937, CZA S100/22, p. 1/5565.

109. *ha-Aretz*, Tuesday, September 28, 1937, p. 1 and Wednesday, September 29, 1937, pp. 1-2.

110. Zeev Jabotinsky, "Ba-Kav ha-Hitnagdut ha-Kala be-Yoter," in Yaakov Shavit (ed.): *"Havlaga" oh Teguva?* Ramat-Gan: Bar-Ilan University Press, 1983, pp. 97-98.

111. David Raziel, "Nagola Herpat ha-Havlaga," in Shavit, *"Havlaga"*, pp. 99-100.

112. Moshe Shertok's Office Diary, Tuesday, November 16, 1937, CZA A245/4, p. 1.

113. Ibid., Saturday, November 13, 1937, p. 1, and Tuesday November 16, 1937, p. 1, CZA A245/4.

114. Ibid., Tuesday, November 16, 1937, CZA A245/4, p. 2.

115. Ibid., Tuesday, November 23, 1937, CZA A245/4, p. 1.

116. Protocols of the JAE, December 19, 1937, CZA S100/22, pp. 4/5628-7/5631.

117. Lustig to Landauer, December 22, 1937, CZA S7/502.

118. Shertok to JAE, December 22, 1937, CZA S100/22, p. 1/5636.

119. Gruenbaum to Kleinbaum, December 26, 1937; "Supplement to *Hamedina*," no date. CZA S44/69B.

Chapter 8

1. Petition for the Democratisation (sic) of the Jewish Agency Submitted on Behalf of the Presidency of the New Zionist Organization, January, 1938, JIA G4/1/5, pp. 1-2.

2. Ibid., pp. 1, 5-6.

3. Ibid., p. 8. The exact figures cited were: 650,000 for the 19th Zionist Congress and 713,000 for the NZO. For their part the JAE leaders rejected such statements uncategorically and declared the Revisionists to be the minority party.

4. Ibid., p. 9. The Authors quote a May 15, 1936 letter by Werner D. Senator to prove their assertion, but do not explicitly name the guilty party.

5. Ibid., p. 10.

6. Ibid., p. 1.

7. Ibid., pp. 1-5.

8. Brodetsky to Kleinbaum, January 3, 1938; Brodetsky to Ben-Gurion, January 3, 1938, CZA S44/69B.

9. Note on a Converstion with Dr. Akzin, December 9, 1937, BGA Protocols. Interestingly, Akzin does not mention these talks in his memoirs.

10. Protocols of the JAE, January 2, 1938, CZA S100/23, p. 12/5675.

11. Protocol of a meeting with Representatives of the Va'ad Leumi and Agudas Israel, February 14, 1938, CZA S25/10109.

12. Ibid., p. 11/5674.

13. Protocols of the JAE, January 16, 1938, CZA S100/23, p. 11/5692.

14. Protocols of the JAE, January 24, 1938, CZA S100/23, p. 1/5714. In August 1941, the Romanians created such a reservation in Transnistria, in Romanian-occupied Soviet territory. By the summer of 1942 nearly 500,000 Jews were deported to Transnistria, where 250,000 were systematically starved, worked, or shot to death. Cf. Abraham J. Edelheit and Hershel Edelheit, *History of the Holocaust: A Handbook and Dictionary*, Boulder, CO: Westview Press, 1994, pp. 83-84.

15. Protocols of the JAE, op cit, pp. 1/5714-2/5715.

16. Ibid., p. 2/5715.

17. Ibid., pp. 3/5716-4/5717.

18. Ibid., p. 4/5717.

19. Protocols of the JAE, February 2, 1938, CZA S100/23, pp. 11/5738-12/5739.

20. Histadrut Cultural Committee to Landauer, January 18, 1938, HIS IV/208/1/1208.

21. Protocol of the Histadrut Executive, March 31, 1938, HIS M34, pp. 2-4.

22. Protocols of the JAE, January 23, 1938, CZA S100/23, p. 1/5707-3/5709.

23. D. Gurevich (comp.): *Statistical Handbook of Jewish Palestine.* Jerusalem: The Jewish Agency, 1947, p. 103; Francis Nicosia: *The Third Reich and the Palestine Question*, Austin: Texas University Press, 1985, pp. 212-213.

24. *Palnews Palestine Economic Annual*, v. 4 (1938), pp. 105-107.

25. Protocols of the JAE, February 27, 1938, CZA S100/23, p. 13/5799.

26. Hexter to Senator, March 16, 1938, CZA S49/265.

27. Ben-Gurion's Diary, January 3, 1938, BGA.

28. Ben-Gurion's Diary, February 20, 1938, BGA.

29. Moshe Shertok's Office Diary, Tuesday, March 1, 1938, CZA A245/6, p. 2.

30. Senator to Alya Department, March 7, 1938, CZA S49/265.

31. Moshe Shertok's Office Diary, op cit, p. 6.

32. Protocols of the JAE, March 6, 1938, CZA S100/23, pp. 3/5802-4/5805.

33. Cf. B. Z. Pinot, "Hitler's Entry into Vienna," *Yad Vashem Bulletin*, # 3 (1958), pp. 15-16.

34. Cf. Herbert Rosenkranz, "Austrian Jewry: Between Forced Emigration and Deportation," in Israel Gutman and Cynthia J. Heft (eds), *Patterns of Jewish Leadership in Nazi Europe, 1933-1945*, Jerusalem: Yad Vashem, 1979, pp. 65-74.

35. Protocol of a meeting with the High Commissioner, March 24, 1938, BGA Protocols.

36. Bernay and Zweig to MacMichael, June 15, 1938, CZA S7/513.

37. Protocols of the JAE, April 3, 1938, CZA S100/23, p. 11/5814.

38. Ibid., pp. 1/5804-7/5810.

39. Jabotinsky to McDonald, no date, JIA Al/2/28. A note in Jabotinsky's correspondence file places this letter in 1938 but offers no more specifics. It should be noted that McDonald, at this point, was a private citizen, having resigned as League of Nations High Commissioner for Refugees in 1935.

40. Zweig to Samuel, March 15, 1938, CZA S7/513.

41. Samuel to Weizmann, April 10, 1938, CZA S25/9713.

42. HOA Executive to JAE, June 10, 1938, CZA S7/513.

43. Cf. *ha-Aretz* Sunday May 1, 1938 (on Hungary), Monday, May 2, p. 1 (on Poland), and Tuesday, May 3, p. I and that day's Evening Supplement, p. 1 (on Vienna). Similar reports were contained in all of the other dailies.

44. Protocols of the JAE, May 8, 1938, CZA S100/23, p. 3/5888,

45. Moshe Sharett, *Yoman Medini*, Tel Aviv: Am Oved, 1971, vol. 2, p. 255.

46. Protocols of the JAE, May 8, 1938, CZA S100/23, pp. 1/5896-2/5897.

47. *The Palestine Post*, Friday, May 20, 1938, p. 6.

48. Ibid., Sunday, May 22, 1938, p. 8.

49. Protocols of the JAE, June t 1938, CZA S100/24, p. 4/5959.

50. Ibid., pp. 5/5960 and 8/5963.

51. Ibid, pp. 4/5959-5/5960. Goldmann was appointed a member of the London JAE in 1935 even though his post was in Geneva. He represented the American Zionists primarily as a result of his involvement with the World Jewish Congress.

52. Ibid., pp. 6/5961-7/5962.

53. Ibid., p. 8/5963.

54. Moshe Shertok's Office Diary, Sunday, July 17, 1938, p. 15.

55. Protocol of a Special JAE Meeting on Youth Aliya, July 18, 1938, CZA S44/95.

56. Moshe Sherotk's Office Diary, op cit, pp. 16-17.

57. Summary of Speeches at a Betar Meeting, May 7, 1938, CZA S44/275.

58. Organization Department to JAE, July 7, 1938, CZA S44/275.

59. NZO to Jevagency, Jerusalem, July 5, 1938, JIA G4/3/1.

60. Circular letter by Jabotinsky, addressed to South African Zionists, no date, JIA A1/2/28.

61. Jabotinsky to Briscoe, July 17, 1938 and Jabotinsky to Haskel, July 18, 1938, JIA A1/2/28.

62. Organization Departmcnt to JAE, July 8, 1938, CZA S44/275.

63. Breuer to Shertok, July 7, 1938, CZA S44/69B.

64. Shabetai Teveth, *Ben-Gurion: The Burning Ground*, Boston: Houghton, Mifflin Company, 1987, pp. 491-492.

65. The text of the agreement is reprinted in Eli Tavin et al (eds): *ha-Irgun ha-Zvai ha-Leumi be-Eretz-Israel: Osef Mekorot u-Mismachim*, Tel Aviv: The Jabotinsky Institute, 1990, vol. 1, pp. 454-457.

66. Ben-Gurion to Golomb, September 20, 1938, BGA Letters.

67. Ben-Gurion to Ussishkin, September 24, 1938; Ben-Gurion to Shertok, September 29, 1938, BGA Letters.

68. David Ben-Gurion's Diary, September 30, 1938, BGA.

69. Ben-Gurion's Diary, October 30, 1938, BGA.

70. Jacobi to Ben-Gurion, October 7, 1938, JIA G4/3/1.

71. Ben-Gurion to Jacobi, October 7, 1938, JIA G4/3/1.

72. Ben-Gurion to Jacobi, October 10, 1938, JIA G4/3/1, p. 2.

73. Idem.

74. Ibid., p. 3.

75. Jacobi to Ben-Gurion, October 16, 1938, JIA G4/3/1.

76. Howard I. Rosenblum, A Political History of Revisionist Zionism, Unpublished Doctoral Dissertation: Columbia University, 1986, p. 404, citing letters from to Leo Lauterbach and other JAE members.

77. Ibid., p. 403.

78. Protocols of the Histadrut Executive, October 20, 1938, HIS M35.

79. "The Political Problem and the Question of Security," address at a meeting of the Yishuv's representatives, September 6, 1938. Mimeographed copy, CZA G33245, p. 2.

80. Ibid., p. 4.

81. David Ben-Gurion, *Zichronot*, Tel Aviv: Am Oved, 1982, vol. 5, edited by Gershon Rivlin, p. 242. Wingate was a British Army Captain who came to Palestine in 1936 and became a close advisor on de-fense matters to the Zionists. He was universally known within the Hagana and the JAE as "ha-Yedid" (the friend).

82. "Security Situation, op cit, pp. 3-4.

83. Ibid., pp. 4-5.

84. Ibid., p. 5.

85. Ibid, p. 6.

86. Ibid., pp. 10-12.

87. Ibid., p. 13.

88. Shhmo Lev-Ami, *Ba-Maavak u-ba-Mered*, Tel Aviv: Maarachot/The IDF Press, N.D., p. 61.

89. "Security Situation," op cit, p. 13.

90. Yaacov Shavit (ed.), *"Havlaga" oh Teguva*, Ramat Gan, Israel: Bar-Ilan University Press, 1983, pp. 105-107.

91. David Niv, *Maarachot ha-Irgun ha-Zvai ha-Leumi*, Tel Aviv: The Klausner Institute Press, 1965, v. 2, p. 66-70.

92. Jabotinsky to Washitz, July 5, 1938, Cited in Tavin, *ha-Irgun*, pp. 32-33.

93. M. Shertok's Office Diary, Thursday, June 23, 1938, CZA A245/6, p. 3.

94. Ibid., Friday, June 24, 1938, pp. 4-6.

95. Ibid., Saturday, June 25, 1938, pp. 6-7.

96. Ibid., p. 9.

97. Niv, *Maarachot*, pp. 71-74.

98. Memorandum of the IZL High Command to the Va'ad Leumi, July 10, 1938, JIA K4/19/2, p. 3.

99. Statement on Partition, December 27, 1937, CZA S25/3614; *Palestine Partition Commission, Report*, London: HMSO, 1938, ch.1.

100. Weizmann to Dugdale, May 14,1938, Weizmann: *Letters*, v. 18, pp. 387-390.

101. *Partition Commission*, p. 114.

102. Ibid., p. 228.

103. Ibid., pp. 114-115.

104. Ibid, pp. 254-255. *The Palestine Post*, Monday, June 20, 1938, p. 6.

105. Moshe Shertok's Office Diary, Thursday, June 23, 1938, CZA A245/6, p. 2.

106. Memorandum of Evidence Placed before the Palestine Partition Commission by the New Zionist Organization, June 1938, JIA G4/1/5, pp. 2-4. Cf. *The Palestine Post*, Tuesday, June 21, 1938, p. 2.

107. Memorandum, op cit, pp. 5-11.

108. Ibid., p. 11.

109. Ibid., pp. 1-2, *Palestine Post,* loc cit.

110. Sharett, *Yoman Medini*, v. 3, pp. 177, 205-206.

111. Memorandum on the International Conference on Jewish Migration, April, 1938, JIA G4/l/5, p. 1.

112. Ibid., pp. 3-4.

113. On Revisionist strategy in 1938 see, Chanoch (Howard) Rosenblum, "The New Zionist Organization's American Campaign, 1936-1939," *Studies in Zionism*, vol. 12 #2 (Autumn, 1991), pp. 170-172.

114. Abraham J. Edelheit and Hershel Edelheit, *History of the Holocaust. A Handbook and Dictionary*, Boulder, CO: Westview Press, 1994, pp. 129, 212.

115. *The Palestine Post*, Wednesday, June 8, 1938, p. 6.

116. Zioniburo, London, to Ben-Gurion, June 18, 1938; Hadassah to Jevagency, Jerusalem, June 23, 1938; Zioniburo, London, to Shertok, June 30, 1938; Goldmann to Ruppin, June 20, 1938; and Memorandum Submitted to the Evian Conference on Political Refugees, July 6, 1938, CZA S46/502.

117. Jabotinsky to Briscoe, June 24, 1938, JIA Al/2/28.

118. Protocols of the JAE, June 26, 1938, CZA S100/24, pp. 3/6053-4/6054.

119. Ibid., p. 7/6057.

120. Ibid., p. 9/6059. The San Remo conference confirmed the Balfour Declaration and granted the Mandate for Palestine to Great Britain.

121. Idem.

122. Note on an Interview with Lord Winterton, signed W(eizmann), June 24, 1938, CZA S46/502.

123. Memorandum, op cit, pp. 6-7.

124. Memorandum of Several Jewish Organizations on the Emigration of Refugees from Germany and Austria for the Evian Conference, no date; and the Memorandum of the World Jewish Congress to the Evian Conference, July 6, 1938, CZA L22/379. I am grateful to Professor Francis Nicosia for bringing these documents to my attention.

125. Golda Meir: *My Life*, New York: Putnam's, 1975, p. 158. In 1938, Meir held the post of Secretary of the Histadrut.

126. *Arthur Ruppin: Memoirs, Diaries, Letters*, edited by Alex Bein, Tel Aviv: Weidenfeld and Nicolson, 1971, p. 294.

127. Protocols of the JAE, August 21, 1938, CZA S100/24, p. 7/6138.

128. Idem.

129. Ibid., p. 8/6139.

130. Protocols of the JAE, August 14, 1938, CZA S 100/24, pp. 2/6127-4/6129.

131. Protocols of the JAE, September 4, 1938, CZA S100/24, pp. 4/6150-6/6152.

132. Idem.

133. Notes of a Conversation with the High Commissioner, September 22, 1938, CZAS25/21.

134. Nicosia, *Third Reich*, p. 144

135. Deborah Lipstadt: *Beyond Beleif*, New York: Free Press, 1986, p. 96.

136. Alfred A. Häsler, *The Lifeboat is Full: Switzerland and the Refugees, 1933-1945*, New York: Funk and Wagnalls, 1969, pp. 28-29. Emphasis added.

137. David Ben-Gurion's Diary, August 31, 1938, BGA.

138. Ben-Gurion's Diary, September 13 and 14, 1938, BGA.

139. David Ben-Gurion, *Letters to Paula*, Pittsburgh: University of Pittsburgh Press, 1971, pp. 183-184.

140. A transcript of the speech is contained in an entry in Ben-Gurion's Diary for September 29, 1938, BGA. To my knowledge, this is the first time a Labor Zionist leader spoke of the need for a Jewish army in such an explicit fashion.

141. Ben-Gurion's Diary, September 30, 1938, BGA.

142. Ben-Gurion to Ben-Zvi, October 1, 1938, Ben-Gurion to JAE, October 21, 1938, BGA Letters.

143. Ben-Gurion's Diary, October 21, 1938, BGA.

144. Minutes of a meeting with Lord Lloyd, October 25, 1938, p. 4, BGA Protocols. Emphasis in original.

145. Protocols of the JAE, September 28, 1938, CZA S100/25, pp. 1/6188-2/6189.

146. Ibid., p. 2/6189.

147. Protocols of the JAE, October 2, 1938, CZA S100/25, p. 5/6194.

148. Idem.

149. Ibid., pp. 5/6194-7/6196.

150. Protocols of the JAE, October 4, 1938, CZA S100/25, p. 2/6198.

151. Protocols of the JAE, October 7, 1938, CZA S100/25.

152. Zeev Jabotinsky: "Mul Tochnit ha-Haluka — Tochnit ha-Asor," *Neumim 1927-1940*, Jerusalem: Eri Jabotinsky, 1948, p. 292.

153. Zeev Jabotinsky: "'Zion-Sejm' le-Hazala Azmit," Ibid., pp. 329-340.

154. Zeev Jabotinsky: "La-Mut oh Lichbosh et ha-har," Ibid., p. 306.

155. Ibid., pp. 305-326.

156. Protocols of the JAE, October 18, 1938, CZA S 10/25, pp. 6/6232-9/6235.

157. Yitzhak Avneri, Ha-Histadrut ha-Zionit ve-ha-Aliya ha-Bilti Legalit le-Eretz Israel, Unpublished Doctoral Dissertation: Tel Aviv University, 1979, pp. 177-179.

158. Dalia Ofer, *Escaping the Holocaust*, New York: Oxford University Press, 1990, pp. 11-17.

159. *The Palestine Post*, Monday, June 6, 1938, p. 1, offers details of one typical case.

160. Herzog to Shetok March 25, 1938, CZA S25/2651.

161. Shertok to Herzog, March 31, 1938, CZA S25/2651.

162. "Zaaka la-Zibur," May 1, 1938, CZA S25/2651

163. Herzog to Shertok, May 2, 1938, CZA S25/2651.

164. Shertok to Mills, May 13, 1938, CZA S25/2651.

165. Mills to Shertok, May 18, 1939, CZA S25/2651.

166. Protocols of the JAE, July 24, 1938, CZA S100/24, p. 8/6104.

167. Anonymous Telegram to the Hagana, June 28/29, 1938, ATH 14/342.

168. Anonymous Telegram to the Hagana, June 29, 1938, ATH 14/342.

169. Report by Sharoni, July 3, 1938, ATH 14/342.

170. Between March and December 1944 the Mossad and Af-Al-Pi collaborated on ten sailings. The ships sailed to Turkey where the ma'apilim disembarked. They then continued to Palestine on foot and entered legally. Cf. Ofer, *Escaping the Holocaust*, pp. 250-253.

171. Stephany to NZO, July 26, 1938, JIA G4/4/12.

172. Abrahams to Stephany, July 28, 1938, JIA G4/4/12/2.

173. Herzog to Shertok, July 6, 1938, CZA S25/2651.

174. Shertok to Herzog, July 10, 1938, CZA S25/2651.

Chapter 9

1. Protocols of the JAE, November 6, 1938, CZA S100/253, p. 1/6282.

2. Idem. See also Eli Tavin et al (eds.), *ha-Irgun ha-Zvai ha-Leumi be-Eretz Israel: Osef Mikorot u-Mismachim*, Tel Aviv: Jabotinsky Institute Press, 1990, pp. 457-466.

3. Karl A. Schleunes, *The Twisted Road to Auschwitz*, Urbana: University of Illinois Press, 1970, ch. 7-8.

4. *Jewish Agency Report*, 1939, p. 29.

5. *ha-Aretz*, Thursday, November 10, 1938, p. 1, and November 10, 1938 Evening Supplement, pp. 1-2. Cf. Joseph Heller (ed.), *Ba-Maavak la-Medina: ha-Mediniut ha-Zionit ba-Shanim 1936-1948*, Jerusalem: The Zalman Shazar Institute, 1984, p. 29.

6. *Palestine Partition Commission Report* (London: HMSO, 1938), pp. 232-247.

7. Heller, *ba-Maavak*, p. 30.

8. Allon Gal, *David Ben-Gurion: Likrat Medina Yehudit*, Sde-Boker: Ben-Gurion University of the Negev Press, 1985, p. 11.

9. *The Palestine Post*, Sunday, November 13, 1938, p. 1, Thursday, November 17, 1938, p. 3, and Tuesday, November 22, 1938, p. 3.

10. *The Palestine Post*, Thursday, November 3, 1938, p. 3, Sunday, November 13, 1938, p. 5, Tuesday, November 15, 1938, p. 6, and Tuesday, November 22, 1938, p. 1.

11. *The Palestine Post*, Monday, November 14, 1938, p. 6.

12. Ibid., Friday November 11, 1938, p. 8; *ha-Aretz*, Thursday, November 10, 1938, p. 2.

13. *ha-Aretz*, loc cit.

14. *Davar*, Wednesday, November 9, 1938, p. 1.

15. *ha-Aretz*, Friday, November 11, 1938, Evening Supplement, p. 2.

16. *Davar*, Sunday, November 13, 1938, p. 1.

17. *ha-Aretz*, Tuesday, November 15, 1938, p. 2.

18. Szold to Senator, December 18, 1938, CZA S7/699.

19. Ben-Gurion's Diary, entry for November 21, 1938, BGA. Cf. Tuvia Friling, "Ben-Gurion and the Holocaust of European Jewry 1939-1945: A Stereotype Reexamined," *Yad Vashem Studies*, vol. 18 (1987), pp. 199-232.

20. Gal, *Likrat*, p. 33.

21. Protocols of the JAE, November 13, 1938, CZA S 100/25, p. 3/6292.

22. Ibid., p. 4/6293.

23. Ibid., p. 5/6294.

24. Ibid., p. 6/6295.

25. Statement by the JAE, November 22, 1938, CZA S25/2519.

26. *Davar*, Wednesday, November 16, 1938, p. 1.

27. Cohen to Executive, November 15, 1938, CZA S25/9809.

28. Rosenblueth to Ben-Gurion, November 18, 1938, CZA S25/9809.

29. Chanoch (Howard) Rosenblum: "The News Zionist Organization's American Campaign, 1936-1939," *Studies in Zionism*, vol. 12 # 2 (Autumn, 1991), pp. 177-179.

30. Robert Briscoe, *For the Life of Me,* London: Longman's Associates, 1958, pp. 263-276.

31. Ben-Gurion to Frumkin, November 17, 1938, CZA S25/9713.

32. Protocols of the JAE (London), November 17, 1938, CZA S100/25, p. 1/6300.

33. Ibid., p. 6/6305.

34. Ibid., pp. 6/6305-7/6306.

35. Shertok to MacDonald, November 23, 1938, CZA S25/2519.

36. Joseph to Shertok, November 23, 1938, CZA S25/2499.

37. Landauer to Ruppin, November 27, 1938, CZA S25/2499.

38. Becher to Cohen, November 28, 1938, CZA S25/2499.

39. *ha-Aretz*, Monday, November 14, 1938, pp. 1, 8.

40. *ha-Aretz*, Thursday, November 17, 1938, p. 1.

41. Cf. *ha-Aretz*, Sunday, November 20, 1938, p. 1, Monday, November 21, 1938, pp. 1-2.

42. *The Palestine Post*, Friday, November 18, 1938, p. 2 and Sunday, November 20, 1938, p. 8.

43. *The Palestine Post*, Sunday, November 20, 1938, p. 8.

44. *Davar*, Friday, November 18, 1938, p. 1.

45. Ibid., Sunday, November 20, 1938, p. 1.

46. Mills to JAE, December 6, 1938, CZA S25/2499.

47. Samuel to JAE, December 12, 1938, CZA S25/2499.

48. Protocols of the JAE, December 11, 1938, CZA S100/25, p. 1/6320.

49. Protocols of the JAE, December 18,1938, CZA S100/25, p. 2/6341.

50. Joseph to Mills, December 19, 1938, CZA S25/2499, pp. 1-2.

51. Ibid., pp. 2-4; Szold to Political Department, January 1, 1939, CZA S44/95.

52. Protocols of the JAE, January 1, 1939, Afternoon Session, CZA S100/25, p. 3/6383.

53. Senator to Joseph, January 4, 1939, CZA S25/9713.

54. Joan Dash, *Summoned to Jerusalem*, New York: Harper and Row, 1979, pp. 269, 273-274.

55. Yoav Gelber, "The Origins of Youth Aliya," *Studies in Zionism*, v. 9 #2 (Autumn, 1988), pp. 168-169.

56. Ben-Gurion to Frumkin, November 17, 1938, CZA S25/9713.

57. *ha-Aretz*, Tuesday, November 22, 1938, p. 1.

58. Cf. *Davar*, Tuesday, November 1, 1938, p. 1 (on protests in America and Argentina), and *ha-Aretz*, Sunday, November 13, 1938, p. 1 (on England).

59. *ha-Aretz*, Tuesday, November 22, 1938, p. 2.

60. David Ben-Gurion, *Zichronot*, vol. 6, edited by M. Avizohar, Beersheba: Ben-Gurion University Press, 1987, p. 62.

61. Discussion on the All-Jewish World Conference in America, January 11, 1939, BGA Protocols.

62. Cf. David Shpiro, Tahalichei Binyanya shel Moezet ha-Herum ha-Zionit ki-Zeroa ha-Peula ha-Ziburit-Medinit shel ha-Zionut ha-Amerikait, 1938-1944, Unpublished Doctoral Dissertation: Hebrew University, 1979, pp. 39-46.

63. In 1941 this unit adopted the name "Gideonites" and operated as a phantom radio network until 1949. Cf. Gabi Sarig, *Ha-Gid'onim be-Oniyot ha-Haapala*, Ramat Efal: Yad Yitzhak Tabenkin, 1988, p. 25.

64. Ibid., pp. 27-34. Sarig also includes the Af-Al-Pi ships in his review but admits that he could not uncover details about their communications system.

65. Report by Mrs. Schmolka, Novemebr 27, 1938, CZA S7/752.

66. Schwartz to JAE, Adar 11, 5699 (= March 2, 1939), CZA S7/752.

67. Ruppin to Rosenblueth, November 17, 1938, CZA S25/9713.

68. Ben-Gurion, *Zichronot*, p. 395.

69. Cf. Arthur D. Morse, *While Six Million Died*, New York: Hart Publishing, 1967, chapter 7.

70. Aharon Kleiman: *Hipared oh Mishol — Mediniut Btitania ve-Halukat Eretz Israel, 1936-1939*, Jerusalem: Yad Yitzhak Ben-Zvi, 1983, p. 110.

71. Protocols of the JAE, Deccmbcr 18, 1938, CZA S100/25, p. 2/6341.

72. Protocols of the JAE, December 11, 1938, CZA S100/25, p. 12/6334.

73. Declaration By Mizrachi, Kislev 21, 5699 (= December 14, 1938), CZA S25/7627.

74. Protocols of the JAE, December 11, 1938, CZA S100/25, p. 13/6332.

75. Shertok to JAE, January 20, 1939, CZA S25/7627.

76. Idem.

77. Protocols of the JAE, December 11, 1938, CZA S100/25, p. 2/6321.

78. Ibid., pp. 2/6321-3/6322.

79. Ibid., p. 3/6322.

80. Ibid., pp. 3/6322-4/6323.

81. Protocol of the Ha-Zach Nessiut, March 29, 1939, JIA G4/l/2. The specific topic of this meeting was the calling of a "Zion-Sejm" to rescue Eastern European Jewry, however, as noted above Ha-Zach's territorialist position was more of a smokescreen than a realistic approach.

82. Protocols of the JAE, op cit, p. 4/6323.

83. Ibid., p. 5/6324, emphasis in the original.

84. Idem.

85. Ibid., p. 9/6328. Cf. Chaim Simons, *International Proposals to Transfer Arabs from Palestine, 1895-1947*, Hoboken, NJ: Ktav, 1988, pp. 9-17.

86. Protocols of the JAE, op cit, pp. 12/6331-13/6332.

87. Ibid., p. 16/6335.

88. Ibid., p. 18/6337.

89. Ben-Gurion to Va'ad ha-Poel ha-Zioni, December 17, 1938, CZA S25/7627.

90. Howard I. Rosenblum, A Political History of Revisionist Zionism, 1925-1938, Unpublished Doctoral Dissertation: Columbia University, 1986, p. 403.

91. Protocols of the JAE, December 18, 1938, CZA S100/25, pp. 3/6342-4/6343, 8/6347.

92. Protocols of the JAE, December 25, 1938, CZA S100/25, p. 11/6363.

93. Protocols of the JAE, January 22, 1939, CZA S100/26, pp. 14/6421-15/6422.

94. These representatives included both Zionists and non-Zionists. cf *AJYB*, v. 41 (1939/1940), p. 335.

95. Protocols of the London Executive, December 16, 1938, CZA S25/7627, pp. 1-5.

96. Ibid., pp. 5-6.

97. Protocls of the JAE, December 25, 1938, CZA S100/25, p. 11/6363.

98. Protocols of the JAE, January 8, 1939, CZA S100/26, p. 11/6389.

99. Ibid., pp. 7/6392-8/6393.

100. Protocols of the JAE, January 8, 1939, CZA S100/26, p. 11/6389; Zioniburo, London, to Jevagency, Jerusalem, January 25, 1939, CZA S25/7627.

101. Administrative Department to JAE, December 5, 1938, CZA S44/69B.

102. Ze'ev Jabotinsky: "'Zion-Sejm' le-Hazala Azmit," *Neumim, 1927-1940*, Jerusalem: Eri Jabotinsky, 1948, pp. 331-332.

103. Protocols of the JAE, December 18, 1938, CZA S100/25, p. 5/6344.

104. Protocols of the JAE, February 5, 1939, CZA S100/26, pp, 8/6443-9/6444.

105. Stenographic Protocol of the meeting at St. James's Palace, Wednesday, February 8, 1939, CZA S25/7630.

106. Stenographic Protocol, Friday, February 10, 1939, pp. 1-4.

107. Ibid., pp.1-2. A slightly different version of this speech is contained in Ben-Gurion, *Zichronot*, pp. 136-140.

108. Stenographic Protocol, p. 3.

109. Idem.

110. Ben-Gurion, *Zichronot*, p. 144-147.

111. Senator to JAE, February 7, 1939, CZA S25/3825, p. 1.

112. Ibid., p. 2.

113. Ibid., p. 3.

114. Ibid., p. 4.

115. Statement made by Mr. Shertok at meeting of the Palestine Conference, St. James's Palace, Monday, February 13, 1939, CZA G14626, p. 5.

116. Ibid., pp. 8-9.

117. Protocols of the JAE, February 26, 1939, CZA S100/26, pp. 2/6472-7/6477.

118 Mapai Central Committee Newsletter #145, March 23, 1939, CZA S25/47, pp. 7-8.

119. Ibid., p. 3.

120. Jabotinsky to Katznelson, November 29, 1938, JIA K6/3/1.

121. Protocol of the Betar Aliya Committee, February 6,1939, JIA K6/3/1.

122. Joseph Schechtman: *The Life and Times of Vladimir Jabotinsky*, New York: Thomas Yoseloff, 1961, vol. 2, pp. 423-424.

123. Expose on the Emigration of the Jews from Romania, January 15, 1939, JIA G4/4/12/2. It is not clear exactly how ROMPALIA intended to get access to Transfer funds, which were in the hands of the JAE. In general, the issue of the Rumanian Transfer agreement requires further study.

124. Presidium of the N.Z.O. in Romania to Director General of Police, Bucharest, January 17, 1939, JIA K6/3/2/1.

125. Constitutive Document of the Association of Organizing the Jewish Emigration from Romania (ROMPALIA), February 20, 1939, JIA K6/3/2/1.

126. Bookspan to Landauer, April 20, 1939, CZA S7/721.

127. Landauer to Bookspan, April 26, 1939, CZA S7/721.

128. Bookspan to Landauer, May 2, 1939, CZA S7/721.

129. Joseph to Mills, January 10, 1939, CZA S25/2512.

130. Mills to JAE, January 27, 1939, CZA S25/2512.

131. Protocols of the JAE, February 12, 1939, CZA S100/26, pp. 6/6452-8/6454.

132. Joseph to Aliya Department, February 2, 1939, CZA S25/2512.

133. Countries marked with an asterisk represent German refugee aliya.

134. Joseph to Aliya Department, op cit.

135. Joseph to Mills, February 3, 1939, CZA S25/2512.

136. Joseph to Battershill, February 9, 1939, CZA S25/2512.

137. Joseph to Shertok, February 19, 1939, CZA S25/2512.

138. Protocols of the Histadrut Executive, March 16, 1939, HIS M36. For a summary of Nazi legislation of that period, see: Abraham J. Edelheit and Hershel Edelheit, *History of the Holocaust: A Handbook and Dictionary*, Boulder, CO: Westview Press, 1994, pp. 306-307.

139. Protocols of the JAE, February 19, 1939, CZA S100/26, P. 9/6468.

140. Schechtman, *Life and Times*, vol. 2, p. 182.

141. Protocols of the JAE, March 15, 1939, CZA S100/26, pp. 6/6483-7/6484.

142. Ibid., p. 1/6478.

143. Ibid., p. 6/6483.

144. Protocls of the JAE, March 11, 1939, CZA S100/26, pp. 1/6493-4/6496,

145. Notes of an Interview with Lord Halifax, February 21, 1939, BGA Protocols.

146. Protocols of the JAE, March 19, 1939, CZA S100/26, p. 2/6510.

147. Ibid., p. 3/6511. Cf. *ha-Aretz*, Friday, March 17, 1939, p.l.

148. Protocols, op cit, p. 8/6516.

149. Protocols of the JAE, March 19, 1939, CZA S100/26, p. 5/6513.

150. Ibid., p. 7/6516.

151. Ibid., pp. 8/6517-9/6518.

152. Protocols of the JAE, March 19, 1939, Afternoon Session, CZA S100/26, p. 1/6519.

153. Ibid., p. 3/6521.

154. Ibid., p. 4/6522.

155. Ibid., pp. 4/6522-5/6523. The specific figures that Dobkin cited were: below 14 — 37,000, 9.6%; 14-25 — 26,500, 7.0%; 25-45 — 104,000, 27.3%; 4560 — 102,000, 26.7%; and over 60 —112,000, 29.4%.

156. *ha-Aretz*, Wednesday, March 15, 1939, p. 1.

157. Ibid., Tuesday, March 14, 1939, Evening Supplement, p. 1.

158. Ibid., Friday, March 17, 1939, p. 1; Tuesday, March 21, 1939, p. 1.

159. Ibid., Monday, March 20, 1939, p. 1.

160. Ibid., Tuesday, March 21, 1939, p. 1.

161. Landauer to Kaplan et al, March 29, 1939, CZA S7/752.

162. William Perl, *The Four Front War*, New York: Crown, 1979, pp. 15-23.

163. Avriel worked for the Mossad in the Balkans, primarily in Austria and Romania. Cf. *Open the Gates!* New York: Atheneum, 1975, p. 31.

164. Zeidman to JAE, April 20, 1939, CZA S7/752.

165. Memorandum Regarding the State of Jewish Academicians in Slovakia, April 20, 1939, CZA S7/752.

166. Landauer to Palcoset, April 30, 1939, CZA S7/752.

167. Hermann to JAE, May 17, 1939, CZA S7/752.

168. Landauer to Transfer Committee, April 20, 1939, CZA S46/302.

169. Landauer to Rosenblueth, April 25, 1939, CZA S7/752.

170. Hermann to Keren ha-Yesod, May 17, 1939, CZA S46/302.

171. Dobkin to Edelstein, May 17, 1939, CZA S7/752.

172. Protocols of the JAE, November 13, 1938, CZA S100/25.

173. Pidyon Shevuyim to Ruppin, October 28, 1938, CZA S7/721.

174. Pidyon Shevuyim to Ruppin et al, January 9, 1939, CZA S7/721, p. 3. This copy was Ruppin's and my comments closely reflect his notes on the text.

175. Ibid., p. 1.

176. Ibid., p. 2. Ruppin annotated almost every line on this page with question marks and critical notes.

177. *Pidyon Shevuyim Bulletin*, # 1, May 17, 1939, CZA S25/9809, pp. 5-10.

178. See the advertisment for this rally in *ha-Aretz*, Friday, December 23, 1938, p. 6 and the news item about it on Sunday, December 25, 1938, p. 1.

179. *Pidyon Shevuyim Bulletin*, p. 13.

180. Ibid., pp. 3-4.

181. Szold to Political Department, January 1, 1939, CZA S25/2499.

182. Szold to Kaplan, January 9, 1939, CZA S25/9715.

183. Mills to JAE, January 9, 1939, CZA S25/2499.

184. Baratz to Political Department, January 11, 1939, CZA S25/2499.

185. Michaelis-Stern to Shertok, January 4, 1939, CZA S25/2499.

186. Szold to Joseph, March 9, 1939, CZA S25/9705.

187. Elimelech to Shertok and Landauer, February 6, 1939; Memorandum on the Transfer of 5,000 Children from Germany to England, February 6, 1939, CZA S25/2499.

188. Landauer to Kreutzberger, March 8, 1939, CZA S25/2499.

189. Martin Gilbert, "British Government Policy towards Jewish Refugees," *YVS*, vol. 13 (1979), pp. 127-167.

190. Note on a Converstaion with Mr. Samuel, Signed by Szold, June 11, 1939, CZA S25/2499, p. .1

191. Ibid., p. 2.

192. Bayth to Landauer, July 23, 1939, CZA S25/2499.

193. Bayth to Poltical Department, August 20, 1939, CZA S25/2499.

194. It should be added here that chicanery at the Passport Control Offices was not unusual. The officers were not regular foreign service employees, but members of MI6 seconded to the Foreign office as a cover. At least one, Major Hugh Dalton, was implicated in a scheme to extort money from Jewish refugees in the Hague. After pocketing £2,896 ($14,400) Dalton was uncovered and committed suicide. Cf. Nigel West, *MI6: British Secret Intelligence Service Operations, 1909-1945*, New York: Random House, 1983, pp. 43-44.

Chapter 10

1. *ha-Aretz*, Sunday, April 16, 1939, p. 1.

2. Ibid., pp. 1, 5-6.

3. Ben-Gurion to MacMichael, April 13, 1939, cited in David Ben-Gurion, *Zichronot*, v. 6, edited by M. Avizohar, Kiryat Sde Boker: The Ben-Gurion Research Center, 1987, p. 227.

4. Protocol of the First Meeting to Clarify the Situation, April 16, 1939, CZA S25/9917, p. 1.

5. Ben-Gurion, *Zichronot*, p. 243.

6. Dalia Ofer, *Escaping the Holocaust*, New York: Oxford University Press, 1990, p. 324.

7. Protocol of the First meeting, loc cit.

8. Ibid., p. 2 .

9. Ibid., pp. 4-5.

10. Ibid., pp. 5-6.

11. Ibid., p. 8.

12. Protocol of the Second Meeting to Clarify the Situation, April 18, 1939. CZA S25/9917, p. 1.

13. Ibid., p. 4.

14. Ibid., p. 2.

15. Ibid., p. 3.

16. Ibid., pp. 7-8.

17. Political Proposals, D. Auster, No Date, CZA S25/59.

18. Report by the political sub-committee, April 19, 1939, CZA S25/59.

19. *ha-Aretz*, Friday, April 21, 1939, pp. 1, 3.

20. *ha-Aretz*, Friday, April 21, 1939, p. 1. *The Palestine Post*, Sunday, April 23, 1939, p. 1 and Monday, April 24, 1939, p. 1.

21. Ben-Gurion, *Zichronot*, p. 264.

22. Ibid., p. 259.

23. Protocols of the JAE, April 23, 1939, CZA S100/26, p. 1/6559.

24. Ibid., pp. 2/6560-3/6561.

25. Ibid., p. 4/6562.

26. *The Palestine Post*, Monday, April 24, 1939, p. 1.

27. Ibid., Tuesday, April 25, 1939, p. 1.

28. *ha-Aretz*, Thursday, April 27, 1939, p. 2; Friday, April 28, 1939, p. 2.

29. *The Palestine Post*, Monday, April 24, 1939, p. 6.

30. *Davar*, Sunday, April 30, 1939, p. 1.

31. Cf. William Perl, *The Four Front War*, New York: Crown Publishers, 1979, pp. 217, 322-323.

32. Protocol of the Third Meeting to Clarify the Situation, April 30, 1939, CZA S25/9917, p. 1.

33. Ibid., p. 2.

34. Ibid., p. 5.

35. Protocols of the JAE, April 30, 1939, CZA S100/26, pp. 1/6566-4/6569.

36. Zeev Jabotinsky: "'Zion-Sejm' le-Hazala Azmit," *Neumim, 1927-1940,* Jerusalem: Eri Jabotinsky, 1948, p. 332.

37. Ibid., pp. 338-340.

38. Protocols of the JAE, May 2, 1939, CZA S100/26, pp. 2/6573-3/6574.

39. Ibid., p. 6/6577.

40. Ibid., p. 1/6572.

41. Protocols of the JAE, May 7, 1939, CZA S100/27, pp. 1/6578-4/6581.

42. Resolutions of the WZO Inner Actions Committee Meeting, May 10, 1939, CZA S25/7652.

43. Protocols of the JAE, May 8, 1939, CZA S100/27, pp. 1/6586-2/6587.

44. *ha-Aretz*, Thursday, May 11, 1939, p. 1.

45. *The Palestine Post,* Thursday, May 11, 1939, p. 1. The Guiana scheme was abandoned in September, 1939, after a small group of refugees had settled there. The editors of the *Post* had no way of knowing what the outcome would be. Cf. Bernard Wasserstein, *Britain and the Jews of Europe, 1939-1945,* Oxford: Clarendon Press, 1979, p. 28.

46. Notes of a Conversation with the Prime Minister, May 11, 1939, BGA Protocols.

47. Cf. Jabotinsky, "'Zion-Sejm'," pp. 329-330.

48. *ha-Aretz*, Monday, May 15, 1939, pp. 1-2.

49. *ha-Aretz*, Tuesday, May 16, 1939, pp. 1-2.

50. Protocols of the JAE, May 14, 1939, CZA S100/27, p. 3/6590.

51. Palestine Statement of Policy, Command 6019, White Paper, May 17,1939, CZA S25/3615.

52. Cited from Yosef Gorny, *The British Labour Movement and Zionism,* London: Oxford University Press, 1983, p. 153.

53. Abraham J. Edelheit and Hershel Edelheit, *History of the Holocaust: A Handbook and Dictionary,* Boulder, CO: Westview Press, 1994, pp. 133, 150-155, and 446.

54. *The Palestine Post*, Tuesday, May 16, 1939, p. 6.

55. *The Palestine Post*, Wednesday, May 17, 1939, P. 1.

56. *The Palestine Post*, Thursday, May 18, 1939, p. 6.

57. Ibid., Tuesday, May 16, 1939, p. 2.

58. Ibid., Wednesday, May 17, 1939, p. 2.

59. *Davar*, Thursday, May 18, 1939, p. 1.

60. *Davar*, Wednesday, May 17, 1939, p. 1.

61. Notes on the Draft JA Manifesto Regarding the White Paper, signed by Dr. Schmorak, May, 1939, CZA S25/7650.

62. Idem.

63. Manifesto of the JA and WZO, Extract from *ha-Olam,* May 18, 1939, CZA S25/7650.

64. *ha-Aretz*, Thursday, May 18, 1939, p. 1, *Davar*, Thursday, May 18, 1939, p. 1; *The Palestine Post*, Friday, May 19, 1939.
65. Examples of the broadsheet version are contained in CZA S25/7650.
66. *ha-Aretz*, loc cit.
67. David Ben-Gurion, "Sefer ha-Ma'al" *ha-Aretz*, Thursday, May 18, 1939, p. 2; Friday, May 19, 1939, p. 2; and Sunday, May 21, 1939, p. 2. An English translation appeared in *The Palestine Post* on Tuesday, May 23, 1939, pp. 7-10. *Davar* published the statement on May 18 (pp. 2-3) and May 19 (p. 2).
68. Cf. the press material cited by the editors in Ben-Gurion's *Zichronot*, vol. 6, p. 321.
69. Yehuda Bauer, *From Diplomacy to Resistance*, New York: Atheneum, 1970, pp. 54-55.
70. Notes of a Meeting Between Ben-Gurion and Representatives of Bnai Akiva, May 31, 1939, BGA Protocols.
71. This remained Senator's position until 1945. At that point, the JAE could wait no longer for the supposed changes in British policy to and agreed to begin military operations, over Senator's opposition. He then resigned from the JAE.
72. Agudas Israel to JAE, Iyyar 23, 5699 (= May 12, 1939), CZA S25/7652.
73. Agudas Israel to JAE, Iyyar 27, 5699 (= May 16, 1939), CZA S25/7652.
74. Thon to Ben-Gurion, May 28, 1939, CZA S25/7650.
75. Protocols of the JAE, May 21, 1939, CZA S100/27, pp. 2/6597-3/6598.
76. Yitzhak Ben-Ami, *Years of Wrath, Days of Glory,* New York: Robert Speller, 1982, pp. 199-212.
77. Protocols of the Histadrut Executive, May 17, 1939, HIS M37, p. 3.
78. Idem.
79. Cf. Peretz Merhav, *The Israeli Left,* San Diego, CA: A. S. Barnes, 1980, pp. 92-101.
80. Ibid., pp. 4.
81. Ibid., pp. 4-5.
82. Eli Tavin et al (eds.), *ha-Irgun ha-Zvai ha-Leumi be-Eretz Israel: Osef Mekorot u-Mismahim*, Tel Aviv: The Jabotinsky Institute, 1990, vol. 1, p. 302.
83. Ibid., p. 296.
84. IZL poster of June 1, 1939, in The EZEL (sic) Movement in Mandatory Palestine, A Microfiche Collection, Geneva: IDC, 1980, Fiche B-44.
85. David Niv: *Maarachot ha-Irgun ha-Zvai ha-Leumi*, Tel Aviv: The Klausner Institute Press, 1965, vol. 2, pp. 234-237.
86. Tavin, *ha-Irgun*, pp. 89-92. In his introductory remarks to the letters, Tavin expressed considerable skepticism regarding their meaning. His specific questions related to three issues: Jabotinsky did not sign the letters (not even with one of his many noms-de-plume); both letters lack any greeting; and the only extant copies originated with Abraham Stern, who made them available to members of the underground after Jabotinsky's death (August 1940). At

the time David Raziel was in prison and the members of IZL were debating how best to respond to the outbreak of World War II. Stern advocated continuing the anti-British struggle, while the majority of the IZL leaders advocated suspending the struggle for the duration of the Nazi threat.

87. Niv, *Maarachot*, p. 237.

88. *Kol Herut Israel*, #4, June 23, 1939, p. 1.

89. *Emor la-Am*, July 29, 1939, p. 1.

90. Ibid., p. 2.

91. Idem. The reference is to the Biblical story of the Exodus from Egypt when God's protection was symbolized by a pillar of smoke during the day and a pillar of fire at night (Exodus 13:22).

92. Observations on the Palestine White Paper, June 1939, JIA G4/1/5. The JAE was involved in a similar effort, independently of Ha-Zach. On this effort, see Protocol of the Mapai Executive, June 14, 1939, ILPA 2/23/39.

93. Protocols of the JAE, May 21, 1939, CZA S100/27, p. 7/6602. The reference is to Jewish self-defense during the pogroms in Russia in 1903-1905.

94. Ibid., p. 3/6598.

95. Ibid., pp. 7/6602-9/6604.

96. Ben-Gurion, *Zichronot*, p. 487.

97. Protocols of the JAE, May 28, 1939, CZA S100/27, p. 1/6615.

98. Ibid., p. 2/6616.

99. Idem.

100. Ben-Gurion said as much at a meeting of the Mapai Central Committee on the evening of May 29th (i.e., after the meeting at the JAE). Cf. Ben-Gurion, *Zichronot*, p. 336. Ben-Gurion's terminology appears to reflect his continuing desire not to repeat the mistake made in 1934, when his agreement with Jabotinsky was defeated by an overwhelming majority of Histadrut members. In other words, he might have been more willing to consider the proposal if it was linked to Ha-Zach' retutn to the WZO.

101. Protocols of the JAE, loc cit. The terms used literally translate to "arise and do" and "sit and not do." The former is a halachic term for the performance of a deed in-tended to repair the breech of a negative command-ment, the latter is a modern adaptation of the Hebrew term. Cf. Mishna Tractate Hullin, 12:4.

102. Protocols of the JAE, op cit, p. 3/6617.

103. Ibid., p. 4/6618.

104. Ibid., pp. 4/6618-6/6620.

105. *ha-Boker*, Monday, May 29, 1939, p. 1.

106. *ha-Aretz*, Monday, May 29, 1939, p. 1.

107. *ha-Aretz*, Tuesday, May 30, 1939, p. 2.

108. Notes of a Meeting between Messrs. Ben-Gurion and Joseph with Dr. Yellin and Mr. Schwartz, May 29, 1939, CZA S25/59, p. 1.

109. Ibid., pp. 5-10.

110. Ibid., p. 15.

111. Cf. Dina Porat, *The Blue and the Yellow Stars of David,* Cambridge, MA: Harvard University Press, 1990, ch. 7.

112. Circular by Ben-Zvi, May 15, 1939, CZA S25/59.

113. Ben-Gurion, *Zichronot,* p. 326.

114. Lines of Action, May 24, 1939, CZA S25/59, p. 1.

115. Ibid., pp. 2-3.

116. Bauer, *Diplomacy,* p. 240, where Bauer analyzed Ben-Gurion's views on possible political options — including continuation of the Mandate, binationalism, or independence — on the eve of the Biltmore Conference.

117. Lines of Action, op cit, pp. 3-6.

118. Ben-Gurion's Diary, entry for May 24, 1939, BGA.

119. Ben-Gurion to Solomon Goldman, New York, May 24, 1939, Ben-Gurion's Correspondence, BGA.

120. Shlomo Lev-Ami, *ba-Maavak u-ba-Mered,* Tel Aviv: Maarachot/IDF Press, ND, p. 125.

121. Tavin, *ha-Irgun,* p. 168.

122. Ben-Gurion, *Zichronot,* pp. 345 and 374-375.

123. Although this document poses some difficulties, I believe it is authentic. The lack of a signature and return address make a precise identification of the author impossible. Nevertheless, his biases — against ha'apala (both Revisionist and Mossad) and opposition to the IZL — are clear. This makes the document more important and does lead to one clear conclusion: that the author lived in Palestine at the time of writing.

124. Anonymous letter to Ben-Gurion, July 20, 1939, CZA S44/69B.

125. Weizmann to Goldmann, May 30, 1939, cited in M. J. Cohen (ed): *Implementing the White Paper* [Rise of Israel Series, vol. 28], New York: Garland, 1989, pp. 8-9.

126. Extract from a letter by Schura, January 23, 1939, ATH 14/343. Although written in code, the reference to farms (= transports) and "a new building" (= a ship) are clear.

127. See the collection of twenty-seven such telegrams, covering operations in Poland, Czechoslovakia, Italy, and Romania between March 24 and July 14, 1939 in ATH 14/343.

128. Anonymous telegram, April 9, received April 11, 1939, ATH 14/343.

129. Cf. Ofer, *Escaping the Holocaust,* pp. 324-325.

130. Romanian Official Society for Tourism to Kanner, March 25, 1939. JIA 116/3/2/1.

131. Testimony on the Sailing of the S.S. *Astir,* no date, LBI(J) #660.

132. Ben-Gurion, *Zichronot,* pp. 454-455, quoting the Vaad Leumi report.

133. Niv, *Maarachot,* vol. 2, p. 149.

134. "The Ma'apilim," no date, CZA S25/2651.

135. Shertok to Wedgewood, June 14, 1939, CZA S25/2651.

136. Circular by Wedgewood, April 8, 1939, JIA K6/9/1.

137. *ha-Aretz*, Wednesday, April 1, 1939, p. 1, for a case of poor treatment of maapilim by a private organizer.

138. Wedgwood to Jabotinsky, June 28, 1939; Wedgewood to Perl, July 12, 1939. JIA K6/9/1.

139. The JDC ban included the Mossad until late in World War II when the policy changed. Cf. Tad Szulc, *The Secret Alliance*, New York: Farrar, Straus, and Giroux, 1991, pp. 3-13.

140. *Yediot Leumiyot*, vol. 1 #4 (April 9, 1939), p. 2.

141. Ben-Gurion's Diary, Wednesday, April 5, 1939, BGA.

142. *Yediot Leumiyot*, loc cit. The Jewish Supernumerary Police were created in 1936 to protect Jewish Settlements from Arab attack.

143. *ha-Aretz*, Tuesday, April 11, 1939, p. 1.

144. Shilton Betar, Circular #20, August 3, 1939, JIA K6/3/1.

145. *The Sentinel*, vol. 1 #1 (April 24, 1939), p. 3.

146. *ha-Aretz*, Friday, June 2, 1939, p. 1.

147. *ha-Aretz*, Monday, June 5, 1939, p. 1.

148. See EZEL Movement, op cit (note 80), fiche B-44 for a description of the strike.

149. Ben-Gurion, *Zichronot*, pp. 374-375.

150. Edelheit and Edelheit, *History of the Holocaust*, pp. 179-185.

151. Abrahams to Rappard, June 2, 1939, JIA G4/I/6.

152. Extracts of the Minutes of the league of Nations Permanent Mandates Commission, June, 1939, CZA S25/3615.

153. Protocol of the Va'ad ha-Poel ha-Zioni, June 27, 1939, CZA S25/59; Resolutions of the Meeting of the Va'ad ha-Poel ha-Zioni, June 27, 1939, CZA S25/7652.

154. Berlin to Shertok, June 29, 1939, CZA S25/7650.

155. Shertok to Berlin, July 2, 1939, CZA S25/7650.

156. *ha-Aretz*, Friday, June 9, 1939, p. 1.

157. There has been some debate as to what Ben-Gurion said at the JAE meeting on September 3, 1939, and some historians doubt if the quote is authentic. In an article he wrote in 1963 Ben-Gurion claimed that this was the formula he actually used. Cf. "Why We Fought for Britain, *Jewish Observer and Middle East Review*, vol. 12 #47 (November 22, 1963): 15-18.

Conclusion

1. *ha-Aretz*, Monday, September 4, 1939, p. 1.

2. Shimon Golan, *Marut u-Maavak be-Yemei Meri*, Ramat Efal: Yad Tabenkin Press, 1988, p. 9.

Bibliography

I. Primary Sources

A. Archival Collections

1. The Ben-Gurion Archive (BGA), Kiryat Sde Boker
2. The Ben-Zvi Archive (BZA), Jerusalem
3. Central Archive for the History of the Jewish People (CAHJP), Jerusalem
4. The Central Zionist Archives (CZA), Jerusalem
5. The Historical Archives of the Hagana (ATH), Tel Aviv
6. The Histadrut Archives (HIS), Tel Aviv
7. The Israel Labor Party Archives (ILPA), Kfar Saba
8. The Israel State Archives (ISA), Jerusalem
9. The Jabotinsky Institute Archive (JIA), Tel Aviv
10. The Leo Baeck Institute, Jerusalem (LBI/J)
11. The Leo Baeck Institute, New York (LBI/NY)
12. Public Records Office (PRO), London
13. Yad Vashem Archives (YVA), Jerusalem

B. Press and Periodicals

American Jewish Yearbook (AJYB)
Betar
Davar
Die Mitteilungsblatt
Doar ha-Yom
Emor la-Am

Jewish Agency Bulletin
Jewish Agency Report
Jüdische Welt-Rundschau
Kol Herut Israel
Moznaim
Palestine Post, The

ha-Aretz	*Palestine Tourist Annual*
ha-Olam	*Palestine Illustrated News*
ha-Poel ha-Zair	*Palestine Review, The*
ha-Zioni ha-Klali	*Palnews Economic Annual*
Haavara Newsletter	*Pidyon Shevuyim Bulletin*
Hazit ha-Am	*Reichsgesetz Blatt (RGBL)*

C. Diaries and Memoirs

Akzin, Benjamin. *Me Riga le-Yerushalayim — Pirke Zichronot*. Jerusalem: The
    Zionist Library, 1989.
Avizohar, Meir (ed.). *Zionut Lohemet: Mavo le-Yoman Ben-Gurion ve-le-
    Zichronotav, 1939*. Beersheba: Ben-Gurion University Press, 1985.
Avriel, Ehud. *Open the Gates!* New York: Atheneum, 1970.
Bein, Alex (ed.). *Arthur Ruppin: Memoirs, Diaries, Letters*. Jerusalem:
    Weidenfeld and Nicolson, 1971.
Ben-Ami, Yitzhak. *Years of Wrath, Days of Glory*, New York: Speller, 1982.
Ben-Gurion, David. *Zichronot*. 6 vols. Tel Aviv: Am Oved, 1973-1987 (vol. 5
    edited by G. Rivlin, vol. 6 edited by Meir Avizohar).
Briscoe, Robert. *For the Life of Me*. London: Longmann's Associates, 1958.
Eliav, Benjamin. *Zihronot min ha-Yemin*. Tel Aviv: Am Oved, 1990.
Frankfurter, David. *Rishon Lohame ha-Nazim*. Tel Aviv: Reshafim, 1984.
Goldmann, Nahum. *The Autobiography of Nahum Goldmann: Sixty Years of
    Jewish Life*. New York: Holt, Rinehart, and Winston, 1969.
Jabotinsky, Zeev. *Autobiographia*. Jerusalem: Eri Jabotinsky, 1948. Collected
    Works, vol. 1.
Lazar-Litai, Haim. *Af-Al-Pi*. Tel Aviv: Hadar, 1957.
Meir, Golda. *My Life*. New York: Putnam's, 1975.
Neumann, Emanuel. *In the Arena: An Autobiographical Memoir*. New York:
    Herzl Press, 1976.
Perl, William. *The Four Front War: From the Holocaust to the Promised Land*.
    New York: Crown, 1979.
Sharett, Moshe. *Yoman Medini*. 5 vols. Tel Aviv: An Oved, 1969-1979.
Warhaftig, Zorach. *Palit ve-Sarid be-Yeme Shoa*. Jerusalem: Yad Vashem,
    1984.

D. Other Primary Sources:

Ancel, Jean (ed.). *Documents Concerning the Fate of Romanian Jewry During
    the Holocaust*. New York: The Beate Klarsfeld Foundation, 1986.
Arad, Yitzhak et al (eds.). *Documents on the Holocaust*. New York: Ktav for
    Yad Vashem and the Anti-Defamation League, 1981.

Atias, Moshe (ed.). *Sefer ha-Teudot shel Vaad ha-Leumi le-Knesset Israel.* Jerusalem: R. Cohen Publisher, 1963.

Ben-Avram, Baruch (ed.). *Miflagot u-Zramim Politiim be-Tekufat ha-bayit ha-Leumi.* Jerusalem: Merkaz Zalman Shazar, 1978.

Ben-Gurion, David. *Letters to Paula.* Pittsburgh: University of Pittsburgh Press, 1971.

———. *me-Ma'amad le-Am.* Tel Aviv: Am Oved, 1931.

———. *The Peel Report and the Jewish State.* London: Palestine Labor Studies Group, 1938.

———. "Why We Fought for Britain." *Jewish Observer and Middle East Review,* vol. 12 #47 (November 22, 1963): 15-18.

Blau, Bruno. *Das Ausnahmerecht für die Juden in deutschland, 1933-1945.* Third Edition. Dusseldorf: Verlag Algemeine Wochen-zeitung der Juden in deutschland, 1965.

Citrine, Walter. "Boycott Most Useful Weapon Against Dangers of Nazism." *Anti-Nazi Economic Bulletin,* vol. 3 #7 (October, 1936): 1.

Eretz Yisrael ha-Shlema. Tel Aviv: N.P., 1938.

Dubnow, Simon M. *Nationalism and History.* Edited by K. S. Pinson. Philadelphia: JPS, 1958.

Duker, Abraham G. *The Situation of the Jews in Poland.* New York: American Jewish Congress, 1936.

Erem, M. *Ba'ad oh Neged ha-Heskem im ha-Fascism ha-Revisionisti?* Tel Aviv: The Action Committee of Opponents of the Agreement, N.D.

Executive of the Jewish Agency for Palestine. "To the Jews in All Countries." *New Judea,* vol. 9 #7 (April, 1933): 93-95.

Feilchenfeld, Werner. *Fünf Jahre deutsche Palestinawanderung und Haavara-Transfer, 1933-1938.* Tel Aviv: N. P., 1938.

Goldmann, Nahum. *From the Danger of Annihilation to the Dawn of Redemption: Four Speeches.* Jerusalem, WZO, 1958.

Great Britain and Palestine, 1915-1945. London: RIIA, 1946.

Gurevich, D. et al (comps.). *Statistical Handbook of Jewish Palestine.* Jerusalem: The Jewish Agency for Palestine, 1947.

Habas, Braha. *Meoraot Tarzu.* Tel Aviv: Davar Publications, 1937.

Heller, Joseph (ed.). *ba-Ma'avak la-Medina: ha-Mediniut ha-Zionit ba-Shanim 1936-1948.* Jerusalem: Merkaz Zalman Shazar, 1984.

Hertzberg, Arthur (ed.). *The Zionist Idea.* New York: Atheneum, 1976.

Hitler, Adolf. *Mein Kampf.* Boston: Houghton Mifflin, 1971.

Hitachdut Olei Germania. *Arbeitsbericht für das Jahre 1938.* Tel Aviv: ha-Aretz Press, 1939.

Huberband, Simon. *Kiddush Hashem: Jewish Religious and Cultural Life in Poland During the Holocaust.* Hoboken, NJ: Ktav, 1987.

Jabotinsky, Zeev. *Al ha-Haluka.* Jerusalem: Ha-Zohar, N.D.

——. *Ba-Sa'ar*. Jerusalem: Eri Jabotinsky, 1953. Collected Works, vol. 13.

——. *Umma ve-Hevra*. Jerusalem: Eri Jabotinsky, 1950. Collected Works, vol. 9.

——. *Neumim, 1927-1940*. Jerusalem: Eri Jabotonsky, 1958. Collected Works, vol. 6.

——. *The War and the Jew*. New York: Dial Press, 1943.

Klinger, Stefan. *The Ten Year Plan for Palestine*. London: The New Zionist Organization, 1938.

Lepecki, M. B. *Madagaskar, Kraj Ludzie Kolonizacja*. Warsaw: Polonia, 1938.

Memorandum Submitte to the Inter-Governmental Conference on Refugees. London: Jewish Agency for Palestine, 1938.

Minutes of Evidence Heard at Public Sessions of the Palestine Royal Commission. London: HMSO, 1937.

New Deal For Palestine, A. Tel Aviv: Tnuat Bnei Chorin, 1938.

Noakes, Jeremy and Goffrey Pridham (eds.). *Documents on Nazism, 1919-1945*. New York: Viking, 1974.

Palestine Partition Commission, Report. London: HMSO, 1938.

"Palestine Ready to Take 100,000 Refugees." *Zionist Review*, vol. 6 # 30 (November 24, 1938): 3.

Palestine Royal Commission: Report, 1937. London: HMSO, 1937.

Petition Submitte to the Permanent Mandates Commission of the League of Nations. N.P.: Union of Zionist-Revisionists in Palestine, 1934.

Rothenberg, Morris. "Palestine's Part in Absorbing German Jewish Refugees." *Jewish Social Service Quarterly*, vol. 11 #1 (Sept., 1934): 58-60.

Sachar, Howard M. (ed. in chief). *The Rise of Israel Series*. 39 vols. New York: Garland, 1988.

Shavit, Yaacov. *"Havlaga" oh Teguva?* Ramat Gan, Israel: Bar Ilan University Press, 1983.

Silver, Abba Hillel. "Why We Boycott Germany." *Anti-Nazi Economic Bulletin*, vol. 1 #4 (May, 1934): 4.

State of Doom or a Jewish State, The. Tel Aviv: Tnuat Bnei Chorin, 1938.

Stenographic Protocols of the 17-21 Zionist Congresses. London/Jerusalem: Executive of the WZO, 1931-1939.

Tavin, Eli et al (eds.). *ha-Irgun ha-Zvai ha-Leumi be-Eretz Israel: Osef Mekorot u-mismachim*. vol. 1. Tel Aviv: Jabotinsky Institute Press, 1990.

Three Congress Addresses: XXth Zionist Congress. New York: Zionist Organization of America, 1937. NYPL Microfilm # *ZP-PV31.

Twenty-Seventh Annual Report of the American Jewish Committee, The. New York: The Committee, 1934.

Warburg, Gustav. *Six Years of Hitler*. London: Allen and Unwin, 1939.

Weinryb, Bernard D. *Jewish Emancipation Under Attack*. New York: The American Jewish Committee, 1942.

Weizmann, Chaim. "The German-Jewish Tragedy and Palestine." *New Judea*, v.9 #8/9 (May/June, 1933): 135-137.

——. *The Jewish People and Palestine*. Jerusalem: The Jewish Agency, 1939.

——. *The Letters and Papers of Chaim Weizmann. Series A: Letters*. 23 vols. Barnett Litvinoff et al eds. New Brunswick, NJ: Transaction Books, 1969-1980.

——. *The Letters and Papers of Chaim Weizmann. Series B: Papers*. 2 vols. B. Litvinoff ed. New Brunswick, NJ: Transaction Books, 1983.

Wyndham, Hugh et al. *Political and Strategic Interests of the United Kingdom: An Outline*. London: Royal Institute of International Affairs, 1939.

Ziff, William B.. *The Rape of Palestine*. New York: Longman's, Green, and Company, 1938.

II. Secondary Sources

A. Reference Books:

Edelheit, Abraham J. and Hershel Edelheit (eds.). *Bibliography on Holocaust Literature*. 3 vol. Boulder, CO: Westview Press, 1986-1992

Edelheit, Hershel and Abraham J. Edelheit (comps.). *A World in Turmoil: An Integrated Chronology of the Holcoaust and World War II*. Westport, CT: Greenwood Press, 1991.

Gutman, Israel (ed. in chief). *Encyclopedia of the Holocaust*. New York: Macmillan, 1990.

Robinson, J. et al (eds.). *Guide to Unpublished Materials of the Holocaust Period*. 6 vols. Jerusalem: Hebrew University, 1970-1981.

—— and H. Sachs (comps.). *The Holocaust: The Nuremberg Evidence*. Jerusalem/NY: Yad Vashem/YIVO, 1976.

B. Biographies

Avi-Hai, Avraham. *Ben-Gurion State-Builder*. Jerusalem: Israel Universities Press, 1974.

Avineri, Shlomo. *Arlosoroff*. New York: Grove Weidenfeld, 1989.

Dash, Joan. *Summoned to Jerusalem: the Life of Henrietta Szold*. New York: Harper & Row, 1979.

Friling, Tuvia. "Ben-Gurion and the Holocaust of European Jewry, 1939-1945." *Yad Vashem Studies*, vol. 17 (1987): 199-232.

Gal, Allon. *David Ben-Gurion: Likrat Medina Yehudit*. Sde Boker: The Ben-Gurion Research Center, 1985.

Hacohen, David. *Time to Tell: An Israeli Life*. New York: Herzl Press, 1985.

Porat, Dina. "Ben-Gurion ve-ha-Shoa." *ha-Zionut*, #12 (1987): 293-314.

——. "Martin Buber in Eretz-Israel During the Holocaust Years, 1942-1944." *Yad Vashem Studies*, vol. 17 (1986): 93-143.

Schechtman, Joseph B. *The Life and Times of Vladimir Jabotinsky*. vol. 2, Fighter and Prophet: The Last Years. New York: Thomas Yoseloff, 1961.

Shaltiel, Eli. *Pinhas Rutenberg: Aliyato u-Nefilato shel Ish Hazak be-Eretz Israel, 1879-1942*. Tel Aviv: Am Oved, 1990.

Shapira, Anita. *Berl: The Biography of a Socialist Zionist*. New York: Cambridge University Press, 1984.

Teveth, Shabtai. *Ben-Gurion: The Burning Ground, 1886-1948*. Boston: Houghton Mifflin, 1987.

Tzahor, Zeev. "Chaim Arlosoroff and his attitude Toward the Rise of Nazism." *Jewish Social Studies*, vol. 46 #3/4 (Summer/Fall, 1984), pp. 321-330.

Weitz, Yehiam. "The Position of David Ben-Gurion and Yitzhak Tabenkin vis-a-vis the Holocaust of European Jewry." *Holocaust and Genocide Studies*, vol. 5 #2 (1990): 191-204.

C. Historiography

Bet-Zvi, Shabbetai B. *ha-Zionut ha-Post Ugandit ba-Mashber ha-Shoa*. Tel Aviv: Bronfmann's Agency, 1977.

Brenner, Lenni. *Zionism in an Age of Dictators*, London: Croom Helm, 1983.

Friling, Tuvia. "ha-Million ha-Shvi'i ke-Mizad ha-Avelut ve-ha-Rishut shel ha-Tenua ha-Zionit." *Iyyunim be-Tekumat Israel*, vol. 2 (1992): 317-367.

Gelber, Yoav. "The Problematics of the Historiography of the Reaction of the Yishuv and the Jews in the Free World to the Holocaust." in *The Historiography of the Holocaust Period* ed. by Israel Gutman, Jerusalem: Yad Vashem, 1988, pp. 581-584.

Hecht, Ben. *Perfidy*, New York: Robert Speller, 1961.

Marrus, Michael R.. *The Holocaust in History*, Hanover, NH: University Press of New England, 1987.

Ofer, Dalia. "The Historiography of Aliyah Bet." *The Historiography of the Holocaust Period*, ed. by Israel Gutman, Jerusalem: Yad Vashem, 1988, pp. 594-595.

Segev, Tom. *The Seventh Million: The Israelis and the Holocaust*. New York: Hill and Wang, 1993.

Shapira, Anita. "Did the Zionist Leadership Foresee the Holocaust?" in *Living With Antisemitism: Modern Jewish Responses*, ed. by Jehuda Reinharz, Hanover, NH: University Press of New England, 1987, pp. 397-412.

Wasserstein, Bernard. "The Myth of Jewish Silence." *Midstream*, vol. 26 #7 (Aug./Sept., 1980), pp. 10-16.

Zertal, Idith. "The Poisoned Heart: The Jews of Palestine and the Holocaust." *Tikkun*, vol. 2 #1 (1987): 79-83.

D. The Holocaust, East European Jewry

Aschheim, Steven E. *Brothers and Strangers: The East European Jew in German and German Jewish Consciousness, 1800-1923*. Madison: University of Wisconsin Press, 1982.

Barkai, Avraham. *From Boycott to Annihilation*, Hanover, NH: University Press of New England, 1989.

——. *Nazi Economics*. New York: Berg Publishers, 1990.

Boas, Jacob. *Boulevard des Miseries: The Story of Transit Camp Westerbork*. Hamden, CT: Archon Books, 1985.

Edelheit, Abraham J. "The Soviet Union, the Jews, and the Holocaust." *Holocaust Studies Annual*, v. 4 (1990), pp. 113-134.

—— and Hershel Edelheit. *History of the Holocaust: A Handbook and Dictionary*. Boulder, CO: Westview Press, 1994.

Friedman, Philip. "The Lublin Reservation and the Madagascar Plan: Two Aspects of Nazi Jewish Policy during the Second World War." *Yivo Annual*, vol. 8 (1953), pp. 151-177.

Greenberg, G. "Orthodox Theological Responses to Kristallnacht: Chayyim Ozer Grodzensky (Achiezer) and Elchonon Wassermann." *Holocaust and Genocide Studies*, v.3 #4 (1988): 431-441.

Grossman, Kurt R. "Zionists and Non-Zionists Under Nazi Rule in the 1930s" *Herzl Yearbook*, v. 4 (1961/62): 329-344.

Gruenwald, M.. "About the *Reichsvertretung der Deutschen Juden*" in *Imposed Jewish Governing Bodies Under Nazi Rule*, New York: YIVO, 1972, pp. 42-47.

Hart-Davis, D. *Hitler's Games: The 1936 Olympics*. New York Harper and Row, 1986.

Janowsky, Oscar I. *The Jews and Minority Rights*, New York: Columbia University Press, 1933.

Johnpoll, B.. *The Politics of Futility: The General Jewish Workers Bund of Poland, 1917-1939,* Ithaca, NY: Cornell University Press, 1967.

Katzburg, Nathaniel. *Hungary and the Jews, 1920-1943*, Ramat-Gan: Bar-Ilan University Press, 1981.

Lestchinsky, Jacob. "The Anti-Jewish Program: Tsarist Russia, the Third Reich, and Independent Poland." *Jewish Social Studies*, v.3 #2 (April, 1941): 141-158.

Margaliot, Abraham. "The Problem of Rescue of German Jewry during the Years 1933-1939; the Reasons for the Delay in their Emigration from the Third Reich." *Rescue Attempts During the Holocaust*, ed. by Israel Gutman and Efraim Zuroff, Jerusalem: Yad Vashem, 1977, 256-259.

Mendelsohn, Ezra. *The Jews of East Central Europe Between the World Wars*, Bloomington: Indiana University Press, 1983.

——. *On Modern Jewish Politics*. New York: Oxford University Press, 1993.

Miller, Richard L. *Nazi Justiz Law of the Holocaust*. Westport, CT: Praeger, 1995.

Poppel, Stephen. *Zionism in Germany*, Philadelphia: Jewish Publication Society, 1976.

Rosenkranz, Herbert. "Austrian Jewry: Between Forced Emigration and Deportation." in *Patterns of Jewish Leadership in Nazi Europe, 1933-1945*. ed. by Israel Gutman and C. J. Haft. Jerusalem: Yad Vashem, 1979, pp. 65-74.

Schechtman, Joseph B. *Zionism and Zionists in Soviet Russia*, New York: Zionist Organization of America, 1966.

Shapiro, *Robert M. The Polish Kehile Elections of 1936: A Revolution Re-Examined*. New York: Yeshiva University, 1988.

Schleunes, Karl. *The Twisted Road to Auschwitz*. Urbana: University of Illinois Press, 1970.

Straus, Herbert A. "The Drive for War and the Pogrom of November 1938: Testing Explanatory Models." *Leo Baeck Institute Yearbook*, vol. 35 (1990): 268-278.

Thalmann, Rita and Emmanuel Feinermann. *Crystal Night 9-10 November 1938*, London: Thames and Hudson, 1974.

Zariz, Ruth. "Officially Approved Emigration from Germany after 1941: A Case Study." *Yad Vashem Studies*, v. 18 (1987): pp. 275-291.

E. Free-World Responses to the Holocaust

Abella, Irvimg and Harold Troper. *None is Too Many: Canada and the Jews of Europe, 1933-1948*, New York: Random House, 1982.

Alderman, Geoffrey. *The Jewish Community in British Politics*, Oxford: Clarendon Press, 1983.

Bartrop, Paul R. (ed.). *False Havens: The British Empire and the Holocaust*. Lanham, MD: University Press of America, 1995.

Bauer, Yehuda. *American Jewry and the Holocaust: The American Jewish Joint Distribution Committee, 1939-1945*, Detroit, MI: Wayne State University Press, 1981.

——. *The Jewish Emergence from Powerlessness*. Toronto: University of Toronto Press, 1979.

——. "Jewish Foreign Policy during the Holocaust" *Midstream*, vol. 30 #10 (December, 1984), pp.22-25.

Cohen, Naomi W. *Not Free to Desist*, Philadelphia: JPS, 1972.

Dinnerstein, Leonard. *America and the Survivors of the Holocaust*, New York: Columbia University Press, 1982.

Edelheit, Abraham J. "Jewish Responses to the Nazi Threat, 1933-1939: An Evaluation." *Jewish Political Studies Review*, vol. 6 #1/2 (Spring 1994): 135-152.

Feinberg, Nathan. *ha-Agudot ha-Yehudiot le-Ma'an Hever ha-Leumim.* Jerusalem: Magnes Press, 1967.

———. *ha-Maavak ha-Yehudi Neged Hitler be-Hever ha-Leumim.* Jerusalem: Magnes Press, 1957.

Feingold, Henry L. *Bearing Witness: How America and its Jews Responded to the Holocaust.* Syracuse, NY: Syracuse University Press, 1995.

———. *The Politics of Rescue*, New Brunswick, NJ: Rutgers University Press, 1970.

Gilbert, Martin. "British Government Policy towards Jewish Refugees. *Yad Vashem Studies*, vol. 13 (1979): 127-167.

Gottlieb, Moshe. *American Anti-Nazi Resistance 1933-1941: An Historical Analysis*, New York: Ktav, 1982.

Häsler, Alfred A. *The Lifeboat is Full: Switzerland and the Refugees, 1933-1945.* New York: Funk and Wagnalls, 1969.

Higham, Charles. *Trading With the Enemy*, New York: Delacorte Press, 1983.

Kubovy, A. L. *Unity in Dispersion: A History of the World Jewish Congress.* New York: The World Jewish Congress, 1948.

Laqueur, Walter. *The Terrible Secret: Suppression of the Truth About Hitler's Final Solution.* Boston: Little Brown, 1980.

Lipstadt, Deborah E. *Beyond Belief: The American Press and the Coming of the Holocaust, 1933-1945*, New York: Free Press, 1986.

Marrus, Michael R. *The Unwanted: A History of Refugees in the Twentieth Century*, New York: Oxford University Press, 1985.

Michman, Dan. "The Committee for Jewish Refugees in Holland (1933-1940)." *Yad Vashem Studies*, vol. 14 (1981), pp. 205-232.

Morse, Arthur D. *While Six Million Died.* New York: Hart Publishing, 1967.

Penkower, Monty N. *The Jews were Expendible: Free World Diplomacy and the Holocaust*, Urbana: University of Illinois Press, 1983.

Rubinstein, W. D. *A History of the Jews in the English-Speaking World: Great Britain.* London: Macmillan, 1995 / New York: St. Martin's Press, 1996.

Sharf, Andrew. *The British Press and Jews Under Nazi Rule*, London: Oxford University Press, 1964.

Steibel, Joan. "The Central British Fund for World Jewish Relief." *Transactions of the Jewish Historical Society of England*, vol. 27 (1978/1980), pp. 51-60.

Wasserstein, Bernard. *Britain and the Jews of Europe, 1939-1945*, Oxford: Clarendon Press for the Institute of Jewish Affairs, 1979.

West, Nigel. *MI6: British Secret Intelligence Service Operations, 1909-1945*, New York: Random House, 1983.

F. Zionism, the Yishuv, Zionist Ideology

Adiv, Zvi. "Iyunim be-Hahskafato ha-Zionit shel Zeev Jabotinsky." in *Ideologia u-Mediniut Zionit* ed. by Ben-Zion Yehoshua and Aaron Kedar. Jerusalem: The Zalman Shazar Institute Press, 1978, pp. 115-134.

Avineri, Shlomo. *The Making of Modern Zionism*, New York: Basic Books, 1981.

——. "The Socialist Zionism of Chaim Arlosoroff." *Jerusalem Quarterly*, #34 (Winter, 1985): 68-87.

Avizohar, Meir. *be-Rei Saduk: Idealim Hevratiim ve-Leumiim ve-Histakfutam be-Olama shel Mapai*. Tel Aviv: Am Oved, 1990.

Bechor, David et al. *Din ve-Heshbon shel Ve'idat ha-Hakira le-Hakirat Rezah Dr. Chaim Arlosoroff*. Jerusalem: The Committee, 1985.

Ben-Yerocham, C. *Alilat ha-Dam*. Tel Aviv: The Jabotinsky Institute, 1982.

Braslavsky, Moshe. *Tnuat ha-Poalim ha-Aretz Yisraelit*. 4 volumes. Tel Aviv: Ha-Kibbutz Ha-Meuhad Press, 1942-1962.

Cohen, Mitchell. *Zion and State*, New York: Basil Blackwell, 1987.

Cohen, Naomi W. *The Year After the Riots: American Responses to the Palestine Crisis, 1929-1930*. Detroit: Wayne State University Press, 1988.

Dothan, Shmuel. *A Land in the Balance: The Struggle for Palestine, 1918-1948*. Tel Aviv: MOD Books, 1993.

——. *Pulmus ha-Haluka be-Tekufat ha-Mandat*. Jerusalem: Yad Yitzhak Ben-Zvi, 1979.

Eliash, Shulamit. "The Political Role of the Chief Rabbinate of Palestine During the Mandate: Its Character and Nature." *Jewish Social Studies*, vol. 47 #1 (Winter, 1985): 33-50.

——. "Rescue Policy of the Chief Rabbinate of Palestine before and during World War II." *Modern Judaism*, v.3 #3 (October, 1983): 291-308.

Golan, Shimon. *Marut u-Ma'avak be-Yemei Meri*. Ramat Efal: Yad Yitzhak Tabenkin, 1988.

Goldstein, Joseph. "Jabotinsky and Jewish Autonomy in the Diaspora." *Studies in Zionism*, vol. 7 # 2 (Autumn, 1986), pp. 219-232.

——. "Mapai and the Seventeenth Zionist Congress (1931)." *Studies in Zionism*, vol. 10 # 1 (Spring, 1989), pp. 19-30.

Hattis, Susan L. *The Bi-National Idea in Palestine during Mandatory Times*. Tel Aviv: Shikmona Press, 1970.

Heller, Joseph. "'ha-Monism shel ha-Matara' oh 'ha-Monisn shel ha-Emzaim?' ha-Mahloket ha-Raayonit veha-Politit ben Zeev Jabotinsky le-ben Ab'a Ahimeir, 1928-1933" *Zion* vol. 52 # 3 (1987), pp. 315-369.

——. *LEHI: Ideologia u-Politika, 1940-1949*. Jerusalem: The Zalman Shazar Institute, 1989.

———. "Weizmann, Jabotinsky, ve-She'elat ha-Aravim — Veidat Peel." *Eighth World Congress for Jewish Studies: Papers*, Jerusalem: WCJS, 1982, vol. 2, pp. 175-176.

——— (ed.). *Ba-Ma'avak la-Medina: ha-Mediniut ha-Zionit ba-Shanim 1936-1948*, Jerusalem: The Zalman Shazar Institute, 1984.

Horowitz, Dan and Moshe Lissak. *Origins of the Israeli Polity*, Chicago: University of Chicago Press, 1978.

Kleiman, Aharon. *Hipared oh Mishol — Mediniut Britania ve-Halukat Eretz-Israel, 1936-1939*. Jerusalem: Yad Yitzhak Ben-Zvi, 1983.

Lev-Ami, S. *ba-Ma'avak u-ba-Mered*. Tel Aviv: Maarachot/IDF Press, N.D.

Merhav, Peretz. *The Israeli Left*. San Diego: A. S. Barnes, 1980.

Niv, David. *Ma'arachot ha-Irgun ha-Zvai ha-Leumi*. Tel Aviv: The Kalusner Institute, 1965.

Norman, T. *An Outstretched Arm: A History of the Jewish Colonization Association*, London. Routledge and Kegan Paul, 1985.

O'Brien, Connor C. *The Siege: The Saga of Israel and Zionism*. New York: Simon and Schuster, 1986.

Orren, Elhanan. *Hityashvut bi-Shnot Ma'avak*. Jerusalem: Yad Ben-Zvi, 1978.

Rosenblum, Howard. "The New Zionist Organization's American Campaign, 1936-1939." *Studies in Zionism*, vol. 12 #2 (Autumn, 1991): 169-185.

———. "The New Zionist Organization's Diplomatic Battle Against Partition, 1936-1937." *Studies in Zionism*, vol. 11 #2 (Autumn, 1990): 154-181.

Rubenstein, Sondra M. *The Communist Movemnt in Palestine and Israel, 1919-1984*, Boulder, CO: Westview Press, 1985.

Schatzburger, Hilda. *Meri u-Mesoret be-Eretz-Israel be-Tekufat ha-Mandat*. Ramat Gan: Bar-Ilan University Press, 1985.

Schechtman, Joseph B. and Y. Benari, *The History of the Revisionist Movement*. Tel Aviv: Hadar Publishing, 1970.

Shapira, Anita. "The Concept of Time in the Partition Controversy of 1937." *Studies in Zionism*, v. 6 #2 (Autumn, 1985), pp. 211-228.

Shavit, Yaacov. *Jabotinsky and the Revisionist Movement, 1925-1948*. London: Frank Cass, 1988.

———. "Realism and Messianism in Zionism and the Yishuv." *Studies in Contemporary Jewry*, vol. 7 (1991): 100-127.

Simons, Chaim. *International Proposals to Transfer Arabs from Palestine, 1895-1947*. Hoboken, NJ: Ktav, 1988.

Slutsky, Y. et al. *Kitzur Toldot ha-Hagana*. Tel Aviv: Maarachot/IDF Press, 1978.

Stein, Joshua B. "Josiah Wedgwood and the Seventh Dominion Scheme." *Studies in Zionism*, v.11 #2 (Autumn, 1990): 141-155.

Teveth, Shabetai. *Rezach Arolosoroff*. Jerusalem: Schocken, 1982.

Tomaszewski, Jerzy. "Vladimir Jabotinsky's Talks With Representatives of the Polish Government." *Polin*, Vol. 2 (1988), pp. 276-293.

Tsur, Zeev: *ha-Kibbutz ha-Meuchad be-Binyan Eretz-Israel*. Tel Aviv: Yad Yitzhak Tabenkin, 1979.

Tzahor, Zeev. *ba-Derech le-Hanhagat ha-Yishuv*. Jerusalem: Yad Yitzhak Ben-Zvi, 1981.

——. *Shorshei ha-Politika ha-Yisraelit*. Beersheba: Ben-Gurion University Press, 1987.

Urofsky, Melvin I. *American Zionism from Herzl to the Holocaust*. Second Edition. Lincoln: University of Nebraska Press, 1995.

Vital, David. *The Origins of Zionism*. Oxford: Clarendon Press, 1975.

Weinbaum, Laurence. *A Marriage of Convenience: The New Zionist Organization and the Polish Government, 1936-1939*. Boulder, CO: East European Monographs, 1993.

Yanai, Nathan. "Ben-Gurion's Concept of Mamlahtiut and the Forming Reality of the State of Israel." *Jewish Political Studies Review*, vol. 1 #1/2 (Spring, 1989), pp. 151-177.

Yishai, Yael. *Siyyot be-Tenuat ha-Avoda: Siya Bet be-Mapai*. Tel Aviv: Am Oved, 1978.

G. The Yishuv and the Holocaust

Bauer, Yehuda. *From Diplomacy to Resistance*. New York: Atheneum, 1970.

——. "Response to Hava Wagman Eshkoli." *The Journal of Israeli History*, vol. 15 #1 (Spring, 1994): 101-104.

Beling, E. *Die gesellschaftliche Eingliederung der deutschen Einwanderer in Israel*, Frankfurt A/M: P. Lang, 1967.

Black, Edwin. *The Transfer Agreement*. New York: Macmillan, 1984.

——. "The Anti-Ford Boycott" *Midstream*, vol. 32 #1 (January, 1986), pp. 39-41.

Brada, F. "Emigration to Palestine" *The Jews of Czechoslovakia*, Philadelphia: JPS, 1971, vol. 2, pp. 595-597.

Esh, Shaul. *Iynnim ba-Shoa ve-Yahadut Zemanenu*. Jerusalem: The Leo Baeck Institute, 1976.

Gelber, Yoav. *Moledet Hadsha: Aliyat Yehudei Merkaz Europa ve-Klitatam*. Jerusalem: Yad Yizhak Ben-Zvi, 1990.

——. "The Origins of Youth Aliya" *Studies in Zionism*, vol. 9 #2 (Autumn, 1988), pp. 147-172.

——. "The Reaction of the Zionist Movement and the Yishuv to the Nazis' Rise to Power." *Yad Vashem Studies*, vol. 18 (1987): 41-101.

Hacohen, Dvorah. "Ben-Gurion and the Second World War: Plans for Mass Immigration to Palestine." *Studies in Contemporary Jewry*, vol. 7 (1991): 247-268.

Nicosia, Francis R. *The Third Reich and the Palestine Question*, Austin: Texas University Press, 1985.

Niderland, Doron. "Back to the Lion's Jaws: A Note on Jewish Return
	Migration to Nazi Germany." *Studies in Contemporary Jewry*, vol. 9
	(1993): 174-180.
Ofer, Dalia. *Escaping the Holocaust*. New York: Oxford University Press,
	1990.
Porat, Dina. "Al-Domi: Palestinian Intellectuals and the Holocaust, 1943-1945."
	Studies in Zionism, vol. 5 #1 (Spring, 1984), pp. 97-124.
———. *The Blue and the Yellow Stars of David*. Cambridge, MA: Harvard
	University Press, 1990.
Sarig, Gabi. *ha-Gideonim be-Sefinot ha-Haapala*. Ramat Efal: Yad Yitzhak
	Tabenkin, 1988.
Szulc, Tad. *The Secret Alliance*, New York: Farrar, Straus & Giroux, 1991.
Viest, A. *Identität und Integration: Dargestellt am Beispiel Mitteleuropaeschier
	Einwanderer in Israel*, Frankfurt A/M: P. Lang, 1977.
Wagman Eshkoli, Hava. "Three Attitudes toward the Holocaust within Mapai,
	1933-1945." *Studies in Zionism*, vol. 14 #1 (Spring, 1993): 73-94.

H. Doctoral Dissertations

Avneri, Yitzhak. ha-Histadrut ha-Zionit ve-ha-Aliya ha-Bilti Legalit le-Eretz-
	Israel, 1933-1939. Tel Aviv University, 1981.
Elcott, David M. The Political Resocialization of German Jews in Palestine.
	Columbia University, 1981.
Rosenblum, Howard I. A Political History of Revisionist Zionism, 1925-1938.
	Columbia University, 1986.
Sagi, Nana. Teguvat ha-Ziburiut ha-Yehudit be-Britania le-Redifat ha-
	Yehudim ba-Reich ha-Shlishi ba-Shanim, 1930-1939. Hebrew
	University, 1982.
Shpiro, David. Thalichei Binyana shel Moezet ha-Herum ha-Zionit ki-Zeroa
	ha-Peula ha-Ziburit shel ha-Zionut ha-Amerikait, 1938-1944. Hebrew
	Univesrity, 1979.

About the Book and Author

For the Jewish world and the Yishuv in particular, the 1930s was a time of escalating crises—the rise of the Nazis and their antisemitic policies, the declining fortunes of Eastern European Jewry, increasing Arab enmity, and the hardening of British Mandatory policies in Palestine. Reexamining some of the most controversial episodes in modern Jewish history, this invaluable study offers the first systematic institutional analysis of the Yishuv's responses to the imperative of saving German and European Jewry from the growing Nazi threat between 1933 and 1939. Drawing on a wealth of archival research and a thorough knowledge of the secondary literature, this informative, important book will be essential reading for all those interested in the history of the Holocaust.

Abraham J. Edelheit is a visiting professor at Kingsborough Community College in New York and is a scholar in residence for the Jewish Association for Services to the Aged.

Index

335